THE NATION'S NEWSBROKERS

VOLUME 1:
*The Formative Years,
from Pretelegraph to 1865*

RICHARD A. SCHWARZLOSE

Northwestern University Press
Evanston, Ill.

No part of this book may be reproduced in any form or by any means
without the prior written permission of the publisher.

Published by Northwestern University Press
Evanston, Illinois 60201
Printed in the United States of America

Composition by Point West Inc., Carol Stream, IL

Library of Congress Cataloging-in-Publication Data

Schwarzlose, Richard Allen.
    The nation's newsbrokers / Richard A. Schwarzlose.
        p.   cm.
    Bibliography: v. 1, p.
    Includes index.
    Contents: v. 1. The formative years, from pretelegraph to 1865.
    ISBN 0-8101-0818-6 (v. 1)
    1. News agencies—United States—History. 2. Journalism—United
States—History. 3. Press—United States—History. 4. Journalists—
United States—Biography.   I. Title.
PN4841.A1S34 1988
070.4'35'0973—dc19   88-37160
                                           CIP

Contents

Preface ix

Chapter
1:      Early News-Movement Stirrings 1
        National News-Movement Efforts 4
        Local and Regional News-Movement Efforts 11
        Discussion 27

Chapter
2:      Technological Imperatives and the First
        Newsbrokerage 33
        Transatlantic Steam and Early Telegraphy 34
        The Journalistic Response 46
        Discussion 72

Chapter
3:      New York City's Newsbrokers Emerge 79
        Early Telegraphic News Activity 81
        The Birth of the New York City Associated Press 89
        The New York City Associated Press and the Early
        Telegraph 108
        Discussion 119

Chapter
4:      Newsbroking Stabilizes 123
        The Jones Administration 131
        The Early News Report 137
        The Halifax Expresses 146
        Discussion 162

Chapter
5:      Conflict and an Associated Press Monopoly 169
        Competitors and Their News Reports 171
        Craig Stalks His Monopoly 186
        Craig Infiltrates Telegraphy 191
        The Editors Perfect Their Partnership 201
        Discussion 206

Chapter
6:      Consolidation on the Eve of War 211
        The American Telegraph Company Menace 212
        New York Associated Press's Internal Changes 223
        Associated Press's Report on the Eve of the Civil War 227
        Discussion 234

Chapter
7:        *Newsbroking in the Civil War* *239*
         Lincoln and the Associated Press *242*
         Other Civil War Newsbrokerages *254*
         The Wartime News Reports *270*
         Discussion *275*

Notes *281*

Bibliography *337*

Index *357*

PREFACE

This volume and its sequel describe and analyze the origins and growth to maturity of newsbroking as a social institution and a cultural force in the United States.[1] Less than two years after Samuel F. B. Morse opened his first experimental telegraph line to traffic, a pattern of journalistic behavior began to emerge in conjunction with that new technology that was novel and, as it turned out, enduring. That behavior was the daily collection and distribution of general news dispatches via communication systems among journalists in several communities, a process controlled by an agent or agency, in other words, a newsbroker. The previous sentence will serve as a definition of newsbroking in this two-volume work.

All but two elements of this definition could also apply to related journalistic activities. The "daily collection and distribution of general news dispatches," for example, could also refer to newspaper publication. The movement of dispatches "among journalists in several communities, a process controlled by an agent or agency" might also describe the activity of special correspondents and feature syndicates. But "general news" eliminates feature syndicates, and "daily," except in moments of unusually high volumes of news, eliminates special correspondents. Likewise, "via communication systems" points squarely at newsbroking's historic use of telegraph, telephone, radio, and now satellite communication, distinguishing it, at least until recently, from transportation-bound feature or supplemental services.

This communication-transportation distinction is a major theme here, especially in the early stages of newsbroking's development. Despite repeated attempts at intercity movement of news via the transportation system before the arrival of telegraphy in the United States, no regular and enduring newsbroking pattern materialized. Rather than being newsbroking's simple and singular cause, telegraphy contributed new forms and organizing concepts to journalistic practices and enabled previously unfulfilled journalistic needs to be met. The telegraph advanced ongoing intercity news movement from its casual, sporadic, expensive, and unsatisfactory condition in transportation to a system of speed, continuity, permanence, and power. Even though all newsbroking is intercity news movement and historically relies on communication technology, intercity news movement encompasses newsbroking and much more by relying on both communication and transportation systems.

Newsbroking's growth to maturity took roughly seven decades, from the mid-1840s to the years immediately following World War I. Except for the first chapter, these volumes focus on those first seventy years of newsbroking history in the United States. Chief among the reasons for this emphasis are the following: first, the evidence unearthed in this project told a fuller, more vivid, and a factually different story about newsbroking's early years than is now available in the literature; second, reliable primary sources are more plentiful and illuminating for earlier newsbroking developments than for those of the twentieth century; and third, the generally steady growth of newsbroking in the past sixty-five years requires only passing notice and analysis compared to the formative years.

This emphasis on the nineteenth century brings the present work into direct competition with Victor Rosewater's *History of Cooperative News-Gathering in the United States*,[2] which, unlike the saccharine house histories of the Associated Press[3] and United Press,[4] is a formidable adversary, still regarded in the field as the authority on news-gathering history up to 1930. Rosewater was a newsbroking insider.[5] His father, Edward, founded the *Omaha Bee* on June 19, 1871, joined the Northwestern Associated Press after a short membership in the American Press Association, and was deeply involved in the AP of Illinois, serving briefly on its board of directors. Victor, armed with an AP franchise, ran the *Bee* from 1906, when his father died, until 1920, when he sold the paper to fuel magnate Nelson B. Updike. The younger Rosewater was chairman of AP's nominating committee in 1916, becoming embroiled in a controversy over the representativeness of AP's board of directors. Between them, father and son experienced nearly fifty years of news-gathering history.

Rosewater's work was the first book-length history of newsbroking that was not also autobiographical. The Rosewater family papers reveal that he labored at length in several Eastern libraries and collections researching his history, and the book's foreword acknowledges that Rosewater's research "extended over many years" and included access to internal corporate documents. Surprisingly, however, the book's narrative does not reflect the intimacy Rosewater and his father obviously had with newsbroking. Moreover, all but about half a dozen of Rosewater's bibliographic entries could be easily located and examined in public depositories. There was disappointingly little in the family papers that cannot be found on public shelves or in other collections.

Although the principal purpose of the present project is to draw together and examine all significant information on the early years of newsbroking in the United States, an important byproduct of this endeavor has turned out to be correcting false and misleading accounts of the subject that now reside in the literature. Because neither historical completeness nor objectivity was the goal of newsbrokerages' house histories, to undertake a point-by-point adjustment of their narratives, especially for the early years, would be to set up a straw man. Many of the corrections in the historical record proposed in this book, however, are expressly at Rosewater's expense. He was, it should be noted, a good scholar, handicapped by not having union lists of manuscript collections, accessibility of microfilm, and his own book as a starting point. On the other hand, some of Rosewater's accounts, as will be seen, have withstood the present writer's research assaults.

*   *   *   *   *

Newsbroking is viewed in these volumes as a techno-journalistic system of policies, structures, political-economic functions, and news content, developing among and interacting with other technological and journalistic systems. The present research seeks to trace newsbroking's growth from inception to maturity as a separate institutional and cultural entity in society, a goal first pursued tentatively by the author more than twenty years ago.[6] In large part such separateness will be measured by the changing dynamic and interactional relationships newsbroking shares with adjacent institutions. Changes in relationships among systems or their components, it is assumed, signify meaningful history. Walter J. Ong lends to this perspective the commonsense tone it deserves:

> Open-system thinking is interactional, transactional, developmental, process-oriented. Terms such as these have by now operated in the discourse about human activity at almost all levels. . . . There had never been any closed system anyhow and the basic insights offered by open-system models were at root even banal. The assertion that everything interacts with everything else is hardly news.

Ong observes that "it has become urgent to exploit this

insight"[7]—essentially, it seems to the present author, because behavioral approaches or causal historical models have failed to comprehend and illuminate the magnitude and complexity of history. Progressivist or leftist revisionist perspectives or historic determinism based on great men, economic factors, technological innovations, or communication media to the contrary notwithstanding, historians remain in the final analysis bounded by and only as good as the evidence available to them.

The test of research now, as always, is the publication of sources and replicability of findings, not a project's kinship to some epistemological labels or trends currently fashionable in the discipline. Stuart Bruchey states the problem well:

> Perhaps there will someday be elaborated a "general theory of society—specifically some sort of sociology of change"...that will be inclusive of economic and all other major sources of change. Until the dawn of that doubtful day, only the total resources of the historian, critical and narrative, can succeed in weaving the thread of growth into the richer pattern of human change. His data may often prove unquantifiable, but history is likely to remain the art of weighing the imponderable.... It will always be true that a Collingwoodite immersion in the uniqueness of the particular may disclose differences that may be justified as more important than similarities. Certainty is unattainable, and we may mince nearer the throne only by shuffling between the particular and the general, man and his whole environment, cause and effect.[8]

In general, the chapters of this work present the development of newsbroking in the United States chronologically, while material within each chapter is arranged under topical headings. Because the chapters attempt multidimensional approaches to relatively complex relationships, even though in reasonably short time periods, they are uncommonly long. In addition to the topical subdivisions, the reader may find assistance in the discussion sections at the end of each chapter.

*   *   *   *   *

The reader will be spared the reasons why newsbroking and its news report are significant forces in society. Those reasons should be obvious to all who know the names Associated Press and United Press International. In addition to being attracted to the signifi-

and post riders that were mired in mud, the eighteenth-century editor and his reader readily acquiesced to having their news hitchhike on transportation systems. What choice did they have? Even though a postal system, designed to maintain communication among the Colonies and emphasizing newspaper exchanges, developed early in America, it relied (and still does) on available transportation technology and thus was the perpetual victim of such inescapable physical conditions as distance, speed, load-weight, prevailing winds, gravity, and the contours of terrain.

Allan Pred, in his study of pretelegraphic urban growth and information dissemination, comments that pretelegraphic news movement in the United States was a function of existing transportation technology, "synonymous with human spatial interaction."

> Thus, the construction of turnpikes, the adoption of the steamboat for passenger and freight purposes, and the initial diffusion of the railroad in the 1830s contributed to the increased rapidity of information dissemination.[5]

But "increased rapidity" remained agonizingly transportation-bound, locked within a technology dominated by "the humble rural road" and augmented only on selected routes by turnpikes, plank roads, and slowly emerging canals and railroads. George Rogers Taylor details the slowness of transportation innovations to take hold and the many financial and engineering pitfalls encountered. And after enormous expenditures to develop inland steam navigation, a canal system, turnpikes, and plank roads in the first half of the nineteenth century, railroad construction supplanted most of these means of transportation on most routes by 1860. But since railroads, like their innovative predecessors, concentrated on linking urban areas along identical, lucrative routes, the rural majority of the population was left to navigate its alternately dusty and muddy rural roads. Taylor says, "The failure of the plank-road movement left most short-haul land transportation literally stuck in the mud, there to remain until the later age of the rigid-surfaced road and the internal-combustion engine."[6]

Pred's formula requires further modification. The transportation alternatives of road, turnpike, steamboat, canal, and railway did not progress simultaneously and uniformly, providing the public and the news consumer with an ever-expanding array of intercity options. Rather, the onset of steam navigation and railroading turned government and business attention away from longer-standing commitments to expand and improve roads, turnpikes, and

3

canals. Wheaton J. Lane reports that "practically no assistance was given to local governments for roads between 1845 and 1903" in Pennsylvania and that

> throughout the country a similar neglect prevailed as local governments, with inadequate revenues, found themselves unable to cope with the problem. The fact that long-distance travel now went by steamboat or railroad, and that industries used waterways and railroads exclusively, left the farmer almost the only element interested in better roads.[7]

As the nineteenth century arrived and with it the new nation's developing political and economic institutions, editors began to seek ways of squeezing more and faster communication out of transportation systems. An increasingly demanding reading audience of political and economic elites, the emergence of the daily newspaper after 1783 and of newspaper competition in major centers, and the improvements in transportation technology were, no doubt, factors in accelerating the search for news.

This chapter describes a representative sample of those early efforts at aggressive news-gathering. None of these efforts, however, led to an enduring newsbroker structure.[8] Most were personal efforts by individual editors; many survived for relatively short periods; none had enduring or regional, let alone national, impact on news movement. As precursors of newsbroking in the United States, they attest to the inadequacy of transportation systems to solve effectively and permanently society's problem of communicating regularly and across even relatively short distances about affairs of general importance. In addition to the pervasive postal service, with its free newspaper exchanges, four news-movement efforts had national dimensions; the rest were local.

NATIONAL NEWS-MOVEMENT EFFORTS

The presence of a large number of postmaster-publishers in the intercolonial postal system, which dated from 1692 and informally permitted free exchanges of newspapers, suggests the existence of a very early newsbrokerage of sorts. Indeed, no other system of intercity information movement existed until the pre–Revolutionary War decade, and, except for human travel and personal correspondence, postage-free newspaper exchanges were the Colonies' only link with each other.

For a century the postage-free newspaper exchange custom was a gentlemen's agreement that occasionally had to be reasserted. In a 1758 notice to postmasters, however, Benjamin Franklin and William Hunter, copostmasters of the Royal Postal Service in the Colonies from 1753 to 1761 and themselves newspaper editors, were the first to formalize a policy of free newspaper exchanges. Congress gave the practice its blessing with passage of the Post Office Act of 1792, which said in part: "Every printer of newspapers may send one paper to every other printer of newspapers within the United States, free of postage, under such regulations as the Postmaster General shall provide."[9] Alfred McClung Lee notes that this law "facilitated the practice out of which modern newsgathering associations and agencies grew."[10] Mott suggests that loss of this exchange system, so pivotal to eighteenth-century news-gathering, would have meant that "many of the western papers would have had to suspend publication."[11]

Anyone familiar with the enormous presence of the party press in the United States between the Revolutionary and Civil wars can appreciate the importance of this exchange system, not only in furthering politics and government, but also in informing the nation's newspaper readers of the nation's news. Dominated by majority party organs in Washington, D.C., state capitals, and the major cities, exchanges disseminated the news and views of state and national leaders down into the hinterlands while communicating ground swells and local grievances upward toward the power centers. Although the postal system moved news slowly and along the parallel tracks defined by newspapers' party affiliations, until the 1840s and telegraphy it was the great conduit for public affairs in the United States.

Obviously important to participating papers, the postal system, however, was only as extensive as the existing road network and the established postal stations, only as frequent or regular as public funds would permit, and only as fast as weather, horses, and coastal ships would allow. A government-sponsored system relying on transportation and responsible to the public at large was not destined to evolve into a newsbrokerage. Even if editors were favored customers of this system, they were still just one of many customers, and, as we shall see, editors later mounted elaborate efforts to beat postal service, which they perceived as being too slow for their purposes.

Although not creating a newsbrokerage, postal service supplied editors with an expanding array of distant newspapers, correspondents' dispatches, and syndicated feature material during the nineteenth century. The practice of clipping the exchanges survived long after telegraphy's introduction. Pred sketches the pretelegraph growth of the postal service as being impressive from the social and journalistic viewpoints, commenting that "A major portion of the information-diffusion role of colonial and United States postal services was accounted for by the delivery of newspapers to nonlocal editors and subscribers, especially after the mid-eighteenth century."[12] Between 1790 and 1840 "spectacular developments" occurred in extending the spatial limits of the postal service.[13]

Significant temporal improvement in the post-road technology developed in the 1830s, prompting introduction of express news routes among major Eastern cities. Postal expresses began in 1833, when the government purchased the New York–Philadelphia expresses operated by the *New York Courier and Enquirer* and by a group of older New York City papers. From then until 1839 the system expanded rapidly, using post riders on round-the-clock schedules, employing railroad and steamer links where feasible, and handling market news and general news items in the form of news slips (proof sheets) printed as a cooperative gesture by editors along the route.

Postmaster and former publisher Amos Kendall ran the express system in 1836–39 in high gear, linking major Eastern cities as far south along the seaboard as Charleston, S.C., and reaching St. Louis, New Orleans, and Mobile. After 1839, railroad expansion and the appearance of private express companies overshadowed the effectiveness of post riders, and the postal service thereafter relied primarily on rail service for regular and express service.[14]

The appearance of this express postal system heightened some big city dailies' urge to beat the government ponies with their own fast expresses, with the *New York Journal of Commerce* and the *New York Herald* leading this competition according to Lee.[15] Moreover, he adds, there is a direct lineage between these early postal expresses of news slips and today's newsbrokerages. "Modern newsgathering associations and agencies trace their inception more directly to this [news slip] effort than to harbor newsgathering or to coffeehouse news books."[16] Lee here links the news slips to the appearance in upstate New York in 1846 of what chapter 2 describes as the first newsbrokerage in the United States.

Somewhat closer to newsbroker status than the postal service were the Committees of Correspondence, another attempt at an early "national" news-movement effort. The committees, "the most formidable revolutionary machine . . . created during the

American Revolution," according to John C. Miller,[17] acquired several missions as colonial relations with England deteriorated: acting as extralegal governing and grievance bodies when town meetings and legislatures were dissolved by the Crown, formulating and disseminating statements of Radical principle, publicizing violations of those principles, and communicating with committees in other towns and thus generating a far-flung intercolonial revolutionary movement.

Samuel Adams secured approval for the first committee in the Colonies at a Boston town meeting on November 2, 1772. Shortly thereafter, similar committees sprang up in towns and regions throughout New England, and by 1774 twelve colonies were represented in the movement. On March 31, 1774, Adams wrote to Benjamin Franklin in London, "Colony communicates freely with Colony. . . . [T]he whole continent is now become united in sentiment and in opposition to tyranny."[18]

While Adams may have exaggerated, the committees did represent an effort to utilize the postal service and their own messengers for the efficient and continuous movement of information of a specific type. An example explains the committees' operation. On June 28, 1773, the Boston committee considered a request from its Connecticut counterpart for "Sundry Letters which the House of Representatives of the Province of Massachusetts Bay have obtained from England of an Extraordinary Nature, tending to Subvert the Constitution of the Colonies."[19] A five-man Boston subcommittee was formed to respond to Connecticut and to correspond the same to all other committees, mailing printed rather than handwritten copies to them. That mailing went out on July 4, and the subcommittee decided four days later to prepare weekly letters for other committees in the network. The news orientation of the subcommittee's operation is expressed in a note in the minutes of a July 29, 1773, meeting: "Some fresh Intelligence being Dayly Expected from Great Britain, it was thought best to defer writing letters to the Several Committees of Correspondence in the neighboring Governments for a few Days."[20] Three weeks later, with further news still expected, "it was thought best still to defer sending the letters."[21]

While initially relying on postal service, as newspaper editors did, the committees occasionally supplied their own delivery system after hostilities became imminent and some postal routes were suspended by the Royal government. Mott, while tracing the path and time-lag of the news of the battles of Lexington and Concord, observes that the committees were "the chief means of communication in the coverage of this news-break" at a time when mail service in New England was temporarily stopped.[22] Mott describes the delivery systems that they employed.

> [T]he Patriot committees of New England saw how important it was that the other colonies should be fired simultaneously from the Massachusetts flame, and that to bring this about it was essential to get the news of the killing of the Patriot minutemen out over the whole country at once. With this object, they hurried the reports southward, sometimes dispatching their own couriers, and other Committees of Correspondence cooperated in sending their messengers on to the next towns, and so the news went at top speed. . . . [T]he Patriot couriers sometimes carried newspapers containing the Lexington story, as well as the official Committee letters; so editors were not wholly deprived of the "exchanges" upon which they so much depended.[23]

Although the committees were more akin to the Liberation News Services of the 1960s in operation and intent than to the Associated Press or United Press International, they had taken a step closer to newsbroking by seeking to eliminate the randomness of newspaper exchanges and bypassing the uncertain postal service when necessary. But they still encountered spatial obstacles for which available technology was no match. Nonetheless, Edwin Emery accurately calls the committees a "primitive news service," commenting

> Samuel Adams'. . . agents "covered" every important meeting as ably as modern reporters gather information for the press services today. In a remarkably short time all such news reached Adams' local committee, which then processed it for effective dissemination where such information was needed.[24]

Curiously, even though news movement enjoyed moderate success via the postal service and under the Committees of Correspondence, American editors totally ignored the semaphore—a successful news-movement system in Europe and the only system prior to telegraphy that was exclusively a system of communication. The semaphore was invented by Claude Chappe in France in 1794; by 1852 his network included 556 semaphore stations stretching over almost three thousand miles of European countryside.[25] Although limited in the volume of information it could handle, semaphore communicated across spatial reaches faster and generally more easily than transportation-bound systems.

In the United States, however, semaphore never amounted to more than a local, and largely privately owned, affair. The first such system, ninety miles of flags on staffs connecting Martha's Vineyard with Boston, was completed by Jonathan Grout, Jr., in November 1801. Devised as a service to Boston's business community, Grout's semaphores transmitted news of ship traffic and weather conditions south of Cape Cod.[26]

One American largely forgotten in communications history lobbied extensively around 1810 for establishment of a national semaphore system. He was Christopher Colles, who is better known for his *Survey of the Roads of the United States of America* (1789), which mapped major roads from Albany, New York, and Newtown and Stratford, Conn., on the north to about fifteen miles east of Williamsburg, Va., on the south.[27] Colles advocated a national perspective on the communication needs of the new American nation, and he lectured, published, memorialized, and advertised on projects of interior improvement, ranging from a canal system linking the Mohawk River system with the Great Lakes to a plan of reservoirs and aqueducts to supply water to New York City.

Convinced of the usefulness of a national semaphore system, Colles proposed in 1812 to link all major U.S. cities by semaphore. His plan envisioned an early-warning system to alert citizens of military invasion at a time when war with Great Britain appeared unavoidable. In July 1812, he took his crusade to the people through advertisements in six New York newspapers inviting public examination of an improved semaphore device displayed "on top of the Custom-House." He followed up with a lecture proposing his idea at the Custom House on July 22.

Within a year Colles had installed a forty-mile string of semaphores between New York City and Sandy Hook, at the lower end of that city's harbor. This system's primary purpose was to signal the city of the approach of ships. (This information appears to have been the only benefit derived from semaphore by newspaper editors.) Improved over the years, it remained in operation until the mid-1840s, when it was replaced by an electric telegraph line from Coney Island to the city.[28]

For Colles, however, the harbor semaphore provided a chance to experiment with speed and to publicize further his scheme for a national semaphore system. In published descriptions of the harbor system Colles claimed a speed of eighty-four characters communicated in five minutes between two semaphore stations ten miles apart. At this rate, Colles calculated, a single character could travel by semaphore the 2,600 miles from Passamaquoddy Bay in northern Maine to New Orleans in fifteen minutes and twenty-eight seconds. The Lord's Prayer, according to Colles, could make that trip in thirty-six minutes and thirteen seconds.[29]

This may seem slow today, but Henry O'Rielly, a champion of Colles's efforts and himself a developer of electric telegraphy, points out that Samuel F. B. Morse's improved electromagnetic telegraph of 1837 was capable of only five words per minute.[30] The public was interested in these semaphore schemes, but outside of the Sandy Hook system, Colles made little headway. Had the United States backed Colles's national semaphore the way France encouraged Chappes's in the 1790s, the nation's first newsbrokerage might have appeared earlier.

(It would be incorrect, however, to say that Agence Havas, the world's first newsbrokerage, arose in France solely because of the presence of a national semaphore network. Charles-Louis Havas established his Bureau Havas in 1832 as a newspaper-clipping and translation service for numerous private subscribers and some Paris and provincial newspapers. Renamed Agence Havas in 1835—a year since recognized as the formal birth of newsbroking—this service expedited delivery of foreign newspapers, established a European network of correspondents, and printed its daily news reports for delivery by courier or mail. Some correspondents' reports were delivered by semaphore, but Havas also used homing pigeons and the mails. He enlisted France's first telegraph line, between Paris and Rouen, when it opened in 1845.)[31]

A news-movement development of sorts on a national scale was *Niles' Weekly Register*, which appeared in 1811. The idea of Baltimore publisher Hezekiah Niles, this publication gathered and reprinted a wealth of facts, statistics, speeches, and documents from throughout the nation. Published with indexes, it offered editors as well as the public a valuable cache of information. Lee calls the paper "a disseminator of nationally significant facts and documents . . . suppl[ying] dailies with an accessible 'morgue' . . . as well as material for current use."[32]

The *Register* declined after Niles's death in 1839 and disappeared in 1849. A Niles biographer and historian of the *Register*, Norval Neil Luxon, notes that in addition to the absence of "an experienced editor with an intelligent grasp of contemporary conditions," the paper's death may be attributed to the rapid increase of news-

adjourned to Topliff's where he might learn of the previous night's happenings, for news of foreign arrivals was quickly wig-wagged to the habitues of the reading-room by a signal system from Long Island in the harbor.[47]

Topliff retired from the business in 1842.[48]

News room enterprises such as Topliff's provided local newspaper editors with substantial amounts of general news—a clearing house or brokerage for harbor news, weather reports, and a scattering of general foreign and national news items. Boston's Exchange Coffee House Reading Room, at the time Topliff joined it, offered a regular news file to five of Boston's six newspapers. From Clarence S. Brigham's list of newspapers publishing in Boston between July 1810 and July 1811,[49] and the names of editors or publishers, five newspaper affiliations on the Exchange Coffee House subscriber rolls for 1810–11 can be identified.[50] The papers, their coffee house subscribers, and the amounts subscribed were

> *Columbian Centinel*, B[enjamin] Russell, $5
> *Boston Gazette*, John Russell and James Cutler, $20
> *Boston Independent Chronicle*, [Abijah] Adams, [Ebenezer]
>   Rhoades & Co., $5
> *New England Palladium*, [Alexander] Young and [Thomas]
>   Minns, $5
> *Boston Patriot*, Isaac Munroe, $35.

A subscription of five dollars or more allowed the patron access to the news books and newspaper files. The *Boston Repertory*, published by John Park and Andrew W. Park, was the only paper not represented on the coffee house roster.

For the sake of chronological order, the reader is reminded that *Niles' Weekly Register* was founded in Baltimore in 1811, and Colles's New York City harbor semaphore went into operation in 1812. Down the coast in Charleston, S.C., Aaron Smith Willington took over the *Courier* in 1813; he became his own boarding office soon thereafter, intercepting northbound ships from Havana, "the duty [Willington] performed in an open boat, eighteen feet in length, with width in proportion; sharp bow, square stern, and rowed by two stalwart slaves," according to William L. King.[51] When Willington retired to the news room, a series of boarding officers followed, culminating with R. A. Tavel, who in the early 1850s met ships for what King calls "the combined daily press" of Charleston.[52]

Lee reports that the *Providence Journal* pioneered in newspaper use of overland horse expresses in the 1820s, running them occasionally, but especially for election returns and presidential addresses.[53]

By the mid-1820s the older generation of New York City papers—the *Gazette, Daily Advertiser,* and *Mercantile Advertiser*—had pooled their harbor news-gathering efforts and, according to George H. Andrews, "were content with transferring to their columns such news as was thus possessed by all alike."[54] (The reader will recall that the *Gazette* and *Daily Advertiser* had run competing news boats in New York harbor, possibly even before the turn of the century.) This combination of New York City newspapers is probably the "Association of Morning Papers" that Lee refers to as existing prior to 1827 and sharing an annual cost of $2,500.[55] Andrews's apparent disdain for newspapers that were "content" with news "possessed by all alike" is a matter of perspective. Andrews here is writing about his boss's (James Watson Webb's) challenge of this association; Webb and Andrews were both later "content" with Associated Press news "possessed by all alike."

The appearance of Webb, David Hale, and Gerard Hallock in the New York City newspaper field late in the 1820s heated competitive waters to the boiling point. Webb became proprietor and editor of the *New York Morning Courier* in December 1827 and purchased Mordecai M. Noah's *New York Enquirer,* forming the *Morning Courier and New York Enquirer* (commonly called the *New York Courier and Enquirer*) on May 25, 1829.

Meanwhile, the *New York Journal of Commerce* had been founded on September 1, 1827, by Arthur Tappan, "a merchant and reformer but," says Mott, "untrained in journalism."[56] His brother, Lewis Tappan, took hold of the paper the next year, entrusting its editorial and business departments to Hallock and Hale, who both had Boston journalism backgrounds. Early in 1829 it was agreed that Hale and Hallock would become the sole proprietors of the *Journal of Commerce* in two years. Both the *Journal of Commerce* and the *Courier and Enquirer* were mercantile (although the latter also exhibited strong tendencies toward political journalism of the Whig persuasion), and, like their older contemporaries, they were eager to please their elite readers with aggressive news-gathering, first in New York harbor and later with horse expresses from Washington.

With the famous Webb versus Hale-Hallock news contest in view, an examination of harbor news-gathering's purposes and methods is appropriate. The prize of journalistic effort in the harbor, of course, was the latest news from Europe, with additional awards for shipping and weather information. Such news was craved by the mercantile reading audience above all else. Robert Greenhalgh Albion's history of the New York port explains that

> To many Americans, the news from abroad often meant something far more vital than the gratification of idle curiosity. A temporary suspension of the British corn laws, which would mean the chance to export flour or grain to England, or a rise of twopence a pound in the price of cotton at Liverpool might mean fortunes to those who learned of it before the general public. This advance knowledge would, of course, make it possible to buy flour or cotton at normal prices before the news produced a boom.... Even when the news was published, New York had a decided advantage over Philadelphia and its other rivals.[57]

Numerous intrigues and charges accompanied the efforts of various newspapers and independent news-gatherers to secure foreign news ahead of the pack. Speculators would scheme and pay handsomely to receive foreign market information in advance of the newspapers and the general public. To counteract the speculator (and to garner favorable public relations), newspapers posted copies of their foreign news in front of their shops even before setting the type and printing the papers that contained the foreign news. Speculators, in turn, armed with the correct news, spread out in areas away from the city, reporting false foreign news to farmers and small-town investors and reaping sizable returns.

Even though the importance of foreign news traditionally was sufficient to goad editors and their agents to take to the harbor in boats, the agonizingly slow progress of transoceanic ships from landfall up the harbor to their berths in the East or Hudson rivers coaxed even more energetic effort from the city's journalists.

Inbound packets encountered an obstacle course, delaying their docking by at least several hours even with favorable tides and weather. At the Narrows, large ships were required to take on a pilot. From their base on Staten Island, the pilot boats would swarm around the inbound vessel, which was fair game and whose pilot fees sustained the twenty-eight or thirty pilots stationed at Sandy Hook. According to unwritten law, the pilot who brought a ship to her wharf was also entitled to take her out again.

While the ship waited at the Narrows for passage across the sand bars and up the crowded harbor, a Customs House officer and a port health inspector were rowed out to examine the ship's papers and the health of crew and passengers. These inspections could take more than an hour; if disease were detected onboard, the ship and its human cargo could be quarantined for thirty days or more. Another delay in European news was caused by the fact that ship captains could release regular mail pouches and bundles of European newspapers only to appropriate postal authorities and only after the ship had docked in New York City.[58] To avoid the mail delay, the alert New York editor arranged with a Liverpool or London agent to prepare a separate package of papers and correspondence carried by a ship's officer. The package was all the editor's intercepting news boat could take offboard without violating postal regulations.

Albion describes the transatlantic traveler's first encounter with the United States. With land still shrouded in mist or still beyond the horizon, specks on the distant seascape grew to become news boats—fifty to one hundred tons and fifty to eighty feet long, and rigged as schooners—bobbing toward the inbound vessel as far as one hundred miles beyond New York City. Their appearance often coincided with that of the slightly larger revenue cutter. Whereas the latter seldom stopped ships, content to prowl the offshore waters for smugglers and ships in distress, it was certain that the news boats would pull alongside.[59]

Webb in the October 3, 1831, edition of his *Courier and Enquirer* describes his news boat's encounter with an inbound ship, the packet *Salem*. The seven-man crew of the news schooner *Courier and Enquirer* patrolling forty miles beyond Sandy Hook had strained for a glimpse of an incoming packet for sixty-one hours before the *Salem* came into view at 9:30 A.M. The news boat moved in as close as prudence would allow and disgorged a yawl into the water, a crewman shouting the name of Webb's newspaper to those on the *Salem* as the yawl rolled up alongside the big packet. Presently the *Salem*'s captain appeared at the rail and dropped a package of tightly wrapped European papers into the yawl. All hands and yawl back onboard, the *Courier and Enquirer* raced for shore, making Coney Island at 1:38 P.M. Here a messenger rushed ashore, mounted a horse, and raced to a semaphore on the Brooklyn side, where a brief summary of the news and markets was transmitted to Webb's office. The European newspapers were brought along later by another of Webb's harbor boats. The schooner *Courier and Enquirer* meanwhile had returned to its vigil in the open sea.[60]

Webb and Hale-Hallock have both been given credit for introducing fast and rangy news-gathering ships in and beyond New York harbor soon after the *Courier and Enquirer* and *Journal of Commerce* entered the newspaper field. The preponderance of evidence, however, supports Webb's claim,[61] which is presented below.

When Webb took possession of the *New York Morning Courier*, he joined the Association of Morning Papers. Late in 1827 the *Journal of Commerce* was also admitted to the association, causing rival Webb to withdraw and inaugurate his own news boat system. Webb's associate, George H. Andrews, says that after leaving the association Webb operated two pilot boats, the *Thomas H. Smith* and the *Eclipse*, one possibly patrolling the waters off Sandy Hook and the other linking the first boat with Webb's Manhattan office. There is also evidence that Webb simultaneously operated smaller boats among the docks within the harbor, gathering bits of shipping and marine information.[62]

The Sabbatarianist and competitive *Journal of Commerce*, to avoid receiving news gathered by the association on Sundays and to challenge Webb's independent harbor initiative, purchased for $3,000 its own news boat late in 1828. The association promptly expelled the *Journal of Commerce*, thus setting up a three-way news boat competition in New York harbor.[63] The Hale and Hallock news boat, christened *Journal of Commerce*, was introduced by the paper to its readers on October 9, 1828, as follows:

> Yesterday our new boat, the "Journal of Commerce," went below for the first time, fully manned and equipped for service. We understand that her rival, the "Thomas H. Smith," is also in readiness for similar duty. An opportunity is now offered for an honorable competition. The public will be benefitted by such extra exertions to procure marine news, and we trust the only contention between the two boat establishments will be which can outdo the other in vigilance, perseverance and success.[64]

Hudson attributes to the news boat *Journal of Commerce* creation of newspaper extras in New York City. Even though many regarded the venture "as ridiculous and ruinously expensive," Hudson reports, "the result proved the wisdom of Hale and Hallock."

> The Semaphoric Telegraph would report the *Journal of Commerce* [news boat] in the offing, and business would be at once suspended to await her arrival. Crowds would then surround the office, as in the days of modern war bulletins,

and the news would soon appear in an Extra. This was the commencement of the New York *Extras*.[65]

Not to be beaten, Webb contracted with Isaac Webb to build, as Andrews reports, "a clipper schooner of one hundred tons berthen, which should beat every pilot boat and schooner in the harbor, or [the editor would] not be compelled to take her."[66] The schooner, constructed at the Webb and Allen shipyards in the East River, was seventy-one feet long with a twenty-one-foot beam and a seven-foot depth of hold. The ship cost Webb's newspaper about $3,000 to build and about $5,000 per year to operate.[67]

The result was the news schooner *Courier and Enquirer*, which Andrews describes as "unquestionably . . . the strongest and fastest craft of her class that had ever been built at that day." Webb operated her seventy to one hundred miles at sea, running the *Eclipse* between Sandy Hook and Manhattan.[68] The *Journal of Commerce*, meanwhile, had added a second schooner, *Evening Edition*, to its harbor service.[69] Willard G. Bleyer estimates that by 1831 the three-way harbor news-gathering rivalry was costing the New York press $25,000 a year to maintain six boats in the harbor.[70]

By 1834, according to Hudson,[71] the excitement over the news rivalry in the harbor had died down; schooners were sold or junked and replaced with rowboats or small pilot boats. The *new* news rivalry was the overland express. In December 1830, three expresses raced to be first to bring President Andrew Jackson's congressional message to various New York City newspapers. The lineup of competitors was familiar: the *Journal of Commerce* versus the *Courier and Enquirer* versus the Association of Morning Papers. The *Courier and Enquirer*'s express was arranged by staffer James Gordon Bennett and went from Washington to Baltimore on horseback, then to Philadelphia by boat, and then on to New York City by horse. It took six hours and twelve minutes and cost the paper nearly $300.[72]

The horse expresses from Washington were prompted, in this instance, by President Jackson's second annual message. The New York editors well remembered the impact of Jackson's first annual message, which had questioned the constitutionality of the Bank of the United States. The second message did not prove worth the effort and expense, but New York's editors had learned to watch the Washington scene more closely and to crank up their expresses as developments in this news-making Democratic administration dictated.

With Jackson's reelection in 1832, strong congressional forces rising to oppose Jackson's bank policy, and Nicholas Biddle of the Bank of the United States tightening credit to pressure the administration, Washington began to look like a news battleground by early 1833.

The *Journal of Commerce* began a regular eight-relay express from Philadelphia to New York City in January 1833 to speed Washington news northward. An irregular *Courier and Enquirer* express begun in 1832 went into high gear, and the Association jumped in with a third express. After eight or ten days of competition, the *Journal of Commerce* express proved to be clearly superior to its competitors, who appealed for help to the postal service, which purchased and operated their express as a government system after January 31, 1833. The *Journal of Commerce* met this challenge by extending its express to Washington; it was then able to beat its government-served competitors by from one to three days, depending on road conditions.[73]

The *Courier and Enquirer*, refusing to rely entirely on the government service, continued more or less regular express runs from Washington, but in 1835 the two old rivals, the *Journal of Commerce* and *Courier and Enquirer*, combined expresses to cut their costs. Even so, during the winter of 1835–36 Webb's *Courier and Enquirer* spent $7,500 monthly on gathering and expressing news from Washington.[74]

Subsequently government expresses of correspondents' letters, news slips, and whole newspapers improved and expanded during the 1835–40 administration of Postmaster General Kendall. As noted earlier, an Eastern pony express linking major Atlantic coast cities and inland to St. Louis and New Orleans operated around the clock from 1836 to 1839, specializing in market quotations and news slips. It was replaced after 1840 by private express companies and an expanding railroad network.[75]

Hudson says that the appearance of the penny press (in 1833 and after in New York City) sent a new competitive shock wave through the city's newspaper press, both in the harbor and with overland expresses.[76] Hudson's own *New York Herald*, a penny paper, is singled out for its harbor enterprise in an 1858 newspaper account of AP's history. "The *New York Herald*. . . soon entered the field, and for a long time, through the enterprise of the proprietor in liberally rewarding the pilots delivering late papers at the office, that journal was enabled to surpass all competition."[77]

In Boston the *Courier, Herald,* and *Commercial Gazette* jointly operated occasional expresses from Washington in 1836 as news warranted. Quoting Isaac C. Pray, Lee says,

> "in one case, an editor nearly lost his life by excitement in riding on the locomotive from Worcester to Boston, about forty miles, in as many minutes." This worthy, in "a state of syncope" was rushed "in a carriage to Congress street where with the greatest difficulty the President's Message was taken from his clutched fingers."[78]

During 1837 and 1838 four major ship-meeting efforts existed in New York harbor, says Hudson: *Journal of Commerce* and *Courier and Enquirer,* served by Captain William Bancker; *Express, Mercantile Advertiser,* and *Gazette,* Captain Hurley; *Commercial Advertiser, Evening Star,* and *American,* Captain Cisco; and the *Herald,* Captain Hamil. The *New York Sun* introduced its own harbor service with Captain William Brogan "later."[79] (Between 1876 and 1878 the letterhead used by the New York City Associated Press asserts that AP was formed in 1837; the literature, however, offers no evidence to support this claim.)

Daniel H. Craig's homing pigeon enterprise can be arbitrarily dated from 1837, the year the *Baltimore Sun* appeared and *Sun* editor Arunah S. Abell called upon Craig to help establish that paper's intercity news-gathering network. By 1842 Craig's pigeon system, headquartered in Boston, served newspapers in New York, Boston, Philadelphia, Baltimore, and Washington, delivering Washington news, reports of various seaboard markets, and dispatches from inbound transatlantic packets and steamers.[80] We will encounter Craig's pigeons in the next chapter in connection with Cunard steamers.

James Gordon Bennett's *New York Herald* led the New York press in harbor and overland expresses during the last half of the 1830s. Hudson, the paper's managing editor, claims that by 1838 the paper operated three news boats—*Teaser, Celeste,* and *Tom Boxer*—and employed five harbor news collectors—Robert Hamil, Robert Martin, William Bassett, Robert Silvey, and John Hall.[81] The paper later added to its fleet the *Fanny Elssler,* a news boat of considerable reputation for speed.

Steam navigation of the Atlantic began in 1838, and Cunard's regular "ocean ferry" service between Liverpool and Boston got under way in 1840. The relationship between transatlantic steam revolution and journalism is explored in chapter 2, but as a pretelegraphic phenomenon, ocean steamers created the last hurrah for Eastern news expresses that relied on transportation.

The arrival in New York City of the *Sirius* from Cork in 1838 marked the first steamer crossing of the Atlantic of consequence. Bennett, sensing a revolution in the offing, booked passage on the return voyage of the *Sirius* to line up letter-writing correspondents in European capitals for his *Herald*.[82] Other papers, notably New York's *Sun* and *Tribune*, followed suit. But Bennett also realized that the regularity of steamer schedules made it unnecessary for editors to station rangy schooners and coastal steamers one hundred miles or so at sea, scouting for the unpredictable sailing vessels. In the late 1830s the paper's news boats prowled the seas off the eastern tip of Long Island, intercepting inbound ships and carrying their news cargo to Montauk Point (at the eastern end of the island), where a railroad express relayed the news to New York City.[83] But by the early 1840s transatlantic steam navigation had two effects on New York's papers, shrinking their news boat operations and redirecting their overland efforts to expresses from Boston, the Cunard line's only U.S. port until late in 1847.

Hudson says that Atlantic steamers "gave the New York papers opportunities to exhibit their enterprise in their own harbor. News schooners were of little use with steam-ships. They became obsolete. Swift row-boats and light sail-boats were the best."[84] The *Fanny Elssler* was of the latter class of sailboats, and its service for the *Herald* in meeting steamers just below Quarantine and running up the bay with the news is depicted in the *New York Herald* of May 18, 1840. This account provides valuable insight into how the *Herald*'s mechanical department handled the news boat's arrival. Docking at the Whitehall Slip (just east of the Battery on the tip of Manhattan) at 2:30 A.M. "Commodore" Martin dashed up Broadway and over on Ann to the *Herald* offices, which was ablaze with lights as the morning edition poured from the press.

> In five minutes all the editors, writers, printers, pressmen were in motion. The immense daily edition of the *Herald* was about one fourth worked off when the news arrived. The press was stopped—the announcement made: this was the second edition. In two hours it was stopped again, and three columns of news put in and sent by the various mails: this was the third edition. In another two hours six columns were put in: this was the fourth edition—also sent by the mails.[85]

A note from Martin to Bennett, dated May 7, 1844, indicates that

Martin was at that time not employed full-time by the *Herald*, a reflection of how the coming of transatlantic steamers had reduced harbor news activity.

> If you will have the goodness to pay my Son the bearer of this note what is due me for six days and nights of collecting Ship News in the Station Boat off Sandy Hook. I owe you three Dollars.... After I left you this time I was down [the harbor] 4 days for another paper for which I got 1.50 per day or 9 Dollars per week.
>
> Yours Respectfully,
> Robert Martin[86]

Meanwhile, each docking of a Cunard steamer at Boston touched off a scramble of messengers and express agents using horses, locomotives, and coastal steamers to reach New York City and beyond with the latest European news. Typically the messenger would go by railway from Boston to Allyn's Point (between Norwich and New London, Conn., on the Thames River), then by steamer across Long Island Sound to Greenport at the eastern end of Long Island, then by rail to Brooklyn. Numerous New York newspaper dispatches of European news during the early 1840s lead off with stirring accounts of news messengers' perilous and record-breaking dashes along this, or some similar, route from Boston. (See, for example, the *New York Herald* quotation at the start of this chapter.)

Thirty-five years later, *Printer's Circular*, prompted by an article by James Parton in the *New York Ledger*, says such "exertions... have probably never been surpassed in the history of the daily press." The *Circular* quotes Parton as saying the cost, as much as $3,000 for a single express effort, was usually shared by half a dozen papers in Boston, New York, and Philadelphia. These expresses, the *Circular* observes,

> made a great stir at the time, for the editors did not fail to blow the boastful trumpet, and the public were gradually worked up to a high degree of excitement. Bets were made, as in the case of other races, and anecdotes were told of the tricks and adventures of the express riders.[87]

One other transportation development that affected news movement needs mention here. The express company business was born March 4, 1839, when William F. Harnden first carried a valise of small packages and letters between Boston and New York. Harnden, and later such express companies as Adams and Co. and Wells Fargo, transported and hand delivered messages, parcels, and packages in a growing network of public and express company–operated modes of transportation. The extent of Harnden's pioneering company is described in an excerpt from his advertisement in the *New York Evening Post* for July 10, 1839.

> WM. F. HARNDEN. . . will run a car through from New York to Boston, and vice versa, for the purpose of carrying specie, packages of goods, small bundles, &c. . . . Responsible agents will accompany the car for the purpose of purchasing goods, collecting drafts, notes and bills, and will transact any other business that may be entrusted to his care.[88]

A sizable portion of the express companies' early business—until introduction of the telegraph—consisted of handling news dispatches and bundles of exchange newspapers for newspapers along their routes. Much of this press traffic was apparently conducted free in order to gain favorable mention in newspapers. One historian of the express business, A. L. Stimson, put it this way: "There were frequent editorial acknowledgements . . . and Harnden seems to have served the press with great zeal for two or three years after he had started his enterprise. In reciprocation, the editors, by their commendations, materially aided him."[89] Hudson nostalgically recalls the days of express-newspaper cooperation just before telegraphy burst upon the landscape. Noting that the express lines "became useful in bringing the latest papers to the newspaper offices," Hudson comments, "those were sparkling days in journalism . . . . Those were times of lively enterprise among the newspapers. They were days to remember."[90]

One final news-gathering development consisted of the gradually emerging "science" of gathering and interpreting election returns. In the pretelegraph days, it was an accomplishment just to amass returns that were accurate and reasonably complete; a journalist's crowning achievement, however, was to interpret those returns correctly. Bennett and Horace Greeley had the knack, according to Hudson, and Hallock acquired it out of necessity after the departure of Richard Haughton from the *Journal of Commerce*.[91] Haughton, whom Hudson calls "the most enterprising newspaper man of his day in New England,"[92] was spirited away from the *Journal of Commerce* by John H. Eastburn soon after the latter founded the *Boston Atlas* on July 2, 1832. In addition to managing the editorial side of the *Atlas*, Haughton established a reputation in Boston for the most comprehensive and comprehensible election returns in the city. Hudson reports that on mornings after elections "[t]hat part of State Street near the *Atlas* office was crowded for hours by people waiting for the news."[93] W. F. G. Shanks explains that Haughton

> established a system by which he was enabled, using horses
> and the few railroads then in Massachusetts, to publish
> election returns from every town in the State by nine o'clock
> [A.M.] of the day after an election. This is nothing remarkable
> [in 1867], . . . but it was not bad for our forefathers, without
> telegraph and railroad lines.[94]

A Haughton, or a Harnden, or a Hudson might have popped up anywhere in journalism at this time, and the chances are good that they did in towns scattered throughout the growing nation. We do know that Harnden's enterprise, as well as other express companies, affected journalism well beyond the major metropolitan centers, but we lack the specifics. While the previous account of local and regional efforts touches on the various pretelegraphic news-gathering systems employed by journalists, it also measures the bias of a literature generated largely by journalists having access to the leading journals, periodicals, and publishing houses in the nation.

This seemingly self-serving literature by and about the New York City crowd has skewed journalism historiography since the appearance of Hudson's history in 1873. Many unsung journalistic pioneers no doubt worked news-gathering miracles beyond the Hudson River; indeed, until 1980 the literature assumed that the nation's first newsbrokerage arose in New York City. The metropolis seemed the natural setting for such a momentous development, especially if backwoods or small-town exploits are unrecorded or are obscured by a history shaped by the strength of the metropolitan pen and press.

By the mid-1840s, it is safe to say, most leading Eastern editors had a taste of competitive news-gathering, its benefits and costs. Regular transatlantic steamer service and the monumental news the steamers brought of a Europe in turmoil and of a Great Britain in transition were about to be linked inexorably by means of Morse's telegraph. The next chapter examines the "technological imperatives" of transatlantic steamers and telegraphy and looks at editors' initial reactions to each. The lessons of the hectic and costly competition for news prior to telegraphy were not lost on the editors of the mid-1840s, as we shall see; the telegraph induced journalistic cooperation without dulling the editors' appetite for fresh news.

DISCUSSION

Half a century of progress, ending in the early 1830s, positioned the daily newspaper press at the center of establishment life in the United States. Paralleling the growth of political and business institutions after the American Revolution, the party and mercantile press bored deeply into the consciousness of the ruling elite and the institutional fabric of the young nation. Alexis de Tocqueville found journalism's "influence in America [to be] immense" in the 1830s. "It causes political life to circulate through all parts of that vast territory."[95]

Only one of several functional media of local and national communication in colonial America, the press by the early nineteenth century had begun to crowd out other media in the nation's marketplace of ideas. Modest technological advances, such as cheaper paper, improved and portable platen presses, and the beginnings of steam-powered cylinder presses, coupled with an impressive growth in the number of newspapers, especially dailies,[96] made the newspaper press a vital component of the nation's lusty, growing institutional system.

Just as the first uses of written language, which was generally employed by 1500 B.C., were governmental and economic,[97] so the first uses made of Anglo-American newspapers, both by editors and readers, were political and economic. This mutual dependence of institutions, which in journalism led to the early emergence of party and mercantile newspapers, was largely a reflection of a new post-Revolutionary society that strove for shape and growth. As Stuart Bruchey observes, "Once government had carved out the channels of a national economy, private interest...could pour into those channels a swelling stream of capital funds, manpower, and constant technological change." Sustaining this stream was "the will of an entrepreneurial people who became increasingly better-educated members of a free society."[98]

Retaining a largely agricultural character, the post-Revolutionary United States strove for better transportation, while reaching for the beginnings of a factory system. Facing a shortage of skilled labor and venture capital in the early decades of the nineteenth century, American entrepreneurs turned to native and foreign inventions to outfit their fledgling factories. One can see in the printing rooms and news-gathering exploits of early nineteenth-century newspapers these same tendencies, for the first time in journalism, to innovate, to experiment with developing technology. For its intercity

news-movement needs, however, the newspaper remained inter-
faced with a transportation system that, while experiencing significant innovation during this period, was better equipped to move
people and goods than it was to move information.

Physically moving information from place to place in one of its
available forms early in the nineteenth century—printed or handwritten on paper or stored in the human brain—required moving
both the message and its medium over distances at the expense of
time. Transportation continually confronts the physical constants of
gravity and the contours of terrain (including water surfaces and
currents) and the unpredictable factors of seasonal and daily
weather. Transportation is a constant test of humans, animals, and
machines to traverse a given distance in the shortest time. Although
the early nineteenth century witnessed great strides in
transportation—the steamboat in 1807, the locomotive in 1830, burgeoning turnpike and canal networks, and the transoceanic steamer
in 1838—the system remained ill-suited to the rapid news-
movement needs of newspapers.

After depicting the rapid growth in speed and volume of intercity
travel between 1790 and 1840, Pred detects a relationship between
trade and information.

> Pretelegraphic long-distance trade was almost always the
> outcome of information acquisitions. . . while at the same
> time it served as a generator of information flow. . . . [T]rade
> was as much the outcome of information flows as it was the
> generator of them.[99]

But Pred's assessment deals with general information more or
less available to all in need of it. A newspaper editor's information
needs, by contrast, are unique in society, peculiar to a newspaper's
self-appointed mission. Anthony Smith thoughtfully sketches that
mission:

> At the start the newspaper situated itself somewhere
> between the historian on one side and the diplomatic,
> financial and military courier on the other. In the information
> which it chose to supply, and in the many sources of
> information which it took over and reorganized, it contained
> a bias towards recency or newness; to its readers it offered
> regularity of publication. It had to be filled with whatever
> was available, unable to wait until information of greater
> clarity or certainty or of wider perspective had
> accumulated.[100]

Thus, interacting with transportation for news movement would always be unsatisfactory for a newspaper. Not only must transportation move both medium and message (as opposed to communication systems, which move only messages), it is operated for general public use by either the government or the private sector. An editor is just another, albeit perhaps a favored, customer of the transportation system, forced to conform to preexisting departure and arrival schedules and to seek the assistance of the nonjournalists who manage and operate transportation systems.

This chapter has depicted several attempts by editors to circumvent such public service by establishing transportation systems of their own, to be used exclusively to move news. While on the whole successful, such schemes proved too costly to operate regularly. The clearest example of this is the news boat rivalry in New York City harbor where a reasonably perfected system crumbled under the weight of its cost, destroying with it newspapers' harbor competition for later news, which was replaced by the more attractive cooperative venture which generated a shared news dispatch. Hudson confirms the rise and fall of this costly, individualistic newsgathering effort.

> After five or six years' enterprise of this sort, however, the New York papers became somewhat tired of the expense, and combined their forces, and finally relapsed to the small row-boats for the collection of ship-news and foreign intelligence.[101]

The editor, thus, faced a dilemma: either he shouldered the extraordinary expense for, and management of, an essentially nonjournalistic transportation enterprise or he received his correspondence and newspapers from abroad at the same time as his readers did. The latter was not damaging to the editor's journalistic mission if the volume of information reaching his newspaper office exceeded that received by most of his readers, but many of these elite readers also frequented the reading rooms and merchant's exchanges, which offered a wide variety of news and correspondence and subscribed to the same European papers the local editor clipped for his own news reports.

Whether the editor relied on public transportation or operated his own system, however, he faced two further dilemmas, speed versus volume and irregularity of delivery. Speed of delivery and volume of information delivered are generally inversely related in transportation. News slips came by express rider, but whole newspapers arrived by slower postal service. Likewise, Craig's pigeons carried brief summaries of European news from Halifax, but the London and Liverpool papers arrived in Boston two or three days later. More recently, when rail and air transportation has surpassed the speed of express messengers,[102] tradeoffs between volume and speed still exist. To meet rail and airline schedules, deadlines have to be adjusted. Evening newspaper press runs suspend the day's news in midstream to avail themselves of overnight mail delivery or late afternoon truck delivery into the streets and suburbs. Conformity to cumbersome transportation systems creates partial accounts of half-finished news events in evening papers. Even today, the end of the line for both morning and evening papers—even for those issuing from regional satellite printing plants—is a truck rumbling down a street or a news carrier bicycling down a sidewalk. A five- or six-hour delay between deadline and delivery remains common, except for metropolitan commuter editions. Meanwhile the electronic messenger on radio and television delivers less news, but does so faster.

It is worth commenting that *speed* is a more useful concept in studying information flow via transportation systems than the time-space dichotomy traditionally used in analyzing the impact of communication media. In the period examined in this chapter, transportation's time and space dimensions were elastic; they expanded spatially as rail, post road, and navigation networks reached out in all directions and contracted temporally as innovations, based mainly on steam technology, produced improved machines to traverse those networks. Speed, the quotient of the distance/time formula, dynamically represents both dimensions of communication in the transportation area.[103] For purely communication systems, such as telegraphy, however, speed has no meaning in information flow, as all electronic transmissions theoretically travel at the speed of light. In the communication era, therefore, only the extent of the communication system's spatial development (distance) affects information flow, and time and therefore speed are applicable only where both communication and transportation systems are combined to move information from place to place.

Irregularity of delivery, the other dilemma confronting editors in the transportation era, is a particularly serious drawback in journalism. Although breakdowns in service are inevitable in new and developing communication systems, a reasonably high level of dependability is eventually attained. Irregularity of service, even today, is, however, the particular province of all transportation systems some of the time and of some transportation systems, it seems, all the time. To an editor steeped in "a bias towards recency or newness...unable to wait until information of greater clarity or certainty or of wider perspective had accumulated," to recall Smith's quote above, the irregularity of eighteenth- and early nineteenth-century transportation carriers of his news was maddening.

Whereas the physical constants of communication systems expedite information flow (see the discussion section at the end of the next chapter), both physical constraints and unpredictable weather factors constantly impede and disarrange transportation's schedules and, in turn, affect the delivery of information. Thus, news boats maintained a constant vigil until they were rendered obsolete by the relatively reliable arrivals of Cunard's steamers. And, horse expresses ideally ran every day in anticipation of important news, rather than relying on the standard transportation system when news did break.

Transportation, therefore, was an institutionalized system of public and private operation, primitive and uncertain as a mover of news. Newspaper editors, having no choice but to move both medium and message, availed themselves increasingly of transportation in the pretelegraph days, at times operating their own transportation networks. In such circumstances a newsbrokerage might have emerged. One can envision an agent for a city's newspapers meeting all arriving ships, trains, and postal deliveries, gathering and collating the news from all these sources, and delivering a news report to each newspaper office. Such a vision, however, is more academic than realistic. A central newsbroker performing these tasks in a transportation-postal setting would only be duplicating the efforts of any alert metropolitan editor whose file of out-of-town newspapers and correspondence would come to hand as readily as an agent could secure the same sources. It seems reasonable to conclude that newsbroking was untenable in a transportation-postal setting because no agent or group of newspapers could regularly receive more or fresher news than the rest or establish monopoly control over the channels by which news reached a community, especially while postal regulations permitted free newspaper exchanges.

In the two decades preceding Morse's telegraph, American editors experienced the significance and impact of aggressive newsgathering. Although newspaper competitiveness would never be totally eliminated by cooperative pony expresses and harbor associations (and the shared newsbroker dispatch that lay ahead), editors surely felt the urge to beat the public's receipt of important news via conventional transportation-postal systems. To fill the streets with an account of a presidential message or news of the repeal of the Corn Laws before the arrival of mail pouches and newspaper bundles with the same news gave a newspaper an aura of worth and immediacy it had not had before, especially among the still largely elitist readers. Of the many claims historians have made for the leaders of the penny and mercantile press movements, none can perhaps be sustained as readily as this one: they succeeded in pushing news-gathering and reporting beyond the public's own accessibility to news.

Editors in these pretelegraphic days had learned to cooperate with each other, to pool resources, to settle for a shared news dispatch. They had learned the importance of controlling the movement of their own news, something that they seldom could do in transportation except at great personal expense. And they were beginning to learn to anticipate the great news of the day either by stationing correspondents at news centers or by running their own expresses selectively. These lessons would serve editors well when the twin technological imperatives of transatlantic steam and telegraphy thrust them into a news-gathering revolution.

Chapter 2
TECHNOLOGICAL IMPERATIVES AND THE FIRST NEWSBROKERAGE

I shall never forget the . . . astonishment, with which, on the morning of the third of January eighteen-hundred-and-forty-two, I opened the door of, and put my head into, a "state-room" on board the Britannia steam-packet . . . bound for Halifax and Boston, and carrying Her Majesty's mails.

That this state-room had been specially engaged for "Charles Dickens, Esquire, and Lady," was rendered sufficiently clear . . . by a very small man-uscript, announcing the fact, which was pinned on a very flat quilt, cover-ing a very thin mattress, spread like a surgical plaster on a most inaccessible shelf.

Charles Dickens, *American Notes for General Circulation*
(1842)

We are in great haste to construct a magnetic telegraph from Maine to Texas; but Maine and Texas, it may be, have nothing important to communi-cate.

Henry David Thoreau, *Walden, or Life in the Woods*
(1854)

The words of two noted nineteenth-century skeptics appropriately introduce this chapter on technological innovation and the press re-action to it. Inventions and change are awkward forces for a society to deal with, phenomena fraught with promise and peril. This chap-ter traces the origins and journalistic meanings of the kind of vessel whose stateroom so astonished Dickens and of the gadget that Tho-reau ridiculed. The mixed press response, including formation of our first newsbrokerage, operation of early transatlantic news-papers, and early press dissatisfaction with telegraphy, will also be sketched in this chapter.

33

April 1838. During that month two quite different and seemingly unrelated events signaled an approaching revolution in newspaper publishing and national news communications.

On April 7, 1838, Samuel F. B. Morse filed for a United States patent for his improved first telegraph device, having labored four years to perfect it and acquiring along the way the technical assistance of two of the eventual copatentees, Alfred Vail and Leonard D. Gale. Morse thus claimed priority in American telegraphy and signaled his readiness to introduce his telegraph to the public. As we shall see, a successful long-distance demonstration of telegraphy lay six frustrating years in the future, and Morse's right to be called the father of the American telegraph would be disputed for years.

On April 23, 1838, the *Sirius* steamed up New York City's harbor, the first vessel of note to cross the Atlantic Ocean under steam power. She was followed into New York six hours later by another steamer from England, the *Great Western*. The era of fast, dependable transatlantic navigation had arrived, and with it the possibility of fresher, more regular news from the Old World.

In the ten years that followed these events, major transformations occurred in both American journalism and communications. Transatlantic steam navigation invited editors' most strenuous efforts yet to gather the latest European news. And, since the news was often extraordinary in the mid-1840s,[1] the nation's leading journals threw horseback messengers, express companies, and locomotives into the breach left by a telegraph system that grew too slowly for journalism's purposes. Meanwhile, telegraphy, our first practical use of electricity and the first successful[2] communication system in North America, struggled toward shape and reliability. Although rushing recklessly through infancy, telegraphy invited editors' hopes of a new era and where possible their participation in telegraphic news-gathering. Even though the press's initial contact with steamers and the telegraph brought mixed results, some journalists quickly grasped the new technologies' possibilities and pitfalls and moved to master them.

TRANSATLANTIC STEAM AND EARLY TELEGRAPHY

The arrival of the *Sirius* and the *Great Western* in New York City's harbor crowned a sequence of gradual improvements in steam transportation stretching back to Robert Fulton's triumphant passage in the *Clermont* from New York City up the Hudson River to Albany on August 17–18, 1807. The few pounds per square inch of boiler pressure in the *Clermont*'s steam engine had to be greatly increased if the Atlantic's three thousand miles were to be traversed without prohibitive fuel use. Two groups of British engineers tackled the problem, and those outfitting the *Great Western* finished first, the ship leaving for New York on April 7, 1838. Their competitors, unable to get their *British Queen* ready in time, chartered the *Sirius*, a coastal steamer, which left for America four days after the *Great Western* and beat the latter by six hours.[3]

England's eagerness to develop transoceanic steam technology arose from the British political and economic communities' desire for closer, more regular contact with the burgeoning American economic and agricultural systems. Indeed, in the wake of the Panic of 1837 Britons lamented that steamships had not been available earlier, many believing, according to F. Lawrence Babcock, "that many of the substantial firms which failed [in the Panic] might have survived...had remittances from America not been delayed by the prevailing easterly winds."[4]

In the two centuries prior to steam navigation, European news arrived in the New World irregularly and haphazardly. But regardless of how old the "latest dates" were, they were eagerly welcomed by newspapers and the public. European news was always an important element of American newspapers.[5] Although Americans often found themselves at the mercy of foreign editors' news definitions and political leanings, nothing could dim the Yankees' appetite for foreign news.

By far the most persistent drawback of presteam navigation was its irregularity. The previous chapter comments that slowness alone is a relative matter. One does not miss, or necessarily even hope for, speed and freshness in news that one has not experienced. But battling the physical variables of daily and seasonal weather was more vexatious than coping with physical constants of prevailing winds, gravity, and friction of the ocean's surface. Nothing frustrated the American editor more than an overdue packet or the infrequency of arrivals during the winter. And when a sailing ship sank, the loss of its news was mourned as sadly as the loss of life and property. As we shall see, the new steam technology, while not conquering gravity, defied most weather and the prevailing westerlies, bringing regularity to Atlantic crossings. This is not to ignore the fact that steam also increased the speed of those crossings.

Frank Luther Mott estimates that in the eighteenth century sailing ships took four to eight weeks to bring British news across the Atlantic. Continental news required an additional two to six weeks to reach England. Thus, foreign datelines in American newspapers were regularly two to three months old.[6] Even with the advent of clippers and faster packets in the 1830s, foreign news was still one to two months old when it reached U.S. newspapers.[7]

Using reports in U.S. newspapers of ship departures and arrivals on westward passages, Robert Greenhalgh Albion offers a picture of the problems that slow and irregular ocean crossings posed for American newspaper editors in the presteam days. Analyzing data on 2,834 westbound crossings[8] from Liverpool, London, and Havre between 1818 and 1848, Albion found the "common range" of passage duration over the entire thirty-year period to be between thirty and thirty-nine days.[9]

Beyond this common range in either direction, the extremely slow passage bedeviled an editor while a fast passage could bestow on him an unexpected news feast. The fastest westbound sailing passage during these thirty years was sixteen days, with five trips made in less than twenty days. The slowest westbound passage was eighty-three days, with eight trips made in more than seventy days.[10]

For many editors the arrival of the *Sirius* and the *Great Western* was just another exciting tidbit of news, but a few sensed that the event signaled the advent of faster and more reliable delivery of foreign news. As previously noted, *New York Herald* editor James Gordon Bennett, for example, booked passage for the *Sirius*'s May 1 return trip to England to arrange for regular European correspondence for his paper.[11]

The success of these first British steamers prompted the British Admiralty to advertise in November 1838 for bids to establish a regular steamer mail and passenger service between England and North America. Samuel Cunard, of Halifax, Nova Scotia, a merchant with experience in transatlantic shipping and a part-owner of a Quebec-Halifax steamer, had been thinking about such service and responded with a bid that soon won for him the exclusive British mail contract in the North Atlantic corridor.

Cunard's bid called for four coal-burning ships with 207-foot keels and 34.2-foot beams. Able to transport 115 cabin passengers (no steerage was available), the one-funnel side-paddle steamers each had a crew of eighty-nine men and one cow (for milk). While their chief power was a 740-horsepower steam engine, the steamers were also fitted with three masts to augment or back up the engine.[12]

Such ships could cross the Atlantic westward in sixteen or seventeen days and eastbound in fourteen to sixteen days.[13] The west-bound passage was accomplished in only 47.8 percent of the time required by the average westbound sailing ship, according to Albion's study. With a fleet of four steamers, Cunard could run monthly departures from both Liverpool and Boston during the three winter months and twice-monthly departures from each city the rest of the year.

The steamer *Britannia* left Liverpool at 1 P.M. July 4, 1840, on the maiden voyage of the new service of the British and North American Royal Mail Steam Ship Company (as Cunard's line was officially called). In addition to the *Britannia* (the steamer referred to by Dickens at the start of this chapter), Cunard's original fleet consisted of the *Acadia*, the *Caledonia*, and the *Columbia*.

The *Hibernia* was added in 1843, and the *Cambria* in 1845. By January 1848 these six steamers were joined by the *America*, the *Canada*, the *Niagara*, and the *Europa*, and westbound passages sailed alternately for Boston and New York City.[14] Belching smoke, their side paddles splashing awkwardly through the water, these Cunarders (as they were called) provided a dependable "ocean ferry," and offered U.S. newspaper editors for the first time regular delivery of foreign news. As we shall see, transatlantic steamers gave rise to transatlantic newspapers and numerous expresses and schemes to move the news once the steamers were at or near American shores. (It must be noted that sailing packets remained steadfastly in service despite the appearance of steamers because many travelers preferred their smoother ride and wider variety and cost of accommodations and many merchants were attracted by their lower cargo rates. Such packets and other steamship companies augmented journalists' reception of foreign news, but Cunard's line was the chief conduit by which foreign news reached American shores and U.S. newspapers until the Atlantic cable was completed in 1866.)

Morse's telegraph received a U.S. patent on June 20, 1840. By then he had already spent two years and most of his money demonstrating the device in New York City and Washington, D.C., eliciting mild curiosity, but not the financial support he had hoped for. In Washington Morse demonstrated the telegraph in 1838 for congressmen from whom he sought funds to erect and test a long-distance telegraph circuit. The chairman of the House Commerce Committee, F. O. J. Smith of Maine, enthusiastic about the Morse demonstration, pushed through his committee a $30,000 appropriations bill for the experimental line. Writing on behalf of his committee in

1838, Smith correctly but prematurely said, "the subject is one of such universal interest and importance, that an early action upon it will be deemed desirable by Congress."[15]

The full House failed to act on the measure, however. Even so, Representative Smith had already, a month before writing the above, signed on as Morse's "counsel, publicity man, and promotional agent," according to Robert Luther Thompson, thereby acquiring a one-fourth interest in the invention's patent rights.[16] Smith finally got around to leaving Congress in 1839 to devote full time to Morse's cause as a lobbyist in Washington. Benjamin Perley Poore later wryly observed that Morse "had to give large shares of [the telegraph's] profits to Amos Kendall and F. O. J. Smith before he could make his discovery of practical value."[17]

The inventor's son Edward Lind Morse more frankly reports that Morse "was, unfortunately, not a keen judge of men," having "an almost childlike faith in the integrity of others." When Smith volunteered to assist Morse, his son continues, "a man of more acute intuition would have hesitated.... Smith did...much in later years to injure Morse, and to besmirch his fame and good name...." He goes on to quote from an 1895 article in which Franklin Leonard Pope says

> Morse in 1843–1844 courteously but firmly refused to be a party to a questionable scheme devised by Smith for the irregular diversion into his own pocket of a portion of the governmental appropriation of $30,000 for the construction of the experimental line.

"Ever after," says Pope, "Smith cherished toward the inventor the bitterest animosity."[18] This brief sketch of the odd Morse-Smith partnership may serve to explain Smith's early role in telegraphy and his later seemingly irrational antagonism toward both the Morse interests and the Associated Press.

In late 1842, Morse was back in Washington giving more demonstrations and again seeking a government subsidy. In the final hours of the congressional session, on March 3, 1843, Morse finally received his $30,000 grant, with which he intended to construct a line from Washington to Baltimore along the Baltimore and Ohio Railroad right-of-way.[19] After one false start (Morse first attempted to construct the line on the ground encased in lead pipe), work on the first successful intercity telegraph line began in mid-March of 1844. By April 2, seven miles of line suspended on poles stretching northeast from Washington were in operation. On April 11 ten miles of line were successfully tested; on April 20 sixteen miles of line worked; and on April 30 twenty-two miles were in operation.[20]

At this point the first of two famous news dispatches moved on the Morse line. On May 1, 1844, Annapolis Junction was the northern terminus of the line and a scheduled stop for the B.&.O. trains. Alfred Vail, a copatentee and the line's chief mechanic, was at Annapolis Junction and had spent most of May 1 conversing by telegraph with Morse, who was in Washington. Late in the afternoon the sounder in Washington began clicking. "The ticket is Clay and Frelinghuysen," it said in code to Morse. The Baltimore-to-Washington train had stopped at Annapolis Junction with that bit of news from the Whig national convention then meeting in Baltimore, and Vail had relayed the news on to Washington. Word spread through Washington, and people rushed to the railroad station to confirm the news with passengers on that train.[21]

By May 22 the line was completed to the Baltimore railroad depot, and two days later "What hath God wrought!" flashed over the line during its public ceremonial opening.[22] The next day saw the second historic news dispatch move on the line. The telegraphic exchange occurred as follows:

> BALTIMORE: Ask a reporter to send a despatch to the Baltimore Patriot at two o'clock p.m.
> WASHINGTON: It will be attended to.
> [One and a half hours elapse.]
> WASHINGTON: Two o'clock p.m.—The despatch has arrived and is as follows:
> One o'clock—There has just been made a motion in the House to go into the Committee of the Whole on the Oregon question. Rejected, ayes 79, noes 86.
> Half-past one—The House is now engaged in private bills.
> Quarter to two—Mr. Atherton is now speaking in the Senate.[23]

On May 27 the *Washington Madisonian* carried a dispatch under the heading "Telegraphic News," an account of the Maryland State Convention at Baltimore. That same day the *Washington Globe* ran telegraphic dispatches from the same convention. The next day Washington's *National Intelligencer* headed a dispatch "By the Magnetic Telegraph."[24]

Newspapers along the new line, thus, began at an early date to use and to experiment with this new form of news communication. Elsewhere, however, editors were reluctant, even antagonistic, about the new device. The following account by a writer for the *Journal of the Telegraph*, reprinted in the *New York Times* in 1872, sheds light on one famous editor's first reaction to telegraphy.

> In order to bring the [telegraph] to the attention of the business interests, Mr. Ezra Cornell, . . . who had superintended the erection of the Washington and Baltimore line, opened for exhibition a short line of telegraph in Boston. Finding but little encouragement in that city, the exhibition was soon abandoned there, and transferred to the City of New-York, where an experimental line was opened in the Autumn of 1844, for exhibition to the public. . . . So little attention did this wonderful invention then receive, even at the modest admission fee of one shilling per head, that Mr. Cornell and his assistant found it extremely difficult to maintain themselves in the most humble manner, upon the entire receipts of their exhibition. Sleeping on the chairs in their exhibition room, they often found it necessary to go to bed supperless. Without the means of paying for advertising, the daily papers were besought to notice the exhibition editorially. Kindly notices were given by the *Express* and the *Evening Post*, as well as some of the other papers of the day, but not a word could the *Herald* be induced to say. Finally Mr. Cornell sought an interview with [*Herald* editor James Gordon] Bennett, and solicited his attention. He was met by the very frank statement from Mr. Bennett that he was opposed to the success of the telegraph. In Bennett's own words, he "had at great expense established his own expresses in such manner that he could beat all of his rivals, and if the telegraph were once successfully established he would lose his advantage."[25]

The account goes on to say that at the end of 1846, with a telegraph line operating between Albany and New York City, Bennett's horse and locomotive express, organized to deliver the governor's message from Albany, was utterly beaten by a telegraphic transcript of the message appearing in the *New York Express*. Bennett was made a believer. Cornell, incidentally, had erected the Albany–New York City line.

Few, however, who saw or experienced the impact of Morse's invention in 1844–45 were able to foresee the massive upheavals it would cause in America's business, government, and news habits. Telegraphy stood on the brink of reshaping national institutions and invading the national psyche, yet most dismissed it as a toy, failing to grasp the significance of transmitting messages among communities and individuals at the speed of light. But since society had had no experience with intercity communication, in contrast to information movement by transportation, such early indifference is understandable.

More directly, the embryonic telegraph—being neither transportation nor a locally based communication system, such as newspapers—had no obvious institutional home in which to mature. Moreover, its electric technology, itself making a maiden voyage in society, offered no guidance as to telegraphy's parentage. Indeed, the telegraph had no lineage, and only a handful of developers and early supporters were on hand at the birth to ponder the infant system's familial future. Congress's $30,000 act of midwifery suggested to these guardians—or at least some of them—that telegraphy might mature better as a child of government, rather than in the private sector.

Morse feared mischief at the hands of private owners. Writing Representative Smith on February 15, 1838, Morse said:

> In the hand of a company of speculators, who should monopolize it for themselves, [telegraphy] might be the means of enriching the corporation at the expense of the bankruptcy of thousands. . . . I will engage to enter into no arrangement to dispose of my rights, as the inventor and patentee for the United States, to any individual or company of individuals, previous to offering it to the Government for such a just and reasonable compensation as shall be mutually agreed upon.[26]

With completion of the first experimental line, Morse in fact offered unsuccessfully to sell his patents to the government for $100,000.[27] Both in May and December of 1844, Morse publicly urged Congress to take control of the invention, but his memorials were ignored. A few newspaper editors publicly shared Morse's fear of private ownership. William Swain, later a heavy investor in the telegraph, commented in his *Philadelphia Public Ledger* of June 20, 1844, that "The Government [should] possess itself at once with this triumph of American genius, and give to every city throughout the Union the advantages which may be derived from it."[28] The *New York Herald* on May 12, 1845, said, "Government must be impelled to take hold of it" and incorporate it in the postal service.[29]

On the other side, just as many journals lined up behind private ownership. Jeremiah Hughes, editor of *Niles' National Register*, will serve as an example.

> We see it asserted by several of the most respectable of
> our public journals, that the people of this country are
> anxious for the general government to take this invaluable
> improvement as a national concern, and regulate it somewhat
> in the manner that the mails and post routes are controlled.
> . . . [Y]et upon the whole, . . . communities would be better
> served and their interests better taken care of, if [the
> telegraph is] in their own keeping, than if submitted to the
> control of the government. . . . Why then should the people
> part with its control?—Why make a government monopoly of
> it?[30]

The twin issues of government regulation and ownership of communication systems, of course, survive to the present day. Those in
the 1840s who feared government control or a government monopoly could not foresee the Western Union monopoly, forged in the
private sector in 1866, and even if they could, many still would have
objected to governmental interference in private contracts and capital, "free trade," and the theory, if not the practice, of competition
in the private sector. Here is the beginning of the classic debate over
natural monopolies and the proper role of private and governmental
interests in development and control.

For telegraphy, this debate burst forth with renewed vigor after
the Western Union monopoly emerged, and it continued to rever-
berate in the halls of Congress, in periodicals, and among businessmen and reformers until World War I. Alvin F. Harlow reports that
between 1845 and 1900 congressional committees eleven times in-
vestigated the possibilities of a "postal telegraph," as governmen-
tally controlled telegraphy was called in recognition of its natural
kinship with the postal system. On nineteen occasions during this
period House or Senate committees publicly expressed opinions on
governmental control of telegraphy, favoring governmental involvement on seventeen of them.[31]

Back in 1844, with his experimental line a success but failing to
generate governmental interest in adopting telegraphy, Morse and
his friends reluctantly began constructing a private sector shelter
for their electromagnetic infant. The blueprint for telegraph's home
in the private sector was an organizing contract, dated March 10,
1845, which identified the rights and obligations of the paten-
tholders. There were four patentees: Morse, who first envisioned a
practical telegraphic system and conducted initial experiments, and
held nine-sixteenths interest; Vail, who tooled the early Morse instruments and improved their initial design, holding one-eighth in-

terest; Gale, a New York University chemistry professor who assisted in designing the system, with one-sixteenth interest; and Representative Smith, the lobbyist who championed Morse's request for federal funds, with one-fourth interest.[32] The interests of the first three men, according to the March contract, were to be administered by Amos Kendall, whose administrative abilities, legal training, and previous experience as postmaster general fulfilled Morse's need for an agent to protect the inventor's personal financial interests while shielding Morse from telegraph's daily affairs. Approval of Smith's one-fourth interest was needed for the Morse interests to convey patent rights.

Kendall set about designing a national telegraphic system and arranging for initial construction contracts by awarding Morse patent rights to regional consortiums of construction and business interests. Drawing on his postal experience, Kendall foresaw five major telegraph arteries. Each would be constructed and operated by a separate company, drawing its officers and financial support from the region through which the telegraph line was routed. All five companies agreed to transfer each others' messages at cities where their lines converged, thus creating a single national system. Each company, however, would be autonomous in its own region, and each was a new creation, organized expressly to engage in the business of telegraphy. Kendall's five trunk lines and the new companies formed to operate them were as follows:

- Washington, D.C., to New York City, through Baltimore, Wilmington, Philadelphia, and Newark. It was operated by the Magnetic Telegraph Company, organized May 15, 1845, by Kendall and others in the name of the three patentees he represented.
- New York City to Buffalo, via the Hudson River Valley to Albany and westward along the New York Central Railroad right-of-way. This was the New York, Albany and Buffalo Telegraph Company, which received the Morse patent rights in a contract on May 30, 1845, between Kendall and John Butterfield, owner of a Utica, N.Y., express company. A Butterfield associate, Theodore S. Faxton, became president and chief spokesman for the company.
- New York to Boston, via Stamford, Norwalk, Bridgeport, New Haven, Hartford, Springfield, and Worcester. This line was run by the New York and Boston Magnetic Telegraph Company, organized on October 22, 1845, with F. O. J. Smith as its chief executive officer.
- The Atlantic, Lake & Mississippi Telegraph Company

encompassed six separate suborganizations, all under the control of Henry O'Rielly, who contracted with Kendall for the Morse patent rights on June 13, 1845. Lines of this company fanned out across the old Northwest Territory: Philadelphia–Pittsburgh–Columbus–Dayton–Cincinnati–Louisville–Vincennes–St. Louis, St. Louis–Chicago, Buffalo-Cleveland-Toledo-Detroit, and Dayton-Indianapolis-Chicago.

• Washington, D.C., to New Orleans, through Richmond, Raleigh, Columbia, Macon, Montgomery, and Mobile. This was the Washington & New Orleans Telegraph Company, contracted to John J. Haley (a cousin of F. O. J. Smith) on November 2, 1846.[33]

Except for the New Orleans line, construction progressed on all routes during the autumn of 1845, with crews erecting poles and stringing lines in several sectors of the routes simultaneously. On the Washington, D.C., to New York City route, for example, Washington and Baltimore, as noted above, had already been joined by Morse's experimental line on May 22, 1844.[34] Newark and Philadelphia were linked on January 20, 1846, and Newark was linked to Fort Lee, N.J. (on the banks of the Hudson River), on January 22, 1846. The Philadelphia-Baltimore section was ready for service on June 5, 1846.[35]

Meanwhile the company struggled with the vexing problem of traversing the Hudson River. Early attempts to lay a submarine cable on the river bottom failed because of seepage and damage caused by ship anchors.[36] And efforts to string a line between tall masts on opposite banks of the river fell victim to high winds and ice storms. Finally in 1852 gutta-percha, a tough plastic substance resembling rubber and containing resin, proved to be an effective insulator for submerged telegraph lines. Until gutta-percha was developed, the company bridged the Hudson by transporting telegraph messages between Manhattan and New Jersey by river ferry.[37]

Kendall's New York City to Washington, D.C., line was the first trunk opened for service, if one winks at the ferry link across the river. Smith's New York City–Boston service opened second, on June 27, 1846. A line from Boston to Washington, D.C., by mid-1846 thus put New York City's leading newspaper editors in touch with two of their most significant and regular sources of news—Cunard steamer landings at Boston and government, chiefly congressional, affairs in Washington. As we shall see in the next chapter, completion of these early telegraph links profoundly affected the content of New York papers at an early date.

The third Morse line opened to the public was the New York, Albany and Buffalo company. Its Albany-Buffalo section was operational on July 4, 1846, and the Albany–New York City section was completed on September 9, 1846. Progressive editors in towns between Albany and Buffalo, anticipating the approaching telegraph line, began setting up the nation's first newsbrokerage in February and March of 1846, mixing telegraphed dispatch and mailed news slip technologies until the Morse line was complete. This will be discussed further later in this chapter.

The web of western lines stretching toward the frontier and under O'Rielly's control materialized more slowly. A look at some of their dates of completion will indicate the difficulty O'Rielly had penetrating and finding financial backing in these less-settled areas: Philadelphia-Pittsburgh, December 26, 1846; Pittsburgh-Cleveland, August 1847; Pittsburgh-Cincinnati, end of August 1847; Cincinnati-Louisville, end of September 1847; Louisville-Vincennes, December 1, 1847; Vincennes-St. Louis, December 11, 1847; and Buffalo-Detroit, March 1848.[38]

O'Rielly's problems were complicated by what he judged to be inferior Morse equipment and overly conservative Kendall management. In the fall of 1848 O'Rielly unburdened himself of the Morse contract and bought the rights to a rival telegraph device, the Bain instrument. Besides setting off a round of legal battles, O'Rielly's move proved damaging to the Morse interests. O'Rielly had acquired a national reputation for constructing durable, dependable telegraph lines and for managing those routes in response to public need, charging low rates and giving press dispatches priority and special low rates wherever possible. These policies had rewarded O'Rielly with a steady stream of good press notices. Editors' growing disenchantment with the Morse system by late 1847 helped, by 1848, to entice O'Rielly into the main Eastern corridors to erect Bain telegraphic routes in competition with Morse lines, as we shall see presently.

The fifth Morse trunk line, Washington, D.C., to New Orleans, frustrated all concerned by not being completed until after the end of the Mexican War. The last of the five companies to organize and the slowest to erect lines, this outfit did not fill in all sections of its proposed route until July 1848. War with Mexico was declared on May 13, 1846, and the Morse people continued to search for a contractor for the Southern line until November of that year. Southern investors cautiously awaited word of the financial success of North-ern lines, and Kendall, desperate to link the powerful New York City press with New Orleans, its source of Mexican War news, turned to the federal government for assistance. Congress was not receptive, and neither was the Eastern press when Kendall proposed that edi-tors invest in the line in exchange for exclusive use of all war and other news dispatches transmitted on it.[39]

A contract with John J. Haley, as noted above, was finally penned on November 2, 1846, and when General Winfield Scott en-tered Mexico City and captured Santa Anna on September 17, 1847, the only operational sections of telegraph were Washington, D.C.-Petersburg, Va., and Montgomery-Mobile. The infant telegraph was having coordination problems, and the hovering editors were not sure whether they should help it, nor what they should expect of it. Amid the confusion, however, the press was engaged in some clear and decisive journalistic activities in response to steam navigation and telegraphy.

THE JOURNALISTIC RESPONSE

When Cunard in 1840 introduced his ocean steamers because the British Admiralty sought a faster, more regular delivery of the mail, journalism entered a transition between transportation and com-munication systems, which would blend and blur these two modes of news movement for the next decade. The arrival of a steamer, but especially a Cunarder, at an Eastern port was a journalistic event of high drama for newspaper people. There were, of course, the partic-ulars of the crossing—its duration, the weather encountered, other ships sighted along the way, notable passengers onboard, and the like—to report. But usually of greater importance was the foreign news the steamer brought in its letter pouches and bundles of for-eign newspapers.

If the steamer's news reached the office of a morning newspaper after about 4 A.M., editors and typesetters would toil to capsulize it for a midday or afternoon edition. Arrivals after noon, unless the news warranted an extra edition, pointed the editorial effort to-ward the regular morning edition; the later the arrival, the more awesome the editorial and composing task, as this passage from the *Boston Herald*'s history indicates.

> "Steamer Nights"... were the especial aversion of editors
> and reporters, and at once the dread and pleasurable
> anticipation of compositors. The former had sometimes to

wait into the morning [for] the papers of the steamer. . . .
Then they had to go over them, pick out and collate the
latest and most interesting items of news, and put them in
shape for the printers. Sometimes the news would be quite
important, and at others flat, stale, and unprofitable. The
interesting news could be easily arranged. . . under long and
often elaborate headings. . . . But when the news was barren,
it was a puzzle how to write headings. . . to catch the eye of
the general reader.

The printers, as a rule liked steamer nights, though they
dreaded a heavy "grist" of copy to set. The later the news
came in, the better it was for them, because for every hour
they waited they were paid at the same rate as for
composition. . . . Sometimes, for economy, the printers would
be allowed to go to their homes after all local matters had
been put in type on a steamer night; the understanding being
that they would be called up if the papers were received in
time to use the news in the morning edition. . . . [T]he
majority preferred waiting, as it gave them an opportunity to
follow the example of their editorial *confreres* and indulge in
dominos, poker, hot Scotch, or in "jeffing" for coppers. . . .[40]

Similar scenes were being played out in newspaper offices all
along the Eastern seaboard, delayed only by the amount of time it
took for messengers, express companies, pigeons, locomotives, the
postal service, or eventually the telegraph to deliver the news from
the steamer's landing site.

While a few other steamers and numerous packets plied the Atlantic, the Cunard service was the centerpiece for journalists—
regular, relatively frequent, carrying the royal mail. Between 1840
and 1847 Cunarders departed from Liverpool monthly in winter and
every other Saturday the rest of the year, bound for Halifax and
Boston. To U.S. editors and readers the steamers' news was a stop-
action view of European affairs, the great events and men of Europe, Asia, and Africa held in fortnightly or monthly suspended
animation—parliamentary debates unfinished, revolutions unre-
solved, ailing statesmen neither recovered nor deceased, market
trends and oscillations abruptly frozen.

With Cunarders calling only at Halifax and Boston, editors in
New York City and to the south eagerly anticipated completion of
the New York–Boston telegraph line, which finally opened for service on June 27, 1846. Continuing friction between the press and
that line's management is discussed in chapters 3 and 4 in terms of
the New York City Associated Press's reception of foreign news.

Meanwhile, a renegotiation of the Admiralty contract in July 1846 permitted Cunard to extend steamer service to New York City. Begun late in 1847, Cunard's new schedule called for Liverpool departures every Saturday, year around, with destinations alternating between Boston and New York City. The *Hibernia* was the first Cunarder to land in New York City, doing so on December 29, 1847. (All Cunarders continued to make the Halifax stop.)[41]

Development of ocean steam transportation touched off another journalistic enterprise—the transatlantic newspaper, a compilation of foreign news presented in newspaper format and published to coincide with the departure of transatlantic steamers.[42] Although it is now impossible to reconstruct the number and variety of such papers, a few examples have survived and the record indicates that transatlantic papers were published on each side of the Atlantic for distribution on the other.

The first person this author has found who attempted a transatlantic newspaper was Dr. John S. Bartlett, editor of the *New York Albion*, a weekly established by Bartlett on June 22, 1822. Calling it "an organ of English opinion," Frederic Hudson notes that the *Albion* "acquired an influential position, and was a useful paper to the British population of the United States."[43]

On January 30, 1841, six months after Cunard began his ocean service, Bartlett announced in the *Albion* a "newspaper on a novel plan."

> *A Journal on a plan entirely new, will be shortly published in Liverpool*, in connection with the "New York Albion," to be called "THE EUROPEAN." Its novelty will consist in being published on the days on which the steamers severally sail, so that it may always bring the very latest news. . . . There is *no single pub'ication* in Great Britain which occupies this ground, and "The European" will combine all the matter of interest to American readers, of half a dozen British journals. . . . The proposed publication will indeed supercede a number of Price Currents, Circulars, Shipping Lists, &c., and will put the merchant, the politician, and the man of leisure in possession of all the European intelligence that can interest him, a few minutes after the vessel shall be in port. . . . Advantage will be taken of Mr. Cunard's Steamers whenever their priority of sailing promises a priority of arrival.[44]

The above announcement was repeated in the *Albion*'s February 6 edition, and the first number of *The European and General Com-*

mercial Intelligencer (subtitled "Published in Connexion with the New York Albion") was published for Bartlett in Liverpool on February 10, 1841.[45] The first number's departure, however, was postponed about a week because the Liverpool printer had mistakenly thought that the *European*, because its total distribution would be outside of England, could escape the British stamp tax on newspapers. In consequence, even before the first number reached American shores, Bartlett (forewarned of the stamp tax problem by his Liverpool printer) had to announce a price rise in the annual subscription to the *European* from $2 to $3 for *Albion* subscribers, but remaining at $4 for nonsubscribers.[46]

Finally on March 6 Bartlett could note in the *Albion* the arrival of the first *European* by the steamer *President*. His comments below about the first issue and his need to go to Liverpool indicate the awkwardness of supervising a publication from three thousand miles away.

> Our agent in Liverpool had many difficulties to contend
> with, independently of those incident to a "First Number,"
> but it is nevertheless a well filled sheet of excellent matter.
> ... [It is] the cheapest British paper ever introduced to this
> country. It is, however, capable of some improvement, and we
> shall send forward by the [steamer] President such
> instructions as may be necessary; it also is the intention of
> the Proprietor of the Albion to proceed shortly himself to
> England in order that the European may be made as perfect
> as possible, and worthy of the patronage of the public.[47]

Luckily Bartlett postponed his own trip to Liverpool, sending only "such instructions as may be necessary" via the *President*. It left New York for Liverpool on March 11, 1841, carrying Bartlett's instructions to his printer, and the ship was never seen again. It was the first transatlantic steamer lost at sea.[48]

The author has been able to locate only one copy of the *European*—volume II, number 38, dated September 20, 1842. A five-column, four-page paper with type pages measuring 14$\frac{1}{2}$ by 22 inches, this issue notes that it was "printed and published, for the proprietor, by Thomas Carter, of Devonshire-Place, Everton, at the Liverpool Mail-Office, Liver-Court, South Castle-Street, Liverpool."

The contents of this extant *European*, and of other transatlantic newspapers published in Liverpool that the author has been able to examine, are summarized elsewhere.[49] Suffice to say that the *European* was similar to copies of *Willmer & Smith's European Times*, described below. Since the paper did not use whole numbers, its publication frequency cannot be reported with certainty. If one assumes that volume II began during the week of February 6–12, 1842, the *European* appeared every six days, on the average, between February and September of 1842.

On September 17, 1842, Bartlett's *Albion* announced the sale of the *European* to Isaac Winslow, a New York City merchant, who, according to Bartlett, intended to continue the publication. Bartlett explains that in "consequence of our other avocations we find it difficult to give the necessary attention to the proper distribution of the European in this country."[50] The *European* suspended publication on November 4, 1842,[51] for reasons the author cannot ascertain.

By all surviving indications the second transatlantic newspaper was *Willmer's American News Letter*, published in Liverpool from September 3, 1842, to September 14, 1845.[52] Unable to locate a copy of this paper, the author can only speculate about its purpose and publisher. If it is consistent with the practice of the day, the title suggests that this paper contained American news for distribution in England, if not all of Europe. If so, the paper's short life may be attributable to the fact that a paper of American news would need to have been published in America in order to be competitive with regular American newspapers once the steamer reached Liverpool. The time required to read, summarize, set type, and print American news in a Liverpool shop would have given the American journals several hours' head start in the British mails.

Indeed, six months after the demise of the *American News Letter* the Liverpool firm of Willmer & Smith announced a new publication, *Willmer & Smith's American Times*, to be published in New York City for Liverpool-bound steamers departing from New York and Boston.[53] Which Willmer is referred to in the *American News Letter*'s title is unclear; two Willmers ran separate printing houses in Liverpool at this time.

Edward Willmer, born in Windsor on October 25, 1793, served a printing apprenticeship in Windsor and went to work in the office of the *Liverpool Chronicle*, eventually purchasing that paper. The *Chronicle* apparently was neither a successful nor a noteworthy venture since it consistently evades mention in English journalism histories.[54] Edward, however, along with David Smith (about whom nothing can be found), was a proprietor of *Willmer & Smith's European Times*, which shall be examined below. Edward died on May 6, 1869.[55]

Charles Willmer, Edward's nephew, was born in 1819 and after apprenticing in his uncle's Liverpool print ship started his own printing business in the same town, founding the *Liverpool Northern Daily Times* on September 24, 1853. The *Times*, which lasted until January 30, 1861, is said to have been the first daily paper published in the provinces. Charles then reestablished himself in the printing and newspaper business in Birkenhead, a Liverpool suburb, where he died on October 18, 1897.[56]

Before focusing on Edward and his *European Times*, it should be noted that Charles, too, tried his hand at transatlantic journalism, apparently in competition with his uncle. *Charles Willmer's European Mail* appeared on January 19, 1847, four years after his uncle's *European Times* began its successful run. Charles's paper lasted until July 11, 1849.[57]

The author could find only number 6 (August 19, 1847) of *Charles Willmer's European Mail*, a four-page, six-column sheet much like Bartlett's *European*. Number 6 was published for the departure of the Cunarder *Caledonia* for America; according to a notice in the paper, the *Mail* published only for Cunard departures.

Edward Willmer and David Smith were engaged in much more than publishing a transatlantic newspaper. Already in business twenty-five years when they introduced their *European Times*, these gentlemen advertised an import-export business. They ran a fast express from Liverpool to London, transporting American newspapers, correspondence, and goods from ships arriving in Liverpool. In the other direction they offered the American public European newspapers, "New and Old Books, Periodicals, Paper, Stationery, Type, and every article used by Booksellers, Stationers, and Printers for a small commission."[58] In 1843 they listed Moses Beach of the *New York Sun* as their New York City agent, but later that year they established their own agency, Willmer & Rogers, in New York.[59]

The first issue of *Willmer & Smith's European Times*, dated January 4, 1843, contained the following prospectus:

> Newspaper editors and readers on the other side [of the Atlantic] find, on the arrival of a packet the impossibility of getting at the correct view of the . . . events which have occurred in the interim except at a considerable sacrifice of time and labor. . . . [In the *European Times*] every item of intelligence worth recording . . . has been condensed according to its relative importance; the facts have been preserved, but stripped of all redundancy. . . . A vast number of interesting

> events...are obliged to be entirely excluded from the
> American press, owing to the diffuseness with which they are
> narrated and the impossibility of finding time, in the hurry
> and bustle attending the arrival of a packet or steamer, to
> condense and arrange them satisfactorily.... It is not
> intended to supersede the London and other papers, but
> rather, by presenting their contents in a striking view, and at
> a glance, to afford the reader of the more voluminous
> journals the choice of perusing their contents when time and
> opportunity enable them to do so with advantage.[60]

The formula worked. The paper continued publishing until September 27, 1868,[61] little more than two years after the successful Atlantic cable opened for service. No reason for the paper's death other than the cable can be unearthed. The author has located eight issues of the *European Times*.[62] Like the other transatlantic newspapers mentioned here, the *European Times* ordinarily devoted about half of its four- or eight-page space to commercial summaries, market tables and stories, and shipping news; about one-third to general and political news; and the remaining one-sixth to advertisements, notices, and the editor's summary of general and commercial news found elsewhere in the paper.

One has no way of knowing the *European Times*'s impact on the American reading public. The paper's longevity and scattered references to the paper in obscure corners of the literature lead one to suppose that it had a rather wide circulation in American political and economic circles. Neither was the paper a stranger to U.S. newspaper editors. In a study of the transfer of stories from the *European Times* to the foreign news columns of New York's *Herald* and *Tribune*,[63] the author found the *Herald* filling an average of 54.7 percent of its foreign news space with copy taken verbatim from the *European Times*. Verbatim *European Times* copy filled 75.8 and 57 percent of the *Tribune*'s foreign file on two Cunard arrivals. The only subtlety in this impact of *Willmer & Smith's* on these leading U.S. dailies in the early 1840s was the reticence with which U.S. editors credited the Liverpool paper as the source of the "adopted" dispatches.

It was noted above that Willmer and Smith announced publication in New York City of an *American Times* for European distribution to begin soon after March 4, 1846, nearly three years after their *European Times* appeared. Two, and possibly three, New York City publishers also inaugurated transatlantic newspapers for distribution in Europe at this same time. Faced with only scraps of evidence, one cannot be certain of these developments, but it appears that Bennett jumped in first with a *Herald for Europe* first appearing on May 31, 1846.[64] Published on "every steam packet day" and claiming a circulation of forty thousand by July 15, 1846,[65] the paper apparently lasted until 1879,[66] two years after James Gordon Bennett, Jr., established the *Paris Herald*.[67]

James L. Crouthamel found in the *New York Courier and Enquirer* for July 14, 1846, a notice that that paper was beginning "a special European edition" for "each steamer's departure for the Continent."[68] The firm of Greeley & McElrath, sometime during late 1847 or early 1848, introduced the *New York Tribune for Europe*, "published on the departure of each mail steamer for Liverpool."[69] No recorded European *Courier and Enquirer* survives, and there is only one *Tribune* recorded as extant.

The author has examined that *Tribune for Europe* and a copy of the *Herald for Europe* and finds them very similar to those papers' weekly editions for domestic distribution. Columns of accumulated telegraphic congressional reports, correspondents' letters, clips from domestic newspaper exchanges, and a week's worth of book and performing arts reviews make up the bulk of their reports. They are very lean on advertising, and, while giving full marine reports, they can muster only about one column on American markets in tabular form, compared with a full page of market tables in *Willmer & Smith's European Times*.

It seems clear from a comparison of Liverpool and New York City varieties of transatlantic newspapers that the New York editors had a far easier time of it, coping with exchanges in only one language, smaller amounts of market data and marine activity, fewer countries, and generally a smaller volume of significant news. Bennett and Horace Greeley covered principally one developing nation in eight broadsheet pages, while Willmer and Smith covered a wider variety of powerful and struggling nations on three continents in eight blanket sheet pages. These disproportionate journalistic tasks and the relative significance of the news they generated explain, in part, why Liverpool beat New York City into the transatlantic newspaper field.

It might fairly be asked why both the Liverpool and New York publishers inaugurated New York-based and European-bound newspapers during a relatively short period in 1846. Any answer will be speculative, but it must be recalled that fundamental changes in Anglo-American relations occurred in that year. Among several U.S. expansionist ventures, the Oregon boundary dispute came to a head early in the year. And on June 26, 1846, British protectionists saw their cherished Corn Laws repealed in the House of Commons, opening the door to free trade between the two countries. Additionally 1846–47 saw New York City begin to enter the transatlantic steam picture. Cunard opened service to New York late in 1847 on the basis of a contract signed with the British government in July 1846, but meanwhile in 1846 the lagging U.S. ship-building industry finally stepped forth with a challenge to Cunard in the form of New York–Liverpool service by the Collins Line. Finally, by mid-1846 New York City was already the hub of the growing telegraphic system, and the city's newspapers and telegraphic reporters, as we shall see in chapter 3, were taking the lead in gathering telegraphic news from all points along the seaboard reached by telegraph circuits. There is no evidence that Boston publishers attempted transatlantic newspapers in the six years of Cunard dockings at that port prior to 1846.

Cunarders and other steamers prompted other journalistic enterprise in America. Augustus Maverick reports that Daniel H. Craig began to fly homing pigeons with Cunard news from Halifax to Boston around 1843.[70] His customers included a few newspapers and some market speculators who would benefit from advance information on European market fluctuations. One of Craig's steady customers in those early days was the *New York Sun*, which on December 14, 1843, mentioned having had a homing pigeon loft on its roof "since we occupied this building," which was in the summer of 1842.[71] Forty years later Craig described his pigeon operation.

> Years before the establishment of the telegraph I had a
> regular News Reporting Business...from Halifax to Boston. I
> carried my birds by land to Halifax to meet the incoming
> Cunard steamers, and then took passage for Boston. After
> gathering news from London and Liverpool journals, I printed
> it on tissue paper, with small type, in my stateroom, fastened
> it to the legs of the birds, and at the proper time flew them
> from the decks or portholes of the steamers. My birds carried
> the news to Boston several hours in advance of the steamers,
> where it was used for speculative purposes, and subsequently
> for publication.[72]

Craig's birds were formidable competition for those newspapers attempting to express mail pouches and dispatches by more conventional transportation systems. Hudson, the *New York Herald* managing editor, comments on the birds' news-moving advantages.

> Carrier pigeons have been more or less used by journalists,
> speculators, and governments. They are swift flyers, and can
> go long distances without intermission. Their speed ranges
> from forty to seventy-five miles an hour. They have been
> known to fly in a few instances, at the rate of one hundred
> miles an hour. Nothing practical but the telegraph can exceed
> this velocity.[73]

Press opposition to Craig's birds at times took the form of direct appeals to the Cunard people. Craig explains:

> When it became known that I was anticipating with my
> birds the news brought to Boston by the steamers, the agent
> of some of the New York journals made representations to
> the Cunard company that I was using the news for
> speculative purposes, and they undertook to prevent me from
> taking my birds on board their steamers at Halifax.
> On one occasion [Cunard] Captain Ryrie seized and held
> [the pigeons] until after the steamer arrived in Boston.
> Apprehending this outrage, I had put one of my birds in my
> overcoat pocket before going on board, and after putting the
> news on his legs, I went on deck and flew the bird close to
> the captain's head. He darted into his stateroom and caught
> his rifle, but before he got a chance to shoot, the bird was a
> mile above him, flying straight to his home in Boston, a
> hundred miles away....[74]

No discussion of Cunarders and transatlantic news movement is complete without mention of the legendary *William J. Romer* episode, an early journalistic effort to hasten news of, and perhaps to affect, affairs of state. The *Romer* incident involved enterprise of the *New York Tribune* to beat the Cunarders and one or more New York papers with news of the Oregon question.[75]

Excitement on both sides of the Atlantic was running high over the disputed boundary of the Oregon Territory early in 1846; dark thoughts of another Anglo-American war could not be suppressed. On January 23, 1846, the Cunarder *Hibernia* reached Boston with news of a new British prime minister and hostile English reaction to President James Polk's December 2, 1845, message to Congress declaring that his administration would settle only for a boundary at 54° 40'. The British, who originally had wanted much of present-day Washington state, according to the *Hibernia*'s news, would entertain an earlier U.S. offer to set the boundary at the 49th parallel (its final location).

The *Hibernia*'s dispatches were raced to New York City by parallel expresses operated by the *Herald* and *Tribune*. The *Tribune*'s express won this time by a wide margin, giving *Tribune* publisher Thomas McElrath the idea of secretly dispatching a fast pilot boat, the *Romer*, to England to deliver the American response to the *Hibernia*'s news and to bring back England's reaction. With the North Atlantic still locked in winter's grip, another Cunarder was not due for nearly a month. On February 9, when Congress directed Polk to notify England that the former convention on Oregon was being terminated, McElrath had the news item to set his scheme in motion. The *Romer*'s unexplained movements in the harbor had been the subject of much gossip and even newspaper articles; equally titillating was the occasional appearance on the *Romer*'s deck of a mysterious man wearing a heavy pilot's coat and a glazed cap pulled down over his face.

Late in the afternoon on February 10 the *Romer* suddenly weighed anchor and shot down the harbor, heading for the open sea and bent on beating all other ships to England with news of Congress's Oregon action. Unfortunately for McElrath and the *Tribune*, the *Romer* did not reappear in New York harbor until April 11, a victim of foul weather on both crossings and without news sufficient to warrant the enterprise. The following account, based on a *Tribune* story by Bayard Taylor, reveals the *Romer*'s ordeal on the high seas.

> On the first evening out she encountered a fearful gale, and her decks and sides were soon encased in ice. On the 12th she encountered a hurricane. . . . For two days she was in constant danger of foundering. And this experience continued with slight variations, through the entire voyage. On March 1st the weather improved, and on the 4th, the twenty-fourth of the voyage, the first dry spot appeared on the deck, and two days afterward the Irish coast was sighted. On the 7th a Cork pilot was hauled on board. . . . Old Neptune seemed determined to put every possible obstacle in the way of newspaper enterprise. On the return voyage, nine days and nights were lost in laying to, and so boisterous was the sea that Captain McGuire finally decided to take the southern passage, which added a thousand miles to the voyage. . . . [T]he Romer did not reach New York until April 11th, a [westbound] voyage of twenty-nine days. The English news brought was only five days later than that which had been already received. . . .[76]

The mysterious man in the glazed cap turned out to be Monroe F.

Gale, assistant foreman of the *Tribune*'s composing room, a passenger on the *Romer* who carried the latest U.S. news from Cork to Liverpool and returned to the *Romer* with the latest English news. Hardly a successful journalistic venture, the *Romer* incident became, instead, a tale of daring and survival.

While the *Romer* struggled to complete its mission, several New York papers employed an agent to meet the next Cunarder, the *Cambria*, at Halifax, secure her papers, race by horseback across Nova Scotia to Annapolis on the Bay of Fundy, take a steamer to Portland, Maine, and a train to Boston. The agent arrived in Boston a little ahead of the *Cambria*. The *Herald*'s agent gathered his paper's mail at Boston, and although departing Boston forty-five minutes after the agent for the other papers, he beat the competitor substantially. Relying on *Herald* accounts, David Budlong Tyler describes the *Herald*'s express.

> Bennett's agent. . . by prearrangement, rode a locomotive to Worcester, another to Norwich, then Commodore Vanderbilt's steamboat *Traveller* to Greenpoint where a relay of three Long Island locomotives, each provided with a hand-car in case of emergency, brought him to South Brooklyn. He had come from Boston in the record time of 7 hours and 5 minutes, thus permitting the *Herald* to get out an extra containing "31 days later" news several hours before the arrival of the other agent on the express steamer from Stonington. This was an expensive victory and Bennett did not attempt to repeat the feat.[77]

When one turns to U.S. editors' response to the telegraph, one is struck by how rapidly some of them employed telegraphy for their purposes. In a previous section it was noted that three weeks before Morse's experimental line was formally opened between Washington, D.C., and Baltimore in 1844 a news dispatch announcing the Whig presidential ticket had been flashed to the capital. And in the days following the line's opening, newspapers along it availed themselves of the droplets of news it conveyed.

Along the emerging routes of the telegraph a scattering of newspapers took the initiative in using its dispatches, making early demands on its service, and showing more reluctant and cautious colleagues its potential. Routine telegraphic news first appeared in New York City papers in early May 1846, even before that city was fully wired to the cities where those dispatches originated. The dispatches had made their way through a mixture of telegraph and transportation links. (Chapter 3 describes early New York City newsbroking, including the appearance of these earliest telegraphic news dispatches in that city.)

Two months earlier, however, America's first newsbrokerage was developing in upstate New York in close alliance with the youthful New York, Albany and Buffalo Telegraph Company. Utica businessmen Faxton and Butterfield, it will be recalled, had purchased the Morse patent rights to erect telegraph lines between New York City and Buffalo, via Albany, through a burgeoning agricultural and commercial corridor already twice favored by transportation developments. The Erie Canal had opened in October 1825 and was paralleled by rail service by 1831. New York's ten-volume history describes changing conditions in this corridor in the 1830s and 1840s.

> A conspicuous line of changing community life across the state was the area immediately along the waterways between Buffalo and New York City.... Most of these communities were built to serve as distribution points to the agricultural population, and, on account of their advantageous location for assembling materials and marketing products, they developed into manufacturing centers. Thus it was that Buffalo, Syracuse, Oswego, Auburn, Utica and Rochester became cities of importance.[78]

Faxton and Butterfield easily raised the financial backing for their telegraphic venture from so fecund a business region. In exchange they gave these communities one of the most dependable, well managed, and profitable of the early Morse lines. Writing enthusiastically to Vail in October 1846, Morse reported receipts on the Faxton-Butterfield line for twenty-three days of $2,900, enough after expenses to show a 14 percent profit.[79] Telegraph historian James D. Reid reports that

> From the time of the opening of the line until March, 1847, it had worked so well and on the whole so uniformly, that Professor Morse spent much of his leisure time in the office in New York, quietly enjoying the fruition of his work, and regarded this as his pet line. Its working quality was superior to most other lines.[80]

The contract with Morse interests for telegraph rights in New York state was signed on May 30, 1845, and by August 27 telegraph wire was on the verge of linking Utica and Little Falls (a distance of twenty miles) and Buffalo and Lockport (twenty-two miles).[81] Work continued on all sections of the Albany-Buffalo line during the winter, and the first major leg (Utica-Albany) was completed on January 31, 1846.

On February 3 the *Utica Gazette*, with Alexander Seward and Rufus Northway as co-owners, carried nearly a column of telegraphic news from Albany. It was the first such journalistic event west of Albany. Looking back on that moment thirty years later, Seward commented that the telegraph "offered great benefits to the local newspapers, but it required a compensation which in their then feeble condition they were unable single-handed to pay."[82]

Immediately after that February 3 column of telegraphic news appeared in the *Utica Gazette*, Northway and Seward received four requests from alert editors to the west for exchanges or *Gazette* subscriptions. On February 5 the *Buffalo Pilot* sent one dollar for the *Gazette* to be forwarded in specially marked *Pilot* envelopes.[83] The next day the *Rochester Advertiser* wrote, "We are desirous of getting an exchange with your daily, for the purpose of making up our legislative summary from your telegraphic postscript."[84] The *Auburn Daily Cayuga Tocsin* on February 7 requested a three-month exchange with the *Gazette*,[85] and on February 12 the *Buffalo Courier* asked to receive the Utica paper.[86]

The following list of all known daily newspapers between Albany and Buffalo in 1846 reveals that these four papers were less than one-third of the dailies west of Utica.

> Albany: *American Citizen, Argus, Atlas, Herald, Journal,*
>   *Knickerbocker*
> Troy: *Budget, Post, Whig*
> Utica: *Gazette*
> Syracuse: *Journal, Star*
> Auburn: *Advertiser, Tocsin*
> Rochester: *Advertiser, American, Democrat*
> Buffalo: *Commercial Advertiser, Courier & Pilot, Democrat,*
>   *Express, Morning Gazette*

(The longevity of the *Albany American Citizen* is unclear; the most recent extant copy is June 17, 1846. In Buffalo the *Courier* and *Pilot* were merged on June 27, 1846.)[87]

Meanwhile two of these upstate editors saw that newspaper subscriptions and exchanges would soon be outmoded by the advancing telegraph. Early in February Isaac Butts, editor of the *Rochester Advertiser*, one of the four papers that had requested the *Gazette*'s telegraph news by mail, went by train to Albany, apparently to see if he could expedite news from the east for his paper. Enroute he stopped in Utica and talked with Northway and Seward, who apparently also had news movement on their minds. Writing from Albany on February 11, Butts told the *Gazette*'s management

> I shall make no arrangements here connected with the telegraph as I understand you will be willing to transmit *all* intelligence to my paper. . . . It is useless to have two conflicting agencies and I hope you will continue to do as you proposed on my way down [to Albany]. [88]

The plan both papers were contemplating consisted of hiring an Albany newsman to compile a daily telegraphic news report for the western papers from whatever was available in Albany. Apparently Northway and Seward had convinced Butts that their paper should organize this enterprise, situated as it was at the western terminus of the then-completed telegraph line.

In the weeks that followed, the *Utica Gazette* sent several circulars to editors west of it, soliciting their support for a plan to hire an Albany correspondent who would compile a report for the *Gazette*, which, in turn, would print proofs of its telegraphic news column to be express mailed on the westbound train leaving Utica during the evening. [89] The mail link, of course, was temporary, the editors anticipating eventual completion of the telegraph to Buffalo. Response to this scheme of a mixed telegraph-transportation newsbrokerage was both enthusiastic and cautious.

The first paper to sign up (after the *Rochester Advertiser*'s Butts acceded to the *Gazette*'s plan) was the *Syracuse Daily Star*, whose editor, James Kinney, wrote on February 17 that he would share in "the expense. . .but cannot at present say how much I can give." The *Star* would pay its fair share "until the experiment had a fair trial." [90] The next day the *Auburn Tocsin* agreed to participate, noting that the *Tocsin*'s editor had contacted Faxton of the telegraph company on the subject of news dispatches and that Faxton had referred him to the *Utica Gazette*. [91] The telegraph people apparently both knew of, and were cooperating with, the *Gazette*'s attempt to form a newsbrokerage.

Other acceptances came more slowly: the *Rochester Democrat* on February 19, [92] the *Buffalo Pilot* on March 4, [93] the *Auburn Advertiser* on March 6, [94] the *Buffalo Morning Gazette* on March 7, [95] the *Rochester American* on March 12, [96] and the *Syracuse Journal* on March 20. [97] By March 7, 1846, therefore, eight newspapers (including the *Utica Gazette*) were sharing the expense of a common telegraph–mail news dispatch and anticipated employing an Albany correspondent. This was 57 percent of the papers between Utica and Buffalo. Letters to Northway and Seward indicate that the *Gazette* began forwarding news slips as soon as a newspaper's notice of participation reached Utica. Here was the embryo of a newsbrokerage.[98] When its members were all connected by the telegraph network (July 4, 1846, as shall be seen), this newsbrokerage was truly born. The author's definition of newsbroking does not require participation by all or any specific portion of the newspapers reachable by communications, but as long as the telegraph was still being extended across New York state, the membership and operation of this emerging newsbrokerage were in flux. The absence on the record of any similar newspaper, telegraphic, or independent enterprise that resembles the author's definition of newsbroking before this time strongly suggests that this was the nation's first newsbrokerage.[99]

During these early weeks it is unclear who in Albany prepared the news dispatches for transmission to Utica, but sometime during March 1846, the *Gazette* engaged William Lacy, an employee of the *Albany Argus*, to compile and file the reports. With Lacy on the job, editors along the telegraph-railway system could expect up-to-date Albany news and a professionally prepared digest of the New York City and Boston papers. Upstate editors paid Lacy $28 in April and $12 in June for his services.[100] Records show that Lacy was still employed by the upstate group in December 1846. In 1851 Alexander Jones, then general agent for New York City Associated Press, listed Lacy as the Albany correspondent for his newsbrokerage.[101]

Ten upstate newspapers had combined forces by April 1, 1846, to forward news from Albany. This was 71.4 percent of the papers between Utica and Buffalo, and was the best Northway and Seward could do until the line was completed from Albany to Buffalo. Much of the resistance to the scheme arose in Buffalo, where, according to letters to the *Gazette*, editors were especially contentious and reactionary. Beyond this, however, Buffalo initially encountered technical problems with the scheme. In February only one train a day reached Buffalo from Rochester, and because of the rail schedule on the Utica-Rochester leg, the *Utica Gazette*'s proof sheets were delayed in Rochester one full day. Early in March, however, a second train began service to Buffalo, giving that city's morning papers the edge on printing the news dispatches. Buffalo's *Pilot* and *Morning Gazette* thus joined the movement early, the rest of the Buffalo press holding out until the telegraph line was opened to that community.[102]

Other sections of the Faxton-Butterfield line were beginning to close ranks. The express mailing of proofs would soon be unnecessary. Utica-Syracuse was the next section opened for traffic. At a meeting on May 28, 1846, in Syracuse—the first recorded newsbroker meeting of editors—the New York State Associated Press[103] editors transferred responsibility for forwarding news slips from the *Utica Gazette* to the Syracuse newspapers. The Albany-Syracuse circuit was opened on June 1.[104]

One month later Buffalo was finally linked to Albany, and the *Utica Gazette* embraced the feat with unbridled enthusiasm. Under the headline "The Hudson Talking to Lake Erie!" the July 4 *Gazette* exclaimed

> The lightning flashed through from Albany to Buffalo, 325
> miles by railroad, this morning at 8½ o'clock. The Telegraph
> now spans the Empire State! The events transpiring at the
> Capital, at one end, are made known at the other extremity
> in "less than no time." . . . This is the longest line of telegraph
> in the world. . . .[105]

Faxton, with his typical promotional flair, telegraphed the following invitation to newspaper editors along the completed line:

> T. S. F.'s compliments to the editors of all the daily papers
> between Albany and Buffalo: will be happy to meet them
> and their friends at the different telegraph stations, on the
> Fourth [of July 1846] between the hours of 4 and 5 P.M. for
> the purpose of interchange of sentiments.[106]

Faxton's "novel party" on the telegraph was covered the next day in the *Utica Gazette* with a two-column account under the headline "Electromagnetic Drama, or a Lightning Sociable."[107] Unlike some of his telegraph contemporaries, Faxton realized the business advantages of cultivating press friendships. The success of the New York State AP can, in large measure, be attributed to the dependability of his telegraph service and to his willingness to recognize the editors' needs and accommodate them.

The New York State AP editors met on August 5, 1846, in Utica and prepared a formal proposal to Faxton's telegraph company for handling a common daily news dispatch for the papers along the completed line. The editors offered Faxton $72 per week to transmit one and a half hours of news daily between 8 and 11 P.M. and a "brief report of the markets together with such facts in the way of news as have become known at New York during the day" between 2 and 3 P.M. If foreign news arrived in New York during the day, "a little more space" was to be given the report. The proposal specified that the editors would furnish a reporter at Albany.[108]

Faxton, though, had the final word, because two weeks later a circular, distributed to the editors, indicated a $100 weekly assessment by the telegraph company for delivery of news report of the above specifications. The circular also announced that George M. Snow of the *New York Tribune* had been hired at $15 per week as the group's New York City correspondent. Snow's salary was to be equally divided among the newspapers.[109] Various letters and records indicate that Snow was attached to the State AP at least up to April 18, 1848, when Snow threatened to sue the *Auburn Advertiser* for libel for charging him with delaying a foreign news dispatch.[110] Snow had been the *Tribune*'s Wall Street reporter for five years in 1846 and continued at that post until 1863.[111]

The New York State Associated Press circular concluded with a warning similar to admonitions that over the years became familiar to editors affiliated with newsbrokerages.

> If any paper or papers decline coming into the arrangement on the above terms, the deficiency thereby occasioned to be assessed equally among the remaining papers. It is the understanding that no paper in the above places which does not come into this arrangement is to be furnished with the Telegraph news.[112]

A handwritten tabulation at the bottom of the extant copy of this circular indicates that there were nineteen members of the New York State Associated Press as of August 18, 1846. Compared with the list presented earlier of all dailies between Albany and Buffalo, this tabulation includes all but three: the *Albany American Citizen*, *Buffalo Democrat*, and *Buffalo Morning Gazette*. The Albany paper may have suspended publication by August; the last known issue of that paper was June 17, 1846.[113] There is no clear explanation for the two Buffalo holdouts—especially the *Morning Gazette*, which had been a participant in the earliest telegraph-railway scheme back on March 7.

Albany was finally linked by telegraph with New York City on September 9, 1846. In the State AP documents is a handwritten financial tabulation for the first five weeks after New York City came on the line. It shows the eight Albany and Troy papers each paying $6.10 per week; the five Utica, Syracuse, and Auburn papers each paying $5.10 per week; and the six Rochester and Buffalo papers each paying $7.10 per week. Appended to these figures is a notation that five full days of service were lost during these five weeks because of telegraph failure.[114]

The news report being received for these prices was seldom a full column of type in the first year. Normally a fifth to a third of the report consisted of the New York City markets. Most items were brief, usually only one-paragraph affairs, and the majority dealt with politics, disasters, and an occasional human interest item or act of violence. For some distant or significant news items, the dispatch would indicate how the information had been acquired. The language, to twentieth-century eyes, is stiff, sentences often laden with digressive phrases and clauses. (Examples of the State AP's news report can be found in the *Utica Gazette* during the last half of 1846 and on into 1847.)

Thus the New York State Associated Press came into being. As subsequent chapters indicate, war broke out between the New York City AP and the Morse telegraph system, and the Morse people in about 1850 began expanding the reach of an allied newsbrokerage, Abbot & Winans, to compete with the AP. Faxton, still a loyal Morse franchisee, arbitrarily delivered all the papers along his upstate New York line to the Abbot & Winans news service early in 1851.[115]

By the mid-1850s an aggressive recruiting campaign, coupled with a better news report and some telegraphic leverage, had retrieved all of these papers for the New York City AP service.[116] The upstate newsbrokerage was incorporated as the "Associated Press of the State of New York" in 1867[117] and maintained its separate identity in the AP structure until 1897, when the death of the old United Press left the Associated Press of Illinois free to create a single national newsbrokerage, eliminating all of the old city, state, and regional associations.[118]

Although newspapers along the Erie Canal may have been pleased with their handiwork and satisfied to have an agent in Albany and New York City looking after their news interests in the world beyond upstate New York, their big-city cousins had long before acquired a taste for more and later news. Indeed, some of those big-time editors had operated news-gathering schooners two hundred miles at sea and had organized expensive pony and locomotive expresses from Boston and Washington, D.C. Thus, it was with growing frustration that these metropolitan editors watched help-lessly as the highly touted Morse telegraph inched through the South as war with Mexico raged on between 1846 and 1848.

What the telegraph had wrought in upstate New York by mid-July 1846 remained beyond editors' reach between Washington, D.C., and New Orleans until mid-July 1848. Above it is noted that this Southern line was the last of Kendall's five trunks to acquire a contractor. Although construction began as soon as the contract was signed on November 2, 1846, and continued at a brisk pace on all sections, the fifteen-hundred mile route proved a time-consuming distance to span with telegraph line. And when the line was finally opened, it disappointed all concerned. Telegraph histo-rian Robert Luther Thompson comments

> The long-awaited line failed to live up to expectations. It
> was a source of grief both to its subscribers and to the public.
> Bad insulation, poor wire, crude transmission—all the
> difficulties experienced by the shorter lines—were multiplied
> a hundredfold on the great 1,500-mile route. Contractor
> Haley may have built the line in good faith, but his primary
> interest in the project had been the construction profits.
> Judged even by the low standards of the day the Washington
> & New Orleans line was inferior.[119]

Although short spans of telegraph line south of Washington could be used to relay Mexican War news (and allow New York City papers to use the "By Magnetic Telegraph" logo over their war dispatches), the slow progress and poor quality of the line left the editors no choice but to rely on the Southern mail or organize horse expresses to beat the mail.

U.S. attempts to negotiate secretly with the Mexicans stretched through the fall of 1845, blocked by technicalities and disagree-ments over negotiation agendas. As tensions grew, the *New York Herald* on December 26, 1845, announced formation of an express, sponsored by the *Herald* and the *New York Journal of Commerce* in cooperation with the *New Orleans Crescent City*, to beat the South-ern mails by from one to four days. It began operation in January 1846.[120]

A sixty-pony express from New Orleans, arranged by the *Phila-delphia Public Ledger* and the *Baltimore Sun*, went into action after the May 1846 U.S. declaration of war on Mexico.[121] At the same time, a 150-mile express to offset slow regular mail service between Mobile and Montgomery was devised by the *New York Sun* and the

Charleston Courier. As Hudson describes it, the *Sun*'s express competed with the *Herald*. This suggests that the *Herald* joined the express of the Philadelphia and Baltimore papers. Hudson's comment on this express competition emphasizes that Mexican War coverage relied on a transitional transportation-communication mix similar to the upstate New York editors' news-movement scheme between March and July of 1846.

> Efforts were made to reach the southern telegraph office first. Sometimes the *Herald* would succeed, and sometimes the *Sun*. Frequently the messengers of these journals would enter the office together. The exclusive use of the wires could not be given to either. They were therefore allowed fifteen minutes each. Not many lines of news could be transmitted in that brief space of time over poor lines, with miserable insulation and inexperienced operators. The result was not favorable to the enterprise of these journals. They spent a good deal of money, but gained very little advantage over each other.[122]

By mid-1847, within a few months of the end of the Mexican War, an association of sorts had formed to operate an express from New Orleans. It included the *Herald, Sun, Journal of Commerce, New York Tribune, Baltimore Sun, Philadelphia Public Ledger*, and *Charleston Courier*.[123] The mixed transportation-communication system engaged in bringing war news to New York led to some odd datelines. The following *New York Herald* lead on the dispatch announcing Mexico's ratification of the peace treaty can be understood only by knowing that the Southern telegraph then extended only to Columbia, South Carolina.

> COLUMBIA, S.C., Feb. 26th, 1848
>
> The daily overland Express package has been received and brings dates from New Orleans to the 21st, Tampico to the 13th, and Vera Cruz to the 16th, the last two brought by the English steamer, which arrived at Cat Island on the 20th instant. . . .
>
> The courier from the English legation arrived at Vera Cruz before the steamer sailed, with dates from the city of Mexico to the 13th.[124]

Even after the above dispatch arrived at the most southerly telegraph office, it was two more days before it appeared in the *Herald*. While many of the participants in these expresses were later organizers and beneficiaries of the Associated Press, the Mexican War was not the vehicle that led the New York City press to devise a newsbrokerage. Some modest order and dependability, such as Faxton's line in upstate New York afforded, may have been a necessary prerequisite to newsbroking.

Delays, line disruptions, inept transmitting and copying, experimental and inadequate equipment—all remained endemic to early telegraphy. For the New York City press, for example, the last lap of their Mexican War dispatches and their pipeline to Washington news was the line of Kendall's Magnetic Telegraph Company between Washington, D.C., and New York. Alexander Jones describes the line uncomplimentarily:

> It was several months after [the line] was opened, before
> scarcely any reliance could be placed on it. . . . This
> irregularity and illegibility was owing to the imperfect
> construction of the early lines, and to the want of experience
> on the part of operators, copyists, &c.[125]

Wherever the telegraph spread its lines, newspaper editors' first taste of the gadget was bittersweet. And editors did not withhold their complaints about telegraphy's early inadequacies. Even among the pioneering New York State AP editors, who relied on Faxton's reliable line, the grumbling began early. From the *Utica Gazette* in late 1846: "The Telegraph got the sulks last night and did as it pleased about holding over the latter part of our report. We managed, however, to get some snatches of, we believe, all the news."[126]

The *Albany Argus* for November 9, 1846, complained of the accuracy of the telegraphic news. News from the Cunarder *Britannia* just arrived in Boston was telegraphed from Boston to Springfield and carried on to Albany by train. A later train from Boston brought *Willmer & Smith's European Times*. Comparison of flour quotations on English markets in the Boston telegraphic dispatch and in the *European Times* showed the former to be inflated. The paper called upon the telegraph company for an explanation.[127]

Another upstate AP paper, the *Rochester Democrat*, on February 13, 1847, minced no words in expressing its frustration with telegraphy's news-movement performance.

> Owing to the frailness of the present [telegraph] structure
> we lose a great many reports; and in order to make up for
> the regular reports we lose, the [telegraph] Company have
> agreed to send us the reports of foreign and any other news
> as soon as it arrives. We are content with this arrangement,

> although we are losers by it—the number of extra reports
> falling far short of those we lose by breaks.[128]

The *Democrat* goes on to raise the old specter of speculation. Reporting that notice of the arrival of the packets *Admiral* and *Sarah Sands* had gotten only as far as Syracuse on the telegraph, the paper said that market speculators boarded the westbound train at Syracuse, detrained at Rochester, "and scattered themselves in various directions, fleecing farmers and holders of produce out of their stocks at low prices."[129]

Back at the pioneering *Utica Gazette*, Northway and Seward's tale of woe grew more melancholy and embittered, as this 1847 comment illustrates.

> The Telegraph is in complete order today, but after
> dancing attendance for hours, we can only get from New
> York the gratifying intelligence, "No report this A.M." So it
> goes. When there is any news, the Telegraph is down; when it
> is in order, there is no report, or "it can't be sent," or it slips
> through without being taken. We pay ruinously, are as
> vigilant as possible, but get little for our pains but vexation of
> spirit. The Telegraph has great capabilities, but its particular
> province seems to be to tantalize those who depend upon
> it.[130]

Aside from technical difficulties, the press and telegraph were at loggerheads at an early date over rates, line priorities, and the use of codes. Should the press have special low rates? Should a rate structure discourage combinations of newspapers (i.e., newsbrokerages) and the use of codes? How much daytime telegraphy should be allocated to press dispatches at the expense of general well paying business? Should telegraphers also serve as local correspondents for distant newspapers or combinations? What was to prevent telegraphers from copying a distant paper's dispatch and handing it over to a local editor? Such questions were hotly debated in newspaper columns between 1846 and 1848. The Morse "monopoly" drew increasing criticism from the press, which vowed occasionally to erect its own telegraph network.

But the Morse people were not oblivious to the potential power and patronage of the press. On November 8, 1845, months before the first line entered New York City, the Magnetic Telegraph Company stockholders unanimously resolved

> That in the present state of our information, it is
> inexpedient to adopt any system to regulate the transmission,
> by Telegraph, of general news and Congressional and
> Legislative proceedings, but being anxious to consult the
> convenience of the Newspaper Press, we invite its managers
> of all sects and parties, to a free interchange of views on the
> subject, that before our line be extended to Baltimore and
> Washington, we may if possible, digest a system which shall
> be just to ourselves and acceptable to them. [131]

In the early days of the company, bills for telegraph news dispatches that arrived too late for newspapers' deadlines were "charged to profit and loss," including $41.29 against the *New York Express*, $2.50 against the *New York True Sun*, and $10.50 against the *New York Tribune*. [132] In another instance, however, the company would not relax its prohibition on "collect" telegrams even though they consisted of news sent from one newspaper to another. The case involved a 997-word dispatch of foreign news from a Cunard arrival on July 17, 1846, sent by the *New York Sun* to the *Washington Union*. Although the *Union* might be expected to pay the $20 charge for the dispatch, the company's directors ruled that the *Sun*, as sender, had to pay. [133]

Despite early efforts to cooperate with the press, Morse lines were reluctant to lower rates generally or to grant the press either preferential treatment or preferential rates. Press criticism against the Morse interests grew steadily during 1847. The next chapter depicts a crescendo of such criticism in early 1848. The Magnetic company, however, was unmoved. Company president Benjamin B. French, addressing the stockholders' meeting on July 11, 1848, recommended reducing rates in order to increase income and to "remove much of the feeling. . .that the Telegraph is a monopoly." French said,

> The press has, to some extent, joined in this cry and seems
> disposed to patronize [telegraph lines competing with the
> Morse system]. That vast engine, the press, powerful for good
> or for evil, is, in this matter, doubtless influenced by motives
> somewhat selfish. Its conductors regard our charges as too
> high, and all they desire is to bring about a reduction. [134]

Neither the stockholders nor the directors were moved by this argument; the company clung to its high rates.

The Morse instrument had held the promise of rapid, national communication, but being the first in the field with an untried system, and facing demanding newspaper customers, telegraphy's youthful awkwardness became the brunt of jokes and earnest criticism. Kendall's master plan for dispersing investment, construction, and management responsibilities among his various trunk routes soon revealed itself as divisive and ineffectual. Contractors and company managers bickered among themselves. Rates and policies varied from line to line, as did the quality of service. A movement was afoot by mid-1846 among some telegraph proprietors to remove Kendall from direction of the Morse system. F. O. J. Smith threatened to invade territory assigned exclusively to other Morse franchisees. Henry O'Rielly's voice was heard increasingly in the West criticizing the Morse equipment and management. Haley's Southern line was so badly constructed that much of it had to be rebuilt within months of the line's opening. Kendall's own Washington–New York City line was constantly in need of repair in the first couple of years. Only the Faxton-Butterfield franchise across New York state regularly showed a profit and approached even occasional dependability.[135] And the upstate editors' disaffection with this best-of-all Morse lines is noted above.

Adding to their internal turmoil, the Morse people were very early faced with the external threat of other telegraph inventions and systems entering the field. In 1846 Royal E. House of Vermont applied for a patent on a printing telegraph system capable of sending and receiving messages twice as quickly as Morse's instrument, and of delivering a printed message, rather than Morse's inscribed dot-and-dash code. Two years later Alexander Bain, a Scottish scientist, introduced an electro-chemical telegraph three times faster than the Morse apparatus. But, like Morse's, Bain's telegraph transmitted code rather than an alphanumeric message.[136] While Morse and Kendall pressed through friendly newspapers to have their own instrument recognized by the public as the true and only telegraph in the United States, they fought competitors in the courts for infringing on their patent rights. The House system survived the challenge and eventually received a patent. Bain's invention, however, lost its court test in November 1851, and several hundred miles of Bain lines were forced to consolidate with Morse companies.

Telegraph operators victimized editors; editors publicly criticized telegraph proprietors. Press and telegraph each reached vainly for strength or some advantage over the other. Neither was satisfied with the other's demands, nor could either at this early stage develop a scheme to control the chaos existing between them. Thompson observes that

> Eager as telegraph and press were to collaborate with one
> another, their early relations were not always pleasant. . . .
> The press contended it was trying to adapt itself to a
> telegraph going through an awkward adolescence; the
> telegraph, for its part maintained it was having difficulty
> serving an industry going through a revolution. Both were
> correct.[137]

These were "early relations," however, overshadowed within a couple of years by mutually beneficial accommodation as each side slowly brought its house into order. Journalism and other mid-nineteenth-century businesses shortly became the chief customers of telegraphy, accounting for 70 to 80 percent of the telegraphic traffic. After surveying the available evidence, Richard B. Du Boff concludes

> In the telegraph industry, business demand was the key to
> increases in the scale of operations and the drift toward
> monopoly. . . . The telegraph possessed autonomous
> cost-saving and internal control features that made it
> particularly suitable for business purposes. These features
> gave rise to intensive business use of telegraph services and
> led to the interplay between customer demand patterns and
> supply adaptation within the telegraph industry, which by
> 1866 became the first major monopoly in the United
> States. . . .[138]

After all, despite the complaints about, and uncertainties within, telegraphy, it was a marvelous new gadget with powers to make the mortal reflect in amazement. Philip Hone's diary on April 15, 1848, quotes the *Milwaukee Sentinel* as saying: "At nine o'clock yesterday morning we had, by telegraph, the news and markets from New York, distant some *fourteen hundred miles,* up to three o'clock of the preceding afternoon! This is, indeed, a startling fact, and may well make us pause and wonder at the agency which has brought it about." Reflecting on this "magical performance of the lightning post, the last miracle of the scientific triumphs of the present age," Hone comments, "I was once nine days on my voyage from New York to Albany."[139]

The awe and expectancy with which journals in the late 1840s periodically traced telegraphy's growth in words, statistics, and even maps remind the modern reader of similar coverage of the nation's early space program. A technological miracle—a nation harnessing "lightning"—was in the offing, and journalists struggled to

find ways of measuring its progress, ranging from long lists of communities reached by telegraph lines to reports of speed and endur-
ance in transmitting presidential and gubernatorial messages.[140]

DISCUSSION

In an institution nearly a century and a half old, one would expect
relatively little progress in just one decade. But between the mid-
1830s and mid-1840s U.S. newspapers nearly doubled their numbers
and some innovative journals aiming at large circulations and the
emerging middle-class reader entered the field and sent shock
waves through the business. In this age of small business enterprise,
when partnerships and handshakes had not yet been replaced by
cold, rigid articles of incorporation, young men armed with novel
ideas and youthful vigor could carve business success and a fortune
out of humble beginnings.

Journalism at this time was swept by tides of broader readership
appeal, a sporadic resurgence of news-gathering competition, live-
lier writing styles, which at times burst into frenzies of pure sensationalism, and visible, personable editors who attracted public
attention, if not admiration. Steam power, the cylinder press, stereotyping, the type-revolving press, and a burgeoning transportation
network were the technological catalysts triggering journalism's
new, persistent assault upon the American consciousness. And no
calm followed the initial storm as circulations continued to rise,
hawking newsboys proliferated, editions and "extras" multiplied,
and editors boastfully made news of their news-gathering enterprise.

Journalism's revolution captured the attention and enthusiasm
of its contemporaries quite as much as it has of historians. Referring
to 1844, when Samuel Bowles entered journalism, his biographer,
George S. Merriam, comments that

> In the great cities a new race of newspapers had begun to
> supplant the older dynasty. The papers of the earlier time
> had been in every sense heavy; big in size, high in price, dull,
> long-winded, intensely partisan, and mainly used as the
> instruments of the party chiefs. Of these journalists... Mr.
> Horace White says... "They were a strong-limbed and
> hard-headed race, but they had never learned that 'variety is
> the spice of life,' and 'brevity the soul of wit.' The railway
> had not reached out its arms, the telegraph had not spread its
> wings for them. They were ruled by their environment, and

the journalism they produced consisted of a diurnal
succession of essays more or less learned, and more or less
bellicose, but as regular as the succession of day and night, or
of seed-time and harvest.''

But within a dozen years there had sprung up in New York
the first of a new class of newspapers, such as the *Sun*...and
the *Herald*.... They were sold for one or two cents...; they
aimed at news more than discussion; their style was lively
and dashing; they were swift to seize and invent new
methods in every direction; they brought steam into their
pressrooms and organized special service by land and by
water for getting the earliest information. They struck into
many veins of social interest—trade, religion, and personal
gossip—which the older papers had ignored. They discussed
politics without asking orders from the chieftains at
Washington and Albany. It was in papers of this class that
American journalism came of age.[141]

But this was not simply a journalistic revolution; the newspaper
and periodical press was but a sector of the American business community, creating and capitalizing on the "age of enterprise." For a
summary of this business context, one can do no better than to bor-
row from the socio-economic history by Thomas C. Cochran and
William Miller, whose sketch is done in broad strokes, both vivid and
intricate.

The growth of the country, the extension and
improvement of transportation facilities, were making
distribution the master key to profits. By producing goods
beyond the needs of their immediate communities, factories
were destroying local industrial monopolies in many villages,
leaving farmers dependent upon outside sources for goods
and services. By drawing thousands of young men and
women into the new manufacturing cities, factories were also
making new workers dependent upon outside sources for
food. A landless population was gathering in many new
towns and older cities, and gradually there were appearing an
urban proletariat and urban paupers.... Quick and regular
communication with distant markets had led to the
shortening of credit terms and more rapid turnover of capital
and goods. More complex business techniques and much
larger office staffs had become necessary to maintain the
new pace of American industry. Thus there appeared, for the
first time in American society in sufficient numbers to be
influential, the urban white-collar worker....

> Dressed in drab alpaca, hunched over a high desk, this
> new worker credited and debited, indexed and filed, wrote
> and stamped invoices, acceptances, bills of lading, receipts.
> Adequately paid, he had some extra money and leisure time.
> He patronized sporting events and theaters, saving banks and
> insurance companies. He read Day's *New York Sun* or
> Bennett's *Herald*—the "penny press" supported by
> advertising, filled with police reports, crime stories, etiquette
> advice for the rising bourgeoisie.... Exploring *Godey's Lady's
> Book* for patterns, patronizing the new industries for
> materials, Mrs. Clerk began to compete with the boss's wife
> in dress and fashion.[142]

Michael Schudson's social history steps to the brink by correctly asserting that the penny press revolution "had its origins in the emergence of a democratic market society" or as he also calls it, "the age of egalitarianism"—the same notions Cochran and Miller are getting at above. But although he finds traditional causal explanations for the penny press inadequate, Schudson fails to take the leap and express the dynamic interaction of these movements.[143] That Bennett perceived a growing middle class and responded to it, there can be no doubt. But Bennett, through his aggressive news-gathering, occasional sensationalism, "money articles," classified advertising, sports coverage, and the rest defined, expressed, and channeled middle-class interests, tastes, and values. His journalism—and that of other new penny editors and those of the more progressive political and mercantile papers—lent intellectual and self-conscious identity to the growing army of clerks and mechanics, a physical manifestation of their collective existence and a daily guide to their significant reality.

Taken all together, this was a social revolution of which journalism was an integral part, not simply a result. It was a revolution advancing on the dynamic interaction among such key factors as innovations in machine and power technologies, broadening participation in political and economic life, advances in education, broadening and diversifying consumption of literature (including daily journalism), increasing investment capital and government support in key public works, the beginnings of a factory system, and emerging metropolitan centers of government and finance.

Into this maelstrom, technology introduced transoceanic steam navigation and telegraphy to gratify and challenge journalism. Steamers fitted comfortably with editors' notions of news movement. Hastening transportation's delivery of news by use of expensive, fast transportation links, such as harbor boats and expresses, had become an annoying journalistic necessity when such stories as the Oregon border dispute and the Mexican War occurred. And editors perceived the transoceanic steamer as a process devised by the transportation institution to relieve editorial frustrations over habitually slow, unpredictable, or absent ship arrivals. Further editorial assistance arose from two sectors: the new express companies and transatlantic newspapers. The old burdens of impoverished and irregular foreign news flow dissolved, replaced by the fortnightly and later weekly flood of foreign news, triggering a massive new process of express messenger, hasty editorial decisions, feverish typesetting, expeditious presswork, and deployment of hordes of newsboys into the streets. This transformation vis-à-vis foreign news released editors from much of their own transportation-bound news-gathering activity to concentrate on purely journalistic processes during "steamer nights."

Transoceanic steam navigation grew within an existing transportation institution, the product of three decades of gradual, inexorable technological trial and error and pushed to fruition by anxious business, financial, and governmental interests. Telegraphy, in contrast, sprang suddenly and singly (so the story goes) to the mind of an artist-turned-inventor, unaided by previous communication technology and unattached to any institutional structure. Only the postal service or its governmental parent held promise as telegraphy's institutional home, but they were disinclined. Telegraphy, thus, was compelled to shape itself into the prototype communication institution, and in doing so it experienced disorienting struggles far more severe than those the journalism revolution was creating for American editors.

Editors, recognizing the kinship between their mission and telegraphy's, expected more from the embryonic institution than it could deliver in its early years. And those expectations were heightened by news events requiring close and frequent journalistic attention, notably the Mexican War, the Oregon question, and European revolutions. Some editors invested in the telegraph; others threatened to erect, or have erected for them, their own telegraph lines. Some telegraph proprietors sought editors' good will and business, rushing the erection of lines to accommodate newspapers' needs, offering reduced press rates, and helping editors gather news.

But all along the newspaper-telegraph interface in the first couple of years, dissatisfaction festered. Editors were frustrated by the early lines' shaky performance, rebelled at the cost of tele-

graphic news-gathering, and resorted to codes to cut costs and protect their dispatches from thieving telegraphers and editors.
Telegraph proprietors retaliated by threatening to eliminate press
rates, refusing to transmit the codes, and as we shall see, eventually
wielding the leverage of an alternative newsbrokerage.

Emerging along this unsettled interface, the embryonic newsbrokerage was conceived by Alexander Seward, Rufus Northway, Isaac
Butts, and Theodore Faxton in upstate New York, even as the interface was taking shape. A compromise for all parties, newsbroking
forced participating editors to share a common dispatch with other
papers, to relinquish editorial control over that dispatch to a distant
agent, and to receive that dispatch at times that were convenient to
the telegraph company. On the other side, telegraph proprietors settled for a brief daily news transmission at a reduced rate rather than
the more lucrative, but uncertain, prospect of every-editor-for-
himself, and agreed to give the common dispatch priority on their
lines at the appointed hour, regardless of other business.

On balance, the newsbroker compromise was conceivable only
because journalism's established institutional strength and ability to
influence community sentiment about such upstart innovations as
telegraphy momentarily gave newspapers the upper hand. When, in
the next few years, telegraphy began to overcome its disorganized
and infantile ineptness, the scales would shift. The new electric
communication technology was, after all, the key to efficient news
movement. Virtually no electric news movement would occur without telegraph's technology and without the assistance of those controlling that technology. Editors could rant about telegraphy's
shortcomings and its "monopoly," and probably influence some of
their readers, but the Morse people, and later the American and
Western Union telegraph companies, could refuse to move editors'
news dispatches. They risked public condemnation with so arbitrary
an act, but business affairs were generally conducted more recklessly and combatively then. Or telegraph proprietors could decide
to set up their own newsbrokerage and transmit only its dispatches.
This tug-of-war between journalism and telegraphy reappeared periodically until editors secured lasting control of their newsbrokerage in the early 1880s.

At the marrow of the infant newsbroker movement was a struggle over the journalistic uses of our first electric communication system. Propelling messages, which have been stripped of their bulky
storage medium, over potentially vast distances at nearly the speed
of light, diminished only by the agility of telegraphers and the ex-

tent of the circuits, nearly eliminates time as a factor in news movement. And once the lines have been strung, distance—which transportation must reconquer with each trip—has been permanently overcome. The old tradeoffs of transportation noted in chapter 1—volume and speed, weight and terrain, performance and weather—evaporate. Assuming the soundness of the electric system, its physical components and its human manipulation, telegraphy's performance is automatic at any distance. Its only physical drawback, until the arrival of multiplex in the 1870s, was its capacity for only one message per circuit at a time. As the volume of traffic or the length of messages increased, the system needed more time or more circuits to perform its task. Within two years after Washington, D.C., and New York City were linked, for example, the Magnetic Telegraph Company operated four lines on that route.

As editors and telegraph proprietors fitfully unsnarled the developmental and control problems attending the onset of this communication revolution over the next decade, two institutions began to take shape: the telegraph, which after its second decade had evolved into a national monopoly, and newsbroking, more variegated than telegraphy and owing its existence to the technology of electric telegraphy and the news needs of the older newspaper institution. In the next decade, newsbroking would grow to occupy a publicly noticeable space along the newspaper-telegraphy interface, as the next three chapters will describe, organizing available technology for the task of constructing a daily news report.

Chapter 3
NEW YORK CITY'S NEWSBROKERS EMERGE

1848! The Year of Hope! You have not forgotten, O reader, the thrill, the tumult, the ecstasy of joy with which, on the morning of March 19th, 1848, you read in the morning papers these electric and transporting capitals. Regale your eyes with them once more:

FIFTEEN DAYS LATER FROM EUROPE

ARRIVAL OF THE CAMBRIA

ABDICATION OF LOUIS PHILLIPPE! [*sic*]

A REPUBLIC PROCLAIMED

THE ROYAL FAMILY HAVE LEFT PARIS

ASSAULT ON THE PALAIS ROYAL

GREAT LOSS OF LIFE

COMMUNICATION WITH THE INTERIOR CUT OFF

RESIGNATION OF MINISTERS

REVOLT IN AMIENS.—PARIS IN ALARM

James Parton, *The Life of Horace Greeley, Editor of the New York Tribune*
(1855)

The imperative of technology challenges man's order. Those caught in the blasts of new technology's storm rush for cover in a fortress of legal paper, or try, usually vainly, to harness the fury. Those reasonably safe on the fringes of the tumult likely survive by shouting self-reassuring criticisms of those being buffeted. Thus, as telegraphy struggled to its feet and strained to articulate its first policies, newspaper editors impatiently hurled insults at it, unaware that they, too, would eventually be drawn into the storm.

The press-telegraph relationship might have gone on like this for several years if the telegraph's birth had not, in fact, produced quadruplets—the instruments of Morse, Barnes and Zook, House, and Bain—and if the birth had not been accompanied by a glut of major foreign news events, growing into the sensation Parton notes above, the 1848 European revolutions.[1] Demanding an extraordinary news-gathering effort, this stream of foreign news drew American newspaper editors steadily and unavoidably toward telegraphy's storm, hastening newsbroking's development. Upstate New York editors provided a model for a news-gathering and distribution system in the first half of 1846 with their limited effort, which relied on whatever news was daily available in Albany and later in New York City.

But down at the mouth of the Hudson River lived and worked some of the nation's most successful and aggressive journalists, men unaccustomed to waiting for the steamer, the train, or the mail pouch to bring news to their offices. Likewise, they might not be expected to wait for the telegraph or some distant correspondent to organize their daily file of news for them. And as the momentous news events of 1846–48 tumbled into newsrooms in growing profusion, concurrent with telegraphy's introduction in New York City, one might expect these editors to reach for control of their daily telegraphic dispatches—to design, in other words, a newsbrokerage. That they were slower than their upstate cousins in taking hold of such a scheme may be because the city's editors, after years of sporadic competition in the harbor and on the post roads and of shifting, short-term news-gathering alliances, could strike a newsbroking bargain only by breaking rigid old habits.

This chapter seeks to untangle the conflicting claims about the origins of the New York City Associated Press.[2] Here the author plunges into the thorny thicket of assertions about who were the moving forces behind the New York City AP's formation and the timing of that formation. Some claims in the literature are mere speculation while others represent loyalty to employers or certain colleagues, but few offer any historical evidence to support their assertions. Meanwhile, the author's repeated efforts to locate evidence of the origins of the city's AP, while making some headway, have fallen short of finding the names, dates, and places of the New York City AP's birth. This chapter, therefore, performs the unsatisfying task of both minimizing much that has been presented as history and offering too little as a replacement.

EARLY TELEGRAPHIC NEWS ACTIVITY

In the collection of the Museum of the City of New York is an 1847 lithograph entitled "Birds-Eye View of Trinity Church, New-York." It is a much reproduced view of the new church on Broadway, its 264-foot spire looming over the western end of Wall Street. In the lower right-hand corner, one can see a pole standing on the northeast corner of Broadway and Wall supporting three telegraph lines as they turn the corner into Wall Street.[3] These were the Morse telegraph lines from Washington, Buffalo, and Boston, converging on the city's commercial and journalistic center.

The city these wires penetrated in the mid-1840s, according to a contemporary guidebook, was "renowned for its wealth, population and commercial importance." The book boasts that New York "derives unrivalled advantage from its position, being on one of the best harbors in the world, and has facilities for inland communication unsurpassed, perhaps, by those of any other city upon the globe."[4] The commercial district, centered on Wall Street, had been rebuilt as modern brick buildings, interspersed with a few neoclassical stone banks, after the Great Fire of 1835, which destroyed seven hundred structures in seventeen blocks from William Street to the East River.[5]

Wall Street epitomized the city, connecting Broadway, New York's "most elegant and fashionable street," its eighty-foot width serving as "the great promenade of the city, being much resorted to in pleasant weather by the gay and fashionable,"[6] and the East River, offering a "scene. . . beyond all description, whilst the noise is incessant and deafening: the sailors' busy songs, and the draymen's impatient ejaculation, being occasionally distinguishable amid the confused and incessant din,"[7] according to the guidebook and an English visitor. Along its north curb, Wall Street housed the major banks, mercantile houses, insurance companies, shops, and express companies, facing a nearly unbroken row of three- and four-story office buildings and dwellings.[8]

On the north side in the first block of Wall Street off Broadway stood a large, coarse building occupied by three express companies.[9] It was in this building, in the offices of expressmen John J. Butterfield and Theodore S. Faxton at 10 Wall, that the Morse telegraph people set up their first office in the city on January 26, 1846.[10]

Some time within the next two years, offices of the Magnetic Telegraph Company (Washington, D.C.–New York) and the New York and Boston Magnetic Telegraph Company moved to 5 Hanover Street, two blocks west and one south of the original office. The new office was one block south of the imposing new Merchants' Exchange on Wall Street.[11] (The first offices of the city's first newsbrokerages, Abbot & Winans and the Associated Press, were located close by on Hanover, as we shall see.) Scattered within a few blocks' radius of the Morse companies' Hanover office were the city's leading newspapers.

One block east of the Merchants' Exchange on Wall and toward the East River were New York's two mercantile powerhouses, James Watson Webb's *Courier and Enquirer* at 70 Wall and, closer to the river amid coffeehouses and warehouses, David Hale's and Gerard Hallock's *Journal of Commerce* at 94 Wall. In the other direction, one block from Broadway at the corner of Wall and Nassau was the *Express* of James and Erastus Brooks. North along Nassau, clustered in their own world apart from the more traditional journals, were the penny papers. James Gordon Bennett's *Herald* and Moses Y. Beach's *Sun* were at the corner of Nassau and Fulton, seven blocks north of Wall; three blocks farther north, on Nassau beyond Spruce, was Horace Greeley's *Tribune*.[12]

Ensconced among journalistic powerhouses in the financial and commercial capital of the nation, the Morse people no doubt expected to be gleefully overwhelmed with telegraphic business. By June 30, 1846, New York City was linked telegraphically to Washington, D.C., and Boston; the Albany-Buffalo line was just closing ranks; and the New York–Albany line was going up rapidly. By September 1846 the *New York Sun* enthusiastically reported 1,269 miles of telegraph line operating on eight circuits, New York in contact with Buffalo, Washington, Harrisburg, and a line extending fifty-five miles north of Boston and pushing rapidly toward Portland, Maine.[13] By the end of 1846 telegraph lines had been strung from Buffalo to Toronto and from Philadelphia to Pittsburgh.[14]

In New York City a few newspapers, notably the *Herald*, *Journal of Commerce*, and *Sun*, made liberal use of the early lines to receive special dispatches from their correspondents, but the community as a whole was lukewarm to telegraphy's arrival. Telegraph historian James D. Reid says, "New York looked at the telegraph baby boy through unimaginative eyes, and glancing at it over its clean shirt collar and close-shaven chin, said, with cold emphasis, 'it isn't mine.' "[15] Not only did New York very reluctantly turn its business over to the telegraph, it also found little investment potential in the new gadget. The telegraph "found no friends in great Manhattan," says Reid. "It was reserved to the inland cities of Rochester and Utica to take hold of the giant child and rear it to national greatness."[16]

Stirring within this cautious atmosphere, however, were the tentative beginnings of newsbroking in the city. Completion of the earliest telegraph lines into the city immediately stimulated the appearance of "By Telegraph" or "By Magnetic Telegraph" labels over dispatches from distant cities in New York papers. Alexander Jones, commonly understood to be the first general agent of the city's Associated Press,[17] provides the only surviving description of those early telegraphic news-gathering activities in New York City.

> At the commencement [of telegraphic service] the papers proceeded to employ [the telegraph] with some caution and hesitation; their dispatches were usually brief, and as much condensed as possible....
>
> It was early in the autumn of 1846, when the writer of this handed in his first message for the newspaper press at [New York City's Magnetic Telegraph Company office]. It contained a brief account of the launch of the U.S. *sloop of war Albany* at the Navy Yard in Brooklyn, and was directed to the *Washington Union*....
>
> At the outset there was a want of system in the collection, transmission and distribution of telegraph news for the press. ...Hence the business of telegraphing brought into requisition Telegraph Reporters. We were among the earliest to engage in the occupation; we commenced with the commencement of telegraphs.... The press at first, owing to the expense, would not agree to receive more than would make from half to one column of the [*New York*] *Sun* newspaper. We then supplied them under a weekly contract, and paid our own tolls and reporters' fees.... Within a year or two after we had engaged in telegraph reporting, an association of three or four reporters was organized, who employed others in various important localities to forward and receive news for the press.... This association only lasted about twelve months, when it was dissolved, and, as far as New-York was concerned, we became the agent of the New-York Associated Press, for all news arrangements of a commercial and miscellaneous character throughout the United States.[18]

Riddled with ambiguity, this only account of the city's newsbroking beginnings has only one straw to grasp at—the launch of the sloop *Albany*—and even that reference presents the historian with a problem. Rather than "early in the autumn of 1846," the *Albany* was launched on June 27, 1846, commissioned on November 6, and sailed for her first naval assignment on November 28.[19] The "brief account of the launch of the... *Albany*" in the *Washington Union* was a telegram sent by Secretary of the Navy George Bancroft, no doubt the official notification sent to President James Polk.[20]

The *Union* contains no dispatch on the fall commissioning of the *Albany*, but the telegraph line between New York and Washington, D.C., was repeatedly in disorder during early November, including the day of the commissioning. It seems more likely that Jones's six-year-old recollection of "his first message for the newspaper press" confused "launch" and "commissioning" than that he incorrectly remembered the season of the year. And the dispatch he sent either failed to reach Washington or was discarded by the *Union*'s editors.

Even if Jones confused the seasons and did file a dispatch on the June 27 launch, he still is incorrect in asserting that "we commenced with the commencement of telegraphs." We have noted that the first Morse office opened in the city on January 26, 1846, four days after the line to Philadelphia was opened, and that the New York–Washington line was operating on June 5, 1846.

By saying, however, that "[w]e were among the earliest to engage in the occupation," Jones seemingly admits that others had taken to the field either before or with him. Based on the date of the *Albany*'s launch and the fact, noted shortly, that the first common telegraphic dispatch appeared in two New York morning papers on May 7, 1846, one must conclude that some pioneer newsbroker preceded Jones in this endeavor.

Continuing with Jones's statement, he notes that he supplied the city's press "under a weekly contract" with news dispatches for some unspecified period, during which the Associated Press apparently did not exist in New York City. "Within a year or two" after either the launch of the *Albany* or the start of his "weekly contract," "an association of three or four reporters was organized." If Jones is correct in reporting that this association "only lasted about twelve months, when it was dissolved," then it seems clear that Jones is not referring to the Abbot & Winans newsbrokerage, which lasted until 1855. The author, unfortunately, can find no record of such an association of reporters. And it *is* unfortunate, because Jones's phraseology suggests that the Associated Press might have come into being while this association was serving the city's press.

Jones continues that when this association was dissolved, "as far as New-York was concerned, we became the agent of the New-York

Associated Press." There is a clear implication here that the AP existed when Jones became its agent. If any reliance can be placed on Jones's references to lengths of time in this sequence of events and we use the *Albany*'s commissioning as the starting point, then Jones became the AP agent in the fall of either 1848 or 1849. Later this chapter traces AP's existence back to late April 1848. Moreover, the author will introduce news-gathering correspondence written by Jones in the fall of 1848 that identifies Jones as an independent reporter and not as AP's agent.

Thus, there is strong circumstantial evidence that a pioneering newsbroker served the New York City press before Jones filed his first telegraphic dispatch to the *Washington Union*. The literature suggests two candidates for this honor. At his death, Francis A. Abbot was credited with having "established the first news agency in Wall Street," in an obituary appearing in the *New York Times*, an AP paper.[21] The obituary for Elias P. Winans, appearing in another AP paper, the *New York Tribune*, credits Winans with having "established the business of telegraphing commercial and general news before regular organization of the Associated Press."[22] Either may have engaged in newsbroking in New York City before Jones, and either may have formed the association of reporters that was dissolved when Jones became AP's agent, an association that might have served the Associated Press before Jones took over the AP job.

Although the first two or three years of newsbroking in New York City are shrouded in uncertainty, it is reasonably certain that Abbot and Winans formed a newsbrokerage around the time the Associated Press was organizing. The historian Alfred McClung Lee accepts the existence of telegraphic reporters prior to Jones, saying Jones was "not the first New York telegraph reporter as some claim." But then both Lee and Victor Rosewater treat the Abbot & Winans operation as an also-ran, just a pesky thorn in AP's tough hide.[23] And, although neither the New York City AP nor A & W can be singled out as the earlier newsbrokerage, it is clear from material presented in chapter 5 that Abbot & Winans was a far more substantial newsbrokerage than our historical literature has indicated up to now.

Between the two of them, Winans is the greater mystery, but this does not mean that Abbot left a clear accounting of himself on the record. Except for a few scraps of information and their obituaries, little remains to lend flesh and activity to these names. Francis Asbury Abbot[24] left behind one insignificant letter,[25] some R. G. Dun & Co. credit notations,[26] and a court record as an unsuccessful defendant in a civil suit in 1875–76 that indicates that he was stealing and selling the market quotations belonging to another man.[27]

Abbot was born in New York City in 1827, but nothing is recorded about his early life or training. Winans, a native New Yorker born in 1824, received some formal education before spending five years as a clerk in a French importing house on Broad Street. Chapter 5 presents evidence that by mid-August 1852 Abbot & Winans delivered a regular news report to more than half the newspapers in the country. Jones's successor as AP general agent, Daniel H. Craig, describes Abbot & Winans as a formidable competitor in the early 1850s. Addressing his New York City editors in an 1863 annual report, Craig says,

> I commenced with you in 1851, at which time all the papers in the city, except the six regular morning journals were violently hostile to the interests of the Association, whilst out of the city, fully four fifths of all the papers sustained an opposition News Association. . . . [T]here never was a time whilst Abbott [sic] and Winans flourished here in opposition, between 1850 and 1855, that they were not able to get hold of any important news within five to thirty minutes after it was delivered at the newspaper offices of the Association.[28]

In addition to the firm's strength and news-gathering acumen, the evidence strongly hints that Abbot & Winans was allied with the Morse telegraph companies, perhaps as an official appendage of the Morse system. If true, this connection would have given A & W added leverage in journalism against the AP. The possibility of such an alliance would also allow the author to pose at times in the next three chapters the question of what would have happened to the infant newsbroker institution if a telegraph-operated newsbrokerage had subdued the AP challenge.

The suggestion of an A & W–Morse alliance, however tentative, is drawn from two sources. First, in an article airing some press grievances about telegraphic service, the *American Telegraph Magazine* in October 1852 cites the *New York Tribune* as characterizing a newsbrokerage then serving upstate New York newspapers as ''a private firm who act in the capacity of general news reporters for the Morse line of telegraph from Albany to Buffalo—the only line connected with [New York] city that makes news a merchantable commodity.'' The article is clear that AP is not the ''firm'' being discussed, explaining that the line's proprietor, Faxton, had refused to transmit AP dispatches and made arrangements for another newsbroker to deliver a report to the papers along his line. Soon after, another article in this magazine listed all the newspapers on Faxton's line as recipients of Abbot & Winans news.[29] The other bit of evidence comes from a New York City directory for 1850 that lists Abbot's occupation as "telegraph" at 5 Hanover, which at that time was also the address of the Morse telegraph office.

The New York City directories[30] provide little assistance in tracing the origins of the city's newsbroking. Winans is listed as a clerk between 1845 and 1847, presumably referring to his tenure at the French import house. He then disappears until 1851, when A & W first appears in the directories. Jones first appears as a "telegraphic reporter" at 3 Hanover in 1849. (As we shall later note, Jones's correspondence in the fall of 1848 shows his office at 28 Merchants' Exchange.) In 1850 Jones's listing was the same as the previous year, and Abbot appears, as noted above, as "telegraph" at the Morse address. In 1851 the Abbot & Winans newsbrokerage first appears, located at $1\frac{1}{2}$ Hanover, and the following year they moved to $4\frac{1}{2}$ Hanover, where they stayed until they disappeared from the directories in 1855. Meanwhile the Jones listing continues until Craig replaced him as general agent in 1851. At no time prior to the Civil War does the name Associated Press appear in the directories.

We are, thus, left with three known early newsbrokers in New York City and two identifiable early newsbrokerages. In the face of a fragmentary record, caution dictates not choosing a first or pioneering individual or association and not ignoring the possibility that there were others in the field, unknown to us today, at or soon after the beginning. It also bears repeating that Jones, by his own description, may not have been AP's first general agent, that honor possibly belonging to "an association of three or four reporters."

Regardless of who ran it, a newsbrokerage that supplied a common news dispatch to New York City's morning papers was functioning in the spring of 1846. Relying on the contents of three of the city's leading news-gatherers,[31] the author has found the *Tribune* was the first of these papers to carry a labeled telegraphic news dispatch. Appearing May 2, 1846, it consisted of two stories, one from Utica, N.Y. (which traveled at least part of the way from Albany to New York via transportation links), and the other from Washington (which had to be transported between the only completed telegraph lines in that region at that time, Washington-Baltimore and Philadelphia–Fort Lee, N.J.).

The second of these three papers to carry a labeled telegraphic dispatch was the *Herald* on May 7. The dispatch it printed was identical to one in the *Tribune* for that same day. This is the first common news dispatch labeled as telegraphic located in these three papers. Datelined Washington, May 6, 6:30 P.M., the seven-paragraph story describes routine congressional business. The two papers continued to run telegraphic dispatches every day or two during May and June, and each time that they coincided, the congressional reports were identical. (Even notices that congressional reports were unavailable because of telegraph line disruptions between Washington and New York contained the same wording in both papers.) The author speculates that this service of congressional news was provided by the Morse telegraph people, in exchange for a reduced toll payment and insertion of "By Magnetic Telegraph" logos in the newspapers.

The third paper studied, the *Courier and Enquirer*, joined the telegraphic age on July 7, 1846, with its first telegraphic dispatch, which was identical to those appearing that day in the *Tribune* and *Herald*. The three papers and other New York papers, the author has since noted, continued the practice of common Washington dispatches thereafter. Again, the author speculates that some time during 1847 the Morse telegraph company either abandoned the service or increased the toll charges sufficiently to cause the newspapers to employ independent telegraphic reporters or reporter associations (as Jones describes) to keep the congressional reports coming.

The New York–Boston telegraph line opened on June 27, 1846, linking New York's papers with the landing site of Cunard's steamers and the all-important foreign news reports. The arrival of the *Britannia* on July 4 caused no change in the papers' handling of steamer news—each ran messengers and compiled individualized summaries of foreign news from the steamer's mail and newspapers, as had been the practice for several years. Two weeks later the *Cambria* was the next Cunard arrival at Boston, and on July 18, 1846, all three New York papers studied carried identical brief first-day telegraphic summaries of the *Cambria*'s news. In fact, one source notes that this was the first common telegraphic dispatch of steamer news and that this dispatch appeared not only in New York City, but also in Boston and Philadelphia. [32]

This fact, coupled with the apparent absence of any press express or arrangement to gather and transmit this dispatch, suggests that the dispatch may have been distributed by an independent reporter or a telegraph company agent. The *New York Herald*, which ordinarily boasted of any news-gathering scheme it participated in, failed to note its own initiative in this instance. The following two paragraphs headed the *Herald*'s reprint of the common telegraphic dispatch of the *Cambria*'s news on July 18.

> There was a bright, brilliant flash of lightning over the telegraph line from Boston yesterday afternoon. Indeed, there was a succession of flashes, that beautifully lit up nearly every newspaper office in this city.
> The first flash announced that the steamship Cambria was off Boston; the next informed us that she was safely moored at the wharf; and the next that she brought some highly important intelligence.[33]

Note that the news reached "nearly every newspaper office in this city," a further indication that a newsbroker was distributing this dispatch in New York City, after another newsbroker had made up the dispatch in Boston.

Second-day coverage, based on the arrival of the *Cambria*'s mail pouches, was individualized in each of the three papers. The author, however, reminds the reader that chapter 2 reveals a heavy reliance by New York papers on *Willmer & Smith's European Times* for second-day coverage of foreign affairs. The *Herald*, it will be recalled, during selected Cunard landings made up, on the average, more than 50 percent of its second-day foreign news file from dispatches lifted verbatim from the *European Times*, and the *Tribune* made even greater use of the *European Times*'s contents.[34]

THE BIRTH OF THE NEW YORK CITY ASSOCIATED PRESS

This section considers two aspects of the birth of the New York City AP—the conflicts and imprecisions of the current literature's depiction of this subject and the only clear and available line of evidence delineating AP's earliest recorded existence in the city.

On close examination, the historical literature presents a bewildering array of assertions and counterclaims about AP's birth in New York City. The evidence that the author has assembled disputes all of these accounts to some extent and disputes some accounts totally. Yet, that evidence is insufficient to pinpoint the moments of conception. Ironically, while the generally overlooked New York State AP, characterized in the previous chapter as our first newsbrokerage, is easily documented, the origins of the New York City AP, which most scholars and writers have mightily sought to illuminate, believing it to be our first, may forever elude students of this subject.

The century-old quest for the beginnings of the New York City AP revolves around three partnership agreements signed by the city's leading newspaper editors, an exchange of letters between the AP's executive committee and the proprietor of the New York–Boston telegraph line, and several maddeningly imprecise accounts by participants in, or observers of, AP's birth. As documents and letters have been unearthed over the years, differing slants have been put on participants' and observers' accounts, leaving us with a range of founding dates stretching from 1837 to 1856.

In addition to founding dates, AP's origins have been clothed in various interpretations according to writers' various perceptions of the legitimate activity of a newsbroker. In New York City one can trace joint harbor activity by some of the AP newspapers back to the late 1820s, and the 1830 and 1840s found most of these AP papers engaged periodically in associations to operate horse expresses. Or does one search for the earliest use of the name Associated Press, or for AP's first uses of the telegraph, or for the editors' first signed partnership agreement? The gradual evolution of the papers' news-gathering efforts, complicated by the continuing activities of independent newsbrokers in the city, presents a baffling array of potential starting points for AP. The author first permits his predecessors to stumble around with the problem before doing so himself.

The earliest account of AP's history that the author has located, an unsigned 1858 story in the *Philadelphia Press*, incorrectly places AP's founding a year too early.

> In 1847 the *Journal of Commerce, Courier and Enquirer,*
> *Express, Sun,* and *Herald* formed an association, and
> purchased a steamboat for $20,000; but after a trial of six
> months, the scheme was abandoned. The association was,
> however, continued, and the establishment of telegraph lines,
> now extended to all sections of the country, has gradually led
> to the present system.[35]

It seems certain that this 1858 article refers to either the *Buena Vista* episode (which involved commissioning the services of a steamer in April or May 1848) or the *News-Boy* episode (which involved purchasing a steamer in May or June 1848). Both episodes are discussed later in this chapter.

Two post–Civil War descriptions of AP operations, one by the New York journalist W. F. G. Shanks in March 1867[36] and the other by AP staffer William Aplin in July 1870,[37] successfully avoid the question of when AP was founded.

Frederic Hudson's 1873 account, chronologically the next and one that should be definitive, disappointingly dates the AP loosely from "1848–'9" adding the following account of a pivotal meeting between the editors of the *Journal of Commerce* and the *Herald*. Hudson gives no date for this meeting.

> One forenoon, after the *Herald* had published some exclusive news, a knock was heard at the door of the editorial rooms of that paper. "Come in!" answered the editor. The tall, gaunt figure of David Hale entered. One of the magnates of Wall Street journalism was actually in the office of a despised penny paper! But Hale was a practical man. He saw the handwriting plainly enough. There was very little circumlocution about him.
>
> "I have called," he said, "to talk about news with you. Have you any objection?"
>
> "None," replied the penny editor. "Am always pleased to talk on that subject."
>
> "We propose to join the *Herald* in getting news," continued Mr. Hale. "Have you any objection to that?"
>
> This led to a brief conversation on newspaper enterprise, pony expresses, and news-boats. This conversation on the establishment of the telegraph led to the organization of the New York Associated Press. This interview was the origin of that institution.[38]

The context of this narrative suggests that the *Herald-Journal of Commerce* alliance preceded the Mexican War and remained a two-newspaper combination until burdensome telegraphic conditions later brought forth the AP. Hudson elsewhere ties AP's founding more directly to telegraphic growth and problems arising after the Mexican War.

> In looking over the ground, it was manifest that the telegraph lines were not equal to the emergency. They did not expand rapidly enough. They could not transmit all the dispatches of the newspapers if the journals acted independently of each other. It was apparent that, with the business of the public, the capacity of the telegraph was not equal to the transmission of single dispatches of one day's news to one paper alone. It became absolutely necessary, therefore, to enjoy the benefit of this miraculous invention, for the newspapers to form an association, in order that their

individual competition should not destroy the early
usefulness of this wonderful means of communication. The
result was, that representatives from the *Journal of
Commerce, Courier and Enquirer, Tribune, Herald, Sun*, and
Express, met at the office of the *Sun*, and formed, 1st, the
Harbor News Association, and, 2d, the New York Associated
Press.... This was in 1848-'9.[39]

On two counts, however, Hudson's oblique narrative leaves much
to be desired. After a long explanation of the papers' necessity "to
enjoy the benefit of this miraculous invention," Hudson lists as the
results, first, the Harbor News Association, which, as we shall soon
see, had nothing to do with telegraphic news dispatches. Rather it
involved association for the operation of a harbor news-gathering
system. One cannot tell from the Hudson passage whether both associations, or just the harbor operation, were formed at the same
Sun office meeting. The preponderance of subsequent accounts
suggests that the telegraphic AP association appeared months or
years after the Harbor News Association. And Hudson's reference to
time is none too precise. The Harbor News agreement was signed
January 11, 1849.

Second, when one puts Hudson's two passages together, one
senses he strains to align AP's formation with a pre-newsbroker arrangement Hudson's *Herald* and the *Journal of Commerce* had
made, an arrangement for expresses that is no different from other
such associations and combinations stretching back into the 1820s.
Hudson's loyalty to the *Herald* here, the author believes, exceeds his
devotion to the historical record.

Following Hudson into print are a couple of sources claiming AP
dates from 1837. New York AP's letterhead stationery between
1876 and 1878 claims this date for the association's founding, and
telegraph historian Reid accepts this claim in his book, which was in
preparation when that stationery was in use.[40] The statistician and
New York State AP editor S. N. D. North more cautiously dates AP's
precursors from 1837 in his 1884 treatise on the U.S. newspaper and
periodical press.[41] These references stemmed, no doubt, from AP's
attempt to attach itself to four or five separate harbor news-
gathering efforts operated in 1837 by different combinations of
New York's leading papers (see chapter 1). The AP's letterhead reference to 1837 may have been a reaction to Alexander Seward's
claims, made at about this time, for an early-1846 newsbrokerage in
upstate New York (see chapter 2).

The same year that North published his press catalogue, a seemingly authoritative voice on this subject was heard from. George Ripley and Charles A. Dana, both attached to the *New York Tribune* during the period of AP's founding in New York (Dana as the paper's managing editor attended several AP meetings), completed editing the *American Cyclopaedia*, a sixteen-volume "popular dictionary of general knowledge." The work's essay on newspapers claims the New York Associated Press was founded in 1849 but provides no elaboration.[42]

James Melvin Lee[43] and L. N. Charles[44] represent one group of 1920s historians who date the AP from October 21, 1856, when the AP editors signed the "Regulations of the General News Association of the City of New York."[45] This group, with a copy of the document in hand, prefers to rely on extant evidence and thus avoids controversy over AP's more informal, obscure, or uncertain antecedents. This 1856 document, however, states that it supersedes two earlier AP documents, the Harbor News Association of January 11, 1849, and "the subsequent Telegraphic and General News Associations, entered into since that time...."

Another group of 1920s historians accepts the 1856 document's reference to the Harbor News Association, triangulated by Hudson's mention of the latter, and dates AP in New York City from this 1849 Harbor News agreement. This group includes George Henry Payne,[46] Willard Grosvenor Bleyer,[47] and Frank H. O'Brien.[48] O'Brien, engaged in writing a laudatory history of the *New York Sun*, understandably focuses on the Harbor News Association because Hudson had reported that this document was signed in the *Sun*'s offices.[49] This school, however, replaces one formal document with another as AP's origin, and in this instance the document they say organized AP was not yet available for examination. The only known copy of the Harbor News agreement was placed in a public depository in 1951,[50] and its significance was not discussed in print until 1968.[51]

Meanwhile, a knowledgeable pair of historians marks AP's founding from that "subsequent Telegraphic and General News Associations" mentioned in the 1856 document and signed after the Harbor News agreement. These writers are William Henry Smith,[52] AP's fourth general agent, and S. N. D. North.[53] Apparently Smith and North viewed the Harbor News Association as a pretelegraph agreement and thus disqualified it as AP's origin. Evidence presented by Rosewater, to be strengthened and augmented by the author on the following pages, suggests, however, that while Harbor News dealt with news boat operations, it was part of a larger, single telegraph-transportation mix of news-gathering efforts reaching back into the spring of 1848, and all sponsored by New York's AP newspapers.

Thanks to Smith and a stray surviving New York City AP document of 1874, however, we have the text of the first paragraph of that "subsequent Telegraphic and General News Associations" agreement and the fact that it was signed in 1851. It says,

> It is mutually agreed between G. Hallock, of the *Journal of Commerce*, J. & E. Brooks, of the *Express*, J. G. Bennett, of the *Herald*, Beach Brothers, of the *Sun*, Greeley & McElrath, of the *Tribune*, and J. W. Webb, of the *Courier*, to associate for the purpose of collecting and receiving Telegraphic and other Intelligence, under the following regulations.[54]

Rosewater's research, appearing in 1930 and the last serious effort to probe AP's origins before the author undertook the task in the 1960s, turns up an exchange of letters between AP's executive committee and the proprietor of the New York–Boston telegraph line, dated May 13, 15, and 18, 1848, and mentioning the "Associated Press" and "the Association" of six morning newspapers in New York City.[55] This important find influences all subsequent historical accounts, which thereafter date AP from May 1848.[56] Rosewater, unfortunately, takes one additional and unsupported step, asserting that the famous organizational meeting described by Hudson as occurring in the *Sun* offices preceded this exchange of letters. Rosewater says that this meeting, "which marked the birth of the Associated Press took place in the month of May, 1848."[57] But Hudson is clear in linking this *Sun* meeting to the signing of the Harbor News Association, which was on January 11, 1849.

These three May 1848 letters relocate AP's birth eight months earlier than the Harbor News agreement, a major breakthrough and one raising the possibility that the AP in New York City may have developed in stages—contracts and arrangements on specific routes or for specific types of news, followed by a formal partnership regarding the then-manageable and stable harbor news-gathering, followed by a more general formal partnership embracing harbor news and telegraphic news when the telegraph system had expanded and stabilized somewhat. This is the view the author entertains in the following pages. It is a view that makes Hudson's casual "in 1848-'9" time reference seem more precise, that is, incomplete, spot arrangements on behalf of these six New York papers in 1848 preceding the papers' first formal partnership, the Harbor News Association, on January 11, 1849.

Neither Rosewater nor this author has seen the May 1848 letters, but both of us encountered them reprinted in 1850 pamphlets authored by F. O. J. Smith and Craig.[58] How much earlier than mid-May 1848 might the first signs of the New York City AP be glimpsed? Rosewater firmly, and correctly it appears, says AP did not exist on November 13, 1847, when Henry Clay gave a speech in Lexington, Ky.[59] And, according to Dr. Tom Reilly, who has conducted exhaustive research on press coverage of the Mexican War, press efforts at reporting that war did not give rise directly to the AP.[60] War was declared on May 11, 1846, and Mexico City fell on September 14, 1847. Editorial frustration and the expense growing out of Mexican War coverage, as Hudson notes, may have been a bitter memory that the editors still harbored when they sat down to form the AP some months after Gen. Winfield Scott hacked his way into Mexico City. Thus, the first signs of an AP in New York City might have cropped up in the six-month period between November 13, 1847, and May 13, 1848.

One such sign is a "proposition made by the Newspaper press of New-York, Philadelphia, Baltimore and Washington, for receiving Congressional Reports and general news by Telegraph" made to the Magnetic Telegraph Company on November 24, 1847.[61] Although the term "Associated Press" does not appear in the company's minutes of these deliberations, the request, it should be noted, was made by the newspaper press of these cities and not by independent telegraphic reporters. The company, in response, expressed to the newspapers of these cities

> the willingness and desire . . . to render them all the facilities
> in [its] power . . . and also [its] willingness to carry out any
> arrangement the press of the said cities collectively may
> make, by which they all can receive the Congressional
> Proceedings and general news by a single transmission.[62]

The company also granted a 25 percent reduction in charges for drop copies of news dispatches at points between Washington and New York, one month later extending the reduction to the New York press as well.[63]

Thomas M. Clark, the only director of the company who consistently opposed such preferential treatment for news dispatches in these meetings, resolved that "every five letters in Communications written in cypher, or in unintelligible language, shall hereafter be charged as a full word." The motion, aimed in part to discourage newspaper use of codes to reduce telegraphic charges, was passed and later modified to apply only to five-letter combinations "not found in the English language."[64] This sent newsbrokers, such as Jones, scurrying back to their dictionaries to rebuild their codes, as we shall see in the next chapter.

Surely this first step by the proprietors of the all-important telegraph line between New York and Washington to accommodate news dispatches was a significant step in newsbroking's development, made even more significant by the fact that newspapers, and not the telegraph company, initiated the proposal, just as the editors between Albany and Buffalo had done sixteen months earlier.

But it is far less certain that this initiative can be called an Associated Press move. After stalking this quarry for two decades, the author can definitely identify the New York City Associated Press only two weeks before the exchange of letters, found by Rosewater, between AP and the New York–Boston telegraph spokesman. The earlier appearance of AP involves the *Buena Vista* episode, which arose in response to the growing excitement in America over news of revolutions in Europe.

Rosewater was aware that these AP papers chartered the coastal steamer *Buena Vista* "in the spring of 1848 to intercept the transatlantic boats at Halifax and put the foreign news on the wire at Boston."[65] And he correctly linked the steamer's activities to the May exchange of letters about the telegraph circuit to Boston. But Rosewater could not date the papers' chartering of the *Buena Vista*, nor trace the steamer's activities on behalf of the AP. And although this author cannot document the actual chartering, he can report the *Buena Vista* began her maiden voyage in the service of the AP on May 2, 1848, almost two weeks before the exchange of letters Rosewater reports as signaling the origin of AP. To understand why the editors would stir themselves to such extravagances as chartering a coastal steamer and arranging for telegraphic transmission of foreign news dispatches, one must realize the extreme sensation news from Europe was creating in America at that time.

In the quotation introducing this chapter, James Parton reminds his reader of the news exploding across New York City's front pages on March 19, 1848. After two paragraphs of traditional particulars about the *Cambria*'s crossing and arrival and how the news boat *Telegraph* brought her news up the harbor in advance of her docking, the *New York Herald* plunges into the cataclysmic news.

The news is of the highest importance.

Intelligence of the most exciting character has been received from Paris. Violent disturbances have broken out, in consequence of the determination of the government to prevent the reform banquets.

The result of these disturbances was:—

The abdication of Louis Philippe, of the throne of France, in favor of his grandson, the Count of Paris.

The refusal of the people to recognize the Count, the regency of the Duke of Nemours, or of the Duchess of Orleans.

The probable flight of the royal family.

The organization of a Provisional Government and the issue of a proclamation to that effect....

And the determination of the people to establish a Republican Government on the model of that of the United States.

All this was accomplished almost by the mere moral force of the people; for, according to the highest estimate, not over five hundred lives were lost, while many, very many more were lost during the trois jours of 1830.

Our special correspondent in Liverpool gives us the details, in brief, of this important revolution in the annexed....[66]

Column upon column of foreign news, letters, speculation, and American reaction tumbled forth in the days that followed. Each steamer and packet was eagerly anticipated; newspapers began printing tabulations of ships' probable days at sea based on supposed departures from Liverpool, Southampton, or Havre. A week after the *Cambria* brought the above news, the *Herald* was calculating the arrival of the next Cunarder.

The whole country is awaiting with extreme impatience the next news from Europe. The steamer Caledonia is now fourteen days at sea, and will bring thirteen days later intelligence from England and France, embracing, no doubt, a solution of the great problem which was unsettled in Paris at the last dates.... [I]t is impossible to predict what the next news may bring us in the way of revolutionary movements, not only in France, but elsewhere in Europe.[67]

But rather than "embracing...a solution of the great problem" in Paris, the *Caledonia*'s news was of wider conflict, a spreading popular revolution. The steamer's news ate up seven columns in the *Herald* on March 28, 1848, four of which concerned France alone.

The dispatch had come over two Morse lines from Boston. It was a time for dropping advertising and trimming editorial columns, for begging the reader's pardon for holding back congressional dispatches because of the rush of foreign news. With each arriving ship the revolution grew or shifted to a new frontier, Americans' earlier anxieties quelled perhaps, but new ones stirred. A month and a half after the *Cambria* had set the revolution in motion in the minds of American readers, the *Herald*, still breathless and amazed, attempted on May 2 to look back and assess what had happened.

> We are overwhelmed with the intelligence from all parts of
> Europe; it comes to us in such quantities, of all kinds—
> revolution, following revolution—with confusion, conflict,
> bankruptcy—representing all the materials and principles of
> the civilized world in an utter state of difficulty and disorder.
> The three days' revolution in Paris has caused a greater
> change in the Continent than might have been produced by
> three centuries of former ages....[68]

Such was the chaotic and frustrating news situation New York City editors faced during the two months between mid-March and mid-May. Only half of the Cunarders were landing in New York City, the others going into Boston; all, however, stopped at Halifax on the way in. The telegraph reached north beyond Boston, but it was no where near Halifax at this time. The only effective course was to intercept the Cunarders at Halifax with a coastal steamer, relieve them of their news, and dash for Boston, where dispatches could be telegraphed on to New York City. It was a system Daniel H. Craig had employed effectively in the past using carrier pigeons, but the magnitude of the anticipated European news required a much longer first-day dispatch than could be carried on a pigeon's leg. The New York editors' answer was the coastal steamer *Buena Vista*.

The *Buena Vista* first appeared in New York harbor on April 4, 1848, making a trial run. Fresh from the shipyard, this new steamer was outfitted expressly to ply the waters of the Gulf of Mexico between New Orleans and Vera Cruz. Her captain was Nathaniel Jarvis, and her passenger accommodations were "spacious,... commodious and well furnished," reported the *Herald*. She was scheduled to leave for the Gulf before April 15, 1848,[69] but she had caught the eye of New York's editors. Her departure for Gulf duty was scrapped at some point in April, and on May 2, 1848, the *Buena Vista* instead headed north for Halifax to meet steamers for New

York's morning press, leaving the editors behind to argue about who should take credit for the venture.

The *New York Sun* on May 8 claimed, "We started the thing ourselves, without any alliances of any kind." The paper noted that its own modesty had "in this, as in other instances, deprived us of the laurels so justly our due."[70] The next day the *Herald* countered that the *Sun*'s claims were "either a falsehood or a misrepresentation," attributing the *Buena Vista* enterprise to the efforts of "four or five other journals of this city" besides the *Sun*.[71]

But the *Sun* had a history of seeking its own news arrangements outside the various associations of New York papers and, like the *Herald* in other situations, of claiming to originate arrangements shared with other papers. In March 1853 the *Sun*, for example, claimed the honor of founding the Associated Press.

> The present Association of the New-York Newspaper Press was started by the present proprietor of the *Sun*, on the occasion of his making arrangements for a daily express to secure the transmission of news from the South, and particularly from the seat of war in Mexico, in advance of all the ordinary channels of communication.[72]

As already noted, a scholar on Mexican War coverage can find no support for the claim that the AP originated during that conflict. If any credence can be given to the *Sun*'s *Buena Vista* claims, the author suggests that the paper may have made the initial move to charter the steamer but, finding the cost prohibitive, sought the help of other papers.

In a pamphlet that in part recounts AP's early history, Craig clearly attributes the *Buena Vista* episode to Associated Press enterprise. Craig quotes a deposition, dated January 24, 1850, and signed by the six original New York City AP editors, which says, "The Associated Press [prior to 1849] had employed the express steamer Buena Vista to run from Halifax to Boston. . . ."[73]

On May 25, 1848, the *Buena Vista* intercepted her first Cunarder, the *Hibernia*, at sea near Halifax.[74] With the *Hibernia*'s news in hand, Captain Jarvis turned the *Buena Vista* toward Boston. En route the *Buena Vista*'s boiler sprang a leak, however, and she limped into New Bedford on May 27,[75] about the same time the *Hibernia* was being met by news boats in New York harbor.

One week before the *Buena Vista* was having her disastrous first outing for New York's morning press, representatives of those papers were arranging with F. O. J. Smith, proprietor of the Boston–New York Morse telegraph line, to have foreign dispatches telegraphed the last leg into New York City. This is the famous mid-May exchange of letters Rosewater first reports, as noted earlier. Henry J. Raymond and Frederic Hudson, managing editors of the *Courier and Enquirer* and *Herald*, respectively, had been named a committee to represent the six morning papers. Writing on May 13, 1848, on behalf of that committee, Raymond informed Smith that the "Journal of Commerce, Express, Courier and Inquirer [*sic*], Herald, Sun, and Tribune, of this city, have agreed to procure foreign news by telegraph from Boston in common." Raymond then proposed:

> 1. Uninterrupted transmission of "all the news we may wish to receive" from "the moment our despatch shall be received at the telegraph office in Boston. . . ."
> 2. Control of the news dispatches upon receipt in New York, preventing "any part of the news from leaving the [New York] office until we choose to send it out."
> 3. Use of the telegraph arrangement for news from steamers docking in Boston and for steamer "news that may reach Boston for us by express from Halifax," a reference to the *Buena Vista*'s activities.
> 4. An arrangement lasting one year from May 13, 1848.[76]

Raymond asked for Smith's terms in "an immediate reply" and Smith, writing on May 15, responded reasonably and positively to the proposition.

> 1. Smith agreed to Raymond's proposal "for the sake of permanency and responsibility" and because "this frequent change of arrangement is annoying to all parties. . . ."
> 2. The rate would be $100 for the first 3,000 words or less of such dispatches and "the usual newspaper charge" of 2 cents per word for the first 100 words beyond 3,000 and 1 cent per word for all beyond 3,100.
> 3. The Associated Press would have exclusive right to permit and refuse other parties the use of the dispatches.
> 4. Additional recipients (beyond the six New York papers) would pay the above newspaper rates for dispatches exceeding 3,000 words.
> 5. The Associated Press would pay for a 3,000-word dispatch even if the dispatch could not be delivered because of circumstances beyond the telegraph company's control,

including the AP's Boston agent electing not to transmit a
dispatch that was in hand.

6. Transmission of a steamer's news, brought by express,
would eliminate further use of this arrangement for
dispatches delivered when the steamer had docked in Boston.

7. The Associated Press would make all copies of the
dispatch when it arrived in New York, and no member of the
AP was permitted to receive its dispatch ahead of the
others.[77]

Smith saw the purpose of this arrangement as "the hastening before the public of the news," but Raymond was more frank: "The
object in making the arrangement proposed, is to prevent the competition, and the frequent changes of which [Smith] complain[ed]."
In a May 18 reply, Raymond accepted Smith's terms and informed
Smith that AP intended to forward its foreign dispatches immediately to the press of Philadelphia and Baltimore.[78]

The "usual newspaper charge" quoted by Smith would have
meant that an individual newspaper would pay $31 for a 3,000-
word dispatch. Smith's tariff of $100 for a 3,000-word dispatch
transmitted to the AP, when divided among the six member papers,
cost each paper $16.67, a savings of almost 50 percent. Although
this was a bargain, one is urged by the exchange of letters to believe
that Smith was not as eager to attract new business with bargain
prices as he was to reduce the chaotic competition among the papers for the use of his lines.

The New York City AP thus proposed to a telegraph company in
mid-May 1848 a permanent scheme of rates, line priorities, and
rights to the news dispatches as property, a proposal that the telegraph company accepted, the latter setting the rates for transmission. Twenty-one months earlier, it will be recalled from chapter 2,
the newspapers in upstate New York had taken precisely the same
step. Both upstate and in the city, initial newsbroking proceeded
amid a mixture of transportation and telegraph systems, but with
the expectation that telegraphy was expanding and would gradually
supplant transportation's role in the process.

The principal difference between these two newsbrokerages was
that whereas the goal of the upstate editors was to secure any news
that daily presented itself in Albany, and later in New York City, the
city's editors had at first the more specific goal of hastening receipt
of foreign news dispatches periodically made possible by the appearance of westbound Cunarders along the North American coast.

Because the city's editors were already in the best position to receive most of the significant domestic news by telegraph, they could set their sights on gathering more rewarding and more expensive dispatches. And with revolution gripping the Continent, these resourceful metropolitan editors would naturally move to expedite the latest from Europe. As we shall see, this first step for the New York City AP was followed by the gradual formalizing and expanding of news-gathering activity—harbor news, acquisition of a general agent, a network of correspondents, and control of telegraphic dispatches. The author believes that the *Buena Vista*'s departure for Nova Scotia waters on May 2, 1848, is the earliest recorded evidence of the existence of the New York City Associated Press.

Meanwhile, back on the high seas, her boiler repaired, the *Buena Vista* resumed her vigil off Nova Scotia in early June, and on the seventh the *Acadia* hove into view, westbound for Halifax. The contact made, the *Acadia*'s news gathered, the *Buena Vista* again turned southwest for the day-and-a-half sprint for Boston. A passenger on the *Buena Vista* was Craig, accompanied by his homing pigeons, still attempting to beat the steamers and newspaper expresses with European news for American speculators. But now he could avail himself of the newspapers' express steamer, rather than booking passage on the slower Cunarders. Craig's birds could beat the *Buena Vista* if he could loft them fifty miles outside of Boston. On this run, however, the *Buena Vista* approached Boston after sundown and, as Craig later reported, he was unable to fly his birds.[79] The *Buena Vista* docked in Boston on June 9 at 11 P.M. and the AP newspapers in New York City the following morning carried identical telegraphic dispatches of the *Acadia*'s news.

AP's express steamer next met the *Britannia* on June 24, and the New York AP papers carried the Cunarder's news in common the morning of June 26. Craig, again a passenger on the *Buena Vista*, this time flew his pigeons from his stateroom porthole and beat the express steamer into Boston.[80] The *Buena Vista* made a third, and final, news run, meeting the *Caledonia* on July 6 and delivering a dispatch in Boston forty hours later. Craig's pigeons, launched from the *Buena Vista*, however, beat the AP dispatch for the second time.[81]

After three successful express runs, though beaten twice by Craig's birds, the AP apparently abandoned the project. Craig reports that the express was costing the AP $1,000 per trip,[82] and probably owing to the expense Captain Jarvis had instructions to meet only Cunarders bound for New York. On June 13, the *America* arrived and on June 30 the *Cambria*, both docking in Boston and neither intercepted by the *Buena Vista*. Although the *Herald* reported that the express steamer was back on station off Halifax on August 24 ready to intercept the next steamer, a thorough search of the newspaper files turns up no indication that the *Buena Vista* ever carried another Associated Press news dispatch. Overland expresses of news from Halifax would appear in February 1849 and would continue intermittently, and at times dramatically, as we shall see in the next chapter, until a telegraph line was completed to Halifax on November 9, 1849.

The Raymond-Smith letters in mid-May 1848 and the *Buena Vista* episode, beginning May 2, 1848, are two vital signs of the AP in New York City. A third sign was purchase of the steamer *News-Boy*[83] in late May 1848 to patrol the New York harbor for five of the six AP papers. The purchase is reminiscent of earlier harbor arrangements. Hudson says "one of the first expensive undertakings" of the Associated Press was purchase of the steamer *Naushon*. Costing $30,000 and renamed the *News-Boy* by the AP, the ship was used by the newspapers, according to Hudson, for about six months and then was sold.[84] (A receipt to James Watson Webb of the *Courier and Enquirer* for payment of an unspecified amount, signed by AP President Gerard Hallock, for purchase of the *Naushon* "now lying at New Bedford" is dated May 30, 1848, perhaps indicating when the purchase was made.)[85]

The *Herald* reported that the *News-Boy* had arrived in New York City on June 1 and would be ready for news service on June 5, commanded by Captain Bancker.[86] A week later the *Herald* said that five New York papers were served by the *News-Boy* and that the harbor arrangement included three other vessels.

> The new ship-news arrangements of the Herald and four of our contemporaries are now complete. The auxiliary fleet consisting of a swift boat at the Narrows, manned by Captain Robert Silvey, and two men; another boat at Quarantine, manned by Captain William Brogan; and another for the East river and harbor service, manned by Captain John Hall, commenced operations on [June 5, 1848]. The new steamer, "Newsboy," commanded by Captain William Bancker, and manned by engineers, firemen, sailors, &c, &c, for outside or sea service, entered upon her duty [the morning of June 9, 1848]. It will thus be seen that the leading journals of New York have now a most efficient Ship News establishment in operation.[87]

Examination of newspaper files after June indicates that the *Tribune* did not participate in this harbor venture, perhaps unable to afford the expense.

After three weeks of operation, the *News-Boy*'s procedures were described by the *Herald*.

> Vessels are boarded by the Captain of the "News-Boy"...
> frequently at a distance of one hundred miles from land. As
> a general thing she beats about, some fifty to a hundred
> miles off, collects all the news, and runs up to the city at
> night, when the Captain distributes the news that he has
> collected during the day, in time for publication the next
> morning.[88]

The first major ship arrival handled by the *News-Boy* was the *Hibernia*, reaching New York on July 21. (This was after the *Buena Vista*'s last interception of a New York–bound Cunarder at Halifax.)

The *News-Boy* apparently did not deliver a common news dispatch; its primary job was to relieve ships' officers of packages and mail pouches addressed to the five subscribing papers. The officers of the *Britannia* refused to hand over the papers' mail to the *News-Boy* crew on October 17, 1848, causing the *Herald* to complain that "some extraordinary arrangements of the steamship company prevented the press from getting their dispatches till the steamer's mail reached the post office."[89] The *Courier and Enquirer* calculated that it received its mail at 1 P.M., three and a half hours after the *Britannia* was sighted at the Narrows.[90] Such press attempts to skirt postal regulations and ship officers' occasional attempts to observe those regulations were grounds for recurring editorial grumbling at this time.

Craig reports that the *News-Boy*'s operation cost the five papers $10,000 for the six months they ran it[91]—this in addition to the ship's $30,000 purchase price. A dispatch of the *News-Boy*'s news was making its way north and south of New York, perhaps distributed by the Associated Press in both directions. A foreign news dispatch in the *Boston Evening Transcript* on September 1, 1848, begins

> BY THE NIAGARA. The Royal Mail Steamership Niagara,
> Captain Ryrie, from Liverpool, whence she sailed on the 19th
> ult. was boarded by the "Newsboy" at New York at 15
> minutes before 4 o'clock on Thursday afternoon, 15 miles east
> of the light boat.

> The Niagara brings. . . 7 days later European intelligence
> than that received by the Britannia at this port.
>   The news began to come through by [telegraph] about 6
> o'clock last evening.[92]

The *Philadelphia Public Ledger* first notes its reliance on the *News-Boy* for news from New York City ship arrivals on July 26, 1848, at the start of a foreign news dispatch from the inbound *United States*.

The *News-Boy* episode ended with the January 11, 1849, signing of the Harbor News Association agreement by the five newspaper sponsors of the *News-Boy* and by the *New York Tribune*. The new agreement, in effect, dispensed with steamer patrols beyond the harbor, falling back to a two-boat configuration: one at the Narrows station "with a News Collector and two men" and the other, with one man, in the East River "and other service near the city."[93] Two days after the agreement was signed, the *Courier and Enquirer* carried a notice offering the *News-Boy* for sale. Rosewater reports that the notice ran for nearly three months.[94] Raymond was named agent for the five newspaper-owners of the *News-Boy* on April 9, 1849, to protect the owners against default of payment for repairs to the steamer.[95] That is the record's last mention of the ship.

With all of this Associated Press activity in New York City in mid-1848, one might expect to find similar developments in other Eastern cities. It has been noted that the New York editors had taken Philadelphia and Baltimore papers under their wing by May 18, 1848, for the transmission of foreign news dispatches. The *Philadelphia Public Ledger*'s involvement in New York City news-gathering efforts dates from Mexican War news expresses. The *Baltimore Sun*, linked through its founders to the *Public Ledger*,[96] seems also to have been intimately involved in New York news enterprise. Hudson may provide a clue to this relationship by reporting that William M. Swain, the *Public Ledger*'s chief editor, lived in New York City "for upwards of fifteen years. He was often met in the streets of that city."[97] The *Public Ledger* received and published all three foreign news dispatches delivered by the *Buena Vista* to Boston for use by the New York City AP, crediting the AP steamer with procuring its dispatches.[98]

Up in Boston the *Transcript* had been complaining of the low quality of news provided by F. O. J. Smith's telegraph company, apparently at no cost to that city's newspapers.[99] Frederick B. Marbut has found that in 1847 the *Boston Atlas* and *Courier* were publishing telegraphic news summaries of congressional news identical to those appearing in New York and Philadelphia papers.[100] If the same congressional dispatches were appearing in the papers of three cities north of Washington, and all of this was happening before any of these cities had newspaper-run newsbrokerages, then either the telegraph companies or a network of locally based independent telegraphic reporters were serving as a newsbrokerage.

An Associated Press came to Boston in April 1848, when nine Boston dailies combined "to buy of the telegraph company a service consisting of a quantity of foreign news, received at New York by steamer," according to the *Boston Transcript*'s historian. The papers were the *Transcript*, *Journal*, and *Traveller* in the evening field and the *Advertiser*, *Courier*, *Atlas*, *Post*, *Whig*, and *Times* in the morning field.[101] This was the origin of the Boston Associated Press—later enlarged and renamed the New England Associated Press. With New York City AP's *Buena Vista* racing for Boston, rather than New York, and with some agency—perhaps the New York City AP—preparing a foreign news dispatch for Boston papers, based at least in part on the activities of AP's *News-Boy* in New York harbor, a degree of reciprocity between the associated presses of the two cities may be suspected, although the record is by no means clear on this point. With a founding period of April 1848, this Boston Associated Press may have been the nation's second newsbrokerage, following the New York State AP by nearly two years and preceding the New York City AP by a few days or weeks.

Even earlier, something was developing in the South, although the author can find only the proposals and not the fruition of the scheme. Several Southern editors, meeting at Stone Mountain, Ga., on August 11, 1847, agreed to meet in Washington on December 15 and consider proposals for organizing telegraphic news delivery in the South. The *Macon* (Ga.) *Telegraph* published a proposal that envisioned telegraphic news service to dailies, tri-weeklies, semi-weeklies, and weeklies.[102] (Including nondaily newspapers in early newsbroking arrangements is unique to this proposal, and made seemingly necessary to the Southern editors by the thinness of the region's daily press.[103] There was little recorded interest, understandably, among the nondaily press in daily newsbroking either at this time or later.)

A daily 300-word report was proposed in the *Telegraph*, half of it originating in New York City, the other half in New Orleans. Agents would be stationed at these two cities and Washington, D.C. A weekly dispatch of foreign news of about 1,500 words was projected, relying, no doubt, on Cunard arrivals. The annual cost for the foreign dispatches would be $97.50 per paper ("a half of the former rates") and the annual cost of daily and foreign news dispatches and agents' salaries would be $414.83 for dailies, $256.16 for tri-weeklies, $203.27 for semi-weeklies, and $150.38 for weeklies, "certainly a meagre sum," says the *Telegraph*, when compared to the over $500 such service would cost each newspaper each week. As we shall see shortly, Amos Kendall in a document dated December 1, 1847, that proposes to bring order to Northern telegraphic news transmission, points to a successful combination of Virginia newspapers then sharing a common news service. Repeated attempts to find more on these Southern developments have failed.

At the same time newspapers west of the Alleghenies availed themselves of the new telegraph as much as possible. William Henry Smith, writing in 1876 while general agent of the Western Associated Press, notes that a line was completed between Philadelphia and Pittsburgh "in the last days of December, 1846." He says,

> Foreign commercial news was then, as now, of great
> importance to business men, and upon the arrival of vessels
> at Halifax, was forwarded as rapidly as possible to Boston,
> New York and Philadelphia, and thence by wire to
> Pittsburgh. From the latter point it was carried by fast riders,
> who changed horses every ten miles, to Steubenville,
> Wheeling, Zanesville, Columbus, Dayton and Cincinnati. [104]

In the spring of 1847, according to Smith, telegraph lines were extended from Pittsburgh across Ohio toward Cincinnati, "and the route of the post-riders grew shorter, and the news fresher, day by day, until the Queen City was reached." This Morse network was soon matched by rival Henry O'Rielly's lines, "and so sharp was the rivalry between the managers, for months there was blood on the face of the moon," says Smith. [105]

Smith also lends support to the notion that the telegraph companies were early surrogate newsbrokers.

> The Telegraph Companies were the pioneers in the
> news-collecting business west of Philadelphia. There was very
> little commercial business done, and few private messages
> sent. The managers of the lines shrewdly directed their
> operators to employ their leisure time in transmitting news
> items for the daily papers, for which the latter paid whatever
> they chose. [106]

THE NEW YORK CITY ASSOCIATED PRESS AND THE EARLY TELEGRAPH

Tracing New York editors' developing association for harbor and high seas news-gathering is relatively easy because of the attendant chartering and purchase of ships and the resulting publication of steamer news, including press explanations of news-gathering efforts. When one turns to the telegraphic system and its news-movement patterns, however, the picture clouds considerably. When did the New York City AP take control of its general daily telegraphic news dispatches and acquire its own telegraphic agent? Was Alexander Jones AP's first general agent, or did someone precede him in that post? AP's contractual relations with the telegraph up to mid-1848 consisted, according to firm evidence, of only (1) securing rates and priorities on the Boston–New York telegraph line for transmission of foreign news dispatches, and (2) securing rates on the Washington–New York line for newspapers along that route. A formal telegraphic news agreement among AP editors in New York City did not appear until 1851. Nonetheless, a steady stream of daily telegraphic reports was pumped into the columns of the New York morning papers after June 1846, reports shared in identical form by these papers.

Although the routine arrangements for delivery of a daily telegraph report from 1846 to 1849 are largely lost or were unrecorded, there is evidence of a serious enmity developing in late 1847 between the press in general (and the New York City AP members in particular) and the Morse system. This antagonism steadily deepened into virtual warfare by early 1848. After a year and a half of operation the Morse system had failed miserably on Mexican War news-gathering, had not expanded rapidly enough for editors' tastes, was proving costly both when it was inoperative and when it delivered dispatches, and continued to employ unreliable equipment and operators.

For their part, the Morse people in the absence of government support had to rely on driblets of investment capital from small communities scattered along projected telegraph circuits and on hesitant and unpredictable public business. Among the Morse people were those who saw telegraphy not as a public service to be rendered but as a technological path to personal wealth. And, still vulnerable in this infantile state, the Morse system encountered press hostility where editorial support and good will were sorely needed, and it faced the challenge of new telegraphic inventions gaining a foothold in opposition to Morse's device.

Surveying the Eastern exchanges in early November 1847, the *Louisville Morning Courier* quoted R. Y. Conrad in the *Philadelphia North American* as saying, "[W]e think Prof. Morse's associates have been too exacting in their wishes and too monopolistic in their aims." The *Courier* then observed,

> The eastern press almost unanimously use the same language about the agents of Professor Morse that Judge Conrad does....The complaint against Morse's agents is general and must be well founded.... F. O. J. Smith and Mr. Kendall have been made almost maniacal by the introduction of House's printing machine.... That House's machine is destined to be the death of their absurd and ridiculous monopoly we entertain no kind of doubt. [107]

A measure of the press-telegraph hostility is a notice by Amos Kendall, "The Telegraph and the Press," dated December 1, 1847, and appearing in several newspapers. Kendall says,

> There is great difficulty in devising any system of charges which will be just to the Telegraph Companies, and, at the same time, bring the use of the Telegraph within the reach of the press on moderate and equal terms. If there be one unchangeable tariff of charges, the numerous presses in large cities combine together and reduce the price very low to them severally, by dividing the cost, while the same tariff is so high to the few single presses in small cities and towns as to exclude them from the use of the Telegraph, or render it exceedingly burdensome. Again, the practical effect of the system of charges heretofore used, has been to confine the use of the Telegraph in the large cities to the stronger presses, while the weaker have been entirely cut off.

Kendall then proposes regulations for general press adoption that, according to this notice, were already in effect south of Washington, D.C., on the Morse line. One such regulation reads:

> Messages for the public press will be sent over the entire line or to any intermediate point upon it, and copies furnished to stations short of their ultimate destination, at one full charge for the whole distance, and five cents for ten words of every copy delivered on the way: Provided, that

> such message shall be in words and sentences intelligible to
> the operator.

Kendall was, thus, inviting the press "to combine together all along the line and, by dividing the cost, get the news at a very low rate." He observes that such a system allowed "the Virginia press, by uniting with the presses beyond to get the Northern news . . . by paying to the Telegraph Company only five cents for ten words and still less where two or more presses in the same place unite and divide the expense."[108]

Even if one allows for the existence of uneven or high tariffs over the Morse system (as was apparently the case)[109] these still are not the words of a grasping monopolist; rather, they seem to offer a peace formula amid a rising din of unreasonable press criticism, which no doubt anticipated telegraphic competition from House and Bain systems. Surely, the response of Kendall's Magnetic Telegraph Company on November 24, 1847, to the proposal from the newspapers of Washington, Baltimore, Philadelphia, and New York City, as noted earlier, was aimed at accommodating press needs and bringing harmony to press-telegraph relations.

But harmony was not to be. Only the *Herald* in New York seemed content with the Morse system, reportedly pouring thousands of dollars into special dispatches and occasionally applauding the Morse system. The *Herald* reported that in the first two weeks of January 1848 it had received 79,000 words of telegraphic news, costing $2,381. One-third of this, the paper said, was received in common with other morning papers, and the remainder exclusively for the *Herald*, "comprehending the debates in the Senate on the Mexican question and other important political movements of all kinds. . . ."[110]

One week later the *Herald* devoted nearly four front-page columns to the Morse system. A four-column cerographic map of operative and proposed lines was accompanied by a laudatory account of Morse's invention. "Of [the telegraph's] superiority, every day is furnishing evidence, both at home and abroad," said the *Herald*. "Let the daily work which it performs testify."[111]

Such comments did not go unnoticed by the Morse people, especially when the rest of New York's papers scolded the telegraph at every opportunity. Enclosing two copies of the *Herald* for January 5, 1848 (which ran nearly ten columns of telegraphic news from the *Caledonia*'s landing in Boston), Samuel F. B. Morse wrote his brother that the *Herald*

has uniformly been friendly to me and to the enterprise,
while *every other* paper in New York that I have seen except
the Sun also, has seemed to take a particular delight in
detracting and crying down, and raising up rivals and
blazening mistakes and giving currency to falsehoods, and
magnifying troubles. The motive of the Herald's course, so
different from all the others, is not for me to scrutinize.
Under the editorship of Mr. Hudson, it was an excellent
paper, having abandoned its objectionable features.[112]

But the month of March 1848, in addition to exploding a European revolution on America's front pages, brought the total unraveling of Morse's flimsy little empire. With a thin, but hopeful, network
reaching out to Portland, Quebec, Toronto, Erie, St. Louis, and Petersburg, Va. (but not to Halifax and New Orleans, where the editors
at that moment needed the telegraph the most), the dreaded competition of other telegraph systems finally appeared.

Henry O'Rielly, whose western lines of Morse telegraph had been
reasonably well built and run in the public interest, had broken
with the Morse people. On March 9, 1848, the New York press reported that O'Rielly's People's Telegraph Line was completed between Nashville and Louisville, with a line projected to New
Orleans. The new line used the "Columbian" telegraphic instrument, a device designed by Edmund F. Barnes and Samuel K. Zook.
Kendall immediately filed an infringement suit in Kentucky, charging the "Columbian" was only a modification of Morse's instrument. The court upheld the Morse claim on September 11, 1848, but
this and similar suits later against O'Rielly served only to make
O'Rielly an underdog and a popular folk hero in the developing telegraphic war. Gathering substantial press support, O'Rielly next
went hunting in Eastern telegraphic swamps, armed with the Bain
telegraphic instrument.[113]

The *New York Journal of Commerce* enthusiastically described
O'Rielly's successful Nashville-Louisville line. Enclosing a copy of
the article, Morse wrote to copatentee F. O. J. Smith

A more contemptible sneaking article never appeared
before in a journal pretending to decency. Their
encouragement of O'Rielly would honor the annals of
incendiarism and burglary. I dare not trust myself to speak of
them as I feel. But we have a portion of the press against us
from the conflict of the Telegraph at present with their
interest, we must be cautious to give them no just cause to
complain. . . .[114]

Although burdened by the adverse press he and his invention received, Morse constantly sought, according to his correspondence, to avoid conflict with the press. Not so with F. O. J. Smith, who was always itching for a fight from which he might profit. We will later encounter Smith's machinations in opposition to the Associated Press, but Morse was regularly having to restrain Smith, as in mid-April 1848, when the inventor wrote Smith, "The Boston Atlas, I perceive, is very hostile. I would give no occasion for them to complain."[115]

On March 10, 1848, the press announced that the House telegraph instrument was being tested between New York City and Philadelphia.[116] Morse wrote Smith on April 18, saying,

> I hear that House is actually sending messages from
> Philadelphia to Paterson. If so what is best to be done? I wish
> you to be on the alert, for what with the prejudice against us
> of the press generally, and the particular and savage enmity
> of some editors, we ought to make an example.[117]

The "example" was another infringement suit, but unlike the "Columbian" and later Bain suits, Morse interests could not convince the courts that Royal E. House's alphanumeric instrument infringed upon Morse's dot-and-dash system.[118] The House line was opened for public service on April 29, 1848, carrying among other messages that day the foreign news dispatches of the Cunarder *America*, which had docked that morning in New York City.[119] "The House instrument works admirably, and is a monument of the ingenuity of the inventor," the *New York Herald* commented.[120] House's invention, after defeating the Morse infringement claim, was awarded a patent later in 1848, retroactive to 1846, when he had first applied for the patent [121] Morse now had a true competitor, and the newspapers had some leverage on the Morse monopoly.

Meanwhile, March 1848 also witnessed perhaps the loudest outburst of anti-Morse press comment yet. The *Buffalo Courier* early in March informed its readers of a *New York Sun* tirade and threat.

> The New York *Sun* roundly abuses the present monopoly
> telegraph lines, and announces that its proprietors are going
> to construct one for their own use, at a cost of $125,000,
> between Boston, New York and Washington, for the exclusive
> use of the New York *Sun*, and states that "the telegraph
> system in this country is nothing but an odious monopoly and
> must be broken up. The companies have derived, and still
> receive more revenue from the Press, than from any other

source; yet they put their screws upon us whenever
opportunity offers. They know we are obliged to have news,
and if we demur at their outrageous charges they will tell us
that 'the wires are broke.' The wires are almost always
'broke' when a steamer arrives, and generally remain so until
the markets are closed; then the newspapers are roundly
bled.'' If this is not a brag, it is a commendable enterprise.[122]

Almost immediately the *Sun* claimed to have concluded the above
arrangements, saying, ''Other newspapers are cordially invited to
join with us in it and share its benefits.''[123]

The *New York Tribune* on March 11, 1848, carried a long letter on
page one heatedly attacking the Morse telegraph, claiming that (1)
Morse had invented nothing, (2) Kendall and Smith charged excessive prices on their lines, and (3) O'Rielly's effort to construct the
People's Telegraph Line in the West was a needed and valid challenge to the Morse system. The letter was signed ''Mercator'' and
appeared one day after the *Tribune*'s dispatch on Senate ratification
of the treaty with Mexico had been delayed because the Morse office in Washington had closed before the *Tribune* correspondent
could file his report.[124] *Tribune* editor Horace Greeley and Washington Morse manager Alfred Vail exchanged angry letters over the incident, concluding with this salvo from Greeley's pen: ''There is just
one remedy for the ills that journals are heir to—Telegraphic Competition. I mean to have it.''[125]

But despite such huffing and puffing, there is no evidence that
the New York City AP editors jointly or individually controlled or
erected telegraphic circuits beyond a line connecting Sandy Hook at
the outer end of Lower New York Harbor with Manhattan. We shall
see Craig as AP general agent buying and selling telegraphic properties in the 1850s (see chapter 5), but he later revealed that he could
not convince his AP editors to do likewise for their own protection.
Apparently the closest AP would come to influencing the development of telegraphy was to offer AP business exclusively to telegraph developers who promised to construct lines in competition
with troublesome Morse circuits.

A case in point is O'Rielly, who in October 1848 signaled his interest in constructing a line between New York City and Portland,
Maine, using Bain telegraph equipment. The O'Rielly line would
parallel the Morse circuit that AP had secured in May 1848 to transmit its foreign news dispatches. In the intervening five months,
however, the Morse proprietor, Smith, had begun to involve himself
in the business of moving foreign news dispatches in a manner that

threatened AP's operations. All six AP papers in New York City printed enthusiastic notices of O'Rielly's plan, but rather than offer O'Rielly financial support for a scheme certain to benefit them, the AP editors resolved to grant him their business exclusively for "at least six months." Five years later, O'Rielly revealed that Moses S. Beach, AP secretary, had

> placed in my hands a statement of the extent and cost of the business telegraphed for the Associated Press between New-York and Halifax, with an approbatory resolution from that Association, declaring that, if I would establish a New Line between New-York and Boston, they would give all their business to that line for at least six months, at such rates of charges as I or my associates might determine, up to the amount or within the rates which they were then paying to the existing Morse Line.[126]

So, while the editors tightly grasped their purse strings, they threw their weight around in telegraph's internal struggle, freely castigating the Morse system and encouraging anti-Morse developments in print. A steady stream of such press notices is preserved at the New York Historical Society in three volumes of mounted newspaper clippings compiled by O'Rielly. He was well aware of press dissatisfaction with the telegraph system Morse had wrought, and, although he was probably not collaborating with the newsbrokers, O'Rielly as a businessman and developer must have been urged by this array of press clippings to invade the Eastern telegraphic field. Historian Thompson reports that by May 1850 Morse, House, and Bain lines paralleled each other from Boston to Philadelphia and Morse and Bain lines ran between New York City and Buffalo and between Philadelphia and Washington.[127]

Greeley had his competition, and the *Sun* did not have to spend $125,000 for its own telegraph line. Slowly the press obtained a more favorable news-movement climate through telegraphic competition. But it was to be short-lived competition for, as the 1850s advanced, the power to purchase and lease circuits and instruments would, by the eve of the Civil War, divide telegraphy into two regional giants—the American Telegraph Company and the Western Union Telegraph Company—and a second-generation telegraph monopoly was on the horizon.

What can be understood about newsbroking from this competition in telegraphy and the continuing barrage of press criticism? Perhaps not much, since while these tides ebbed and flowed, newspapers in many communities continued to receive and print a daily file of domestic telegraphic news and the latest from Europe by weekly steamer. But at second glance, these battles made up the context in which editors were deciding how and where they should take hold of their news-gathering activities. From a late-1840s perspective, the scraps of evidence presented here depict a progression of newsbroker developments in New York City extending over probably three years and embracing a widening scope of activities as news events and technological growth dictated.

It seems safe to observe that even in the fourth decade of the nineteenth century, European news remained the most sought-after commodity for the newspaper editor. Clearly the papers wanted their steady diet of congressional and state legislative accounts, but, judging from their style of presentation and placement in the paper (usually sketchy and chronological and on inside pages), such accounts were largely formularized records, a telegraphic token gaining early currency among Eastern newspapers and unchanged after several years. And if the telegraph did not exist or was out of order, such legislative reports, and most other domestic news items, would eventually find their way into a newspaper's office via the newspaper exchanges, which, as we shall see, continued to supply a substantial diet of domestic news well into the telegraphic era. But steamer news usually went on page one, called for extensive space in news columns, required multiple headline decks, and defied formulas for writing and presenting. Steamer and packet news solicited the kinds of news-gathering efforts, both before and after the appearance of the telegraph, commonly not used for domestic stories. An indication of the functions foreign news performed for American readers was that European markets received at least summary treatment at the top of the foreign dispatch, as did parliamentary actions affecting American trade. Sources of similar congressional actions were multiple and easily accessible to the American reader interested in such things.

To editors, who habitually pursued the European dispatch far more aggressively than the domestic dispatch, the new telegraph in its first few years offered primarily an expeditious link in a foreign news-gathering process still conducted via transportation systems. And when those foreign dispatches became overlaid with news of European revolution, editors of means and fame made the supreme effort to hasten them to their newsrooms.

Thus, in March of 1848 when word of revolution reached the United States, the New York City editors cranked up the old harbor news-gathering machinery, dating from the 1820s, of sharing the expense and benefits of an association. But in the intervening quarter-century the machinery had been drastically changed. Steam and telegraphy gave editors cause to expect more and fresher news and demanded of editors greater expenditure and a more complex set of arrangements with suppliers of news and technology. This time a Liverpool agent prepared the dispatch for telegraphing at Boston; this time the editors needed a steamship, rather than a schooner, to scout the horizon off Nova Scotia, rather than off Long Island; this time the editors required a contract with the telegraph company, rather than an open wharf in New York harbor.

Beyond the reach of most cities' collective newspaper press, such expenditures and arrangements could be mustered only by the wealthy New York City press. And by definition, this meant the city's established morning papers, competition and penny, political, and mercantile labels notwithstanding. Off and on for twenty years such distinctions had not stood in the way of news-gathering associations generated by the city's press, and they did not in 1848. A month or so after European revolution was first reported in the United States and with no signs of the news subsiding, the New York editors chartered the *Buena Vista* as their express vessel to race between Halifax and Boston. Eleven days after the express steamer embarked for Nova Scotia waters with instructions to intercept only New York–bound Cunarders, the editors approached the Boston–New York telegraph proprietor with a scheme for expediting their dispatches from steamer to newsroom. This, the author believes, is the origin of the New York City Associated Press.

Ill-fated, beaten by Craig's pigeons, and expensive to the point of being able to meet only every second Cunarder, the *Buena Vista* was released by the editors in July when the sensation over European revolution died down. Meanwhile late in May, five of these six editors purchased a fast coastal steamer, the *News-Boy*, to patrol the waters off Long Island. Although successful, the *News-Boy*, too, was abandoned in January 1849, at the time the six powerful morning editors penned the Harbor News Association agreement in the *New York Sun* offices. This agreement, the earliest surviving partnership document of the city's AP, describes a simpler harbor operation. Also, it implies protection for each signatory from the aggressively competitive inclinations of fellow partners, and it probably anticipated the approaching completion of telegraph lines between Boston and Saint John, New Brunswick, and eventually Halifax. (Chapter 4 notes that AP signed an agreement with New Brunswick telegraph officials on February 9, 1849, to expedite foreign news dispatches from Saint John. The line from Saint John to New York City was opened four days later.)

While the editors personally looked after receipt of their foreign news dispatches, a handful of independent and telegraph company newsbrokers—Francis A. Abbot, Alexander Jones, Elias P. Winans, and perhaps others—attended to the less important movement of domestic news dispatches over a rapidly growing, but carelessly operated and competitively self-defeating telegraph system. These newsbrokers had occupied the field for nearly two years when New York's editors responded to the European crisis with their steamer and telegraph association. The New York papers had regularly received and printed a common domestic telegraph dispatch since June 1846, a practice that continued throughout 1848 and into 1849. The author reads Jones's account of early newsbroking as saying that the New York editors were served by a succession of independent or telegraph company newsbrokers before Jones began to organize AP's telegraphic news-gathering, probably some time during 1849, the year he first appears in the city directories as a "telegraphic reporter" at 3 Hanover. That address, it is clear, is the AP's first office; it was the business address of Craig after he succeeded Jones as AP's general agent in 1851. On the other hand, Jones's correspondence in late 1848 places him at 28 Merchants' Exchange, corner of Hanover Street and Exchange Place, almost a block south of the Hanover address. The Merchants' Exchange address appears on letters to Henry O'Rielly on October 3, 4, and 5, and November 2, 1848. Jones signs his letter of October 3 "Alex Jones, Firm—Jones the Telegraph Reporters." The last two letters deal with telegraphic news-gathering, but, rather than mentioning the Associated Press anywhere, they are signed "A. Jones" and "Alex. Jones" and speak in terms of Jones's own business. [128]

The October 5 letter requires additional attention. The letter transmits a printed "Circular. To Telegraph Correspondents, Reporters and Operators" and explains that its "object is to avoid confusion and to obtain greater uniformity in the transmission of election returns by Telegraph." (A presidential election, the first to be conducted nationally on the same day, occurred on November 7, 1848.) Jones asks O'Rielly's help in distributing the circular along his lines. Neither the letter nor the circular mentions the Associated Press (which the reader will recall was the name given the six morning newspapers by Raymond in correspondence with Smith nearly five months earlier). Instead, the circular says: Jones "in behalf of the Journals of this City, associated in obtaining Telegraphic and other intelligence'' and later ''in behalf of the New York Press and their associates in other cities.'' Jones signed the circular: ''Jones & Co., 28 Merchants Exchange.''[129] It seems to the author that Jones at this time was contracting as an independent newsbroker with the New York press for transmission of domestic reports. Bringing Jones into the AP organization as general agent, which if the city directories are true was in 1849, was like naming a captain for one of AP's news boats. More than a mere contractual arrangement with an independent reporter, naming an in-house newsbroker was a move by which AP editors reached for greater control over the gathering and distributing of telegraphic dispatches, as distinguished from harbor or ocean interception of transatlantic ships.

After two years of toil, Jones had devised a network of correspondents and was generating a daily news report not much larger than that received by New York papers before 1849. (Chapter 4 discusses Jones's administration and news report in detail.) Also after those two years, with Craig either in New York or shortly moving there to replace Jones, New York City's AP editors finally sat down and formalized their partnership with the 1851 document discussed earlier in this chapter.

Thus, when viewed in this broad perspective, slowly developing newsbroking in New York City contrasts sharply with the New York State AP, which bloomed immediately and fully with the completion of the telegraph. The difference, of course, was the absence along the Albany-Buffalo line of independent telegraph reporters whose reports of domestic affairs in the early years freed the New York City editors to concentrate on affairs in Europe, affairs that were more newsworthy in March 1848 than in the summer of 1846.

Far less, unfortunately, can be said about the development of Abbot & Winans in New York City. This suggests to the author that A & W may have been a creation of the telegraph companies. It clearly was not a product of newspaper-based initiative; no newspaper this author has examined praised itself for helping to develop A & W the way the *Herald* and *Sun* in New York City vied for credit for the *Buena Vista* and other AP ventures, either at the time or in later treatises on the subject. Moreover, and on reflection this is striking: not a single contract or conflict has come to light between A & W and the telegraph companies. Significantly most of what the author, and his predecessors, have learned about the origins of the New York City Associated Press is revealed either in editors' published comments about their news-gathering handiwork or from pamphlets and magazine articles arising from subsequent conflicts between the newspapers or AP and the telegraph companies.

DISCUSSION

Among the three institutions, established and emerging, in this and the previous chapter—newspapers, newsbrokers, and telegraphy—only newspapers had a defined institutional structure and function in the last half of the 1840s, and even that institution's contours were being altered by new production technologies of speed and volume, new notions of audience and news report, and new distribution concepts.

Telegraphy's physical presence on the landscape, even though mitigated by faulty construction and operation and by competing patents, offered the false impression until the late 1850s of being a fully developed institution. Telegraph historian Thompson observes that the average telegraph company in the early 1850s "was dangerously near bankruptcy."

> Aware of the crisis within the industry, a number of
> far-seeing individuals urged a grand combination of lines, but
> the time was not ripe. Nearly a decade was to elapse before
> competition gave way to consolidation, and the telegraph
> industry emerged from the era of methodless enthusiasm into
> one of order and prosperity.[130]

Newsbrokers, suspended between the other two institutions and only marginally operational at this time, were the least developed of the three, their news report maturing very slowly and their structure still very much in doubt. One detects in the evidence four possible newsbroker structures emerging: (1) in New York City, editors personally and heavily investing in transportation equipment to augment public transportation and to supplement fragmentary telegraphic facilities for themselves and a few Philadelphia and Baltimore friends and Boston colleagues; (2) New York state editors forming an association of newspapers along a new telegraph line, handing daily control of the news report over to a distant agent and negotiating with the telegraph company for times and rates of delivery; (3) independent telegraphic reporters under contract generating a news report for newspapers and striking their own arrangements with the telegraph company; and (4) a telegraph-based newsbrokerage supplying newspapers with a news report at times and rates set by the telegraph companies. We shall find that only the telegraph-based brokerage failed to survive, a victim of editors' persistent demand to receive a news report at least constructed by journalists—if not controlled by the editors themselves.

The crucial relationship in this chapter is between newspapers and the young telegraph, the former increasingly wanting regular, dependable telegraphic news but finding telegraphic service unreliable and expensive, and the latter wanting the press's news business and good press notices, but not yet able to provide sound service at low rates in a settled institutional setting. With the powers of commentary to influence public opinion about telegraphy and of expenditure to encourage telegraphic competition, in the short run major Eastern newspapers could and did dominate this relationship, despite their occasional posturings as victims.

Concepts of news, as we shall see in the next chapter, had not yet changed as the result of early telegraphy and newsbroking; that would come later. But for the moment, telegraphy either was simply an alternative system of news-gathering that paralleled and supplanted old transportation systems or was plugged into old transportation routes of news movement to speed delivery of special types of news that would also arrive later by traditional transportation systems. Domestic reports by telegraph were simply shorter versions of articles eventually coming to hand in the newspaper exchanges. The gathering of foreign news by telegraph, however, required much effort of editors, especially the demanding metropolitan editors. And the motivation for such effort was threefold and stretched way back into the pretelegraphic days: to secure, print, and sell foreign news before it could come into the possession of the general population by ordinary postal service, to limit the impact of market speculators armed with foreign news in advance of the general population, and to maintain a standing for foreign news enterprise that was equal to (but increasingly not necessarily superior to) that of journalistic colleagues.

The appearance of newsbrokers in conjunction with the new telegraphy was largely journalism's recognition that single telegraph lines, restrictions on transmission times at economical rates, and the potential threat of telegraph companies entering the news business all required a journalistic structure and process for gathering, organizing, and delivering a news report via telegraph. That editors would use telegraphic news in some form, there can be no doubt, judging from the rapidity with which such news appeared in papers along new telegraphic circuits. And that editors would settle for a common dispatch among them seems to have been a painless decision. A common dispatch protected each editor from the aggressive tendencies of his local colleagues in the city and kept each editor abreast of his colleagues down the road in the countryside. Moreover, the common dispatch signaled the existence of a pool of participating editors whose combined financial resources could control and deliver that which individual editors were incapable of.

That the upstate organizers were *editors* Seward, Northway, and Butts and that the initial New York City organizers were *reporters* Abbot, Jones, Winans, and perhaps others, is of some historic significance, but of no long-range consequence. After 1855 either editors took a hand in shaping newsbroking, or the effort was doomed to failure. But despite editors' guiding hands at the outset, creation and operation of a newsbrokerage increasingly deprived an editor of the ability to make daily decisions on selecting and editing stories from beyond his community. Newsbroking centralized the gathering, assembling, and distributing of news stories in the hands of the broker, who might be many miles away and was functioning with motivations or perspectives differing from those of the local editor. Such tendencies toward centralization and monopolization of news movement are a continuous theme of newsbroking's history, and find parallel expression in each of a succession of national communications systems, of which telegraphy was only the first.

Chapter 4
NEWSBROKING STABILIZES

Dr. Jones undertook the management of the news in the infancy of the Association, and when the telegraph lines were few in number. He was an indefatigable worker.

Frederic Hudson, *Journalism in the United States*
(1873)

The [Associated Press] business required our personal attention day and night, Sunday and Monday. Often on stormy nights in winter. . . have we gone round at twelve and one o'clock, and delivered messages with a snow or sleet storm beating in our face. . . .

Our services were thus continued until. . . we resigned the general news agency after having devoted from five to six years of unremitting health-wearing toil to the business. . . .

Alexander Jones, *Historical Sketch of the Electric Telegraph*
(1852)

''Dr.'' Alexander Jones was indeed a physician with a scientific turn of mind, and, as these quotes suggest, not the aggressive news hawk needed to coax a newsbrokerage to its feet in the nation's journalism capital. One suspects after examining the record that Jones was attracted to the telegraph as a scientific innovation rather than as a device for delivering news dispatches. Journalism and even his own involvement in the Associated Press take a back seat to telegraphy's development and telegraphic codes in Jones's *Historical Sketch of the Electric Telegraph*, published one year after he stepped down as AP general agent.

This chapter examines Jones's tenure as general agent—the organization he operated, the news report he prepared, and the changing telegraphic scene he coped with. On balance, Jones's role in the

AP was limited to expanding slightly and formalizing the telegraphic news practices already in place for the morning press in New York City. The conflict during Jones's two or three years with AP, as this chapter describes, occurs not in New York City, but along America's North Atlantic coastline, where competing telegraphic interests and warring news factions threatened to disrupt the pipeline of European news to the nation's leading editors. Jones processed and delivered the news reports and devised telegraphic codes while AP's executive committee negotiated and contracted with telegraph's officialdom and while AP's firebrand, Daniel H. Craig, occupied the territory between Boston and Halifax, regularly slaying telegraphic dragons and bringing home the foreign news that AP so dearly wanted.

Nonsense abounds at places in our literature about newsbroking history. Consider, for example, Oliver Gramling's stage-setter for that meeting in the *New York Sun* office which reportedly sowed the seeds of the New York City Associated Press.

> But, aside from Hale and Bennett, the overlords of the
> New York press were suspicious and reluctant. Hale outlined
> his plan and saw marked signs of resentment. The rival
> publishers had not been pleased with the strides of the
> *Herald* and *Journal of Commerce* through their co-operative
> efforts. There were gruff questions and vigorous dissents.[1]

Four paragraphs of narrative follow purporting to describe the discussions and disagreements of the six founding editors of the New York City AP in the course of that meeting. The drama of conflict, unfounded but infused into this account, lends to AP's birth the aura of a miracle rather than a business proposition. Such are the dangers of relying on house histories—two of which exist for American newsbrokerages[2]—and one finds such accounts more useful in detecting corporate mentality than in discovering the historical truth.

The more he reads in journalism history, the more the author realizes that these six editors were not the cutthroat competitors that the literature describes. Then, newspaper success rested on finding a niche of untapped readership, whether through style of news presentation, mix of news content, political slant, price per paper, or amount of sensationalism. Early in March 1848 the *New York Herald* reported New York newspaper circulations as follows.[3] (Asterisks indicate original AP papers.)

Penny Papers		Political-Mercantile Papers	
*Sun	40,000	*Journal of Commerce	7,500
*Herald	17,280	*Courier and Enquirer	7,000
*Tribune	11,500	*Express	6,000
True Sun	9,000	Commercial Advertiser	3,000
		Evening Post	1,300
		Globe	480
	All Others	2,000	

These figures are important to an understanding of the origins of the New York City Associated Press, but since the reader may suspect the *Herald*'s reporting of its colleagues' circulations, we can turn to an independent source, J. C. G. Kennedy, who reports essentially the same picture for the New York journals in 1850,[4] thus supporting the *Herald*'s report during the crucial year for AP of 1848.

Original AP Papers		Papers outside AP	
Sun	55,000	Morning Star	15,000
Herald	32,640	Commercial Advertiser	3,500
Tribune	19,480	Mechanics' Day Book	2,000
Express	10,700	Evening Post	1,500
Courier and Enquirer	5,200	Evening Mirror	1,500
Journal of Commerce	4,800	Democrat	1,200
		Deutsche Schnellpost	1,150
		Globe (defunct in 1850)	591

By the *Herald*'s tabulation, AP papers' circulations in 1848 were 85 percent of the city's total daily circulation, and, according to Kennedy's 1850 figures, AP papers controlled a similar 82.8 percent of the city's total daily circulation. Two common threads among all six AP originators were substantial circulations and a respectable longevity.

Beyond these common threads, however, each of the six AP papers was an identifiable news package, different from the other five. Within the penny press group the *Sun* was a shade more sensational than the *Herald*, appealing to the mechanics and laborers, although both the *Sun* and the *Herald* leaned in differing degrees at different times toward Democratic politics. The *Herald* was the most exciting and diversified of the pennies, introducing its middle-class readers to a wide variety of news subjects, occasionally making news with its own news exploits, and exploiting innovation and short bursts of sensationalism. The *Tribune*, only seven years old and still struggling to catch up to the pack in 1848, held to the Whig-Republican standard and tried to steer a higher intellectual course than its fellow AP pennies, seeking solutions in the ethereal reaches of philosophy to the worker's plight. All three pennies, however, through their street hawkers, low prices, and cash sales, catered to middle-or lower-middle-class readers.

For members of the political and commercial elites, able to pay the higher prices (usually by subscription), AP's three political-mercantile papers presented as wide a choice as the pennies did for their audiences. Among the three elite papers, the *Journal of Commerce* can be classed as almost totally a mercantile paper, its Democratic leanings taking a back seat to aggressive and accurate news-gathering. The *Courier and Enquirer* presented a mix of mercantile and political fare, its Whig-Republicanism playing a more pronounced role in the news report than did the *Journal*'s touch of Democratic politics, but less than the *Express*'s obvious Whig-turned-Know Nothing-turned-Democrat politics. The *Express* was a political paper of the old school, even though it was the youngest of the political-mercantile AP papers. These were not largely overlapping news packages of "competitive" newspapers; they were, if one looks again at the figures above, the city's most successful and established newspapers, able to underwrite a news-gathering association from the profits derived from comfortably large and diverse readerships.

The New York City AP was a product of the city's journalistic "haves," not of editors swallowing their pride or ignoring the competitive urge. Even with common domestic and foreign news dispatches there would be plenty of room for competition among the papers' news emphases, political leanings, letter-writers, and correspondents. At stake here were financial matters—the saleability of newfangled telegraphic news, the excessive cost of gathering of telegraphic news by individual newspapers, and the perception of a monopolistic Morse telegraphic management. The solution for these papers was equally financial: one must invest in a structure that would control the journalistic portion of the no-man's-land created by telegraphy. This was merely good business sense, based on the city's twenty-year history of news-gathering associations and expresses. There is nothing especially visionary, heroic, or—in light of the earlier New York State AP—novel about what these New York City editors accomplished with their AP. Simply put, their AP bought these editors protection on important news channels at a time when technological innovation was making those channels more unpredictable.

In fact, a close reading of the record reveals that at least some of these great men of New York journalism had very little to do personally with creating or shaping the AP. It was, of course, their money that floated this AP ship, but its navigation through some treacherous waters was left to underlings. The reader will recall that two managing editors—Henry J. Raymond of the *Courier and Enquirer* and Frederic Hudson of the *Herald*—constituted the committee that, on behalf of the new AP, approached F. O. J. Smith in May 1848 about foreign news movement over his Boston–New York City telegraph line.

Hudson's sketchy diaries[5] give our best glimpse of AP's governing personnel in those early years. Regulars on AP's executive committee were Hudson; Raymond, until 1851 when he founded the *Times* and ascended to editor status; George H. Andrews, Raymond's successor on the *Courier and Enquirer*; and Charles A. Dana and George M. Snow of the *Tribune*.

Even at regular meetings of AP's members, according to the diaries, editors were apt to be represented by managing editors. Here are the papers' representatives at three such meetings, as recorded by Hudson. (Editors are indicated by asterisks.)

Newspaper:	AP Meeting of Jan. 28, 1851	AP Meeting of Jan. 17, 1854	AP Meeting of April 26, 1854
Courier and Enquirer	George H. Andrews	Andrews	absent
Express	K. S. Townsend	Stansbury	*James Brooks
Herald	Frederic Hudson	Hudson	Hudson
Journal of Commerce	*Gerard Hallock	*Hallock	*Hallock
Sun	*Alfred E. Beach	*Moses S. Beach	*M. S. Beach
Times	nonexistent	*Henry J. Raymond	*Raymond
Tribune	George M. Snow	absent	Charles A. Dana

Hallock was AP's president from the start until he relinquished control of the *Journal of Commerce* on August 31, 1861. The Beach brothers took charge of the *Sun* in December 1848 from their father,

Moses Y. Beach. Moses S. Beach was AP's secretary in the early years. When the presence of these officers at the above meetings is noted, the reader finds very few other editors in attendance.

Also, it was a reasonably young crowd of journalists who shaped AP's early development. Those for whom biographical material can be located are listed below according to their ages in 1848. (Asterisks indicate those most active in the AP organization between 1848 and 1860.)

Age
57—David Hale, *Journal of Commerce* editor
53—James Gordon Bennett, *Herald* editor
*48—Gerard Hallock, *Journal of Commerce* editor and AP president
48—Moses Y. Beach, *Sun* editor to December 1848
46—James Watson Webb, *Courier and Enquirer* editor
*ca. 46—Alexander Jones, first AP general agent of record
41—Thomas McElrath, *Tribune* publisher
38—James Brooks, *Express* editor
37—Horace Greeley, *Tribune* editor
*37—Daniel H. Craig, second AP general agent of record
*33—Erastus Brooks, *Express* editor
*29—Charles A. Dana, *Tribune* managing editor
*29—Frederic Hudson, *Herald* managing editor
*28—Henry J. Raymond, *Courier and Enquirer* managing editor to 1851, then *Times* editor
*26—Moses S. Beach, *Sun* editor after December 1848 and AP secretary
22—Alfred E. Beach, *Sun* editor from December 1848 to 1852.

In fact, many of those above who were not active in AP, although considered the Founding Fathers of AP, were busy with other pursuits during the crucial formative months for AP in 1848, as the following notations indicate:[6]

- James Brooks, who had been in the New York Assembly, was elected to Congress in November 1848.
- Greeley in that same election was named to fill a three-month vacancy in Congress.
- Hale was stricken with paralysis on June 11, 1848, and died on January 20, 1849.
- Dana was on a European tour for eight months beginning in June 1848.
- Webb's wife died during 1848.

• Hudson's diary notes on May 25, 1847, that Bennett was to leave for Europe in a few weeks and would be absent for several months. Bennett biographies note that he spent much time in the late 1840s and 1850s traveling in the United States, Europe, and the West Indies. Hudson is credited by Frank Luther Mott in the *Dictionary of American Biography* with organizing, guiding, and improving the *Herald*'s operation with little intervention or direction from Bennett.

• Morton Borden comments that "Dana—more than Greeley—was responsible for many of the improvements and standards set by the *Tribune*." The more Greeley became interested in politics and the onrushing debate over slavery, the more he "abdicated the guidance and editorship of the paper...in favor of Dana."[7] Beman Brockway, who was a *Tribune* staffer for two years after 1853, would have agreed with Borden. Calling Dana the paper's managing editor "because he looked after the conduct of the paper, directing what matter should go in and what not," Brockway says, "I make this explanation because it was the general supposition that Mr. Greeley performed that duty, whereas he knew little of the contents of the paper previous to its publication."[8]

These editors were, however, by no means oblivious to their Associated Press memberships. Addressing London publishers in 1851, Greeley observed

> The Telegraphic dispatch is the great point.... I should say that a hundred thousand dollars a year is paid by our association of the six leading daily papers.... We telegraph a great deal in the United States.... We have a report every day, fifteen hundred miles, from New Orleans daily; from St. Louis too, and other places.[9]

The organizational pattern chosen by these editors, one declining in popularity but still prevalent in the mid-nineteenth century, was the partnership, at first documented in the joint chartering of the *Buena Vista* and the joint ownership of the *News-Boy*, and then in the Harbor News Association agreement of 1849, the "telegraphic and other intelligence" agreement of 1851, and the Regulations of the General News Association in 1856.

Although later regional Associated Press organizations were incorporated, as noted in Volume 2, the New York City AP throughout forty-five years of operation never incorporated. James W. Simonton, New York City AP's third general agent of record, in 1879 described the advantages of such a partnership. The New York City AP, Simonton said,

> is not a corporation. It derives no element of success from special legislation, State or national. Its every source of power and strength is the direct creation of its owners and controllers and their associates in the press, and use of their combined capital, experience and skill. . . . It is . . . a great mutual benefit or co-operative association of business men who, having common interests and common needs, work together for efficiency and economy. . . .[10]

Although Simonton was engaging in propaganda before an audience of U.S. senators, there were practical reasons for AP to maintain a partnership. Corporations appeared in the middle decades of the nineteenth century as a shield against increasingly ruthless business practices; as a means of raising large sums of development and improvement capital while protecting investors; and as a self-sustaining legal entity that identified its purposes in its charter, an "artificial person" capable of owning property, engaging in litigation, and surviving the deaths of members and officers.[11]

The AP, however, had no telegraph lines to erect, no presses to buy. Except for purchase of the *News-Boy*—a disastrous early financial venture—the AP required only a few salaries, a small amount of office equipment, office rental, and a couple of boat charters. The vast bulk of its cash flow was the weekly assessments of partners and client newspapers, which were immediately turned over to telegraph companies to cover telegraphic tolls as set by contract. The New York City partners apparently gave no thought to extracting profit from their venture, content to operate it principally as protection from news-gathering competition, happy not to be paying anymore for their news.

Moreover, the partnership at first allowed participants the latitude of making individual telegraphic and harbor arrangements outside of the AP. Consequently, one finds the *New York Sun* seeking its own telegraphic contract with Ezra Cornell in September 1849.

> Can we make an arrangement with the N.Y. & Erie and Erie & Mich[igan] Tel[egraph] lines for the transmission of *news* messages from the various stations on the line . . . the whole not to exceed say 1500 words per week?
> Our purpose would be to employ correspondents at the various stations, each to forward any news he might have.[12]

One week later, the *Sun* "found so much difficulty in arranging with other lines" that it abandoned the idea "for the present, certainly." [13]

As the 1850s progressed, however, the partnership, as we shall see, increasingly limited participants' individual news-gathering activities. The purpose of this partnership, beyond the daily delivery of news, increasingly appeared to be the protection of each paper against the potential enterprise of its local partners.

THE JONES ADMINISTRATION

As AP's first recorded general agent, [14] Alexander Jones made his way to this distinction by an unlikely route. The son of a North Carolina planter, Jones received a medical degree from the University of Pennsylvania in 1822 at the age of twenty. [15] He went to Mississippi to practice his profession and acquired an interest in the cultivation of cotton, becoming a well-known authority on the subject. He is credited with making several improvements in the cotton gin that were still in use when he died in 1863.

The British East India Company sought his help in expanding the Indian cotton industry and paid for his passage to London to finalize arrangements for his employment in India. In London, however, Jones was gripped by the thought, as his *Herald* obituary writer says, "that it would not be patriotic for an American to go into a foreign country and there give his time and attention to the cultivation of an article which was one of the most important staples of his own country." Jones, therefore, declined a $5,000-a-year job, plus expenses, and returned to the United States, settling in New York City because its climate was more favorable to his health than the South's.

Upon his return, at about age thirty-eight, he became a correspondent for several British and American newspapers and wrote a popular series as "Sandy Hook" for the *New York Journal of Commerce*. His activities as an independent telegraphic reporter, beginning in the spring or fall of 1846, are described in the previous chapter. His *Herald* obituary says he was appointed AP general agent "about the year 1850." His own account in his book, *Historical Sketch of the Electric Telegraph*, could be interpreted as dating his AP appointment anywhere from late 1848 to the end of 1849.

Jones apparently continued to practice medicine in New York City while engaged in his various journalistic pursuits. He first appears in a New York City directory [16] in 1845, listed as a physician located on Lexington Avenue above 25th Street, which was also his residence. This listing continues until 1847, when he moved to 39 East 25th Street. He continued his medical practice, according to the *Herald*, "with some degree of success until his health broke down" in 1862.

Meanwhile, the 1846 city directory shows an office for Jones at 16 Wall Street, adjacent to the first Morse telegraph office in New York. Presumably this is where his independent telegraphic reporters' bureau operated. The directories locate Jones's first office as "telegraphic agent and reporter" at 3 Hanover beginning in 1849.[17] By this time the Morse office was at 5 Hanover. Jones's own correspondence, as noted in the previous chapter, indicates his reporter's office in the fall of 1848 was at 28 Merchants' Exchange.

Jones describes his Associated Press activities as follows:

> We received and distributed the news, paid all tolls and other expenses necessary to conduct the business. We employed reporters in all the principal cities in the United States and Canada, and, on receiving it in New York, would make about eight or nine copies of it, on manifold paper—six for the New York press, and the remaining copies for reforwarding to the press in other cities and towns. To this had daily to be added the New York local and commercial news, ship news &c. The remuneration for services was made to depend chiefly upon what we could obtain from papers in other cities, such as Boston &c., for the news of all kinds reforwarded, including the local intelligence. . . . The agent had an office separate from the press, but centrally located, where he employed generally an assistant, besides one or two other parties as clerks and aids with an errand boy or two.[18]

As out-of-town correspondents, Jones lists:

C. C. Fulton, Baltimore	William Lacy, Albany
George W. Brown, Buffalo	George Bennett, Cincinnati
Mr. Davidson, Buffalo	Richard Smith, Cincinnati
Eugene Fuller, New Orleans	Edward Goff Penny, Montreal
Joseph Palmer, Boston	Charles Linds[e]y, Toronto
William [?] Stimson, Boston	J. B. Skinner, Norfolk, Va.[19]

Most of these correspondents were newspaper reporters or editors in their respective communities. The reader will recognize William Lacy as the Albany agent for the New York State Associated Press after March 1846. Lacy, as chapter 2 notes, was apparently on the staff of the *Albany Argus*. Richard Smith later became proprietor of the *Cincinnati Gazette* and was a leading figure in the Western Associated Press after it was incorporated in 1865. Palmer was with the *Boston Atlas*. The author cannot find a William Stimson in Boston city directories, but does find a Henry M. Stimson listed as a reporter for the *Traveller* at this time.[20]

Charles C. Fulton was at this time managing editor of the *Baltimore Sun*.[21] He continued as an AP correspondent in Baltimore long after leaving the *Sun* and purchasing a half-interest in the *Baltimore American* on June 30, 1853.[22] Efforts to identify other U.S. correspondents listed by Jones have failed.

Both of Jones's Canadian reporters rose to some prominence in Canadian journalism. Both were born in 1820 in England and came to Canada within a year of each other. Penny joined the *Montreal Herald*, eventually becoming its editor and one of its proprietors. He later served in the Canadian Senate. Lindsey was on the staff of the *Toronto Examiner* when reporting for the AP. In 1853 he was named editor-in-chief of the *Toronto Leader*, and in 1867 he was appointed registrar of deeds for Toronto, a position he occupied until his death in 1908. Lindsey authored six books and was a charter member of the Royal Society of Canada.[23]

Although he acknowledges "many other excellent men, in other less important localities, with others employed as occasional reporters for conventions, public meetings, &c.,"[24] Jones lists no correspondents in Washington, but explains that

> In reporting Congressional proceedings, the usual plan was
> to employ two reporters in Washington; one for the House of
> Representatives, and another for the Senate. The reports of
> the House would be sent by one line, and those of the Senate
> by the other.[25]

AP's Oliver Gramling states that AP's Washington bureau chief from the founding of the organization was Lawrence A. Gobright.[26] But, although Gobright was AP's Washington bureau chief by the end of the 1850s, historians have been more cautious than Gramling in dating the start of his AP service. Frederick B. Marbut links Gobright to AP no earlier than 1853.[27] Gobright's own writings fail to connect him with AP until 1857.[28] Perhaps, like Jones, Gobright worked as an independent reporter or, like Abbot, he was associated with the telegraph company when AP was young. Gobright is introduced in the next chapter. Someone, however, was filing AP dispatches from Washington from the start of the newsbrokerage if the following comment by a Washington historian can be believed.

> A year after the senate arranged in 1848 for reporting its debates, the New York [City] Associated Press was formed. One of its functions was to supply its members with the regular proceedings of both houses, which left the letter-writers entirely free to choose their subjects.[29]

Jones estimates the average annual cost of the AP operation to all six of its newspaper proprietors at between $25,000 and $30,000. "During long sessions of Congress it exceeded this amount," Jones notes.[30] Telegraph companies submitted weekly bills to which were added the office and other incidental expenses. The aggregate was divided into six parts and assessed by the AP treasurer. Penalties for defaulting on AP charges were severe: "In case any [New York City member] paper had failed to pay, its news would have been stopped," says Jones. Newspapers supplied with AP news in Boston and other communities outside of New York City paid monthly bills, and AP's distant correspondents' salaries and expenses were paid monthly.[31]

The Associated Press office also processed requests by individual AP papers in New York City, according to Jones, for "long and expensive reports of meetings, speeches, conventions, &c." Such reports were automatically made available to the other five AP newspapers. Those choosing to use the dispatch shared in the telegraph tolls; if no other paper wanted the dispatch, the requesting paper shouldered the entire expense. Jones says that the *Herald*, being the only daily of the six to publish on Sundays, "takes all the telegraph news which is received on Saturday afternoon and night, and pays the whole expense of the tolls."[32]

The bulk of the New York City Associated Press news report was transmitted late in the evening, after telegraph lines had cleared the day's lucrative business and personal messages. Lockup for New York City's morning press was, in the 1840s, about 1 or 2 A.M., requiring Jones to gather his dispatches at the telegraph office by midnight or 1 A.M., take them to his AP office, decipher them, scribe them on manifold paper, and deliver copies to his New York members and to the telegraph offices for retransmission to out-of-town clients. (Stereotyping, faster presses, and a larger volume of typesetting caused by Civil War news pushed lockup to 3 or 4 A.M. by 1864 when a bogus presidential proclamation printed in the *Journal of Commerce* and the *New York World* [the *Courier and Enquirer's* successor in AP] called into question AP's method of hand-delivering news dispatches. The incident is described in chapter 7.) A much shorter midday file of a few brief news items provided a telegraphic "Postscript" for AP papers' afternoon editions.

Transmitting the bulk of the report during the late evening hours, when other telegraph business was lean, ensured cheaper rates for the press and saved the telegraph companies from suspending their midday business of private messages for transmission of the lengthy newspaper dispatches. Such a transmission arrangement clearly favored morning papers.

Press transmission rates during Jones's administration ran one-third to one-half below regular charges,[33] and special arrangements with newsbrokers, press consortiums, and individual newspapers granted "bulk rates" for specific types of dispatches. The general public rate for telegrams was reasonably high, as an 1849 register of Morse charges for business on AP's frequently used lines indicates.

> Washington to New York: 50¢ for the first 10 words and 5¢
>   for each additional word; $3.30 for a 66-word message.
> Philadelphia to New York: 25¢ for the first 10 words and 2¢
>   for each additional word; $1.37 for a 66-word message.
> New York to Boston: 50¢ for the first 10 words and 3¢ for
>   each additional word; $2.18 for a 66-word message.
> New York to Albany: 37¢ for the first 15 words and 15¢ for
>   each additional five words; $2.02 for a 66-word message.
> New York to Buffalo: 52¢ for the first 15 words and 20¢ for
>   each additional five words; $2.72 for a 66-word message.[34]

Early newsbrokerages did not have their own operators but relied on the telegraph companies to transmit their dispatches.

To further reduce telegraph rates for press dispatches and to protect dispatches' news, reporters devised codes that loaded sentences and even paragraphs of meaning into single words. Jones developed several such codes in his tenure as a telegraphic reporter. In his pre–Associated Press days he used a system of abbreviations that could reduce a 100-word market report to just twenty transmitted words. Early in 1847 he unleashed a more elaborate code on the telegraph company, freighting some rather grandiose "words" with a paragraph or more of meaning.[35] The "words" Jones transmitted, for example, were: "Caserovingedsable," "Rehoeingedableness," "Rehairiringed," and "Retackmentativeness."[36] Telegraph proprietor F. O. J. Smith eventually decided such a code abused the price-per-word rate structure and taxed his telegraphers' ability to transmit rapidly. So Smith ordered his operators to count the letters in such messages, divide by five, and apply the per-word tariff to the quotient. As noted in the previous chapter, the Magnetic Telegraph Company adopted a similar plan in November 1847, later modifying it to apply only to words not found in an English-language dictionary.

Jones then dug into his dictionary and compiled a list of as many words not exceeding five or six letters as he could find. Arranging them in alphabetical groupings, he assigned to each word a phrase or sentence of meaning. A group of words, for example, beginning with "b" referred to conditions in the flour market: "baal" meant "The transactions in flour are smaller than yesterday" and "baby" meant "Western flour is firm, with moderate demand for home trade and export." A sixty-eight word market report could be transmitted in nine such code words.

Later he devised a similar code for Washington news, using the same words used in his market code. "Babble," for example, in the market report meant "There is good business doing in the flour market," and in the Senate report it meant "From the committee on finance, reported...." Since the market and congressional dispatches were expressly labeled in the news report, no problems should have arisen in doubling up on the code words.[37] Copies of the code were printed and distributed to New York City AP correspondents.[38] Jones observed that

> When we received a scrap of news we endeavored to make the most of it the facts would justify, by writing it out as full as possible. Thus often, from a small page of manuscript of congressional reports in *cipher*, have we written out enough to fill a column of the Sun.[39]

The daily file of Associated Press news varied usually between 700 and 1,000 words in mid-1849, to which must be added the weekly foreign dispatches of about 3,000 words prompted by Cunard arrivals. The report, however, began to expand gradually early in the 1850s. At a conventional transmission speed with Morse equipment of about thirty words per minute,[40] a 1,000-word news report, sent steadily in its published form, would require slightly more than half an hour to transmit. When reduced to code, the report might take only ten minutes of circuit time.

Thirty-word-per-minute speeds were attainable only when operators received by sound. The original Morse receiving instrument was a register that recorded dots and dashes (the Morse code) on long strips of paper. The register slowed reception, and operators soon learned that they could "read" the clicking noises made by the register. By 1850 the Morse companies reluctantly allowed their operators to jot down messages by ear since it was easier, faster, and more economical.[41] Hudson reports that as of 1873 the highest attainable speed on Morse equipment was 2,731 words per hour (or 45.5 words per minute), transmitted for a full hour without break in May 1868 between Boston and Providence. "On short lines sixty or seventy words per minute have been transmitted," Hudson says.[42] Thirty words per minute of manual transmission, one must remember, is not puny compared to the 60-word-per-minute Teletype and 45-word-per-minute Teletypesetter news circuits of the 1960s.

THE EARLY NEWS REPORT

The news report[43] that sprang from this new communication technology was a picayunish thing indeed. Sporting a label headline like "NEWS BY TELEGRAPH" or "Telegraphic Reports" or "THE LATEST NEWS BY MAGNETIC AND PRINTING TELEGRAPH" in the newspaper columns, the AP's domestic news report seldom filled more than one broadsheet column of type until the mid-1850s, when one begins regularly to find two or three columns of daily domestic telegraphic news in the New York papers. (The reader may peruse the New York City AP report by examining the files or films from 1848 to the Civil War of New York's *Herald*, *Tribune*, or *Times*.) The report's three mainstays were legislative summaries from Washington and Albany, grain and produce market quotations, and marine and harbor shipping news. The shipping news was usually broken off and placed in the back of the paper; the legislative and market dispatches, along with a sprinkling of newsy shorts, appeared together, usually on pages two or three of a four-page metropolitan daily. The shorts, which grew with time to become a fourth staple of the news report, included such occurrences as political party meetings and activities, one- and two-sentence notices of laws enacted by distant state legislatures, fires, ship and rail disasters, murders, violent weather, duels, and the activities of prominent persons. As the report grew over the years, each of its major components grew proportionally, the congressional summary, for example, becoming longer by the mid-1850s than the entire news report was in the beginning.

Predominantly focused on New York state and the Eastern seaboard between Boston and Washington, the report daily mustered only a couple of items originating west of the Alleghenies. Except for the daily mainstays noted above and the weekly foreign news dispatch from a Cunarder, one gets no sense of continuity or completeness from scanning a series of these reports. The report seems to have arisen daily from haphazard or chance coverage by Jones's correspondents and telegraphers. And such newsbroker coverage appears in many cases to have resulted from a distant AP correspondent condensing accounts published in local newspapers outside of New York City. Reporters were not dispatched to disaster scenes; news was not anticipated, except for such regular and obvious events as annual presidential messages, congressional proceedings, and Cunard arrivals.

Many events that are today regarded as historic went unreported in AP dispatches. Henry Clay's compromise on the slave question in 1850 was left to Washington letter-writers to sort out, but California's admission to the Union on September 9, 1850, was part of AP's regular congressional summary. The AP reported President Zachary Taylor's death on July 9, 1850, in a series of dispatches, but most of the presidents' proclamations and programs were covered by special correspondents, unless they surfaced in congressional proceedings. Political conventions were largely letter-writers' territory, the AP filing only very brief summaries of votes on platform planks and nominees. The Ripon, Wis., meeting in 1854 that led to formation of the Republican Party reached the New York City press via exchanges and letters. AP had no coordinated campaign coverage. Lincoln's fifty speeches in 1856 for Fremont are not in AP's report, nor are the Lincoln-Douglas debates of 1858. (Many such occurrences, of course, acquired much of their historical significance only in retrospect.)

Brief, sketchy, riddled with holes, the AP and Abbot & Winans reports were a far cry from what we expect today. On the one hand, antebellum definitions of news were less stringent and demanding than they are today. Whereas editors exerted themselves to secure news that presented itself—ship arrivals, presidential messages, and the like—unanticipated events, it was believed, would eventually find their way into public print somewhere. If the telegraph failed to report an event, and if distant colleagues or special correspondents were not able to fire off a letter or telegram, the newspaper exchanges would eventually bring the event to an editor's attention. And if after even several days in transit, the account of the event still struck the editor as important, he put it in his paper. If the event went unnoticed by all of these sources, it simply was not news. This suggests a collective determination of what was news—local editors relying on the individual decisions of many far-flung journalists outside the local community. The more journalists who picked up and retold a news story, the more compelling was the story's newsworthiness to the local editor. Today, in contrast, an editor's or newsbroker's centrally imposed news beats and correspondent assignments give shape to news even before it occurs, ignoring some potentially newsworthy events while concentrating on sources and events that may not always be significant.

This mid-nineteenth-century system of survival of the fittest (or the "newsworthiest") stories shaped the contents of all newspapers, tinted only by the local editor's political leanings, personal proclivities, or natural human reactions to certain subjects. Sailing disasters, which were numerous, had little newsworthiness beyond the site of the accident, unless a distant editor was a sailor or simply liked such stories, the ship was bound to or from the editor's community, or the disaster resulted in an extremely high death toll. Likewise, bizarre deaths—falling into a well, being buried by snow sliding off a roof, or tumbling over the American side of Niagara Falls while attempting to navigate the channel in a skiff filled with vegetables—regularly made the rounds of newspaper columns, as did cholera and smallpox outbreaks and fatal family arguments and the ensuing murder trials.

But beyond the struggle of such violent or human interest stories to survive, on the other hand, was the editorial assumption that certain types of stories—business and financial affairs, legislative proceedings, and the activities of parties and politicians—should automatically survive, routinely, even ritualistically, being reprinted even though to the twentieth-century eye some of these reports are dull, fragmentary, and lacking in newsworthiness. Although usually one or more days old and often lacking perspective and apparent significance, these accounts nonetheless seem to have appealed to editors as being their stock-in-trade, the basic stuff of which a newspaper record should be made. This notion of newsworthiness survives today in less ritualistic form in journalists' preoccupation with government and has its roots in this country in the colonial press and in the post-Revolutionary political and mercantile press movements.

The same processes of survivability for some classes of events and rigid inclusion for other classes shaped the newsbrokers' reports. The telegraphic dispatches were a microcosm of editors' long-standing judgments in clipping the newspaper exchanges, the only differences being that the telegraphed stories arrived a day or so earlier and were selected by a distant agent. The benefits of newsbroking, thus, may seem to have been hardly worth the expense. Why let someone else select your news when your own selection will arrive shortly by mail? And why settle for the same selection being printed by your fellow local newspaper leaders? The "NEWS BY TELEGRAPH" headline, however, must have been a bit of magic for editors whose newspapers could now harness a piece of this "lightning," often at a fraction of what previous transportation expresses had cost the newspaper. These editors took pride in being modern and in bringing even fragments of the day's news to their newsrooms at the speed of light. And Associated Press editors as the 1850s progressed could take increasing pride in their association with a front-running newsbrokerage, an organization representing the leading and established newspaper properties in the East. By the mid-1850s a daily newspaper without telegraphic news was a second-class citizen.

The previous discussion focuses on newsbroking's similarities to the long-standing system of clipping exchanges. Newsbroking, however, did introduce a new dimension to that system. When an event occurred where newsbrokers or their correspondents were located, the news report could bring the first news of a breaking news story and could stay with, and update, such a story day after day. Such a telegraphic bulletin service was occasionally interwoven with clips from exchanges arriving later from the site of the event. A case in point is the murder of a prominent Boston doctor, George Parkman, in November 1849.

In the *New York Herald*[44] the story broke on Monday, November 26, as a one-paragraph AP short, datelined Boston, reporting that Parkman had been missing since November 23 and police were out in force looking for him. On November 28 an AP item said Parkman was still missing, that his brother-in-law offered $3,000 for information leading to his recovery, and that murder was feared. The next day the AP reported that the doctor's friends offered $1,000 for the recovery of his body, they having given up hope that he was still alive. An AP correspondent in Boston had moved these items on the telegraph as a summary of information printed by the Boston newspapers. The *Herald* editors, of course, were also following the story in their Boston exchanges but had determined not to reprint any of those accounts up to this point. AP's short summaries of published accounts of diffuse elements of an event, the significance of which remained unclear, would suffice in New York City for the time being.

On Saturday, December 1, the AP reported still no trace of Parkman; the Charles River had been dragged near the bridges, and the countryside scoured in a thirty-mile radius around Boston. Then on Sunday the grisly Parkman murder story began to unfold for New York readers. The *Herald* on page three used eight paragraphs from the Saturday morning *Boston Times* about how police had discovered some of the remains on Friday night. The *Herald* also summarized the week-long effort to find Parkman, and carried four brief one-paragraph AP dispatches dated at various times on Saturday, a succession of updates on events from Boston. The principal coverage on Sunday was provided by an account copied from the *Boston Times* for Saturday morning. The telegraphic dispatches served primarily to inform the New York editor and reader of the few, relatively insignificant, developments that had occurred since the *Times* account reached New York by train. (It should be noted that the *Herald*, the only AP paper in New York publishing a Sunday edition at this time, had the jump on its colleagues with this story and shows some restraint confining the coverage to page three. But, since the story had broken in Boston, the bulk of gory details could first be reported in Boston's Saturday evening papers. But they did not reach New York in time for the *Herald*'s Sunday edition, and thus all of the New York press had a fair shot at the story Monday morning.)

On Monday morning the Parkman murder was up on page one of the *Herald*, occupying the first two columns and a bit of the third. The coverage consists of accounts taken from Boston's *Transcript*, *Journal*, and *Traveller* editions for Saturday night. An AP dispatch, dated Sunday, is tacked on the end of these clips in the *Herald* reporting that

> Further discoveries have been made tending to fasten the murder of Dr. Parkman upon Professor Webster. In his own laboratory has been found a chest in the bottom of which, covered with straw, were found further portions of the body.
>
> All the body has now been found, save the head, feet and arms. The accused is quiet this morning. The inquest will commence on Wednesday. The police assert that they have further information against the accused which will not be made public until the Coroner's jury sits. A number of chemists and physicians are now engaged in analyzing the ashes in the grate of the room and placing the recovered fragments of the body in their true position. The military were out last night.

Again the telegraphic dispatch served to update the basic coverage provided by Boston newspapers delivered overnight by train. This arrangement would hold for the *Herald*'s front page for the next four days—a composite story incorporating clips from the Boston press, leaning toward the evening papers and filling from one to three columns of type, followed by a brief telegraphic update at the end. Early telegraphic news-gathering appears, in the Parkman instance and others the author has examined, to have acknowledged the continuing economy, readability, and detail of exchanges. Telegraphic dispatches served primarily to update the clips where necessary and otherwise to reassure the distant editor and reader that nothing new had happened since the local papers were printed and shipped.

A national presidential election—in which events move too swiftly for an editor to wait on distant newspaper exchanges for his first-day coverage—gave the telegraph a head start. The election on November 7, 1848, the first conducted on the same day throughout the nation, was the first presidential race to be covered on any kind of national scope by the telegraph. Alexander Jones complains that during this election, "we remained up for three nights consecutively" and the telegraphic tolls to the New York morning press exceeded $1,000.[45] The election was made more complicated by a three-way race—Zachary Taylor for the Whigs, Lewis Cass for the regular Democrats, and Martin Van Buren for the Free-Soilers. In addition there was a Barnburner-Hunker split in the New York State Democratic Party.

Jones, who may still have been an independent telegraphic reporter in late 1848, distributed printed instructions to "telegraph correspondents, reporters and operators," indicating how "the New York Press and their associates in other cities" wanted their 1848 election returns filed. It said,

> 1. You will of course, send returns by *Counties*, so far as is practicable.... When we hear that "Mobile," "Montgomery," "Albany," or "Philadelphia" has given so much majority, we shall understand that it is the *County* so entitled, the term county being superfluous....
>
> 2. You need not attempt to compare the vote of any whole County with that cast at any former election: We have the means of making such comparisons here.... In all cases, we shall understand "gain" to mean that the vote is by so much more favorable to Taylor or Cass, than it was to Clay or Polk in 1844.

3. Send us County *majorities* only at first; they are less liable to become confused or intermingled than full votes for each candidate. And, when you have returns to send from several Counties send all the majorities for Cass first; then those for Taylor, distinguishing them carefully. Afterwards, as soon as you have leisure, you may send the full vote for each candidate.

4. Send the Presidential results first in all cases; first, the actual returns, then reports in circulation; lastly, the probabilities or rumors as to the vote of the State. You may then say who is chosen to Congress from any District, with his politics; then who the Legislative has given, &c. . . . It will generally do to say, "—— for Governor runs —— better than —— for President in the above counties."

5. Write the majorities in words uniformly; thus: "Coswell, six-hundred and fifty-three for Cass;" "Guilford fourteen hundred and seventy-eight for Taylor," &c. &c.

6. Should you while Telegraphing county or other partial returns, receive information which settles the vote of your state, in the judgment of intelligent men, beyond a reasonable doubt, you may break off everything to say, "Returns from —— Counties, clearly indicate that —— (name the State), has gone for —— by —— majority." And this message must take precedence over all others at every station in the route through to this City.[46]

Turning again to the *Herald* of November 8, 1848, for an example of this first widespread telegraphic election coverage, one finds most of the election returns on page two. There is a column-long, ward-by-ward table of New York City returns for president and some congressional seats, a half-column, double-leaded list of candidates elected in New York City, and a two-column general wrap-up story headlined "Incidents of the Election. The Effect of the Result in the City." There is no evidence, when one compares the *Herald* with other AP papers, that any of this local coverage came from the AP or an independent newsbrokerage.

Slightly more than two columns of returns, headed "Telegraphic Returns from the Several States," was a newsbroker's, possibly Jones's, contribution to the night's proceedings in the *Herald*. Arranged under state headings, the dispatches were presented in the order in which they were transmitted to New York City by telegraph. The states represented there and the number of dispatches received from them between 7 P.M. and 1:30 A.M. were: New York, 13; Pennsylvania, 9; Massachusetts, 5; Ohio, Michigan, Virginia,

Delaware, and Maryland, 4; Connecticut, 3; Vermont and South Carolina, 2; and Indiana, Illinois, New Jersey, Missouri, Maine, and New Hampshire, 1. These dispatches measure, apparently, the extent of the telegraph and correspondent systems nationally in early November 1848. The sampling of the New York state dispatches offered below looks sketchy and inconsistent to the twentieth-century eye, but they must have been fresh and valuable to readers used to getting their election returns by mail.

THIRD DESPATCH   Albany, Nov. 7-7-1/2 P.M.
   The vote for Taylor in Albany 3,563; for Cass 1,807; for Van Buren, 1,402. Taylor's majority over all, 354. Majority for Cass over Van Buren, 405.

FOURTH DESPATCH   Buffalo, Nov. 7-8 P.M.
   The vote in the city of Buffalo is for Taylor 2,741; for Cass, 1,412; for Van Buren, 820.
   Lockport has given Taylor a majority of 179.

FIFTH DESPATCH   Poughkeepsie, Nov. 7-10-1/2 P.M.
   Returns from six towns in Dutchess county show a majority of 1,256 for Taylor.
   Hudson city gives Taylor 467, Cass 423, and Van Buren 115.

NINTH DESPATCH   Syracuse, Nov. 7-Midnight
   Syracuse gives Taylor 1,199, Van Buren 721, and Cass 449. Gott, whig, for Congress, has a plurality of about 300 in the city.
   The reports from Onondaga county are all favorable to Taylor, where majority will probably be from 1,000 to 1,200 for the county.

ELEVENTH DESPATCH   Carmel, Nov. 7-Midnight
   Returns are received from all the towns in Putnam county except Phillips. These give Taylor 633, Cass 600, and Van Buren 309. For Congress, Green, democrat, has 636; Halloway, whig, 602; and Baily, free soiler, 306. A whig member of Assembly is elected.

THIRTEENTH DESPATCH   Schenectady, Nov. 8-1 P.M.
   This county will give about 500 whig majority. The vote in the city was, for Taylor 713; Cass, 413; and Van Buren, 164.

Jones was disappointed by the night's journalistic efforts. Writing Ezra Cornell afterwards, asking for the election night charges on the Albany-Buffalo line, Jones took the occasion to complain that

Only a portion of [the returns] ever came exclusively to me as the operators have on the Buffalo line claimed the

priviledge [*sic*] (as they came free tolls) to give them broad
cast to all papers and nearly all persons. . . .
  Please send along accounts as soon as practicable; you
have my sincere thanks for your attention to the business,
although I did not reap the full benefit of your services.[47]

Zachary Taylor, of course, won the election, beating Cass by
140,000 votes; Van Buren ran far behind. Less than two years later,
however, Taylor lay dying, a victim of cholera morbus. It was an
event for which AP's system of periodic brief update dispatches was
perfectly suited. AP's coverage, offered below as it appeared in the
New York Tribune for Wednesday, July 10, 1850, provided only new
information in each dispatch and assumed that all dispatches would
be printed.

FIRST DISPATCH   Washington, Tuesday, July 9–1 P.M.
  The President passed a very bad night, and the physicians
report him no better this morning. His position is very
critical.

SECOND DISPATCH   Washington, Tuesday, July 9–P.M.
  No change for the better in the President's condition,
though fever has abated.

THIRD DISPATCH   Washington, Tuesday Afternoon, July 9
  A message has just been received from the President's
Home, stating that he is no better and that his friends despair
of his recovery. The Senate and House adjourned in
consequence.

FOURTH DISPATCH   Washington, Tuesday Evening, July 9
  The report received this moment from the White House is
that the President is dying. Congestion has commenced, and
the sufferer is beyond the power of human skill. The White
House is thronged with anxious inquirers, and sorrow is
visible upon every countenance.

FIFTH DISPATCH   Washington, Tuesday, July 9–10 P.M.
  The physicians attending the President have announced
that he is sinking fast, and it is impossible for him to recover.
A congestion of the stomach, brain and lungs have [*sic*] set
in.

SIXTH DISPATCH   Washington, Tuesday, July 9–10½ P.M.
  The President is breathing his last, surrounded by his
family, Cabinet, Vice-President, Mayor, and Marshal of the
District, together with the medical attendants. He is not
expected to live 15 minutes.

SEVENTH DISPATCH   Washington, Tuesday, July 9
  The President died to-night at 35 minutes past 10 o'clock.
His death was calm and peaceful. The Vice-President,

Cabinet, Mayor, Marshal of the District, the attending
physicians, and his family surrounded the bed. His last words
were, "I am prepared. I have endeavored to do my duty."

During the Jones administration, AP's domestic news report
roughly doubled in size when compared with mid-1848 news reports. Although a few more short items of general news contributed
to the expansion, the bulk of the increase came from more detailed
congressional reports and expanded market reports. By June of
1850, for example, the AP report took nearly two columns of type in
the *New York Herald*. It was a marked increase, but with only two of
twenty-four columns of type devoted to telegraphic news, the *Herald* still relied primarily on local staff, special correspondents,
letter-writers, and newspaper exchanges for most of its news.

THE HALIFAX EXPRESSES

Even though the domestic telegraph report gradually and routinely
expanded under Jones's direction, foreign news, which remained
the primary object of the New York City papers' newsbrokerage,
continued to cause conflict and anxiety. After the first telegraph
line linking New York City and Boston was opened in June 1846, a
system of news-gathering emerged that put the European news carried by the Cunard steamers in the hands of New York City and Boston newspapers with reasonable dispatch. John Turel Smith, lessee
of the Boston Merchants' Exchange, would meet the Cunarder at its
Boston dock, collect the European papers, cull and summarize their
news, deliver this summary to the Boston press, and telegraph the
summary to the New York City press. Sometime during 1847 Daniel
H. Craig surprised Smith and his newspaper patrons of both cities
one morning by having delivered a summary of foreign news to an
obscure Boston newspaper before the Cunarder had docked in Boston. Craig had unexpectedly put on a display of his homing pigeons'
prowess and caught the press napping.[48] The reader will recall from
chapter 3 that again during 1848 the New York City AP's use of the
Buena Vista to meet Cunard steamers proved costly and was too often beaten by Craig's birds. The *Buena Vista* yielded to the less
rangy, but more expensive, *News-Boy* in July of 1848, which, in
turn, gave way to two small boats according to provisions of the
Harbor News Association, signed on January 11, 1849. At first
glance this may appear to have been an AP retreat in the foreign
news field abetted by Craig's aggressiveness, but the AP editors had
a long-range strategy for collecting foreign news that eventually

would bypass chartered ships and homing pigeons with a telegraph line running all the way to Halifax.

The telegraph by January 1849 had pushed past the Canadian border into New Brunswick and was inching toward Saint John, a port on the Bay of Fundy, which separates southern Nova Scotia and mainland New Brunswick. The line would ultimately extend around the bay to Halifax. So unlikely a telegraphic route as one linking the U.S. metropolitan centers of Boston, New York, and Washington, D.C., and the remote and commercially middling Maritime Provinces would seem to have been a lucky break for New York's editors. But as telegraph historian James D. Reid notes, the project bore the heavy imprint of New York City journalism.

> The telegraph lines through the eastern provinces of the Dominion of Canada owe their origin largely to the influence of the New York Associated Press.... [T]he Associated Press agent offered to guarantee the payment of a liberal sum to any company who would construct lines of telegraph between Calais [Maine] and Halifax, which they could use for their business.... For this guarantee the press stipulated for the exclusive use of the wire, thus erected, on the arrival of a steamer from Europe long enough to transmit a dispatch of 3,000 words. Without this guarantee the lines in that region would probably have long remained unbuilt.[49]

It was fortunate for the New York City AP editors that many of the Maritime residents, displaced colonial Tories who had fled to Canada during the American Revolution but retained strong personal and business ties to the States, preferred a telegraph link with the United States to one with their Canadian neighbors to the west. In fact, a proposal to link Saint John with Quebec had failed to secure local investment capital, but AP's proposal for a line to Calais easily drew financial backing in Saint John.[50]

AP's long, flimsy telegraphic thread to Saint John, and eventually to Halifax, enlisted or created the services of five separate telegraph companies: New York–Boston, F. O. J. Smith's New York and Boston Magnetic Telegraph Company, operating since June 27, 1846; Boston-Portland, a second Smith company, operating by the end of 1848; Portland-Calais, the Maine Telegraph Company, operating by early January of 1849; Calais-Sackville, New Brunswick, the New Brunswick Telegraph Company, operating by early October of 1849; and Sackville-Halifax, Nova Scotia Telegraph Company, a provincial line completed on November 9, 1849.

While this shaky technical and corporate edifice eventually did deliver the news, the conflict[51] that developed over its policies and operation altered the course of AP by singling out Daniel H. Craig as having the mettle to become the New York City AP's second general agent of record. The conflict also was a chapter in the continuing saga of whether journalistic or telegraphic interests would control foreign news movement.

Lawson R. Darrow, superintendent of the New Brunswick line, recently completed between Calais and Saint John, negotiated a news-movement contract with the New York City Associated Press on behalf of the four other telegraph companies that would participate in transmitting the foreign news dispatches. The agreement, signed on February 9, 1849, by Darrow for the telegraph companies and Henry J. Raymond and Frederic Hudson for the city's AP, contained the following basic points:

1. The foreign news dispatch of the Associated Press and other papers served by AP will have priority over other dispatches all the way to Boston at a rate of $200 for the first 3,000 words and pro rata for anything over 3,000 words. (Presumably the nine-month-old AP-Smith agreement for moving news dispatches from Boston to New York City was still in force.)

2. The Associated Press will establish "a good and sufficient" express relay between Halifax and Saint John and will pay the amount even if the express is operated with "carelessness, neglect, omission, want of energy, or unnecessary delay."

3. One copy of the dispatch will be supplied to the Associated Press at Boston from which other copies may be made for distribution to Boston papers and for retransmission south and west.

4. Copies of the dispatch may be taken by the telegraph companies north of Portland "for their own benefit," but if these are handed over to newspapers in those communities, some reasonable assessment will be paid by the papers to the Associated Press.

5. The New York City papers will be required to post the dispatch in public as soon as practicable, and every effort will be made to guard against the dispatch being used for private speculation in advance of publication.

6. The agreement will be in effect one year, and in the meantime when the line is extended to the Nova Scotia boundary, the express will operate from Halifax to that

terminus and the expense to the Associated Press will be
increased on a pro rata basis according to the additional line
distance embraced. Once the line reaches Halifax, the express
will be eliminated and additional pro rata charges will be
assessed to the Associated Press.

7. If the lines are broken and cannot be speedily repaired
when the foreign dispatch is available, the telegraph
companies will operate an express at their own expense to
bridge the gap in the circuit.[52]

F. O. J. Smith, after examining the contract, wrote Raymond on
February 15, 1849, asking that the foreign dispatches be made available to all Boston and Portland newspapers interested in having
them. The Boston press, he said, would pay its share of the expense.
Smith also refused to operate an express at times of line failure as
specified in no. 7 on his portion of the telegraph network. Raymond
grudgingly accepted Smith's exceptions four days later.[53]

(It bears noting here that, as this narrative subsequently indicates, Darrow and the telegraph companies he represented sought
by this contract not so much to favor the AP as to eliminate market
speculation by transmitting the dispatch to the respectable New
York City press on a priority basis and also to avoid the chaos of
competition for the line, a notion F. O. J. Smith had expressed to the
AP's executive committee back in May 1848.)

From the start the Morse telegraph companies, as well as most
other telegraph firms, had operated on a first-come-first-served basis, and not even this contract could circumvent that rule. Information reaching Boston's and New York City's AP papers indicated that
Craig was in Halifax arranging for a horse and steamer express to
get his foreign news summary to the Saint John telegraph office
ahead of the AP's. AP's foreign news agent, John Turel Smith, thus
obliged to journey northeast and follow Craig's example, soon discovered, as an unnamed source later reported, that

the Commodore, the fastest and best steamer in the bay had
already been chartered by his opponent, and had left for
Annapolis or Digby on the Peninsula side. Following in the
next best boat he could procure, he was just too late in
reaching Annapolis to hire anything except some second-rate
horses for his express....[54]

Craig had made promises of foreign news for his speculator-clients
and probably a few smaller newspapers, but it is likely that he also

entertained the notion that by beating Smith and the AP he could replace Smith as AP's foreign news agent.

Smith and Craig, therefore, awaited the arrival of the first Cunarder, the *Europa*, in Halifax after the line was completed to Saint John. That arrival occurred on February 21. With "desperate energy . . . relays of galloping horses" shattered the tranquility of the Nova Scotia countryside, separate strings of express horses engaged by Smith and Craig pounding through post-villages along the 146-mile route from Halifax to Digby Gut on the Bay of Fundy, John W. Regan reports. Riders changed at Kentville, and fresh horses were spotted every twelve miles along the route. As the riders passed Annapolis Royal, five miles from the express steamers' berths at Digby Gut, a cannon was fired, signaling the steamers to get up steam and make ready to cast off. [55] The *Europa*'s news was thus conveyed by two expresses over this untried route. Never had so many given so much for what turned out to be so routine a collection of European dispatches.

Craig won the first outing handily and was immediately offered, and accepted, the post of AP's Halifax agent. Smith stayed on for one more try, the arrival of the *America*, but was once again beaten by Craig, and retired for the moment to Boston. (The two would face off again in a few months.) The *New York Tribune* summarized Craig's express of the *America*'s news at the top of its foreign news file as follows:

> St. John, N.B., Thursday, March 8
> The steamer *America*, Capt. Shannon, from Liverpool, Feb. 24, arrived at Halifax at 2¾ this morning. Our express started immediately and arrived at Digby at 11:40 AM in 8 hours and 50 minutes. Arrived across the Bay of Fundy in steamer *Conqueror* in 6½ hours being detained nearly two hours in the Bay by immense fields of ice. [56]

The *Halifax British Colonist*'s contemporary news account of the expresses gives a graphic description of the event.

> On Thursday morning (8th March) immediately after the arrival of the steamer from England, two expresses (one on behalf of the Associated Press of Philadelphia, New York, and Boston [Craig's], and the other got up in opposition by some mercantile gentlemen in the United States [Smith's]) left this city travelling at a rate of speed that is, we believe, unprecedented in this country. The parties engaged here to

convey the rival expresses overland to Digby, were Mr. Hyde [for Craig] and Mr. Barnaby [for Smith]. Hyde's express arrived at Digby Neck at 28 minutes past 12 o'clock accomplishing the distance of 146 miles in 8½ hours—having met with several accidents and interruptions. At Windsor a delay of 20 minutes occurred, and after starting Mr. Hamilton, the courier from that place, when crossing the bridge broke his stirrup, and was thrown from his horse with such force, that he lay insensible for some time; he, however, remounted, and, though lamed, with one stirrup performed his route with astonishing despatch. A distance of 18 miles from Kentville, was performed by Mr. Thad Harris in 53 minutes. The steamer "Conqueror", chartered to convey Hyde's express to St. John, was waiting in readiness when the express arrived. Barnaby's express arrived 2½ minutes before Hyde's, but the steamer "Commodore," engaged by his party, had not made her appearance at the latest accounts.[57]

On through the spring, summer, and early fall of 1849 Craig ran the AP express each time a Cunarder arrived in Halifax, meeting a total of twenty-eight steamers, but after the first two, Craig had the field to himself. Meanwhile, telegraph construction continued around the upper end of the Bay of Fundy, north of Saint John and Halifax. Although the first telegraph poles appeared in Halifax on June 8, the next link to be completed was from Saint John to Sackville, on the Nova Scotia border, opening on October 3, 1849, and causing Craig to reroute his expresses northward to Sackville and to abandon the Bay steamer. The *Caledonia*'s news, arriving at Halifax on October 10, was the first test of the new route, and although the dispatch apparently made it down the long strand of telegraph circuitry in fine shape, a fire in the Morse New York office kept the dispatch from the New York City papers. Craig, however, successfully telegraphed the news from four other Cunard arrivals in October and early November from Sackville.

Craig's expresses, first to Saint John and then to Sackville, had supplied AP's foreign news needs during most of 1849. Completion of the line to Halifax on November 9, 1849, gave F. O. J. Smith new hope of controlling Cunard news flow. Without the need of an express to reach some distant telegraph terminus, control of the press's foreign news dispatches revolved around the question of who would be recognized by the telegraph company as the New York City AP's Halifax agent and who could traverse the short distance between the waterfront and the Halifax telegraph office. With the line opened all the way from Halifax to New York City, John T. Smith reappeared in Halifax and began scurrying around representing himself to telegraph authorities as the true AP agent and arranging to collect AP's bundle of papers from the steamer. Craig watched, believing he was still AP's agent, but realizing that retaining his AP position might require beating Smith again.

F. O. J. Smith's desire to interpose himself through John T. Smith on the collection and transmission of foreign news may have sprung not only from the potential power and profit of such control but also from a fear of losing the agreement he had with the New York City papers to transmit their weekly foreign news dispatches over his Portland–Boston–New York City telegraph lines. Especially along the Boston–New York route, competing telegraph lines had begun to appear. In fact, by the autumn of 1849, when the Nova Scotia line was closing ranks, two competing lines were operating between Boston and New York. A House line, the Boston and New York Printing Telegraph Company (commonly called the Commercial line), was up, but because it was so hastily and cheaply built, it proved no immediate threat to Smith. But a Bain line, the New York and New England Telegraph Company (commonly called the Merchants' line), had been carefully constructed by Henry O'Rielly and threatened to take the press business away from Smith.

F. O. J. Smith's hope was to get John T. Smith reinstated as AP's agent, not for AP's benefit, but so that the latter's dispatches would have preference in the Nova Scotia office, arrive in Portland and Boston ahead of all competitors' dispatches, and thus be carried exclusively on Smith's lines to both the Boston and New York City press, ensuring Smith the weekly profit and general goodwill, vis-à-vis his House and Bain competitors.

Arrival of the *America* on November 15 set the stage for the new Craig–John T. Smith confrontation. The rivals had procured horses for the short dash from the dock to the telegraph office; townspeople gathered as much to watch the Yankees race each other through the streets as to see the *America* dock. As the steamer eased toward the dock, the purser stepped up on the paddle-box and threw a bundle of European papers directly into Smith's outstretched arms. Craig had been done in by a paid-off purser, and Smith, for the moment at least, was again AP's Halifax agent.

Since both men had presented themselves to the Halifax telegraph agent as the bona fide AP correspondent and the telegraph agent applied the first-come-first-served rule, Craig had to devise a scheme to beat Smith to the telegraph office if he hoped to reclaim the AP agency. To that end, Craig let it be known publicly that he was planning to meet the next Cunarder in two news boats stationed at different points below Halifax and attempt to express the bundle of papers by horse from the shoreline to the telegraph office. Privately, Craig instructed the AP Liverpool agent to send via special messenger aboard the next Cunarder two identical bundles of European papers.

Sometime before the end of the year[58] Craig's plan matured. As a Cunarder approached Halifax, the AP messenger tossed the newspaper bundles to the two Craig news boats as expected. At the same time, however, another Craig operative, stationed at the water's edge and armed with a bundle of old European papers, rolled and wrapped so that no dates showed but prominently displaying the nameplate of *Willmer & Smith's European Times*, dropped this bogus bundle in the water and gave it a good soaking. He then raced with it to the telegraph office, burst in breathless, threw the dripping bundle onto the counter, and announced that it was Craig's European news bundle.

A few minutes later John T. Smith arrived at the office, armed with his bundle, procured as before from a helpful purser. But when told that Craig's bundle had beaten him to the office—and the wet evidence still lay wrapped on the counter awaiting Craig's arrival—Smith returned to the Cunarder and booked passage for Boston, a defeated man. The victorious Craig sauntered into the telegraph office later with one of the true bundles of the latest European news under his arm and casually assembled and filed his Associated Press dispatch.[59]

John T. Smith was a beaten man. But F. O. J. Smith was not, and his Halifax news agency was next taken over by E. S. Dyer.[60] The timing of dispatches to favor either morning or evening papers next became the critical confrontation. It cannot be determined whether Craig timed the dispatches to favor New York's morning press or Smith timed the relay of Craig's dispatches to favor the morning or evening papers, but the dispatches' timing split the Boston Associated Press into factions. On November 27, 1849, Boston's morning papers—the *Advertiser, Courier, Post, Atlas, Times,* and *Bee*—regrouped as the new Boston Associated Press, aligned with the New York City AP. Boston's evening papers—the *Transcript, Journal,* and *Traveller*—broke away, aligning themselves with Smith's newsbrokerage.[61]

The *Boston Journal* for January 12, 1850, expressed the grievances of Boston's evening press.

> Not a line of the [foreign] copy could be procured from the
> Boston [telegraph], without the consent of the New York
> Association being first obtained. Neither can the evening
> papers of this city obtain the news, except upon conditions
> which make it worthless to them.... It is true that on the
> arrival of the news by the last steamer, a meager statement
> of the market—only a few words—was sent on by the agent—
> and published at one o'clock, though the steamer arrived in
> Halifax at six in the morning, and whole despatch might
> easily have been published at the same time; but it was
> withheld from the public until the next morning.[62]

The splintering of the Boston press gave Smith at least part of the
press patronage, with Dyer filing a report for the evening papers in
Boston, and perhaps elsewhere, while Craig continued to file for the
morning paper in Boston, New York City, and elsewhere, using the
Bain lines between Portland and New York City. But Smith could
still see his way to controlling the movement of news along the
North Atlantic seaboard if he could get the Associated Press to dis-
claim Craig as its Halifax agent. Unwittingly Craig almost gave
Smith the opening he needed to oust Craig.

In the weeks following the opening of the telegraph to Halifax,
while he plotted to defeat John T. Smith with that soaking dummy
bundle of European papers, Craig had sent John T. Smith an impetu-
ous letter, apparently intended as psychological warfare. In it Craig
threatened to return to flying pigeons, announcing he was contemplating

> a personal and private enterprise, in the results of which the
> press and the public will fully and fairly participate if they
> choose to pay me a quid pro quo; if not, I shall assume it as a
> right to sell my news as I would a string of onions, i.e., to the
> highest bidder.[63]

Meanwhile, the competition at Halifax had heated to the point
that telegraph wires were being cut, telegraph officers assumed, by
the party unable to get the telegraph line for his dispatch first. Darrow of the New Brunswick Telegraph Company in a letter on December 20, 1849, to F. O. J. Smith spelled out the problem.

> The Halifax papers stated to the world that the
> government had adopted the principle, "first come, first

served," in all cases. Advantage of this is taken by parties.
Great opposition is raised. If one party gets in first, the other
is sure to cut the wires and vice versa; and this is continually
being done.... Are we to go on in this manner...or are we
to adopt the strict rule that the whole public press, that will
pay their portion of the expense, shall first be served at all
hazards?[64]

Whereas Darrow seemed eager to be done with the competing
news agents at Halifax, and may even be trying here to convince
Smith to recall Dyer, Smith put this letter and Craig's to John T.
Smith together, to imply that Craig was the wire-cutter and to dis-
credit Craig because of his old homing pigeon days of trafficking
with speculators.

Associated Press editors on December 29, 1849, attempting to
hang onto their foreign news pipeline, sent a new proposal to the
telegraph companies between Halifax and New York City. Prominent in the proposal was a 12.5 percent increase in the rate AP was
willing to pay for receipt of its foreign news dispatches, bringing the
base rate to $225 for a 3,000-word dispatch. The proposal also al-
lowed evening papers to publish dispatches until 3 P.M., called for
the time that a dispatch actually arrived at the Halifax telegraph office to be transmitted along with the news, and dropped the earlier
requirement that the telegraph companies run expresses to circumvent breaks in their lines.[65] AP thus sweetened the pot on its own
behalf and appears to have given evening papers an equal break on
the dispatches.

On December 31, 1849, however, F. O. J. Smith served notice on
the New York City Associated Press decrying "Craig's reckless system of business," and stating, "Until [Craig] totally abandons the
use of carrier pigeons, I shall refuse transmitting any despatches
from him over either the Portland, or the Boston and New York line
of telegraph."[66]

AP immediately contacted Henry O'Rielly about extending his
Bain line (already in place between New York and Boston) from Boston to Portland so that Craig and the AP could bypass Smith's telegraph circuits altogether. On January 23, 1850, O'Rielly agreed to
proceed, but warned that it would take until spring or early summer
to get a line through to Portland.[67] The next day found Samuel F. B.
Morse writing to Smith.

I see you are at war with the Associated Press. I am sorry
that the war has occurred just at this time, but know not that

155

> it could have been avoided. It is unfortunately a contest
> where defeat is disastrous and victory itself a defeat.[68]

The Nova Scotia Telegraph Company commissioners wrote Smith on January 28, 1850, acquitting Craig of the charges Smith had leveled against him.

> No evidence is before us that Mr. Craig has yet resorted to
> any such unfair expedient, and we cannot overlook the fact,
> that he is now the agent of a press, eminent alike for its
> talent and influence on this continent. It would be
> unreasonable in us to infer, that a gentleman, clothed with
> such large responsibilities, and holding so important an office,
> would be permitted by his employers to resort to the
> practices to which you allude.[69]

Even in the absence of substantial support, Smith pressed his case in a forty-six-page pamphlet, dated February 22, 1850, addressed to the commissioners of the Nova Scotia line, in which Smith elaborately seeks to advance and document Dyer's claim as press representative while discrediting Craig with insults and innuendos.[70]

Craig responded with a twenty-nine-page "review" of Smith's pamphlet, published March 16, 1850. Seemingly sure of his position, Craig smugly told the commissioners, "I cannot doubt but that you will spurn the senseless remarks" of Smith. No person, "save a knave or a fool, would presume to urge objections against the arrangements between the Telegraph and the Press." To add bite to his argument, Craig reprinted his letter to John T. Smith, containing his "string of onions" line. The reprinted letter said indirectly what Craig dared not say directly to the commissioners: "neither F. O. J. Smith, any portion of the public press, yourself or friends, nor the devil himself, shall ever drive me from any position that I may see fit to assume." He observed that only one first foreign news dispatch could be first, and he and his AP patrons were the logical ones to transmit it southward and dispense it among the press.[71]

Four days after publication of Craig's pamphlet, Smith retaliated by calling on other companies in the Morse system to join in his fight against Craig and the Nova Scotia company. A notice from Smith asked the Magnetic Telegraph Company (operating between New York City and Washington, D.C.) to "send no more messages, until further orders, to go beyond St. John, New Brunswick, unless they are to be mailed at Portland."[72] Smith would punish the Nova Scotia company for its alliance with Craig by denying it telegraphic business from the south. Magnetic's directors, meeting next on April 12, 1850, urged Smith to rescind his blockade of both north- and south-bound telegraph messages at Portland, asserting that the policy is "calculated to bring odium on the Morse Lines, forfeit the public confidence in them, and endanger the privileges they derive from Morse's Patents."[73] Owing to unavoidable delays, Magnetic's official response was not communicated to Smith until April 28,[74] but in the meantime actual conflict continued.

O'Rielly pushed forward with his Bain line between Boston and Portland on behalf of the AP, which by late March was transporting its steamer dispatches by a locomotive express between those communities to circumvent Smith's blockade.[75] And although his Magnetic Telegraph Company's official response took a month to reach Smith, Amos Kendall unofficially and angrily wrote Smith on April 1, demanding,

> What is your position? A message comes to your line after having passed over three legitimate Morse lines and you assume a right to stop it—to send it no further. For what reason? . . . Simply because the Agent of the Associated Press at Halifax is in your opinion a bad man, not to be trusted by the Public; that he has avowed his purpose to employ carrier pigeons and that he has threatened under certain circumstances to cut down the Lines. No overt act has been traced to him; it is not shown that he has employed carrier pigeons or cut the wires.
>
> You assume a high prerogative. . . . [You] attempt to dictate to the customers of the telegraph whom they shall not employ as their Agents and in what manner their business shall not be done.
>
> You have against you the authorities of Nova Scotia, the legislature of Maine, all the Morse lines east of Portland and I may add south and west of New York, a powerful portion of the public press and growing public opinion.
>
> I feel it an imperative duty to implore you to abandon it. As it is not your property and interests alone that are hazarded, I respectfully insist that you have no just right to persist.[76]

Smith, no doubt, ignored Kendall's irate letter, but soon after a new policy on the Nova Scotia line could not be ignored. The commissioners ordered the suspension of all other transmissions south from Halifax until Craig's foreign news dispatch to the AP had reached Boston via the AP locomotive express from Portland. The

Nova Scotia people had not only respected Craig's credentials as AP agent, they had undertaken to preserve the integrity of the AP foreign dispatches from coded private messages that might announce changes in European markets to speculators in advance of AP's press reports.

The fatal blow to Smith's scheme, however, finally came on June 22, 1850, when O'Rielly's Bain line between Boston and Portland was completed,[77] ending AP's expensive locomotive express by making it possible for the press dispatches to bypass Smith's circuits totally between New York City and Portland. New York City's morning press had survived its first serious confrontation with the telegraph by throwing much money at the problem and by setting telegraph's weak and immature components against each other. There would be other confrontations between press and telegraph over control of news movement, and as time passed such clashes menaced the press increasingly as telegraphy, growing increasingly monopolistic, was less susceptible to a divide-and-conquer strategy.

At stake in the Smith-AP confrontation was control over vital foreign news dispatches from Europe. European revolutions may come and go, but the critical market and business reports from Europe were steadily prized in the American commercial community. Craig and Smith accused each other of scheming to feed market information by code to speculators in advance of the press's published dispatches. Charges of such skulduggery made good pamphlet copy for each man's attempt to convince journalism, telegraphy, and the public of the other's mean and sinister nature.

The outcome of this war of words and wires hung in the balance for several months because such charges would automatically be taken seriously by many people, speculators having too many times reaped a bountiful harvest on the basis of privately obtained advance information about European markets. The Nova Scotia authorities were willing to make the AP dispatch the first and principal source of news from Europe if the recipient newspapers would continue their habit of posting the essentials of the European market as soon as the dispatch reached their offices. To this extent, the press assisted in defeating speculators' schemes.

But had Craig reformed? His history of trafficking with speculators via pigeons had been recently resurrected by his "string of onions" comments, even though he had proved extremely resourceful and competent in the service of the Associated Press since February 21, 1849. To the press, on the other hand, control of its foreign news dispatches to any extent by the telegraph, but by Morse interests in particular, was an increasingly distasteful prospect. Telegraph operators and proprietors in a few short years had proved themselves ineffective as journalistic correspondents and unable to protect the press's dispatches from unauthorized editors and speculators. And the telegraph management had balked at transmitting press dispatches in codes that would have shielded the dispatches' contents from prying eyes. AP was more comfortable associating with Craig, whose energy, journalistic ability, and resourcefulness discounted a shady past, than with agents of telegraph proprietors, who, despite their vital role in transmitting news dispatches, had exhibited neither journalistic aptitude nor sensitivity to journalism's mission.

O'Rielly, who, as we shall see, continued in the next few years to preoccupy himself with the fair use of telegraphic facilities in the public interest, came to AP's rescue, not as an ally of the New York press but as a businessman seizing upon an opportunity and as a fair-minded man endeavoring to serve the widest public need. Although his Bain line between New York and Portland tipped the scale for Craig and the AP, O'Rielly did not construct a line paralleling Smith's only because Smith was a competitor. O'Rielly, one of the original Morse contractors, had for more than a year viewed Smith and the entire Morse management as inept, conservative, and monopolistic. In O'Rielly's view the public would be better served by a foreign dispatch controlled by the editors than by Morse telegraphic interests.

F. O. J. Smith, although the singular source of AP's headaches in this situation, was clearly the best enemy the editors could have had. His repugnant reputation preceding him, Smith, simply by donning his battle dress, would force his supposed allies into the opposing camp. We glimpsed Smith, the bellicose schemer, at the birth of Morse's telegraph, and we have heard Morse's son report that Smith did "much in later years to injure Morse and to besmirch his fame and good name."[78] Such was the net effect of this blockade in 1850, but one might inquire whether Smith, the Morse interests notwithstanding, could reasonably have benefited from this war with AP, which broadened into war also with the Morse interests to the south, other telegraph companies to the north, and an emerging rival O'Rielly line on his flank.

With the blockade still in force and AP operating its locomotive express, Smith wrote at length to the officers of the Magnetic Telegraph Company, explaining his position. Stating that his blockade was an act of "self-defence," he asserted that the Nova Scotia line had violated one of telegraphy's most important laws—the law of first-come-first-served—by granting a priority to AP's foreign news dispatches. Smith said Nova Scotia's policy imposed "upon my Lines the necessity of becoming the mere tool of a particular class of customers," claiming that preference was given to the "highest bidder," rather than to the first to deliver a news report.[79]

The gist of Smith's argument, however, revolved around the presence of Craig in Halifax and the split in the Boston press over delivery of foreign dispatches that caused the evening press to bolt the AP. Championing the cause of an "excluded class of the public press," Smith claimed to have "urged the favored portion of the press to permit the other portion to unite with them in terms of equity," but to no avail.[80] As for his old nemesis, Smith had only few and pointed words: "From what has transpired, I do object to yielding any *special privilege* to any parties, who will employ as agent, the present agent of the presses by the Nova Scotia Line—*Mr. Craig.*"[81] Passionately Smith urged his position upon the directors and officers of the Magnetic company.

> I shall neither retract, nor modify my position while I have
> a post, or rod of wire left under my charge between the cities
> of New York and Portland. I will wait until the one shall rot
> down, and the other be consumed with rust, and my own
> ability to replace them shall have been exhausted, before I
> shall change this policy. . . .[82]

After so resolute a show of firmness on May 1, however, Smith abruptly turned around on May 22 and offered to lease his entire New York and Boston telegraph company to the Magnetic company for ten years. The Magnetic's directors after much discussion refused Smith's offer.[83] O'Rielly's Bain line between Boston and Portland was closing ranks, and Smith sought vainly to rent his sinking ship to others rather than ride it down into a competitive quagmire with O'Rielly.

Smith's method was an opportunistic changing of horses in midstream; his motive, aside from money, was "self-aggrandizement," according to Morse's son.[84] Or, as Kendall observed in a letter to Morse, Smith "is so utterly unprincipled and selfish that we can expect nothing but renewed impositions as long as we have any connection with him."[85] Telegraph historian Thompson flatly states that "Smith's ambition [was] to establish a foreign news monopoly over the important Halifax–New York route."[86] Thompson explains that

> Smith's defense of the Boston press interest had not been prompted solely by love of fair play and justice. Since the time of his first arrangement with the New York journals, Smith had become aware of the tremendous value of the telegraph to the press. The guaranties made by the Associated Press to anyone who would undertake to push a line on toward Halifax served to confirm his belief that ultimately the great volume of European news would be transmitted by telegraph from Halifax to New York, and that the individual who controlled its transmission and distribution would have a monopoly at once powerful and profitable. Believing such a goal within his reach, Smith quietly [created] an independent foreign news agency [in which] John T. Smith [was] merely a puppet of F. O. J. Smith.[87]

Smith had changed from congressman to Morse's counselor, lobbyist, and copatentee virtually overnight in 1838, and in 1850 he attempted in quick succession to enter journalism and then to rid himself of his telegraphic property. Such erratic behavior may be, in part, dismissed as the unpredictable course of a notorious forty-three-year-old scoundrel. But it was also characteristic of antebellum business for individuals to move rapidly through a variety of jobs in search of security, or wealth, or power, or all three. If Craig could be a printer, the editor of a city directory, and a news-gathering agent in a few short years, Smith could be reasonably expected to try to rent or sell a young telegraph company facing hostile new competition and having lost a lucrative news contract. Moreover, Smith's attempts to involve himself in foreign news gathering and disseminating were symptomatic of journalism's new-found immediacy and importance. Many others, besides F. O. J. Smith, were attracted during this period by the power or profit offered by telegraphed foreign and domestic news. The war over control of news dispatches had only begun in 1850. Craig and the New York press had won this early skirmish, but hostilities continued into the 1880s.

Craig stayed on in Halifax as AP's agent for nearly a year before moving to New York City and replacing Alexander Jones as general agent of the New York City Associated Press. Throughout this episode, Jones seems not to have taken any significant role, merely processing the news reports as they arrived from the north while Hudson and Raymond as AP's executive committee wrote the letters, signed the contracts, and issued the public statements.

In spite of his modest role, Jones found the work stressful. "For months at a time we seldom retired before twelve or one o'clock, and then had to be on duty through the next day," Jones recalls of his AP days.[88] He left the post on May 19, 1851, to become a commercial reporter for the *New York Herald*. "This change," Jones observed, "has relieved us of night work and many annoyances which seemed in a measure inseparable from the business."[89]

Jones died on August 22, 1863, still employed by the *Herald* and having given up his medical practice about a year before. A decade later Hudson described Jones as "an indefatigable worker,"[90] and Hudson's successor, Thomas B. Connery, called Jones "a man of considerable force of character, if a little erratic."[91] In the *New York Herald*, Jones's obituary calls him "very energetic in the cause of the [AP] association, never sparing his labor and time when they could be used with advantage for its success." It sketches him as "a man of the strictest integrity, and honorable in all his dealings. . . . He was never known wittingly to wrong any one. . . ."[92]

Craig's past aggressiveness both as competitor and as agent of the New York press foretold changes for AP when he arrived in New York City. This forty-year-old man, who could assert that not anyone "nor the devil himself shall ever drive me from any position that I may see fit to assume" and who outmaneuvered Smith's minions at Halifax in a reckless winner-take-all struggle, arrived in New York City to tackle an Abbot & Winans competitor that was numerically stronger than his AP, to take responsibility for the telegraphic news reports of the nation's leading journals, and to combat the growing monopolistic tendencies of telegraphy. The early years of Craig's administration are the subject of the next chapter.

DISCUSSION

The newspaper institution in the United States was measurably extending itself at the start of the 1850s. In the 1840s the total number of dailies increased 84.1 percent and that of all newspapers, regardless of publication frequency, increased 64 percent. Population rose only 35.9 percent during this time. New printing and power technology, linked with a new cash street distribution system, gave the metropolitan press a reach and a presence previously unknown to editors and their communities. An estimated total daily circulation of newspapers in 1850 of 758,454 represented only 3.3 percent of total population, which was about forty-four percentage points less than the contemporary school enrollment rates. But at its height in the twentieth century, total daily circulation represented about 37 percent of population, which was about forty percentage points less than the contemporary school enrollment rates.[93]

Perhaps the only check on newspaper growth was the slow emergence of urban centers and of an aggregate urban population at mid-century. In 1850, 254 dailies and 2,048 papers of less frequent publication were scattered among and in between 236 urban centers, and urban population that year was only 15.3 percent of total population. Without a concentration of residents to create an easily accessible market, such as began to appear in the 1890s, some editors needed the weekly mail edition to retain the financial edge. But, unlike the more homogenous general circulation newspaper of today, antebellum papers could succeed by being more specialized, offering well-defined personalities, politics, or contents.

"Perhaps the most potent new influence of all" in the growth of journalism, suggests Anthony Smith, was the invention of the kerosene lamp, "which meant that the reader had access to printed material during the hours of leisure."[94] It also meant that the editorial, composing, and printing tasks in a newspaper office could be performed well into the night for a morning paper. And Alexander Jones could decode and manifold six copies of his telegraphic news report around midnight in his Hanover Street office. The question posed by much of this chapter was whether Jones's kerosene would be paid for by the telegraph companies, by the press of the city, or out of the receipts of his own independently run news agency.

Despite newspapers' striking growth in numbers and technology in the 1840s, journalism continued as the only relatively stable institution of the three being examined here, exerting pressure on telegraphy to generate the desired circuits for its news movement, protecting those circuits with financial power and preferential contracts, and inducing telegraphic competition where it benefited the press. Within political and mercantile circles and on the street, newspapers were respected and feared, especially in New York City. Their hold on public opinion and on the potentially lucrative news movement business they controlled caused telegraphy to treat powerful editors solicitously. Read again the words of the Nova Scotia telegraph commissioners as they defended Craig against F. O. J. Smith's charges.

> We cannot overlook the fact, that [Craig] is now the agent of a press, eminent alike for its talent and influence on this continent. It would be unreasonable in us to infer, that a

gentleman, clothed with such large responsibilities, and
holding so important an office, would be permitted by his
employers to resort to the practices to which you allude.[95]

We have seen Morse and Kendall writhe under adverse press comment and we have watched Greeley attempt to bully Alfred Vail. If
only a fraction of the accusations made by a contemporary observer
of the press, Lambert A. Wilmer,[96] can be believed, the press was
entrenched, efficacious, feared, perhaps greedy.

That telegraphy's and newsbroking's infancies were thus enormously affected by editors' needs and desires is not surprising. But
these twin institutional infants, in turn, affected editors' perspectives. Certainly in the smaller towns along the growing telegraphic
network, newsbroking delivered news with a new immediacy and
speed from more distant locations. In his *Springfield* (Mass.) *Republican* in January 1851, Samuel Bowles noted the change.

> Nothing can be more evident to the public, and nothing
> certainly is more evident to publishers of newspapers, than
> that there is a great deal more news nowadays than there
> used to be. . . . Publishers of country weeklies used to fish
> with considerable anxiety in a shallow sea, for matter
> sufficient to fill their sheets, while dailies only dreamed of an
> existence in the larger cities. . . . Now all is changed. The
> increase of facilities for transmission of news brought in a
> new era. The railroad car, the steamboat, and the magnetic
> telegraph have made neighborhood among widely dissevered
> states, and the Eastern Continent is but a few days' journey
> away. These active and almost miraculous agencies have
> brought the whole civilized world in contact. The editor sits
> in his sanctum, and his obedient messengers are the lightning
> and the fire.[97]

More than two decades later another editor, Frederic Hudson, a
practitioner in journalism's mecca, New York City, pondered telegraphy's impact on, and continuing challenge to, journalism.

> What will be the effect of the universal extension of the
> telegraph on the Press? . . . What has been the effect thus
> far? Will not the common property in news compel journalists
> to employ better, brighter, broader brains? With the events of
> the world hourly placed before the conductor of a leading
> newspaper, will he not have to be a man of greater and more
> comprehensive grasp of intellect than has yet been seen?
> With dispatches from every quarter and nation of the earth

tained control of policy and membership matters. Thus, the threat of a monopoly lodged either in an independent agency or in the telegraph system might be kept at bay. That threat, nevertheless, hung over Jones's administration as the AP of the New York City press rushed toward a journalistic monopoly. Jones's successor, Daniel H. Craig, moved rapidly and forcefully to solidify AP's gains and to push ahead into news frontiers, as we shall see in the next chapter.

Chapter 5
CONFLICT AND AN ASSOCIATED PRESS MONOPOLY

When organizing the Associated Press, I visited all the leading editors of the country and the managers of the numerous telegraph companies, and explained to them my purpose to establish a complete system for reporting the details of all important news by telegraph.... It required several years to force our news reports onto the editors of the country.

Daniel H. Craig, *Answer...to...the U.S. Senate Committee on Education and Labor* (1883)

D. H. Craig... did not increase the number of his personal friends; but amid all the trials he fought the battles mildly, pleasantly, and gentlemanly in conversation, but savagely, bitterly, and ruthlessly on paper. His correspondence was always a full-charged galvanic battery... but he was a faithful worker, a prompt news collector, an excellent executive officer, always on duty....

Frederic Hudson, *Journalism in the United States* (1873)

Compare the above quotes with those heading the previous chapter, and the reader may sense that Daniel H. Craig's ascent to the leading administrative post in the New York City Associated Press pointed that newsbrokerage in a new direction. Craig, the defiant, independent, pigeon-expressman and later AP's scrappy Halifax lieutenant, put a new face on the Associated Press after the mild-mannered Alexander Jones stepped down as general agent. This chapter surveys AP's new face as reflected in Craig's fight for an AP monopoly, in his news report, and in his personal involvement in telegraphy.

Craig was born November 3, 1811, in Rumney, N.H., the son of a War of 1812 veteran and grandson of a Revolutionary War soldier, and learned the printing trade as an apprentice at the *Plymouth* (N.H.) *Gazette* and *Lancaster* (Mass.) *Gazette*. He tried his hand at publishing a business directory in Baltimore in 1842–43 and in 1844 settled in Boston to make a living using homing pigeons to anticipate the foreign news for a few newspapers and speculators. Named AP agent in Halifax in February 1849, as the previous chapter describes, after having regularly beaten AP's news-gathering arrangements there over the previous few years with an assortment of pigeons, horse expresses, and telegraph schemes, Craig was summoned to New York City to replace Jones, who stepped down as AP general agent on May 19, 1851.[1]

While Craig took charge of the AP office at 3 Hanover Street, just off Wall Street, he moved his family into a house in Brooklyn. An AP staffer, Lewis H. Bridgham, whose name first appears in the city directory when Craig's does, roomed with the Craigs during 1851–52 before finding other Brooklyn accommodations. Two years later another AP staff member, Richard Stuart, also took up residence in Brooklyn.[2] To reach their Hanover Street office this AP staff rode one of the five steamer ferries plying the East River between Brooklyn and New York City, a four- to six-minute trip costing two cents per trip or $10 for a one-year pass.[3]

The year Craig arrived in New York City, the Associated Press underwent its first significant realignment—the six original newspaper partners signed a telegraphic news-gathering agreement and a seventh morning paper, the recently founded *New York Times*, joined the partnership. Some authorities date AP's existence from that 1851 telegraphic agreement. William Henry Smith, AP's general agent from 1882 to 1893, referring to this telegraphic agreement writes that "in 1851 the present 'New York Associated Press' was organized."[4] The document's first paragraph (all that survives) stated:

> It is mutually agreed between G. Hallock of the *Journal of Commerce*, J. and E. Brooks of the *Express*, J. G. Bennett of the *Herald*, Beach Brothers of the *Sun*, Greeley and McElrath of the *Tribune*, and J. W. Webb of the *Courier*, to associate for the purpose of collecting and receiving telegraphic and other intelligence.[5]

No date is attached to this fragment, but it was signed in 1851 before the September 18 founding of the *Times*. Its title, "The Telegraphic and General News Association,"[6] suggests that it organized AP's business broadly.

Henry J. Raymond was in AP's inner circle—a member for three years of its executive committee and the managing editor of James Watson Webb's *Courier and Enquirer* throughout AP's formative years. So it was natural that when Raymond, George Jones, and Edward B. Wesley introduced their *New York Times*, the paper joined the newsbrokerage partnership. Without directly referring to the AP, the paper's first number, under the heading "A Word About Ourselves," says, "As a *Newspaper* presenting all the news of the day from all ports of the world, we intend to make The Times as good as the best of those now issued in the City of New York...." This presumably meant sharing the common telegraphic dispatches then received and printed by the other six morning papers.

AP's historian, Oliver Gramling, asserts that the admission of the *Times* broke a deadlock between the three penny papers, which "believed that the activities of the association should be increased," and the three mercantile-political papers, which "were satisfied with things as they were."[7] There is no support for such a claim. Indeed, provisions of both the 1849 Harbor News Association agreement and the 1856 reorganization document of the AP, the latter discussed later in this chapter, indicate that significant decisions required unanimous or six to one votes of the papers. Factionalism of the type Gramling describes did not arise until after the Civil War.

COMPETITORS AND THEIR NEWS REPORTS

We glimpsed in chapter 3 AP's chief newsbroking competitor at the time Craig came to New York City. Abbot & Winans apparently enjoyed ties to the Morse telegraph system and served numerous Eastern newspapers, including the evening press of New York City. Craig, addressing his AP editors in 1863, recalled that

> I commenced with you in 1851, at which time all the papers
> in the city, except the six regular morning journals were
> violently hostile to the interests of the Association, whilst
> out of the city, fully four fifths of all the papers sustained an
> opposition News Association.... [T]here never was a time
> whilst Abbott [*sic*] and Winans flourished here in the
> opposition, between 1850 and 1855, that they were not able
> to get hold of any important news within five to thirty
> minutes after it was delivered at the newspaper offices of the
> Association.[8]

With significant telegraph routes amounting to a few or single strands of wire—especially along the North Atlantic coastline to

Halifax and certain corridors to the West—competing newsbro-kerages, each wishing to file lengthy dispatches at the same time over the only available lines, constantly threatened each other. Both morning and evening papers could publish extra editions for significant breaking news, and the papers whose extras reached the streets first were determined by the newsbroker who could get his dispatch first to the telegraph office and across the single-line circuits into his clients' newsrooms. For Craig, the Abbot & Winans competition was magnified by the latter's alliance with Morse telegraph interests. Craig's fears of a telegraph-controlled news conspiracy against him were fueled by an incident in upstate New York.

It will be recalled that the papers between Albany and Buffalo formed the nation's first newsbrokerage in 1846 when Theodore Faxton's New York, Albany and Buffalo Telegraph Company, a Morse franchise, was opened. Much of the papers' daily news report came from their New York City agent, the *New York Tribune*'s George Snow, who came to rely increasingly on the New York City Associated Press news report being assembled by Alexander Jones. As Jones describes this episode,[9] some upstate editors continuously grumbled about Faxton's telegraphic service, and when House and Bain lines started going up between New York and Buffalo in 1849 and 1850, these editors asked Snow to transmit their daily report over one of the new lines. Snow and Jones in New York City, of course, were comfortable with such a request, the city's AP having used Bain lines to fend off F. O. J. Smith's aggressions between New York and Boston.

Faxton retaliated on January 1, 1851, announcing that unless his line received all the AP business to communities he served, he would charge the upstate AP papers public rates, paid in advance, for whatever business the city AP sent up his line. For a while the city AP used whichever line the distant editor requested, ignoring Faxton's threat, but soon Faxton notified the New York City AP that his line would no longer transmit AP dispatches to upstate papers and that he had made other arrangements for a daily news report to be sent to the papers in the communities along his line.

Faxton's other arrangement was to employ Abbot & Winans to feed a news report to the papers he served. Jones comments that F. O. J. Smith's lines and "a portion of the Boston papers" also patronized Abbot & Winans at this time.[10] Another version of this incident, published in the *American Telegraph Magazine*, says that dissatisfaction among upstate editors arose, not with the telegraphic service, but with "irregular and unsatisfactory" AP news reports. "In self-defense," the magazine continues, the editors arranged with Faxton "to furnish them the current news of the day at a very low price."[11]

Ignoring for a moment his fierce competition with Abbot & Winans, it perhaps mattered little to Craig, at least in the early days of his administration, whether his news report reached small daily newspapers in upstate New York, although a certain prestige would result for him, but Craig would have had the journalist's worry that foreclosure of his report on Faxton's telegraph also meant denial of vital news items from Faxton's region for Craig's patron editors in New York City.

For Craig, assembling the daily report for the New York City AP papers was the first priority, but if a competitor and some hostile telegraph proprietors jeopardized the New York State portion of that report, he would have to fight his battles in the countryside and small towns as well as in New York City. Craig would have to build a news monopoly on at least the principal telegraphic arteries, and probably on the entire system, if the New York City partners' news report was to be protected. Telegraph proprietors had to be stripped of their ability to choose among newsbrokers on behalf of editors imprisoned along their telegraphic monopoly. The only way to do so was to develop a superior news report, with one hand, and to crush Abbot & Winans, with the other.

A fracas on one of those key single-line circuits—the familiar Halifax to New York City corridor for moving Cunard steamers' foreign news—early in Craig's regime provides a stark example of the pressures moving Craig to build a news monopoly. The reader will recall from the previous chapter that AP, with the help of Henry O'Rielly's Bain line, had fought off several attempts by F. O. J. Smith during 1849–50 to control the flow of news southwest of Halifax.

In 1852–53, however, AP and Craig faced off against Abbot & Winans and O'Rielly, whose concern for service to the public had led him to challenge Smith in 1849 to AP's benefit and in 1852 led him to challenge an AP monopoly on that line on behalf of Abbot & Winans. O'Rielly may have been additionally influenced by a new circle of friends he acquired in 1852. In November 1851 the Bain instrument was declared an infringement of the Morse patent, and O'Rielly and his Bain holdings in New England were ordered to merge with F. O. J. Smith's Morse telegraph system in the region, creating by July 1, 1852, the New York & New England Union Telegraph Company.[12]

The 1852–53 clash began in August 1852, with a request from

Francis A. Abbot to O'Rielly for assistance in getting equal treatment from the Nova Scotia line for transmission of Cunard news to the United States. In the preceding "six or eight months" Abbot & Winans and their newspaper clients had vainly sought a first-come-first-served policy from the Halifax telegraph office, a policy A & W had gained in various regions through passage of several state laws. Abbot is quoted as saying he approached O'Rielly because of the latter's assistance to AP in a similar situation two years earlier. [13]

The Nova Scotia line, originally built as a government-owned monopoly friendly to the aims of the Associated Press, had been converted by the provincial parliament into a private stock corporation, the Nova Scotia Electric Telegraph Company, on March 31, 1851. The new company's first president was Samuel Cunard, developer of the Cunard steamer system in 1840 and still a Halifax resident. [14] On September 6, 1852, O'Rielly addressed a letter to Cunard, enclosing remonstrances from the Baltimore press, Abbot & Winans, and an A & W agent in Baltimore and requesting "equal and exact justice in the transmission of despatches. . .in the order in which they are furnished at Halifax. . . ." O'Rielly claimed to represent "a major portion of the American Press." [15] By mid-November of 1852, some Boston merchants were publicly expressing concern about New York City's control of the foreign news. [16] Boston was at this time largely an Abbot & Winans stronghold.

Commenting that O'Rielly was "pouring forth his venom upon me through the pages of the [American] Telegraphic Magazine," Craig responded with a pamphlet calling O'Rielly a turncoat who, after securing these privileges for AP three years earlier, had now joined the opposition. Craig also claimed in his pamphlet that O'Rielly had attempted to get the New York AP editors to fire Craig, and, failing that, O'Rielly had turned to attacking the AP as a whole. [17]

Apparently Craig stood alone in the viciousness with which he approached this scuffle, his patron editors taking a more subdued role in the growing controversy. During March 1853, an anonymous author published a pamphlet entitled The Associated Press versus Henry O'Rielly and F. O. J. Smith, which vigorously denounced the telegraph proprietors. The writer claimed to be writing "wholly on his own responsibility, without consultation with any" AP newspaper editors, but he expressed indebtedness "to an individual in their employ for some facts here set forth." [18] Moses S. Beach, AP's secretary and editor of the New York Sun, disavowed any AP connection with the pamphlet. The March 25, 1853, *New York Sun* commented that the "extremely ungenerous and disgraceful attack" on O'Rielly in a recent "scurrilous pamphlet" suggests the contents belonged to the AP. The *Sun* continued, "Our only purpose in alluding to [the pamphlet] is to *deny*, in the *fullest and broadest sense, any knowledge of, or complicity in, the publication of it by the 'Associated Press.'* " The newspaper went on to assure its readers that the AP had always sought and received the confidence of the whole community.[19]

A proposal to lay a submarine cable from Halifax to the New Brunswick coast to compete with the land lines of Cunard's Nova Scotia company might have defused the situation by stripping AP of its Halifax monopoly, or it might have moved the quarrel to the New Brunswick telegraph system. But the Nova Scotia Parliament rejected the plan, 67 to 16, on March 17, 1853.[20]

Meanwhile O'Rielly was drafting two "Memoranda" for publication in the *American Telegraph Magazine*, the first reviewing his relations with the press over the past eight years and the second restating his case for an open policy on the Nova Scotia line. Dated June 13, 1853, the documents reiterated O'Rielly's desire to see fairness at Halifax, answered the anonymous pamphleteering "libeller," and sought to make clear that he had no vested interest in the matter beyond the principle involved.[21]

As O'Rielly described the dilemma, partisans cannot be easily identified. A few complaining editors received the favored AP dispatches, but felt aggrieved because their natural desire to receive the earliest dispatches available forced them unwillingly to align with the AP. New York City AP editors were described as being less eager to support publicly the preferential line treatment than was Craig, who at the height of this controversy published a business card claiming that AP's London agent, John Hunter, could forward European news dispatches to the United States "*in advance of all other private communications,* on the arrival of the steamers at Halifax. . . ."[22]

Anti-AP grievances, it seems, were justified; O'Rielly's long-standing preoccupation with the public interest in telegraphy was intact. AP's contract with the Nova Scotia line gave AP priority on the line for its average 3,000-word dispatch, even if a competing agent submitted a foreign dispatch ahead of AP. Moreover, no other foreign news dispatch could be sent from Halifax until AP newspapers had *published* their dispatch! If the steamer arrival and subsequent AP transmission occurred so as to just miss the early morning deadlines of New York's morning AP papers, and those papers found too little in the dispatch to warrant extra editions, Abbot & Winans would have to wait nearly twenty-four hours to transmit its dispatch. The logic of such an arrangement is found in the telegraph companies' fear that their facilities would be used by speculators to influence U.S. markets. An alliance with AP guaranteed a wide public distribution of the first European news dispatch.

Duplicate telegraph circuits would have permitted both newsbrokers to file their dispatches at their own speeds. But beyond the U.S. newspapers' foreign news dispatches, telegraphic business north of Portland did not warrant duplicate lines, and the provincial parliament had protected the existing private line by defeating the submarine cable plan. Failing a technical solution, one was left with a choice between AP and A & W. Which was stronger? Which represented the public interest better? Contemporary statements of both Craig and O'Rielly, as we shall see, sustain the impression that whereas AP represented the established, financially successful metropolitan press, A & W represented the vast majority of those daily newspapers receiving a newsbroker report. Although New York's six AP papers had acquiesced in sharing a common telegraphic dispatch seven years before, they now looked down from their superior position and refused to share facilities with A & W for transmission of a common foreign news dispatch for both newsbrokerages, and for the benefit of a substantially larger reading public.

The controversy's final resolution remains a mystery. Between June and November 1853, when AP and the Nova Scotia telegraph officials penned a new five-year contract reaffirming priority for AP's foreign dispatch, the record is totally silent on the matter—no newspaper comments, no pamphlets, no magazine accounts. The chief reason for the record's failure here is that the confrontation's battleground, the *American Telegraph Magazine*, suspended publication with its sixth issue, dated April-May-June 1853. The preferential treatment previously given AP at Halifax continued under the new contract, which had two new features: its five-year duration and the doubling of AP's payment to $450 for a 3,000-word foreign dispatch.[23] One suspects that, as before, the reputation of the metropolitan press, liberally buttressed with financial inducements, tipped the scales toward AP.

Even though AP had survived this second challenge in five years to its foreign news dispatches, it could not tolerate newsbroking competition. Abbot & Winans had to be crushed, and Craig mounted a three-pronged assault on that firm and its Morse allies.

He personally involved himself in telegraphic development in opposition to Morse interests by discovering and promoting the Hughes telegraph instrument, purchasing and leasing telegraph lines, and working his way into Cyrus W. Field's American Telegraph Company. Craig also worked the field along every telegraph line, convincing or coercing editors, telegraph operators, and owners to cooperate with the AP, and then holding his clients together with constant pressure and stringent rules. Finally, he enlarged and improved AP's news report until it seemed indispensable to American newspaper editors. [24] In addition to augmenting his report for morning papers, which favored his New York City patrons, Craig expanded his report for evening papers. Many larger morning papers by the late 1840s had begun publishing afternoon editions for the few news dispatches dribbling in over the telegraph during the day. (Some papers headed these late dispatches "Postscript.") Craig would eventually be so successful at developing two news cycles that one of the New York City partners, the *Express*, could switch its primary edition to the afternoon in the early 1860s without being denied a substantial report of telegraphic news.

Improving the news report was Craig's first order of business, no doubt at the constant urging of his patron editors. The author compared the complete news reports of AP and Abbot & Winans for January 9 and 10, 1852. The morning AP report was collected from New York's *Herald*, *Times*, and *Tribune*; the A & W report was found in its evening cycle in the *New York Evening Post* and *Boston Evening Transcript*[25] for January 9 and in its morning cycle in the *Utica Gazette* for January 10. Even when two cycles of A & W copy are compared with one AP cycle, the latter is much longer and more complete. By transcribing the news dispatches by typewriter into two parallel 40-character columns on typing paper, the author compared the lengths and contents of stories in the two reports. The AP's report was 996 typed lines long (roughly four newspaper columns long), whereas A & W's report was only 221 lines (about three-fourths of a column long). The AP report contained twenty-seven stories, and A & W's contained twenty.

Only three stories—all routine and short—appeared with identical wording in both newsbrokers' reports. Another nine stories were similar in substance, but not in wording, in the two reports. The AP moved fifteen stories not found on A & W, and this group amounted to 748 typed lines or 75 percent of AP's total report for January 10. Abbot & Winans moved eight stories not found on AP, and this group totaled about 28 percent of A & W report. Its largest linage

(63 percent) consisted of the nine stories appearing in similar form in AP. The Associated Press report was longer, containing more stories, more complete stories, and more stories not found on its competitor's report. And this completeness extended across all categories of news—politics, government, disasters, even weather. A historian of the *Boston Herald* confirms these findings, reporting that although "on a number of occasions" Abbot & Winans would "'beat' the Associated Press by eight to ten hours" on a story, AP's report was usually much longer than A & W's, the latter averaging "scarcely more than a 'stickful' or two" of type per day.[26]

One key to improving the news report was to maintain a strong list of correspondents. An AP business card appearing in two early-1853 numbers of the *American Telegraph Magazine* lists Craig's correspondents as in Liverpool, John Hunter, No. 2 Paradise St.; in Halifax, R. Nugent, editor of the *Halifax Sun*; in Boston, W. G. Blanchard, office of the *Boston Mail*; in Philadelphia, W. W. Fulton, *Philadelphia Public Ledger* building; in Baltimore, C. C. Fulton, *Baltimore Sun* building; in Charleston, A. Carroll, *Charleston Courier* office; in New Orleans, Eugene Fuller, Merchants' Exchange; in Louisville, J. W. Clarke, *Louisville Courier* office; in Cincinnati, Richard Smith, Merchants' Exchange; and in Buffalo, A. D. Levien, *Buffalo Commercial* office.[27] Compared with Jones's correspondents, listed in chapter 4, this group contains only three holdovers, Fulton in Baltimore, Fuller in New Orleans, and Smith in Cincinnati. Consulting standard American, Canadian, and British biographical sources sheds no light on the new names in Craig's list.[28]

By 1854, according to James Parton, AP's New York office had three staff members (Craig, Lewis H. Bridgham, and Richard Stuart, according to city directories), correspondents in Liverpool and Halifax, and "fifty reporters in various parts of the country." The AP's New York City harbor news operation included superintendent John T. Hall and twelve agents and reporters.[29] Neither Jones's nor Craig's list gives Washington, D.C., correspondents. Someone was in that service, but it apparently was not yet the famous Lawrence A. Gobright, who appears to have taken command of AP's Washington bureau late in 1853, after the above list was published.

Lawrence Augustus Gobright was born May 2, 1816, in Baltimore, where he learned the printing trade. After operating a Martin Van Buren campaign paper, the Batavia *Ohio Sun*, he moved to Washington, D.C., and reported Washington news for the *Baltimore Clipper* and other papers. With two partners, Gobright edited a penny paper, the *Washington Daily Bee*, during the summer of 1845. It lasted only one month.[30] He was known as "Larry" or "Father Gobright," and, as an intimate of many leading political figures in the capital from 1841 until his retirement in 1879, he was ideally suited to head Craig's Washington bureau.[31] Ben Perley Poore in 1874 observed of Gobright that "probably no one has enjoyed to an equal extent, during the past quarter of a century, the confidence of the statesmen, diplomates [sic], politicians, and financiers who congregate at Washington."[32]

Frederick B. Marbut finds Gobright's earliest identification with the AP on an unofficial list of reporters admitted in 1853 to Congress, where Gobright held a seat in the Senate gallery for the AP and James W. Sheahan was in the House gallery for the AP and the *Washington Republic*.[33] A "first list of correspondents," dated 1859, shows Gobright in the House for AP and J. T. Piggott covering the Senate for AP.[34]

A *Philadelphia Press* writer observed in 1858 that "during the session of Congress, the reports of its proceedings by the able reporters of the [Associated Press] are doubtless the only ones that are read outside of the political world."[35] Gobright's oft-quoted description of his AP duties, given in testimony to a congressional committee, bears repeating here:

> My business is to communicate facts. My instructions do not allow me to make any comment upon the facts which I communicate. My dispatches are sent to papers of all manner of politics, and the editors say they are able to make their own comments upon the facts which are sent to them. I therefore confine myself to what I consider legitimate news. I do not act as a politician belonging to any school, but try to be truthful and impartial. My dispatches are merely dry matter of fact and detail. Some special correspondents may write to suit the temper of their organs. Although I try to write without regard to men or politics, I do not always escape censure.[36]

Although Gobright tried to walk the straight and narrow, his patron editors, who occasionally ventured down to Washington, D.C., and looked over his shoulder, tried to nudge him this way or that. Here, for example, the *Tribune*'s Horace Greeley, writing to his managing editor, Charles A. Dana, from Washington sought to pressure Craig to free Gobright's hands on a matter of urgency to Greeley.

> Dana,
> Will you please have an earnest talk with Craig? I went to

the Senate yesterday in purpose to hear the additional
Crampton documents. On hearing them, I saw that they
needed to be sent over *verbatim*, and sent every copy for
Gobright to tell him to send them to the Associated Press. . . .
He hesitated, but telegraphed to Craig. Craig answered that
he need only send the substance. I saw Gobright again early
in the evening, and still again at 10 o'clock, and he assured
me that he had sent all but a few unessential phrases. So I
could do no more with him, as he was acting under orders
from Craig. . . . I want you to ask Craig distinctly whether I
may not expect to be listened to in another contingency like
this. . . .[37]

Craig ran a tight ship, knew what he wanted, and firmly steered
his news report toward a compromise between expensive completeness and inadequate brevity. An 1854 printed circular from Craig attempting to recruit and instruct AP agents indicates AP's definition
of newsworthiness—a definition that in its essentials would suffice
today for much of the wires' news report.

In regard to the character of the news required, we would
say that we want *everything that is* IMPORTANT and
everything that would be of *General Interest* in this City,
State, or the country at large.

In preparing dispatches for transmission, it is desirable
always to bear in mind that we want only the *material facts*
in regard to any matter or event, and those facts in the
fewest words possible compatible with a clear understanding
of correspondent's meaning. All expressions of opinion upon
any matters; all political, religious, and social biasses; and
especially all *personal feelings* on any subject on the part of
the Reporter, must be kept out of his despatches. . . .

What we should consider of sufficient importance for
Telegraphic news would be notices of serious Railroad
accidents; fires, resulting in large losses of property;
shipwrecks, and other serious maritime accidents; mutinies
and piracies; duels; fracases of a serious nature, between
individuals distinguished in any way; murders; serious
accidents, occurring to individuals well known in the
country; movements of the President, or of his cabinet, or of
other high Government officers; notices and results of trials
of unusual interest; important election news; ship news;
notices of proceedings of National, State, political or religious
Conventions; extensive robberies; extensive forgeries and
swindles; extensive failures; news by foreign arrivals at your

place, if of importance; important Legislative proceedings; passages of important laws; riots on a large scale, etc.

What we *do not want* is, news of a merely local consequence, such as accidents to individuals not known out of their immediate vicinity; small fires; small robberies, small assaults; small local political matters and personalities, etc.[38]

Along with Jones's instructions for filing returns of the 1848 presidential election, this document exhibits AP's early reliance on flat factuality, political impartiality, and national emphasis. Indeed, this 1854 circular may be journalism's first expression of the principle of objectivity, the origins of which for journalism as a whole some scholars trace to newsbroking.[39]

Although the author does not seriously contend that this circular installed objectivity in AP's news report, objectivity was prevalent, if not pervasive, in the early news report. Gobright in Washington and other AP correspondents in politically sensitive assignments were learning that slavishly recording the words and actions of newsworthy people without context or commentary suited Craig's and the leading New York City papers' needs. Craig could offer a politically inoffensive news report to newspapers occupying a wide political spectrum; the newspapers, in turn, could editorially make of this objective report whatever their political leanings dictated. A chronological account, only summarizing proposals, amendments, and final actions and stripped of emotion, personality, and judgment, the objective dispatch required far fewer words, and thus lower telegraphic tolls, which was good financial news to both Craig and the AP newspapers.

But AP's early news report was neither uniformly objective nor interesting. The following two dispatches illustrate the extremes that AP transmitted, ranging from an enthusiastic account from Cincinnati to a dry and colorless item from Boston.

Cincinnati, March 8, 1854

A great meeting of citizens was held last night in opposition to the Nebraska bill. Although the rain fell in torrents the large hall of the Mechanics' Institute was filled. Prominent men of all parties took part in the meeting, which was addressed by Judge Walker, Bellamy Storer, Charles Reemlin, and others. A series of ten resolutions, opposed to Douglas' Nebraska bill, or any further extension of slave territory, and expressed in strong language, were adopted with but one dissenting vote.

Twenty delegates were appointed to the State convention
to be held at Columbus on 22d March.[40]

Boston, Nov. 12, 1856

The Fillmore American Council for Massachusetts met in
this city yesterday afternoon. About fifty Delegates were in
attendance. A series of resolutions were discussed and finally
adopted, acknowledging the supremacy of the National
American Organization, and declaring in favor of the
purification of the ballot-box, and the prevention of any
interference of Church hierarchies in politics; the protection
of American men, American rights and American interests;
an open Bible and Free Schools; a Registry law in every
State; a modification of the Naturalization laws, and in fine,
for the general principle that "Americans should rule
America."[41]

In general, however, the AP dispatches were straightforward,
factual, and exceedingly brief. Most events covered by the AP were
flattened by undistinguished, terse treatment. Even events anticipated by correspondents and for which there was much public interest and emotion could not escape AP's blandness. Such coverage
recorded events as they happened, leaving the reader to sort out
the meaning of the event.

AP's news report for January 10, 1852, analyzed above by the author filled about four columns of type in the New York papers. Surveying AP newspapers later in the 1850s, one finds a sharp
reduction in Craig's report to one or two columns between 1854 and
1858, perhaps an effort to keep telegraph charges down and perhaps, after 1855, a response to the death of the Abbot & Winans
agency. In 1859, however, the report shot up to a regular three-or-
more columns of type daily in the New York papers.[42] During these
periods of reduction and expansion, the report's essential charac-
teristics—types of stories (government, politics, disasters), regular
stories (congressional sessions, market reports, shipping news), and
the report's style of presentation—did not change; only the brevity
and selectivity of dispatches did.

This news report, Craig reported thirty years later, cost each of
the seven New York AP papers between $200 and $230 per week
during the 1850s. The evening New York City papers that eventually
became AP clients paid about half those rates and received a
shorter news report. Toward the end of the decade, when Craig virtually controlled the news flow to American newspapers, charges to

all out-of-town clients totaled between $10,000 and $12,000 per week.[43] There is no indication that Craig or the New York partners realized a profit from the out-of-town revenue, but the impression is left by all sources that all of AP's revenue beyond operating expenses flowed right through AP into the pockets of the telegraph operators.

By no means were newspapers relying exclusively on Craig's or Abbot & Winans's news report for their coverage of news beyond their immediate communities. Reprinting from exchanges continued universally and voluminously. Often on major stories, exchange clips were intercut with newsbroker dispatches (as we saw in chapter 4 with the 1849 Parkman murder coverage in the *New York Herald*) during the 1850s, a practice that, in fact, increased during the Civil War. On a major breaking story it is often impossible to decide whether the principal coverage was from the exchange clips or the telegraphic dispatches, the clips generally providing important background and the bulk of the factual matter about an event and the newsbrokers providing sketchy accounts or fragmentary new facts. The sources of much of the early telegraphic news were local editors, reporters, or telegraph operators relying on the local newspapers.

Two scholars examining newspaper content between 1820 and 1860 and using the same raw data present a picture of news reporting consistent with the above observations. Donald L. Shaw notes two significant trends in his data: the advance of the telegraph between 1847 and 1860 resulted in newspapers nationally "focusing on the same news sources, looking more alike, performing a similar functional role" and a "retarded development of Southern newspapers. . . in using the telegraph to bring in the outside world," apparently because of slower urban development and diffusion of communication systems in the South.[44] David H. Weaver, four years later, notes an "overall similarity of news emphasis between the newspapers of various regions of the country, even before the invention of the telegraph and the use of syndicated news services."[45]

An extensive study of nineteenth-century newspapers confirms Weaver's suggestion that even just before the Civil War, in terms of subjects reported, "They concentrated on general political, general community and intellectual and cultural news, while downplaying news of slavery and abolition, sectional differences, and territories and expansion."[46] Telegraphy in its early years had no appreciable effect on the news values, prominent subjects, and approaches taken by journalists in the United States. The pretelegraphic news values were transferred in briefer format into the newsbroker's daily report. The AP's and A & W's dispatches, although shorter, followed the prevailing patterns of defining and portraying news except where partisanship might permeate newspapers' political coverage. And yet, the arrival of the telegraph, as Shaw found, did heighten the significance of those news sources and urban areas reached earliest by telegraph lines. The nation's attention was being focused on the major centers where newsbrokers assembled the telegraphic reports or where newsbrokers had positioned correspondents or agents who filed regularly. The daily bundle of newspaper exchanges might have made Indianapolis or Portland, Maine, the momentary site of significant news in many newspapers across the county, but the daily telegraphic dispatch from New York City called all subscribing editors' attention to that city's thoughts and actions, plus those of a handful of other Eastern urban centers.

Editors, many of whom were already swept up in a technological revolution in their pressrooms, found they and their readers needed the product of this new news-moving technology if their newspaper was to be "modern," if they were to keep up with the Greeleys and Bennetts. No longer available only to those papers located along the old pioneer telegraph routes, but not yet capable of comprehensive national news coverage, the newsbrokers' reports in the 1850s offered speed on selective stories from selected cities. They also were a badge of an editor's allegiance—either to the boisterous Craig and his crowd of big city patrons or to the middling Abbot & Winans enterprise and its telegraphic ally.

Between 1851 and 1855, if AP's news report could be termed modest and uneven, Abbot & Winans' report, as we have seen, was puny and spotty. Craig's affiliation with the cream of New York City journalism may have attracted to his service correspondents and cooperative Eastern papers of better talent and energy. Abbot & Winans found its strength in the allies and operators of the Morse telegraph system, surely a matter of concern for Craig. If telegraph proprietors, such as Faxton, could deliver the entire flock of editors along their lines into A & W's hands, Craig's competitor was formidable.

No record of AP's membership during the 1850s exists, but A & W's reach may be ascertained from an 1853 article in *American Telegraph Magazine* that examined the competing claims of AP and A & W for priority on the Nova Scotia telegraph line.[47] The article reprints letters from Abbot & Winans and from John Wills, their Baltimore agent, in which sixty-two newspapers are listed by name as clients of A & W as of mid-August 1852, with comments that other papers were dependent upon some of those named for their telegraphic dispatches.[48] Wills asserts that "So far as I am able to judge, my firm impression is that MORE THAN ONE HALF THE NEWSPAPERS IN THE UNITED STATES are supplied with Telegraphic news by myself and the several agents and correspondents [including A & W] with whom I am connected."[49] The list embraces some substantial Eastern newspapers and lists subscribers in New Orleans, Pittsburgh, and St. Louis. The papers along Faxton's New York, Albany and Buffalo Telegraph Company line are all on the list,[50] as are three evening New York City papers.

Initially A & W and AP were not necessarily competitors for news dispatches—thus accounting for some duplication of dispatches appearing in the two wires' news reports on January 9 and 10, 1852, noted above. Frederic Hudson's diary notes on March 14, 1851, that "the Boston Associated Press could employ F. A. Abbot as their agent in New York exclusively and take the news of the New York Associat[ed]" Press or "could send an agent [to New York City] if they chose to do so."[51] Amiable reciprocity, however, could not long endure as the battle for a news monopoly heated up. Eventually on May 10, 1854, Hudson recorded in his diary that "It was resolved [by the New York AP] that in the future Abbott [sic] & Winans, nor any other newspaper agent, should be employed by any member of the Association."[52] Nonintercourse had set in, and sometime during 1855, according to Craig and city directories,[53] the Abbot & Winans newsbrokerage disappeared from the scene, leaving Craig, for the moment, alone in the field.

Soon after the breakup of A & W, Francis A. Abbot moved to Harrison, New York, but he remained active in the city as a commercial reporter for several out-of-town newspapers. During the Civil War Abbot was on the staff of the *New York World* (which by then had replaced the *Courier and Enquirer* as an AP member). After the war he resumed his correspondence for distant papers, notably the *New Orleans Picayune*, *Baltimore Sun*, *Philadelphia Record*, and *Galveston News*, and conducted some advertising business on the side.

Regarded as highly religious, Abbot was credited with founding chapels in Harrison and Bryan, Conn. At the time of his death, May 25, 1898, he was a financial reporter in New York City for the *Philadelphia Record* and *Galveston News* and was reported to have left a "comfortable fortune."[54] As for Abbot's financial picture and something of his character, one can glean some understanding from R. G. Dun & Company's occasional notations on him.

Oct. 30, 1866. 68 Wall St. He says he is an editor & connected with sev[era]l papers in the city. Has been so for a long time & considers himself fully respons[ible] & good for any contracts he enters into. We learn outside that he has been in the telegraph bus[iness] in the firm of Abbott [sic] & Winans and is principal correspondent for the New Orleans Picayune. Very indust[rious] & energetic but no bus[iness] means. He however means well & parties think he would be good if he gave a note for 1000 $.

April 15, 1879.... We find him spoken of as a man of fair character, but of very little money strength. Is not in a condition to ask a credit except on the strength of honest intentions.

April 7, 1880. 26 Broad. He...is spoken of as a very respectable man. Lives up to engagements and tho[ugh]t to have some little money but cannot est[imate] worth. Is said to be doing fairly well and saving more money than he spends....

May 9, 1883. In fair credit and is in good repute with the press....[55]

R. G. Dun ignores Elias P. Winans, who became a commercial reporter for the Associated Press after the Abbot & Winans firm died and continued as a reporter for the *New York Commercial Advertiser*, a post he held during his days with Abbot. In 1876 Winans joined the *New York Tribune* as its produce markets reporter, retaining his position as a commercial reporter for the AP. He died on January 29, 1887, still a staffer for the *Tribune* and AP.[56]

CRAIG STALKS HIS MONOPOLY

By his own account Craig was the victim. He comments that the Associated Press general agent

presents a mark to the open bully and to the lurking assassin. He encounters the rage of baffled selfishness; he sustains as well as he can the inexorable malignity of that envy to which his success is the unpardonable grievance, and the better he performs his duty to the press and the public, the more deep and the more bitter is the exasperation of the disappointed monopolist. Such, at least, is my experience.[57]

Victor Rosewater, on the contrary, surveys the activities of this maligned agent and concludes that "Craig was to hold the place and wield a power in the realm of news service akin to that of absolute monarch."[58]

A Craig contemporary and telegraph historian, James D. Reid, gives this penetrating view of the AP agent. Craig was

> a cool, shrewd, indefatigable man, to whom processes were valuable only as they secured success.... He preserved at all times the placidity of a summer's morning. His speech was as gentle and suave and courtly as if the world had made him its exceptional favorite, and he was its benignant son. Beneath this calm exterior there was a fertility of resource, a capacity of terse Saxon, especially with his pen, and an energy and force of will, which, for a time, made him a very prominent factor in the telegraphic enterprise of the period.[59]

After Abbot & Winans retired from the scene in 1855, an editor got his reports from Craig or got none at all. In addition to developing an unmatchable news report, Craig acquired his power by leaning heavily on the nation's editors and telegraph owners and by directly participating in telegraphy's development wherever it benefited his news schemes.

Craig in 1883 described for a U. S. Senate committee his campaign to recruit the nation's editors in the 1850s.

> I visited all the leading editors of the country and the managers of the numerous telegraph companies, and explained to them my purpose to establish a complete system for reporting the details of all important news by telegraph. I found a large majority of the editors violently opposed to my views, and among the telegraph managers, such men as Amos Kendall, F. O. J. Smith, Professor Morse and their associates, did all in their power to defeat my purpose of combining the whole daily press of the country in sustaining one substantial telegraph news organization, their selfish and absurd idea being that each individual editor should telegraph all the news he desired to publish, and thus bring a larger grist to their mill.... [But] until I retired from the management of the Associated Press at the close of 1866, every daily journal in the country and in Canada was compelled to submit to our rules in regard to telegraphic news reports.[60]

In 1876 William Henry Smith, the occupant of Craig's AP throne between 1882 and 1893, was no kinder toward Craig's efforts in the 1850s than Craig himself. Observing that the New York AP entered the Western field "in the person of D. H. Craig" when the area "began to give promise of an abundant harvest," Smith says that for

1,500 words per day the New York AP "squeezed out of the papers from Buffalo to Milwaukee, and from Pittsburgh to St. Louis, all of the money they could spare after paying expenses." The original "equitable system" by which "certain news necessary to all newspapers" could be gathered for all at a savings in telegraphic tolls, Smith continues,

> was abandoned for one which should make outside papers. . . bear the largest share of the cost of the news. Thus the [New York AP] not only determined the character of the reports, adapting them to their own needs, but assessed such sums as they pleased upon their customers, and absolutely refused them all voice in the management of the business.[61]

Here was a monopoly in the making, and, though Craig is our principal source on the subject, there is no evidence of a serious challenge to AP's empire between 1855 and the end of the Civil War.

A few glimpses of Craig's methods survive. Ezra Cornell, for example, controlled the New York & Western Union Telegraph Company (later shortened to Western Union) in the wake of bankruptcy proceedings on the line in 1852.[62] An engineer and developer for the Morse system from the early days, Cornell had broken with the Morse people in 1849 and by 1853 presided over a western network that stretched from Erie, Pennsylvania, and Cleveland to Toledo, Detroit, South Bend, Chicago, and to Pittsburgh, Steubenville, Zanesville, Fort Wayne, Columbus, Cincinnati, Indianapolis, and St. Louis.

With Abbot & Winans out of the picture and knowing that the AP contract with the New York and Mississippi Valley Printing Telegraph Company (a rival of Cornell's) had expired the previous November 1 and was being carried over temporarily until February 1, 1856, Cornell wrote "Craige" on January 4, 1856, proposing to transmit AP's reports of "average quantity of last year" to Cleveland, Sandusky, Toledo, Detroit, Chicago, and Milwaukee, copy and deliver the report to each AP newspaper named by Craig for $6,000 per year, all to be levied by the telegraph company on a weekly basis against the receiving papers. Cornell further proposed to "transmit news messages from any of our offices Eastward for the Assd. Press at a deduction of one half from our regular rates."[63]

Two and a half weeks later Craig accepted, saying that "there is neither mystery nor great art required to prepare the copy for the compositors of subscriber newspapers." Craig then went into his war dance:

> When you get careless or neglectful, you and your whole
> tribe will get blowed up, privately and, possibly, publicly, and
> if that don't answer, we will *plot treason* against the State
> and especially against Telegraphic monopolies. Recollect
> always that you are on your good behavior. [64]

The new contract took effect February 1, 1856, and after only eleven days had passed, Craig wrote Cornell with numerous requests. Craig wanted a line to Syracuse, connecting there with Oswego. (Syracuse "for us is more important than any other place between Albany and Buffalo on account of conventions.") He also wanted to see Cornell's contracts with the Erie Railroad Company and with the Mississippi Valley Telegraph Company, commenting "you know I have to talk here to men who never take anything for granted, and I want to be able to prove all I assert." [65]

Craig here was exploring the possibilities of using Cornell's line from New York to Buffalo, constructed primarily for use by the Erie Railroad Company, for experiments with the new Hughes telegraph instrument, in which Craig owned an interest. Craig subsequently saw the railroad contract and, noting that Cornell's rights were not exclusive on that line and that Cornell could not assign the line to others (such as Craig and his Hughes patent friends), chided Cornell. "It seems to me you were not as sharp as usual in drawing up that arrangement with the R. R. Co. See if you can't get the Co. to make your rights *exclusive* on their tracks." [66] Ten days later Craig playfully asserted the invincibility of the Hughes instrument. "The Hughes instruments are to be *completed*, so Phelps says, this week. Good—then you and some other telegraph woodenheads will have an opportunity to realize what consummate apes you have made of yourselves." [67] While Craig worked his angles and charm on Cornell on behalf of the Hughes instrument, he enlisted and instructed Cornell's telegraphers on behalf of his Associated Press business.

The day before he sent the above letter to Cornell, Craig dispatched a long telegram to the Chief Clerk of the Western Union saying that while Craig would retain his own few correspondents in the field, he and Cornell had agreed

> that the Chief Operators, Clerks, and their Assistants should,
> as far as in their power, and consistently with their duties,
> aid our local agents and myself in collecting and transmitting
> promptly to us and to our Editorial friends at regular report
> hours all news of real and general interest....

Craig enclosed a circular defining "news of real and general interest."

But in addition to converting telegraphers into correspondents, Craig turned Cornell's "tribe" into AP bill collectors, instructing them to present AP editors with AP bills every Saturday and to expect payment every Monday "without fail." Craig predicted, "I do not apprehend you will have any trouble upon this point, as every editor will readily admit the propriety of our demands, and will, doubtless, pay the trifling sums as they fall due, and cheerfully. . . ." Failure of one paper in a community to pay meant not only cutting off the paper's AP news, but forcing other AP papers in the community to shoulder the additional telegraphic charges previously paid by the defaulting paper. A paper leaving AP and then returning, according to Craig, was required to pay "all arrearages and also pay the same sum for the time they may have been out, as they would have paid, if they had been in."

Craig also advised the operators on enlisting new AP subscribers. "If new papers apply for the reports, their publishers should satisfy you by security or otherwise, that they will honorably receive and pay for the reports, for at least one year. . . ." Finally, the operators were admonished that "all news embodied in our reports is to be regarded by you and your assistants as strictly private until published in the regular Edition. . .of your papers."[68]

Hardly a cohesive, well-controlled structure, Craig's Associated Press was relying on nonjournalist employees of the telegraph companies to perform some fundamental newsbroking chores—gathering and transmitting news dispatches, soliciting, evaluating and billing subscribers, and even imposing Craig's punishment for nonpayment. There were no applications to fill out, no decisions by New York's morning press on admitting new members, and not even Craig would know immediately that a newspaper had been recruited. On a lean budget, Craig probably had no choice but to rely on telegraphers and agents to conduct much of his business along the lines. And it led to abuses.

Jacob Barns, editor of the *Grand Rapids* (Mich.) *Enquirer*, a new daily in a town of six thousand people, wrote Craig on February 10, 1856, wanting clarification of AP's policy. Barns explained that he sought the AP report and was told it would cost him $12 per report. Answering that he could not afford it at more than $1 per report (about half of the actual rate for the AP report), Western Union's Kalamazoo telegraph operator sent the report to Barns at the $1 rate for a while. Then the operator wrote Barns accusing him of receiving the report "by stealth" and saying that if the *Enquirer* wanted more AP reports, it would have to pay $20 per week.[69]

Craig's answer to Barns is lost, but Craig enclosed Barns's letter when he fired off this broadside at Cornell:

> See how your wild cat swindles leak out. I suppose our reports are *used* at about 40 places at the west where they ought not to be, and I shall now rely upon *you* to stop the thieving system and make all who use the reports pay *something* for them, and one third or one half of the amount paid *must come to us*. DO YOU HEAR THAT, and will you try and redeem your *tribe* by acting honestly in regard to this whole business. I'll do whatever you suggest, for a while and see what sort of d——d mess you'll get us all into out west.[70]

Craig may have struck a blow for honesty above, but it was honesty on behalf of an AP monopoly. From the western editors' viewpoint, Craig was as much a menace as the "swindling" telegraph operators he relied upon. From the rostrum of AP's annual banquet in 1896, Joseph Medill looked back on the hard days when, as a twenty-nine-year-old editor, Medill struggled to keep a new daily newspaper afloat in Cleveland.

> Mr. Craig was the boss and dictator. He had a short and effective way of enforcing discipline and maintaining his authority. If any of us grumbled at the lateness of receiving his news, or its quality, or talked back to his autocracy, he cut us off, stopped our news, and after we had begged his pardon and promised never to repeat our offense, he would let up, but fine us to the amount of the cost of the news as if we had received it.
>
> When I embarked on published a morning daily paper in Cleveland in 1852, I found the Craig rule sharply enforced, including one which cut off any paper which became delinquent in paying its bills for the telegraph news. I was sometimes more bothered in obeying the last-named rule than any of the others. When advertisers were slow in paying their bills, I had to "shin round" for the money with which to pay Craig, for to go to press without his news, thin and scanty as it was, would be to go broke and suspend publication. . . .[71]

CRAIG INFILTRATES TELEGRAPHY

From time to time, Craig roused himself when a telegraphic opportunity came along that might benefit either him personally or his

AP business. Such was the case with the Hughes telegraph instrument, which was leverage he could bring to bear on telegraph companies for the benefit of his news operation. But Craig's involvement in telegraphy went well beyond owning a piece of the Hughes device, or enlisting news clients through contracts with telegraph companies. By the early 1850s there was talk of an Atlantic cable, and by mid-decade Western Union and the American Telegraph Company were emerging as telegraph's two giant monopolies. If Craig was to keep his news reports flowing freely in and out of New York City, especially those important foreign dispatches, Craig would have to involve himself directly in telegraphy's business. He would have to determine which of the giants had the better chance of eventual success, both with a cable to Europe and with eliminating domestic competition, and throw his considerable weight behind his chosen ally.

There is no evidence that his New York AP newspaper patrons participated in Craig's telegraphic forays in any way. We saw in chapter 3 that in October 1848 when Henry O'Rielly announced his intention to neutralize F. O. J. Smith's New York–to–Boston telegraph monopoly with a line of his own, O'Rielly received only a covert promise from the AP secretary that he would get AP's news business "for at least six months"—nothing more, no financial assistance from the city's press lords to erect poles and wires. The New York editors did, of course, pump considerable money into contracts with telegraph companies along the North Atlantic coast to guarantee priority delivery of foreign news dispatches. Jones estimates these dispatches' annual cost to AP at between $25,000 and $30,000, almost all of it for telegraph tolls. In the fall of 1850 AP requested the Magnetic Telegraph Company to release one of its four lines between New York City and Washington, D.C., for AP's exclusive use. Although the company's directors failed to act on the request, this first leased news wire on so heavily used a route where so few lines existed no doubt would have cost AP's New York members substantially.[72]

The AP editors in New York City, thus, were willing to spend heavily on weekly telegraphic tolls, but, except for a short telegraph line between Manhattan and Sandy Hook, they would not own or invest in telegraphic lines as a group, even though in the long run it might have proved the cheaper, and surely would have been the more secure, course of action. Cornell on July 14, 1851, approached the AP editors for a loan to complete construction of his Erie and Michigan line, projected to serve Ohio, Indiana, Illinois, and Michigan from a terminus in Buffalo. Responding on August 29, however, AP secretary K. S. Townsend wrote Cornell that after due deliberation the AP declined to grant the loan, "on the ground that it was a subject foreign to the real object of the Press of New York in associating together for the purpose of obtaining news." This apparently had not been the first such proposal, because Townsend commented to Cornell that "All matters of this kind has [*sic*] been avoided heretofore as beyond their power, as an association."[73]

On the other hand, there is no evidence that these editors either encouraged or discouraged Craig's personal involvement in telegraphic development. His first telegraphic outing, coming soon after he was installed as AP's general agent, was to erect a line of telegraph between Sandy Hook and Manhattan to expedite the delivery of foreign news dispatches carried by ships approaching New York harbor. Telegraph historian Reid implies that Craig received financial help for this venture from the AP newspapers, which may have seen this project simply as an extension of their 1849 Harbor News Association agreement. To this harbor news line Craig added his own trademark—homing pigeons, which flew to the Sandy Hook telegraph terminus from AP's newsboats intercepting inbound ships beyond the Narrows. AP relied on this system, which was Craig's property, until the Atlantic cable was successful in 1866.[74]

In 1853 the New York AP editors faced a Craig proposal to purchase the faltering Commercial telegraph line between New York and Boston. This was House's Boston & New York Printing Telegraph Company line, which had assisted the AP after the autumn of 1849 in overcoming F. O. J. Smith's Morse monopoly on that route. Craig's proposal had special significance. By 1853 the courts had declared the Bain instrument an infringement on the Morse patent and had swept Bain lines into the Morse family, including O'Rielly's New York–Boston line, the New York & New England Telegraph Company. The result of this marriage, consummated on July 1, 1852, was the New York and New England Union Telegraph Company with Morse people holding two-thirds interest and Bain people holding the remaining third. This left only House's Commercial line to compete with two Morse-operated lines between the two cities.

November of 1852 found Craig negotiating, perhaps half-heartedly, with Marshall Lefferts of the new Union company for transmission of AP dispatches over the Union's lines. The two men could not settle on a weekly rate for delivery of the AP report to Boston's evening papers—they were five dollars per week apart—

and Lefferts reported to his board of directors on December 14, 1852, that

> It is unnecessary...to explain the reasons why the
> [Associated Press] of New York took from us their business,
> and compelled the Boston Association to do the same.... It
> cannot fail to be perceived that [in negotiations with Craig]
> we have done every thing that could be reasonably expected
> from the Company, and to have gone further would have
> shown a want of knowledge of what was just towards us, and
> a sense of proper dignity.[75]

The company had even proposed that Craig alternate transmission of his report between the Union and Commercial lines each week, but Craig, in the end, held out for an extremely low rate, knowing that the Commercial was also there to move his report.

But that was not totally consoling knowledge. Craig knew that the Commercial line might fall into the hands of Freeman M. Edson and Robert W. Russell, who Craig feared would make arrangements with the Union people to create a new Morse monopoly between New York City and Boston. Russell had even made public statements favoring union among the telegraph companies, and, as later events would reveal (and perhaps Craig knew as early as 1853), Russell violently opposed the growing AP news monopoly.[76]

In any event, lean receipts and faulty equipment continued to plague the Commercial line. It declared bankruptcy in 1852, was reorganized and renovated by new owners, but still did not pay expenses. The owners, therefore, offered the line to the New York AP for $40,000.[77] Craig urged the AP papers to accept but was forced to report that although the New York editors "had two long sessions to consider my programme," they decided that telegraphing was outside the association's business. Thirty years later Craig observed:

> Had they assented to my wishes, the Western Union
> Telegraph Company would have been buried in its infancy, or,
> if permitted to live, it would have been as the tail to the
> Associated Press' kite, instead of the Association's being in
> that relation to the Western Union Company as it is....[78]

On July 23, 1853, Craig and two associates, John McKinney and Charles Spear, purchased the Commercial line to Boston, and soon thereafter the East and West, Troy and Boston, and Nahant and Boston lines, all tributaries of the Commercial and worked with House instruments. Craig had a half-interest in all the acquisitions;

the purchases were made expressly in the interest of the Associated Press.[79]

Purchase of telegraph lines to ensure his employers' receipt of news and his own power in Boston was an extreme, even if eventually profitable, step for Craig, but the general agent's infiltration of telegraphy continued. Craig became intimately associated with the Atlantic cable movement at an early date both to protect AP interests and for personal gain.

At the age of thirty-three, Cyrus W. Field[80] retired from the wholesale paper business in 1852 with a modest fortune, and, casting about for investment potential, he became intrigued with the possibilities of a submarine cable between the United States and England.[81] It is not clear how, but Craig gained the confidence of Field and his associates and, along with his newsbrokerage, continually figured in the plans and arrangements of Field's enterprise, right up to the 1866 success of the cable.

Field began his cable venture on May 8, 1854, by forming the New York, Newfoundland & London Electric Telegraph Company, incorporated in Newfoundland for the purposes of landing a transatlantic cable on that province's eastern shore and constructing a land-and-submarine link southwestward from the cable head to Halifax, connecting with the then-completed Canadian and American telegraph system. Reid indicates that Craig owned stock in this company although it was voted by proxy.[82]

Field and his associates next formed the American Telegraph Company in New York state on November 1, 1855, to assemble and operate a U.S. telegraph network as a feeder system for the cable. They planned to lease existing House and Morse-Bain lines wherever possible rather than construct lines among Eastern commercial centers. For their plan to work, the Field people needed leverage to force telegraph proprietors to release their lines to Field under lease. A chaotic telegraphic scene in the mid-1850s with too many proprietors making too little profit, even after elimination of the Bain system, might have been reason enough. But Craig administered the coup de grâce for Field with a two-pronged attack. First, he unleashed through the Eastern press a merciless anti-Morse propaganda campaign, discrediting the Morse system's operation as shoddy and attacking the effectiveness of the Morse instrument. Second, and shortly after the press attack began, Craig publicly introduced the Hughes instrument he had unearthed. Telegraph historian Robert Luther Thompson has aptly captured the subtle relationship between Craig and Field at this moment.

> Craig...now attempted by means of a flood of propaganda
> and vilification to discredit the Morse patent and the
> companies operating under it. While Field and his colleagues
> emphatically denied any association with the press campaign
> of Craig, they exhibited a lively interest in the new [Hughes]
> printer....[83]

Thus on November 1, 1855, the same day the American Telegraph Company was born, the Field interests and Craig's Commercial telegraph company purchased the rights to the Hughes instrument for $100,000. And as Craig's press campaign for Hughes and Field and against Morse and Kendall continued, the American company began receiving early in 1856 the line leases it needed so badly. It leased the Maine Telegraph Company (Portland to Calais) on January 1, 1856; it acquired leasing rights to the New Brunswick line (St. Stephens to Sackville) in February 1856; and on May 30, 1856, it leased the Commercial line from New York to Boston from Craig and his associates.[84] (Two years later American bought the Commercial from Craig.)[85] The Hughes instrument was shortly introduced on all the leased American lines and in the succeeding months was improved and refined to the point that it was granted a patent on September 23, 1857.

While he worked his way closer to the emerging locus of power in Eastern telegraphy, Craig worked his propaganda machine in the West. When the Morse people were the common enemy of both the American company in the East and the Western Union lines in the West, Craig could beat the same drum in both regions, as this Craig letter to Western Union's Ezra Cornell on August 2, 1857, indicates.

> I judge that we shall soon see the western lines
> co-operating with the Am[erican] Co. & part-owners of the
> Hughes patent—and on the other side, we shall see Fog
> Smith, old Fogey Kendall, Drunken blackguard [William M.]
> Swain & that party in opposition. This is as it should be, and
> the result cannot be doubtful nor be long delayed. Telegraph
> matters look better to me than they ever did before. The old
> fogies of the Morse party must go by the board. They have
> disgraced themselves and cursed the business quite long
> enough.
>
> Swain is frothing mad & old Kendall is *virtuously*
> indignant! Poor old superannuated fool!...
>
> P.S. I *repeat* to you that the Hughes invention has been
> proved to be *fully* up to the representations of Hughes and
> his friends in every single particular.... Don't you believe

anybody but *me* in regard to the Hughes machine. I *never*
lie.[86]

Meanwhile Field's cable plans matured. A telegraphic link between Halifax and St. John's, Newfoundland, involving four hundred miles of land lines and submarine cable at a cost of more than
$800,000, was completed in the summer of 1856. In England Field
had formed the Atlantic Telegraph Company, selling there, at one
thousand pounds each, 262 of the 350 shares issued. Finally the
first attempt at a cable-laying came in the summer of 1857—at the
same time that an American Telegraph Company-inspired Treaty of
the Six Nations against the Morse interests was consummated. (The
Alliance is discussed in chapter 6.) After three hundred eighty miles
of cable had been laid westward from Valentia Bay, Ireland, the line
snapped, leaving Field to plan for another try the next summer. On
June 25, 1858, ships from each side of the Atlantic met in mid-
ocean, spliced their cables, and departed for their respective shores.
After eighty miles, the cable broke, and the ships returned to their
meeting point, respliced, and tried again. This time two hundred
miles of cable were paid out before the cable snapped. Finally on
July 17 the ships met once more in the mid-Atlantic, spliced their
lines, and headed for both shores. On the evening of August 4, 1858,
England and America were finally linked by cable.[87]

Craig and his Associated Press enjoyed preferential treatment by
the Field people during this first Atlantic cable's short life. Americans first learned of the successful cable-laying in the afternoon
press on August 5 from a dispatch telegraphed by Field at Trinity
Bay, Newfoundland, directly to the Associated Press in New York
City. According to several accounts, Field preceded this dispatch to
the AP only with personal telegrams to his family, advising them of
his safe arrival at Newfoundland.[88]

The *New York Herald* the next morning spread a collection of
news items, backgrounders, reaction pieces, diagrams of the cable
and the ocean floor, and lists of the ships' crews across all six
columns of both its first and second pages. The paper editorialized,

> We look confidently forward to the time when the Herald
> will contain, besides its local and city intelligence and
> advertisements, nothing but a mass of faithful telegraphic
> reports of the events in the whole world of the present day,
> with our editorial comments thereon.

But protocol dictated that news take a back seat to queens and presidents, as the *Herald* noted: "No news can be obtained of affairs on the other side until the message of Queen Victoria and President Buchanan has been transmitted and the reply sent."[89]

Meanwhile Craig ordered AP agents from New York City to Trinity Bay to relinquish use of the lines the night of August 5 to allow Field to file progress reports or to get on with ceremonial exchanges of messages between the two heads of government. Except for some domestic reaction dispatches, all Craig could garner from the event for his August 6 news report for the evening papers was a three-paragraph congratulatory telegram from President Buchanan to Field.[90]

Tests on the cable proceeded slowly, and Field attempted to placate an increasingly impatient public with messages telegraphed to the AP for distribution to the papers.[91] Not until the evening of August 16 did Queen Victoria's message to Buchanan flash through the cable, down the coast, and into the Washington office of Associated Press. Many, including the President, doubted the authenticity of the message. The tone of the *New York Sun*'s coverage of the message was typical.

> We received last night and publish to-day what purports to be the message of Queen Victoria, congratulating the President of the United States on the successful completion of the Atlantic telegraph. We are assured that the message is genuine, and that it came through the Atlantic cable. It is not surprising, however, that the President, on receiving it, doubted its genuineness, as among the hundred who crowded our office last evening the doubters largely preponderated.[92]

If the detached observer had his doubts, consider the plight of the Buchanan administration, which did not want to be caught publicly replying to a telegraphic hoax. AP's Lawrence Gobright describes the scene at the White House that night.

> [The President] sent for me, and I repaired to the White House, where I found all the members of the Cabinet talking over the matter and speculating as to whether telegrams *could* be sent by cable!
> Secretary [of the Treasury Howell] Cobb, lying on a sofa, disbelieved everything of the kind; but the majority of them were less incredulous. Mr. Buchanan asked a number of questions, wanting to be certain that the Queen had sent him the message. He was properly exercised as to its truth, not wishing to show his gallantry in the absence of a proper

invitation to do so; in other words, he was afraid of being "hoaxed." I satisfied him that he ran no risk in responding to the lady. Then he showed me what he had written, and read it to me. . . . He then asked me how I liked it, and I replied in terms that pleased him. . . . Mr. Buchanan again read it, and finally he handed it to me, to be telegraphed to Her Majesty. "It is yours," he said.[93]

Gobright sent Buchanan's reply through the AP system to the North American cable head.

While this ceremonial exchange created some news, the first actual news dispatch arrived in New York on August 26. Datelined Valentia, August 25, it appeared two days later in the New York morning press, delayed because the Nova Scotia line had closed its Halifax office early, holding up transmission of the dispatch until the next morning. This first cable news dispatch appeared in the New York City papers Friday morning, August 27, 1858, and consisted of six short paragraphs. Ironically, it noted the pending departure of the Cunarder *Asia* "with the mails for Halifax and Boston," as if the cable had not the power to supplant the old transatlantic steam and mail services for news movement.

Between 1851 and the brief success of the 1858 Atlantic cable, Craig relied for most of his foreign papers on brief summaries prepared and mailed by his London agent and on European newspapers, including such news compendiums as *Willmer & Smith's European Times*. Robert W. Desmond reports, however, that in 1857 England's Reuters news agency and the New York AP struck an agreement to exchange their raw news dispatches,[94] thus augmenting each newsbrokerage's flow of transatlantic newspapers. There is no evidence that this arrangement was converted to a telegraphed exchange while the 1858 cable operated. Steamer exchanges of Reuters and AP dispatches continued throughout the Civil War. A more permanent telegraph news exchange among the leading international newsbrokerages, and including the New York AP as a second-class participant, was finally established in 1870 when the international "Ring Combination" was formed (see Volume 2).

The nation celebrated the new cable on September 1, and the papers on September 2 were full of accounts of "the cable carnival," processions, "glorious recognition," "the metropolis overwhelmed with visitors," "a bouquet in every window," and the like. But by the time of this celebration, the signals on the cable had faded into silence, this first cable having handled only 269 messages from the United States and ninety-seven from England. The celebration therefore was followed by public derision of Field, who, although the Civil War would intervene, persevered and opened a permanently successful transatlantic cable to the public in 1866.

When the cable fell silent, Craig scampered around to protect his foreign news flow by linking Field's coastal network with Cunard steamer crossings. He leased the Newfoundland-Halifax line from Field, extending it from St. John's to Cape Race (the Cunarder's Newfoundland landfall) where he maintained news boats to intercept westbound steamers.[95] A press description of AP's postcable foreign news operation, dated November 27, 1858, gives this picture:

> The Associated Press has an agent at Liverpool who, upon the departure of each steamer...places in the hands of the purser a tin cylindrical can, containing the latest news prepared for transmission by telegraph. These cans are thrown overboard on the appearance of the news boats stationed off [New York, Halifax, St. John's, Quebec, or Portland]....[S]teamers are frequently overhauled off Cape Race by the steamer Victoria, employed by the associated press. If at night, rockets are fired by the steamers, and the news dispatches, enclosed in a keg, are thrown over, so that the Victoria can pick them up....[96]

This system was continued until completion of the successful Atlantic cable in 1866, and on that cable the AP would also occupy a favored position.

The suspension of Abbot & Winans, Craig's direct involvement in telegraphy even though his patron editors felt that telegraphy was "beyond their power, as an association," and improvements in the news report had made AP by late 1858 a power to be reckoned with in both journalistic and telegraphic circles. A contemporary account of AP's operation in 1858 gives the following overview:

> Our telegraphic Association has agents in every important city in this country, and intelligent European correspondents; its news yachts are stationed at every point where it may be possible to intercept a steamer; and during the session of Congress, the reports of its proceedings by the able reporters of the Association, are doubtless the only ones that are read outside of the political world. Virtually, it collects, at an annual expenditure, all told, of over one hundred thousand dollars, the fullest and most reliable news from every quarter of the globe.... The bills of the entire association are properly audited by members of the press, duly elected for

that purpose, and the whole sum collected is expended for
the legitimate purpose, the reporters and other employees
receiving reasonable, but by no means extravagant, salaries
for their labor.[97]

Extravagant salaries or not, with so many pies to dip his fingers
into, Craig was one AP employee who realized considerable personal wealth from his affiliation with the newsbrokerage. R. G. Dun
& Co. credit notations on Craig during his AP tenure are revealing.

> June 28, 1858,...a shrewd, sinewy, indefatigable man,
> receiving a large salary, now supposed to be well off, is
> engaged in various schemes for making money.... [H]e
> gen[eral]ly looks out for "No.1"; it is difficult to get from him
> any am[oun]t wh[ich] he regards as a loss....
> April 3, 1860,...Owns a handsome house in Brooklyn
> wh[ich] he has just built and owns stock in the "American
> Telegraph Co." as does also his wife. She is w[orth] from
> 40,000 to 50,000 $ and reg[arde]d good for any engagement
> he is likely to make.
> June 10, 1866,...Agent of Assoc. Press, gets a go[od]
> salary and has go[od] chances of making money and is a
> successful man. Owns largely of Telegraph Stock and is
> w[orth] very probably 75 to 100,000 $ and quite reliable.[98]

THE EDITORS PERFECT THEIR PARTNERSHIP

Meanwhile, the New York morning newspapers that sponsored his
activities stood on the sidelines reaping the news benefit of Craig's
private schemes. The editors' only sign of progress during this period was to formally recast and consolidate their two earlier partnership agreements—the Harbor News Association of January 11, 1849,
and the telegraphic and general news associations of pre-September
18, 1851—into a comprehensive, tightly structured association.
Adopted on October 21, 1856, the "Regulations of the General News
Association of the City of New York," as the new partnership agreement was called, spelled out in detail the regulations among the
seven AP papers, the AP staff, and other papers receiving AP
news.[99] How many of these rules and restrictions were carried forward from the 1851 agreement, of course, cannot be determined
without a copy of the earlier document, but as we shall see in Volume 2 these rules, with a few significant amendments, were still in
force in 1874. Below is a summary of the 1856 agreement's provisions, organized topically:

Officers—president, secretary, and executive committee elected by and serving during the pleasure of a majority of New York AP partners. (Incumbents' terms were to continue: Gerard Hallock, president; Moses S. Beach, secretary; and George H. Andrews and Frederic Hudson, executive committee.)

Executive Committee—duties were (1) to audit the association's accounts, bills, and expenses; (2) to withhold news from parties in arrears; (3) to supervise the general agent and marine news collector; (4) to make all regulations necessary for the reception of news; (5) to designate the times when various types of news reports could be published; and (6) to enter contracts on behalf of the association.

General Agent—chosen by the association and paid by the week for his services. His duties were (1) "to receive all Telegraphic communications for the Association, and to transmit them immediately, by manifold copies, to each of the parties who may be entitled to receive the same"; (2) "to provide for the reception and immediate delivery, to each paper, of all Telegraphic despatches arriving at any hour of the day or night"; (3) to "collect the weekly bills of tolls and other expenses—after having submitted them to such auditor or committee as may be appointed for the purpose by the Association—and when collected, shall attend to the payment of all bills and accounts after they shall have been approved"; (4) "to keep a regular account of his outlays and incomes for the inspection of the members of the Association"; and (5) to "perform such other duties connected with the Telegraphic business of the Association as the Executive Committee may direct."

Marine News Collector—appointed by the association and paid by the week for his services. His duties were (1) "to collect all marine and other news, which may transpire at the port of New York, and transmit the same by manifold copies" to the association members; (2) to complete a weekly statement of all expenses incident to the duties assigned to him to be submitted to the association for payment; (3) "to make efficient arrangements for the prompt delivery of all packages of newspapers and other news, which may arrive at this port addressed to any members of the Association"; and (4) to "perform such other duties connected with the collection and delivery of the Marine and other harbor news of the port as the Association or the Executive Committee may from time to time direct."

Correspondents—shall be stationed at Washington and

Albany "to furnish, by telegraph or otherwise, the Congressional and Legislative proceedings," and shall be appointed at such other places as may be designated by the executive committee.

New Members—"No new member shall be admitted to this Association, without the unanimous consent of all the parties hereto; but the news obtained may be sold to other parties, for the general benefit of the Association, on the vote of six-sevenths of its members."

Withdrawal of Members—"Any member . . . may withdraw . . . by giving six months previous notice, in writing, and paying up his proportion of any expenses and debts owing by the Association up to the day of his withdrawal." No member may dispose of his interest in the small boats and other association property to any other person than the other members of the association without the unanimous and written consent of the other members. If a member indicates a wish to dispose of his association property, "it shall be the duty of the other members to purchase the same at two-thirds of its value," relying on three appraisers, "selected in the usual way." Only visible property will be appraised, "but not any supposed value in the share itself."

Liability—"Expenses occasioned by or growing out of the arrangements of this Association, shall be borne, in equal proportions" by the members, except for the following: (1) special reports, ordered through the general agent by one member (but under AP rules available to all members), will be paid for by those members accepting those reports for publication; (2) members declining regular segments of the daily news report "as they think proper" will not be assessed for such declined news; and (3) only papers with Sunday editions will be assessed for news reports received too late for Saturday publication and before regular Monday deadlines.

Nonpayment of Bills—Parties failing to pay an AP bill beyond one week after presentation will have their news report cut off at the discretion of the executive committee, but will be responsible for the expense of the cut-off report as if it were delivered. After thirty days of nonpayment "the defaulting . . . parties shall forfeit all rights pertaining to this Association."

Nonintercourse—"No party receiving news from this Association shall enter into any arrangement with rival Telegraphic news agents in this or any other city, or with any person in their employ, nor shall they receive from them any

Telegraphic news, from Washington, Albany, or any other part of the country, nor shall such parties, nor any persons not connected with this Association, be permitted to avail themselves of the facilities of the Association, for the reception of California or European newspapers, circulars, or other intelligence arriving at this or any other port."

Members' Enterprise—News received by individual members from their own correspondents by telegraph or special express regarding California, Europe, election returns, or other events must be tendered to the other members of the association for their use as well. Exceptions to this rule are: "reports of conventions, political meetings, trials, executions, public dinners, sporting intelligence and the legislative proceedings of other States" and the telegraphic dispatches of members' separate correspondents in Washington and Albany.

Noncompliance—If a member violates a rule of the association, "and shall continue to do so after being remonstrated with by a committee appointed by this Association for that purpose, or a majority of the members, the other associates shall have the right to exclude him from the Association, and take possession of his interest in the property of the Association" at two-thirds of appraised value. "This provision shall not apply to an honest difference of opinion as to the meaning of any rule or article; but in case of such honest difference of opinion, a majority of votes shall decide what the meaning is" and "the member or members in the minority shall acquiesce, and govern themselves accordingly."

Clearly this was a rigid, yet delicately balanced, covenant. The partners held themselves, each other, and the rest of the subscribing newspaper press in check, using as leverage the worth and uniqueness of the daily news report generated by the partners' employees. Each original member had little room to maneuver without the approval of his partners. The AP staff was constantly audited financially and journalistically. Upstart New York City newspaper competitors could not join the partnership without unanimous consent of the original seven, and nonmember clients of the AP service needed a six-sevenths approval to get the report. This provision was enacted roughly a year after Abbot & Winans abandoned operations, a year during which Craig added the bulk of AP's nonmember subscribers.

Members wishing to leave AP could sell their interests to an outsider only with unanimous consent of the other six, but more likely, the other six would take possession of the withdrawing member's interests at two-thirds of their face value. They expressly disallowed any value attaching itself to the membership, hoping to forestall bargaining on the name of the association. This was successful in New York City, but it failed miserably elsewhere. As we shall see, the value of a membership in a regional AP would soon be routinely measured monetarily when newspapers were being bought and sold. The nonintercourse provisions, in the absence of a competing newsbrokerage, were intended to discourage partners from striking out on their own and additionally to discourage the development of other such agencies.

Perhaps the most fascinating limitations, however, were imposed on the partners' own journalistic enterprise. Except for some specific types of dispatches—Washington and Albany correspondence, reports on conventions, political meetings, trials, executions, public dinners, sports and legislative proceedings in other states—the members were prohibited from securing and using telegraphic news dispatches without offering them to their morning partners in the association. Implied here, it seems, is the fear that among the partners lurked some aggressive news-gatherers whose individual efforts might heat up the old news-gathering war that had proved so expensive and unsettling to the combatants. The fear was strong enough to make the partners state expressly what *could* be done independently of the AP, rather than to state, as one might expect, what the partners expected of the AP, leaving the rest unsaid and up to individual initiative. These fears achieved additional bylaw expression in the decade following the Civil War when the postwar fracture of the membership into four weaker papers and three potentially aggressive papers turned this nonenterprise rule into a source of internal friction and public derision for the New York AP.

One glimpses here a structure for mutual protection that insulated the partners against the icy blasts of journalistic misfortune. These partners would be served by *their* news apparatus in all seasons according to *their* policies, and any other editor, with *their* permission, could accept and live with what these partners offered as news. The alternative was to attempt to survive largely in telegraphic isolation from the news events of the day. Craig's news monopoly was in place when this partnership was signed, and this document, from 1856 forward to the absorption of the partnership by the old United Press in 1893, advertised AP's New York City press to the journalism fraternity as both impenetrable and fearful. The powerful or well-established journals would control the flow of telegraphic news through their city, a center of finance, commerce, transportation, and communication, and their control would be jealously withheld from newcomers. At the same time these leading and powerful journalistic lights would settle for a common dispatch of daily news and limit the brightness with which each other's journalistic enterprise might shine.

DISCUSSION

When it moved its patronage from AP to Abbot & Winans in 1851, the *Boston Evening Transcript* editorially chirped, "Business is business, Mr. Craig." He did not need to be reminded, for seldom has journalism harbored a craftier, more determined businessman than Daniel H. Craig, not only in the business of journalism, where he developed an effective system for gathering, processing, and delivering a daily news report on a large scale, but in the business of telegraphy, where luck as well as cunning and capital mattered. Craig beat his journalistic competitors with muscle and money and held the advantage with vigilance and an improved news report. Meanwhile he boldly approached the telegraphic arena, where too many combatants were flailing each other mercilessly, chose his allies carefully, and entered the games with a new weapon—the Hughes instrument—that tipped the scales in his chosen allies' direction.

In any age this would be no mean accomplishment, but in the decade before the Civil War, the "golden age" of new small business, when someone with a new idea, a modest stipend, and a little luck could strike it rich, but when many practiced business sharply, shrewdly, and recklessly, Craig's feat was even more remarkable. Beyond a moment's applause for this newsbroking legend, what, in the end, can be made of Craig's first few years at AP? To some historians the story of powerful Eastern editors assuming a judiciously low profile while the bullying, sharp-tongued general agent of their partnership built a news monopoly for them represents business as usual where raucous, vicious, profit-oriented capitalism stalks like a predator among its potential prey, unrestrained by ethics or government. Other historians will, by smoothing Craig's rough edges and concentrating on the press leadership exercised by his patron editors, those esteemed public servants and men of vision, recognize in Craig another milestone in journalism's long journey toward press perfectibility and social significance.

Viewed from an institutional perspective, however, Craig presided over the critical early stages of structural growth. A pragmatic and combative presence, Craig contributed the driving force from within journalism to extend AP's frontier to the outer limits of the daily press and to supervise and perfect AP's vital processes. This, however, required him also to transport his talents into telegraphy, on which newsbroking vitally depended. Alexander Jones stood on the sidelines observing and writing about telegraphy's growth; Craig jumped in and helped shape telegraphy's growth. While Craig's unique abilities and his seemingly firm allegiance to journalism vouchsafed a newspaper-controlled newsbrokerage, at least for the moment, his patron New York City editors contributed a firm, even iron-clad, partnership to the emerging structure. The regularizing of financial and news product functions began in the Jones years, but perhaps with the 1851 agreement, and surely the 1856 "regulations," these functions were joined by politically self-limiting, yet enfranchising, accords among the editors that lent stability and protection to AP's processes.

The outcome might easily have been otherwise on the eve of the Civil War; the nine or ten years of conflicts and confrontations for AP of New York City thus far discussed suggest alternative scenarios that might have dramatically altered newsbroking history. If Craig had fought both the press and the telegraph with his assortment of expresses and pigeons, independent newsbroking might have gained strength along the North Atlantic coastline and might have thrived under independent contracts with telegraphy, at least for a while. Had Abbot & Winans or F. O. J. Smith possessed Craig's acumen and drive, or if Craig had not had those qualities as AP general agent, telegraphy's foothold in newsbroking might have been assured. In either case journalism's course would have been more difficult when and if it later decided to take control of newsbroking.

Those who view these alternatives as merely academic are either too conscious and accepting of newsbroking's subsequent history or unmindful of the business climate in which Craig and his editors operated. Ends justified means; the only end for most was wealth, acquired as quickly as possible, even at the expense of one's own corporation. As Henry Steele Commager put it, "Whatever promised to increase wealth was automatically regarded as good, and the American was tolerant, therefore, of speculation, advertising, deforestation, and the exploitation of natural resources. . . ."[100] The nineteenth-century American "resented government interference with private enterprise," Commager continues, "far more than private interference with government enterprise."[101] F. O. J. Smith's bid for newsbroking dominance is recalled by this Commager comment: "It was easier to skim the cream off the soil, the forests, the mines—or business investments—and go on to something new, especially when new was so often synonymous with better."[102]

Rather than the dark side of human nature, this was the bright side of sharp new business practice. "Face-to-face personal transactions and well-known business associates," Leonard D. White observes, "were giving way to impersonal dealings with banks and corporations, and with men in distant cities and of unknown character."

> The temptations to ruthless and unscrupulous operations
> in the business world were constantly greater as rich prizes
> in railroad construction, shipping, and manufacturing took
> shape.... The decline in morals was accelerated by the
> impersonal life of city dwellers, as traditional village and
> small-town existence gave way to the anonymity of urban
> life.... [103]

If New York City newspaper editors could devise personal horse, locomotive, and coastal steamer expresses, thereby replacing the postal service, express companies, and portions of the transportation system in the pretelegraph days, then Theodore Faxton, the Morse interests, and F. O. J. Smith, armed with vital technology, could replace journalism in its own long-distance news-gathering practices. The struggle over control of newsbroking in the decade preceding the Civil War—a struggle we again encounter in the next chapter—reflects the fluidity of business practice in general then and the uncertainty attending new technologies and intercity news movement in particular.

The superior position of the established New York City press attracted the newsbroking services of Craig, who, in turn, further strengthened his patron editors' hand in the news field. Newsbrokers employed by and allied with telegraphic interests stood reasonably little chance of representing these leading journals during Alexander Jones's administration, and virtually none once Craig was in control. The deciding factors were the journals' habitual desire to conduct their own news-gathering enterprise, backed up by inordinate financial strength and national esteem. The same cannot be said for the newspapers of the New York State AP between Albany and Buffalo; geographically dispersed, financially middling, respected largely only within their communities, they could be arbitrarily delivered into the hands of Abbot & Winans by the proprietor of the telegraph line that was their link with the world beyond their communities.

Developments swirling around newsbroking between 1859 and 1866 would continue to threaten the newspaper-controlled newsbrokerage, as the next two chapters and Volume 2 indicate. Well after the Civil War one finds newsbroker leaders still fretting about the possibility of a takeover by Western Union. Craig's and journalism's newsbroking strength relied in large part on unsettled conditions in telegraphy, but as telegraphy consolidated itself and began amassing corporate and territorial strength, the New York City journals had to assume a more conciliatory posture toward the emerging technological giant in order to preserve their national news apparatus.

the principal East Coast trunk routes had begun to unnerve proprietors of many independent or regionally dominant telegraph companies. Representatives of four concerned telegraph companies—the Magnetic, the New York, Albany & Buffalo, the New York & New England Union, and Western Union—were invited by Amos Kendall to a meeting in New York City on June 30, 1857, to draw up an offensive-defensive pact protecting the four companies' territories from encroachment by others, discouraging further competition among lines, and requiring each company to connect exclusively with the lines of other signers of the agreement. Except for the Western Union, the contingent was dominated by Morse interests. Kendall hoped that such an agreement would present a united front to American's aggressive moves.

When the principals gathered, however, Kendall found the American, the New Orleans & Ohio Telegraph Company, and the Illinois & Mississippi Telegraph Company also in attendance, although uninvited. Undaunted, Kendall pushed ahead with his plan and by the second day participants had hammered out a proposal that the delegates were to take back to their respective boards for ratification. Throughout the two-day meeting the American said it would enter the agreement only if the other companies would help it purchase the Hughes patent. Seeing an opportunity to bind his enemy to an agreement intended to shackle the latter, Kendall reluctantly agreed to assist in the purchase, even though he represented the competing Morse patent. The work of the meeting finished, Kendall returned to Washington, D.C., on July 1, satisfied that he had taken a stand against the American on behalf of his Morse interests.[4]

But a select group of telegraph representatives stayed on in New York and by July 7 had drawn up a second agreement, the "Treaty of the Six Nations" (also called the "Six-Party Contract"). Telegraph historian Robert Luther Thompson characterizes this select group as "carefully chosen delegates," bent on "a revolt of second generation telegraphers against the pioneers." At the instigation of Western Union, according to Thompson, a "concerted effort was on foot to rid the industry of 'Amos the pious' and the 'fraudulent Fog'," referring respectively to Amos Kendall and F. O. J. Smith.[5] A thirty-year treaty requiring annual meetings, the Six-Party Contract divided the United States to the western borders of Minnesota, Iowa, Missouri, Arkansas, and Louisiana among six telegraph companies—the American; the Atlantic & Ohio Telegraph Company; the New York, Albany & Buffalo; Western Union; the New Orleans & Ohio; and the Illinois & Mississippi.[6]

The companies were granted exclusive operation in their assigned territories (except for a few designated lines of one "nation" intruding upon another's territory), and were required to traffic exclusively among themselves. Finally, the contract bound all six companies to share in the purchase of the Hughes instrument, a total cost of $56,000 with American shouldering 45 percent of that price tag.[7] The American's territory under this contract coincided with Morse companies' lucrative seaboard and southern circuits. Purchase of the Hughes instrument (superior by all accounts to Morse's or House's) by all six "nations" meant its eventual introduction in telegraphy throughout the nation. Samuel F. B. Morse, Kendall, Smith, and their patent would thus be excluded from most of the country's telegraphic business.

Looking around, Kendall found only Smith's New York & New England Union company, an old Morse company, as an ally. Long-standing animosity between Kendall and Smith was forgotten in the face of younger telegraph associates' duplicity, and together the Morse leaders moved briskly to invade the western and southern states and the Canadian Maritime provinces with new lines. The Kendall-Smith scheme, unaffected by the noncompetitive provisions of the Six-Party Contract, was to challenge the six "nations" with competing circuits along key routes everywhere east of the Mississippi River. At the same time Kendall lent support to the transatlantic cable project of Tal. P. Shaffner, who intended to link England and North America by hopscotching from northern Scotland to Iceland, Greenland, and Labrador[8] in competition with Field's Atlantic cable venture. Such a show of force on all fronts would either bring the six "nations" back to the negotiating table or sustain Morse interests through the protracted competition ahead.[9]

By October 20, 1858, when the six "nations" convened for their first annual meeting, they were already feeling pressure from Kendall and Smith. The American company had moved too slowly to erect and acquire lines along the East Coast; Field had by this time failed twice to lay an Atlantic cable; and western telegraph companies, unaccustomed to serious competition, feared Kendall's encroachment on their territory. The six "nations" reorganized as the North American Telegraph Association, admitting the Montreal Telegraph Company as the seventh partner on equal terms with the first six. But principally the new association determined that peace with Kendall-Smith must be secured with all reasonable speed.

Tortuous, complex negotiations between the association and

should take over all news-gathering and news-selling activities along its circuits,[20] and it appeared that Johnson and Zabriskie would become American's house newsbrokerage for achieving Russell's goal. There immediately flared up a natural animosity between Russell and Craig, and, as Reid describes it, an "insane contest" ensued.

> Russell...instinctively sought to rule. He was an Englishman, able, imperious, willful and persevering. Russell and...Craig...read fight in each other's eyes the moment they met. The cool grey eye of the New Englander, his placid assertion of power, his merciless saxon, made all the blood of the Englander hot. From that moment Russell commenced a scheme to make the telegraph company a purveyor of all news, the retailer of foreign and domestic markets, and to make the Associated Press dependent on the telegraph not only for the transmission, but the matter of its news.[21]

The Johnson and Zabriskie newsbrokerage appears to have been Russell's concoction, quite as much as E. S. Dyer was F. O. J. Smith's newsbroking creation a decade earlier.

No information has survived on Johnson and Zabriskie beyond the predictably abusive comments by Craig. In a pamphlet dated July 7, 1860, Craig calls the USAP a "bogus 'Associated Press'... consist[ing] of two individuals." Craig then unlimbers his "merciless saxon."

> Mr. Johnson has for the past ten or twelve years originated not less than from fifteen to twenty brilliant schemes for 'smashing the Associated Press machine,' in most of which schemes he has been vigorously backed up by Fog Smith and the Union line, together with [among others] all the insolvent and beggarly newspapers which have, from time to time, been kicked out of the [Associated Press] for the non-payment of their bills. Mr. Johnson has generally managed thus to raise a new hat, a pair of boots, one or two shirts, and sometimes even a coat; but always after getting largely in debt to the Telegraph Companies, quietly subsiding, and for a brief period returning to his old quarters under the shadow of the small beer shops of Philadelphia.[22]

As for Zabriskie (whose name Craig repeatedly misspells "Zabriski," similar to his habit of misspelling another competitor's name, Francis A. "Abbott") the AP general agent notes that

> The junior manager...is, I believe, a very worthy youth
> from some fishing village on the coast of New Jersey, a State
> which, the world over, is celebrated for its *land pirates*. It is
> also the congenial home of R. W. Russell.... This youth...
> who appears to have more money than brains has, according
> to his own statements, been pretty severely fleeced during
> the past year through the joint agency of Fog Smith and the
> late Halifax telegraph managers.[23]

Johnson seems to have been operating a newsbrokerage of sorts as early as December 21, 1858. On that date four Philadelphia papers, the *Inquirer, Journal, North American*, and *Press*, circulated a notice supporting an opponent to AP, claiming that it is in

> the interest of the press of this city that a permanent
> opposition should be sustained to the New York Associated
> Press. We can by this means get more reliable reports, and be
> better served. In order to do this we will join with our
> brethren of the press, if they will all combine, and pay the
> extra ten dollars per week for Congress reports to Messrs.
> Carr & Johnson, of this city, instead of paying, as at present,
> that amount for the reports furnished by the New York
> Associated Press....[24]

Johnson and the mysterious Mr. Carr appear to have had the backing of Philadelphia's press, outside of the *Public Ledger*, Swain's paper and a collaborator in NYAP's development since the days of the steamer *Buena Vista* a decade earlier.

Thus, with Johnson and Zabriskie's USAP waiting in the wings to unseat Craig and the NYAP, Russell, with a controlling majority on the American board and executive committee,[25] and his friends pushed hard early in 1860 either to bring the newsbroking business within the telegraph empire or to establish Johnson and Zabriskie as an independent competitor to Craig. The American's executive committee in late June 1860 openly expressed its opposition to AP.

> It is very clear that if we remain quiet, and allow this
> [Associated Press] monopoly to go on increasing in strength
> from day to day we shall soon find ourselves dependent for
> existence on the mere will and pleasure of the agent or
> manager of the news monopolists.[26]

Russell added his own attack on the AP.

> There is no business in this country more effectually
> secured against competition than [the American Telegraph

Company] will be after we shall have put down the monopoly
of the New York Associated Press, and that we can do to a
certainty without any difficulty whatever.[27]

When the above comments were published in mid-1860, the
American's executive committee was already well under way with
its assault on AP. On February 18, 1860, the committee terminated
the company's special contracts with the AP, increased its rates for
news dispatches for morning papers by 75 percent and those for
evening papers by 150 percent, established equality of rates between AP and non-AP newspapers, and asserted the principle of
first-come-first-served, consistent with Kendall's demand for joining the North American Telegraph Association. This bitter pill for
Craig and the AP was to take effect March 1. Historian Thompson
observes that the old rate had been too low, but these new terms for
press dispatches were "nothing less than an outright declaration of
war."[28]

Craig and the AP screamed in protest, petitioning American's full
board for relief. The board, not wanting to interfere with executive
committee action, empaneled a special committee that reviewed
the executive committee's proposed rates and declared them fair
and in effect as of April 23. The board approved the special committee's report.[29] The howls of protest went up again, freighted with
invective, dire threats, and predictions of damage to the public interest, both in the daily newspaper columns and in a series of pamphlets.[30] For each participant in the quarrel, the issue was primarily
one of survival. Russell saw the defeat of AP and telegraphic control of newsbroking as vital to American's future prosperity and
profits. Craig sought to preserve the AP monopoly he had so carefully built up over nine years. Other telegraphic officials feared either a continuation of the quarrel or a Russell victory, which might
trigger new efforts to construct competing telegraphic lines with
AP backing, thus possibly unraveling the North American Telegraph
Association cartel. From a historical perspective the argument concerned whether newsbroking would be the province of journalists
and their agents or would be controlled by the telegraph industry.

Making a last-ditch effort to modify the company's press policies,
the minority on the American board sought and received a special
board meeting on June 29. Henry J. Raymond of the *New York
Times* spoke on AP's behalf, numerous resolutions were proposed
on both sides, but in the end the meeting proved inconclusive. After
extended debate, further company policy-making regarding the

press was deferred until American's executive committee and press representatives could negotiate their differences.[31] In these private meetings, according to biographer Francis Brown, Raymond "debated long with Cyrus W. Field and others concerned with telegraph business in prolonged night sessions at the Astor, in private rooms at Delmonico's in William Street, or at Peter Cooper's brick and brownstone house off Gramercy Park."[32]

Meanwhile two of the moderate directors from the pre-1859 American company, Cyrus W. Field and Abram S. Hewitt, disgusted with the outcome of the June meeting, allowed themselves to be bought out by Russell, relinquishing their directorships. To replace them on the board, Russell handpicked Cambridge Livingston and Edwards S. Sanford, a move that would later backfire for Russell. By October 31, 1860, the American menace was ended, as Kendall reports in a letter to Morse.

> Russell is checkmated by his own moves.... Both Sanford
> and Livingston, though Directors of his own selection,...as
> soon as they understood his policy, took decided ground
> against it. The best of the joke is that he paid Field about
> $8,000 more than his stock was worth to get him out of the
> Board, and now finds the very man he selected for the place
> as much opposed to his views as Field ever was! He is now
> discouraged and proposes to sell out.[33]

In short order American's executive committee consisted of Livingston, Sanford, and Barnum, with Sanford elected president and Livingston named secretary.

So dramatic a shift in American's power balance made agreement with the Associated Press a relatively easy matter, and a decided relief to the AP people, as *New York Herald* managing editor Frederic Hudson explained more than ten years later.

> On the night of a monster torch-light procession of the
> unterrified democracy of the metropolis...there met, on an
> early November evening in 1860, at a room at Delmonico's...
> Amos Kendall, Edwards S. Sanford, Cambridge Livingston,
> and Zenas Barnum, on the part of the telegraph companies,
> and the executive committee on the part of the Associated
> Press. These gentlemen, comprehending the situation, at this
> and three or four subsequent meetings concluded a treaty
> and a contract by which the rights of the public, of the
> telegraph, and of the Press were fully recognized.... [I]n
> accomplishing this happy result too much credit can not be

given to Colonel Sanford for the efforts he made to preserve the *entente cordiale* between the telegraph and the Press.[34]

The contract does not survive, but we know that it extended for five years,[35] long enough to carry the AP through the looming Civil War.

NEW YORK ASSOCIATED PRESS'S INTERNAL CHANGES

Those anxious relations between AP and the American company during 1860 served, among other things, to solidify further Craig's ties to the Western Union. It is hardly coincidence that in 1860, despite the North American Telegraph Association compact that limited Western Union's territory to west of Pittsburgh, Western Union moved its headquarters from Rochester, N.Y., to New York City, occupying a six-story building, the Old Wilkes Building, at "Kiernan's Corner" (on the southwest corner of Wall and Broad streets.)[36] Meanwhile Craig moved AP's offices from 58 Beaver, where they had been since 1857, to 7 Broad, across Broad from Western Union and a few steps south.[37]

The next year, however, the American moved into a six-story building at 145 Broadway,[38] and that same year found Craig moving AP offices into that same building.[39] When Western Union swallowed the American company in 1866, Craig was still there, and thus began an arrangement that saw AP occupying space in two Western Union buildings along Broadway,[40] except for a brief period in the 1890s, until 1914. Beyond such superficial changes, however, AP at the start of the Civil War experienced its first serious membership changes since the *New York Times* became the seventh AP partner in 1851. The changes involved AP's three political or mercantile papers, including the two oldest newspapers in the partnership, the *Journal of Commerce* and the *Courier and Enquirer.*

The *New York World* first appeared on June 14, 1860, organized by Alexander Cummings, a successful Philadelphia journalist, supported by $200,000 from stockholders, and intending to be a highly religious, or at least a moral, morning newspaper. It shunned theater and lottery advertising, the gory details of crimes, and sensational news in general. "It advertised church and Sunday School supplies," Frank Luther Mott reports, "and was itself advertised in the backs of hymnals."[41] This editorial policy, however, could not attract sufficient readership. Hudson analyzed the paper's problems this way:

> The *World* had all the telegraphic and all the shipping
> intelligence that the other papers had, and, with its
> contemporaries, it had the world, physically and mentally,
> before it.... But the universal world was Pandora's box to
> the *New York World*. It refused to give any details of the evils
> that filled the box, and waited patiently and expensively for
> the appearance of that sleeping beauty, Hope....[42]

Hudson implies above that the *World* from the outset had secured, as a nonmember subscriber, receipt of AP's regular news report, a point in dispute in the literature,[43] but if not in 1860, surely
by mid-1861 the *World* was receiving AP's news. On July 1, 1861, the
World purchased James Watson Webb's *Courier and Enquirer*. Webb,
after over thirty years of publishing the paper, had just entered the
U.S. diplomatic service,[44] and, although the merged paper published under the title the *World and Courier and Enquirer*, the name
was soon shortened to the *World*. The acquisition, while giving the
paper full NYAP partnership privileges (reportedly at a cost of
$100,000 to the *World*),[45] did not substantially improve the paper's
situation, a feat accomplished only when Cummings relinquished
control to Democratic owners who elevated night editor Manton
Marble in 1862 to full editor and part-owner of the paper.

One month after the *World* bought the *Courier and Enquirer*,
Gerard Hallock of the pro-South *Journal of Commerce* ran afoul of
Union loyalty in the city. As historian Robert S. Harper describes it,
the Lincoln administration was in a precarious position by August
1861, after the rout of Union troops at Bull Run on July 21 and a
Confederate show of strength in Missouri and Kentucky. Northern
Democratic editors demanded an end to bloodshed by compromise,
if not full recognition of the Confederacy. These first skirmishes,
however, had quickly converted many Northerners to Lincoln supporters and had placed Northern Democratic papers in some communities at the mercy of mobs. Only in New York City and New
Jersey did the citizenry turn to the courts for relief against anti-
Union newspapers.[46]

On August 16, 1861, a federal grand jury issued a presentment
naming five New York newspapers, including the *Journal of Commerce*, that "are in the frequent practice of encouraging the rebels
...by expressing sympathy and agreement with them, the duty of
acceding to their demands, and dissatisfaction with the employment of force to overcome them."[47] Even though the Federal District Court failed to act upon the presentment, federal officials

seized upon the grand jury's findings as an excuse for stripping the papers of their mailing privileges on August 22.[48] Hallock's antebellum editorial policies, says one biographer, "supported the rights of the South in the fugitive-slave law controversy, opposed the election of Lincoln in 1860, after the election sought to avert war between the states, and as soon as hostilities had begun, urged measures of peace and conciliation."[49]

One of the government's terms for restoring the paper's mailing privileges was the retirement of Hallock from the paper.[50] With the intervention of friends of the paper in Washington, D.C., Secretary of State William Seward indicated that privileges would be restored if Hallock sold the paper to David M. Stone and William Cowper Prime.[51] This Hallock did on September 1, 1861, and, according to his obituary in 1866, Hallock "never contributed a line to its columns" after that day.[52] Stone had joined the *Journal of Commerce* in 1849 as a reporter and gradually assumed the duties of editor in chief. When he purchased the paper, Stone enlisted the financial help of Prime, a friend and a New York lawyer. Stone became publisher and Prime dropped his law practice to become editor in chief.

Prime also replaced Hallock as president of the New York AP, a post that apparently automatically went to the *Journal of Commerce*'s editor in chief, regardless of his background.[53] During the roughly twelve-year "calm guidance" of AP by the "amiable and venerable" Hallock, according to Hudson, "there was never a ripple" in AP's operation, but "there has been an occasional flurry within the past few [post–Civil War] years."[54] Stone purchased Prime's share in the paper in 1869, becoming editor in chief and, thus, president of the NYAP.

It seems odd that such journalistic power as was represented in AP's membership would not wish to elect its leadership, but perhaps AP's first president inadvertently put his finger on the reason after Webb's *Courier and Enquirer* was absorbed by the *World*. The *Journal of Commerce* "is now the only paper of its class in the city," Hallock wrote in 1861, "all the other[s]...being now defunct, or metamorphosed into some new form of physical existence."[55] Of the three political or mercantile papers joining the AP's original partnership, only the *Journal of Commerce* retained its mercantile mission on the eve of the Civil War, Webb's "blanket sheet" having been caught up in the *World*'s transformation from morality to marketability and the Brooks brothers' *Express* having shifted its party allegiance so frequently as to be undeserving of the title "political paper" in the eyes of the public.[56] In other words, the *Journal of Commerce*, its elitist mercantile readership reasonably secured and unchanging, found itself by 1861 in calm, shallow water by the shore, while most of the city's journalism was swept along in faster currents of high circulations and appeals to the fickle middle class. The paper, an odd vestige of the past, could serve AP well as mediator and presiding officer.

A final adjustment in AP's New York membership occurred when the *Express*, which had been a morning paper since its founding on June 20, 1836, moved its principal edition into the evening field. With the advent of telegraphic dispatches, the news from Cunard arrivals and the rush of prewar domestic news, metropolitan papers increasingly published extra editions, both to keep up with the flood of news and to satisfy additional reader interest. The *Express* so muddled its publication schedule that eventually it found it easier to jump to the evening field. Hudson says,

> The numerous editions of the *Express*, containing the spirit of the morning and evening papers, the latest telegrams to the Associated Press, and the arrivals at the hotels, gradually destroyed its regular morning issue, till it was decided to make the paper an evening one exclusively. . . . [57]

Both Lee and Mott state that the *Express* moved to the evening field in 1858,[58] in contrast to Hudson's recollection of "1864 or thereabouts." Providing no additional insight, Winifred Gregory lists the *Morning Express* as existing June 20, "1836–64?" but below in the list of available files only a single issue, September 2, 1864, is located for the period after April 1861. The *Evening Express* is listed in Gregory as existing "1839?–Dec. 1881," when it merged with the *New York Evening Mail*.[59]

From AP's viewpoint, the *Express*'s shift to evening publication foreshadowed a post–Civil War explosion of evening papers and the consequent necessity of developing news services accommodating both fields of publication. From its earliest days on through most of the nineteenth century, the AP system sent the bulk of its news report around midnight for use in morning papers, providing brief, updated "postscripts" during the day for morning papers' later editions. The *Express*, not noted for its aggressive news-gathering, could survive in the evening field on AP's sketchy daytime "postscripts."

ASSOCIATED PRESS'S REPORT ON THE EVE OF THE CIVIL WAR

Election night, Tuesday, November 6, 1860. The nation's fate hung on the outcome of a four-way presidential battle, and the New York Associated Press did its best to report the results. Although Wednesday morning's *Herald, Times, and Tribune* could tell New Yorkers that Lincoln was elected, AP dispatches in those papers occupied only one or two columns of type and were no less sketchy than those assembled by AP's agents in 1848. (See chapter 4.) Gone were the numerous brief update dispatches of 1848, filed periodically through the evening from distant states and cities and faithfully reprinted in the New York papers. They had been replaced in 1860 by single late dispatches covering statewide trends with a few specific vote totals in key towns or districts. Three examples of AP's coverage will indicate the report's election night tone.

NORTH CAROLINA
Wilmington, Nov. 6

Partial returns from this city and county show uniform gains for Breckinridge.

Raleigh gives Bell 231 majority.

The State has probably gone for Breckinridge.

MARYLAND
Baltimore, Nov. 6

The Union men claim the State by not less than 2,000.

Baltimore City complete: Breckinridge 14,850; Bell, 12,619; Douglas, 1,562; Lincoln, 1,082.

Returns from various Counties show considerable gains for Bell, but not sufficient to overcome the heavy Breckinridge majority in the city. The result is doubtful.

Returns from Allegany County indicate 800 for Bell over Breckinridge, a gain of near 1,000.

CONNECTICUT
Hartford, Nov. 6

Mr. Lincoln has 276 majority and 1,348 plurality. Six towns, including Hartford, show a Republican gain over last Spring, of 1,015. Lincoln's majority in the State will be several thousand.[60]

From New Orleans the AP could only furnish the news that, "The election in this city passed off quietly. The result is not yet ascertained." The *Times* topped this notice with a 6 P.M. special dispatch datelined Richmond reporting: "A dispatch just received here announces that New-Orleans has gone for Bell." The AP dispatch from New York state in the city papers gave county-by-county returns, but mentioned only a few towns and districts. Various reporting methods were used for tallying returns, and there were scattered attempts at interpreting vote totals on the basis of previous elections, as these examples of AP copy indicate:

> CAYUGA COUNTY—Auburn City gives Lincoln 449 majority—a Republican gain over the previous vote of 149. Eleven Election Districts give 415 Republican gain over 1859.
>
> ONONDAGA COUNTY—Thirteen towns give a Republican majority of 1,283; Republican gain over last year of 250. Both Republican Assemblymen elected.

All told, AP supplied election dispatches from only twelve[61] of the thirty-three states in 1860. Four other states[62] were represented by special dispatches to one of the three papers used in this analysis. AP's election report took only one column in the *Herald*, $1^{1/2}$ columns in the *Times*, and $2^{1/4}$ columns in the *Tribune*.[63] To accommodate the election returns, Craig had cut his regular domestic file back to five or six short items, including the arson destruction of a factory near Troy, N.Y.; a shoe factory file at Natick, Mass.; counterfeit five-dollar bills being issued by a Philadelphia bank; and a steamer from Liverpool to Quebec sighted en route. Complicating AP's election coverage, the Cunarder *Persia* appeared in New York harbor at 11 o'clock on election night, dumping two columns of generally insignificant but nonetheless obligatory European news in Craig's lap.

Adjacent to the election returns on the *Herald*'s front page is a special dispatch datelined Columbia, S.C., saying the state legislature had postponed for two days consideration of the governor's "suggestion to arm the State," awaiting final word on the presidential canvass. The item notes, "There is a supposed majority for prompt action. . . . There is no excitement; secession regarded as a foregone conclusion, coolly awaiting results of Northern elections." On December 20 the South Carolina legislature unanimously dissolved the state's ties with the Union, followed in January and early February by ten other Southern states. The Confederacy had been formed.

Meanwhile, the well-recorded saga of Henry Villard's assignment to cover president-elect Lincoln in Springfield, Ill., began on November 16, 1860.[64] Although Villard claims in his *Memoirs* to have been sent to Springfield by the New York Associated Press, editors of the volume correctly note that he was employed by the *New York Herald*, whose special dispatches, under AP's rules, were made available to other members.[65] A careful examination of the telegraphic news in the New York City AP press between November 1860 and February 1861 reveals that other AP papers rarely used the Villard copy, and if they did, the half-column or so of the Villard material in the *Herald* shrank in other papers to a mere paragraph.

Neither the *Times* nor the *Tribune*, both Republican voices, carried the Villard copy up to Lincoln's departure for Washington, nor did they arrange for their own specials from Springfield. Four days before Lincoln left Springfield the *Herald* gloated editorially,

> Ever since the 6th of last November Old Abe Lincoln has been a historical personage, and we have fully recognized the fact by giving to the public the fullest and most accurate intelligence as to his movements. . . . We are only endeavoring to give accurate news about Lincoln, no matter how far we may disagree with him, politically, as part of our duty to the public as a journalist. The spoils, so dear to Greeley, Webb, Raymond and the rest, have no temptation for us. . . .[66]

Villard had won the Springfield assignment on the basis of his reporting of the Lincoln-Douglas debates in 1858, his reported personal acquaintance with Lincoln, and his general knowledge of the Midwestern Republican situation.[67] Villard recalls that on first contact with Lincoln after the election, the president-elect "gave me a very friendly welcome, and authorized me to come to him at any time for any information I needed."[68] In August 1861, Villard, preparing to tour Memphis, Richmond, New Orleans, and other points for the *Herald*, wrote offering to supply the administration "with whatever information of usefulness. . .I shall be able to collect. . . ." Lincoln's endorsement, written on the reverse side of the letter and dated August 14, is not as warm as earlier: "I have only a slight acquaintance with Mr. Villard, as a gentlemanly correspondent; and as such I commend him to others."[69]

One Villard dispatch that received extensive use through the AP was Lincoln's departure from Springfield, containing Villard's text of Lincoln's famous Farewell Address. It is one of four texts of the address that have survived.[70] The lead on the AP dispatch, datelined Springfield, Feb. 11, reads:

> Mr. Lincoln left home at 7½ A.M., accompanied by a large
> concourse of people to the Depot where nearly 1,000 citizens
> had already collected. After he had shaken hands with a
> number of friends, he took his stand on the platform of the
> car, and spoke as follows.[71]

There followed in the AP dispatch the one-paragraph Villard text of Lincoln's Farewell and chronologically arranged dispatches from Decatur and Tolono, Ill.; the Illinois-Indiana state line; and Indianapolis, where Villard reported a long Lincoln speech verbatim. The AP coverage took a full page-one column in the *New York Times*. Meanwhile, in the South, Lincoln's departure received a less fulsome treatment, as the following full account, buried in a column of telegraphic news in the *Richmond Dispatch*, indicates:

> SPRINGFIELD, Feb. 11—Mr. Lincoln left at 8 o'clock this
> morning on his trip to Washington. He made some brief
> farewell remarks, but with no political allusions.[72]

An AP news report for the South was financed by an association of Southern editors dating from late 1847.[73] The report moved south over two telegraph routes.[74] One route was the American Telegraph Company's trunk line from New York through Washington, Richmond, Raleigh, Columbia, Macon, Montgomery, and Mobile, with spurs to coastal ports and some inland communities and a special connection to New Orleans across the territory of the Southwestern Telegraph Company.[75] The other AP route was the Southwestern company's main circuit from Louisville south through central Kentucky and Tennessee, northern Alabama and central Mississippi, to New Orleans. The Southern papers received the report from New York as relayed through Washington, and newspapers along the Southwestern lines were fed their report at Louisville by the Western Union, which simultaneously was delivering the same report to papers in Ohio, Indiana, Michigan, portions of Illinois and Missouri, and Wisconsin.

To examine the workings of the AP news network on the eve of the Civil War, the author studied the telegraphic dispatches of six morning newspapers for April 12, 1861. Three papers were AP partners in New York City—the *Herald*, *Times*, and *Tribune*—and the others were regionally scattered AP recipients—the *Chicago Tribune*, *Richmond Dispatch*, and the *New Orleans Picayune*. This date, just prior to hostilities, was selected because the nation's telegraph network was still intact and because significant prewar news was occurring at several places in both the North and South. In fact, the editions of these papers being examined were being printed early Friday morning, April 12, at about the time that shots were first fired on Fort Sumter in Charleston, S.C., harbor.

Looking first at the three New York City papers, the author finds a report that fills about three columns of type in the *Tribune*, and is roughly 50 percent longer than AP reports on an average day during the previous few months. Unlike earlier years, two of these papers were regularly crediting AP—the *Times* used "Dispatch to the Associated Press" and the *Tribune* "To the Associated Press." These same papers interspersed AP dispatches with their own specials, labeled "Special Dispatch to The N. Y. Tribune" or "OUR CHARLESTON DISPATCHES" and "OUR WASHINGTON DISPATCHES" in the *Times*. (The *Herald*, acting on the other hand as if the Associated Press did not exist, sprinkled phrases, sentences, and even paragraphs from AP dispatches in its own dispatches to create a briefer, more unified story that contained no indication of source.) All three papers, however, ran a column of short telegraphic dispatches on a variety of subjects and separated by short label headlines, a practice in place in these papers since the 1840s.

The AP handled the breaking news in Charleston harbor in a sequence of dispatches, all of which appeared in print, another policy long employed by the AP. The main Washington dispatch, in six paragraphs of quite widely differing lengths, embraced three subjects, one of them presented chronologically in one very long paragraph. All three subjects of this dispatch related to the mounting hostilities—the mustering of troops, the organizing of a Zouave company, and the movements of a Confederate Commission in Washington. A second Washington dispatch summarized several routine governmental matters—the treasury balance, bids on treasury notes, a circular on customs collections, and various administrative appointments and diplomatic recognitions.

Taken as a whole, the AP report totaled twenty-one dispatches and on this day was heavy with Southern news (ten dispatches, including four from Charleston on the Fort Sumter siege). Otherwise the report's dispatches were distributed as follows: Washington, D.C., two; North, six; Midwest, one; and West, two. All but one (from Galveston on April 9) bore an April 11 dateline. Subjects of Southern dispatches were troop movements and morale, municipal self-defense, and military limitations of vessel movements. War preparations were reported from most of the cities in the report, making this report unusual in relation to the past but a portent of things to come. The single exception is a brief Boston item that announces the death of Joseph T. Buckingham, former editor of the *Boston Courier*.

When one turns to the Chicago and Southern papers for AP news, one finds an absence of AP credit lines. Otherwise, these papers carried the same items as found that morning in the New York City papers. Short dispatches were identical in all papers. Longer dispatches in New York papers were sent west and south in shortened form. Craig's staff also rewrote and shortened the specials appearing in New York papers for the hinterlands reports. The special dispatches appearing in New York's evening papers, such as the *Evening Post* and *Commercial Advertiser*, were especially useful to the AP staff because their afternoon publication brought late commentary at a time when the morning report was being compiled at AP offices. The following dispatch, appearing in both the *Chicago Tribune* and the *Richmond Dispatch* the morning of April 12, illustrates the point.

> NEW YORK, April 11—A special dispatch to the Times, dated Charleston, the 10th, states that the Floating Battery is now in position, and commanding the Barbette guns at Fort Sumter. It carries two 32-pounders, two 52-pounders, and sixty-four men.
>
> The Federal steamers are expected to-night.
>
> The city is filled with troops.
>
> SECOND DISPATCH
>
> The *Post* says the agents of the Confederate States have been rebuffed in their efforts to get a part of their Government loan taken here.
>
> A special dispatch to the *Commercial Advertiser*, from Charleston, dated noon to-day, says the rumor has been confirmed that President Davis has issued orders that vessels conveying provisions to Fort Sumter are not to be fired upon.

Wholly or nearly, identical dispatches appeared on Friday, April 12, in New York AP papers and in one or two of the regional papers. Interestingly, whereas a few dispatches like the one above were prepared only for transmission and publication beyond New York City, every dispatch appearing in all three of the regional papers also appeared in New York's AP press. The *Richmond Dispatch* was served by the American lines, and the *Chicago Tribune* and the *New Orleans Picayune*[76] were served by a combination of Western Union and Illinois & Mississippi Telegraph lines in Chicago and Western Union and Southwestern lines in New Orleans. Thus, the dispatches in the *Picayune* are more similar to those in the *Chicago Tribune* than to those in the *Richmond Dispatch*.[77] In fact, whereas the *Picayune* and *Dispatch* shared two or three dispatches, the *Picayune* and the *Chicago Tribune* shared sixteen or eighteen dispatches. Meanwhile the *Tribune* and the *Dispatch* shared eight dispatches. Of the twenty-one dispatches appearing in New York's morning AP press, nine also appeared in the *Chicago Tribune*, ten appeared in the *Dispatch*, and eleven appeared in the *Picayune*.

Perhaps the most striking find in the regional papers is the extent of AP's dominance over their telegraphic news columns. Associated Press accounted for fourteen of seventeen (82.4 percent) of the *Dispatch*'s items, the other three being special reports to the paper, two from Charleston and one from New York City about the Fort Sumter situation. In the *Chicago Tribune* twenty-two of twenty-four (91.7 percent) were dispatches from AP, the others being reports from Greensburg, Ind., and of river levels at LaSalle and Rock Island. Twenty of twenty-one (95.2 percent) telegraphic dispatches in the *Picayune* came from AP, the exception concerning the river level at Louisville.

Unquestionably Craig and his correspondents exercised enormous influence over the national flow of news, indeed over the public's perception of the day's issues and events in the months preceding the war. Telegraph historian George B. Prescott provides a contemporary view of AP's operation in 1860. Noting that "the press from Maine to Texas [is] supplied with every important event which transpires in any part of our vast country within a few minutes of its actual occurrence," Prescott observed that "nearly all of the daily newspapers in the United States" had become associated with the New York AP.

> Everything of interest occurring in any part of this country is telegraphed at once to the general office in New York, copies being dropped at all intermediate points on the route, and the other parts of the country being supplied from the central office.[78]

Thus, the system worked primarily for the benefit of the New York editors, distant points filing copy to Craig's office. From there copy was refiled for other AP clients in, as the April 12 report reveals, a somewhat selective and abbreviated form. Prescott continued his description of filing procedures at AP.

The larger share of the press reports comes over the wires during the night,—commencing about 6 o'clock P.M. and concluding generally about 1 o'clock A.M., but not infrequently continuing as late as 4 o'clock, and sometimes all night. We have sometimes been occupied in sending press news when the sun descended below the horizon and when it arose the next morning, having continued at our post during the entire night. During the sessions of Congress the reports are the fullest. . . .[79]

DISCUSSION

The snug little news empire that Craig and his patron editors had assembled during the 1850s, the telegraphic cartel dating from mid-1857, and the growing interdependence between newsbroker-customer and telegrapher-supplier—all offer glimpses of a national revolution in technology, commerce, and manufacturing sweeping the nation on the eve of the Civil War. Like dance partners who only infrequently stop to argue about who will lead, newsbroker and telegrapher found their own interests served by waltzing on in ever-wider circles, gradually improvising steps and flourishes that made each partner's success dependent on the other. Meanwhile the dance floor was filling with other dancers—bankers, speculators, corporation directors, investors, accountants, manufacturers, clerks, mechanics, and the like. And the tune they danced to was the steady chug of steam presses and the staccato of telegraphic instruments.

George Rogers Taylor, reflecting a transportation viewpoint, describes the "new orientation" of the national economy in 1860.

The great cities of the East no longer faced the sea and gave their chief attention to shipping and foreign trade. Their commerce centered increasingly now at the railroad stations rather than at the docks, and the commercial news from Mobile, Memphis, Louisville, Cleveland, and Chicago was awaited with greater interest than that from Liverpool, Marseilles, or Antwerp. . . . [T]he leaders of the emerging era of financial capitalism were beginning to appear. By means of well-placed investments, by speculation and manipulation on the stock and produce exchanges, and by membership on the boards of directors . . . these rising entrepreneurs, the successors of the older sedentary merchants, were soon to play the directing role in the emerging national economy of stocks and bonds and debentures.[80]

The nation was beginning to "take in its own laundry." Growing cities filled with unemployed rural youths, hopeful immigrants, and go-getters with skills, inventions, and get-rich-quick schemes. Traders bought and sold goods and produce with but samples or grade designations at hand. Contracts were negotiated between strangers who never left their offices, which were separated by many miles or even states. Payment and shipping orders arrived minutes after their transmission from centers hundreds of miles away. Corporations were rapidly formed, their stock sold and resold, and then they were reorganized, merged, or absorbed just as rapidly.

The impetus for such accelerating activity was the nation's new-found ability to communicate more rapidly, more widely, and more voluminously with itself. Telegraphy and journalism, especially newsbroking, were obvious contributors to this ability. Daily newspapers, with the help of Craig's daily news reports, were informing a widening circle of mercantile, political, and middle-class readers about the nation's pulse and progress. It was the first stages of a democratization of general news that late in the century would shape a national marketplace of information, a daily nationally shared experience that the society had with its own particulars. Meanwhile, telegraphy was unlocking a national marketplace of goods and services in which businessmen and manufacturers, armed with their favorite newspaper, could participate with no greater effort than it took to send a telegram.

In the transportation industry, as well, network expansion, technical improvements, and growing patronage signaled a spiraling acceleration of old-style communication, through both letter-writing and traveling. Allan Pred's examination of urban growth and economic activity between 1840 and 1860 depicts a rapid growth of various transportation systems and the telegraph as conduits for the flow of "specialized economic information." An inescapable finding in Pred's work is that expansion in all forms of electric and steam communication principally suited the needs of business people.[81] The "spatial bias" of developing rail, water, and telegraph networks favored business interests by linking established centers for business, manufacturing, and shipping. Moreover, tariffs and fares up to 1860 remained prohibitive for all but the business and political communities. The only concession to the non-elite individual who needed to communicate was an 1851 postal service rate revision that replaced high distance-graduated postal rates with a prepaid rate of three cents per sheet delivered anywhere within three thousand miles. Even though the new rate system accounted for increased mail use by non-business people, Pred finds evidence that "businessmen. . . remained the leading. . . users of the official mails throughout the antebellum period."[82]

The new mid-nineteenth-century technologies of steam and electronics rather than resurrecting the town meeting, as James Russell Lowell had predicted,[83] produced systems of communication that only the business and political communities could and did use extensively. The average individual, amid this national technological, manufacturing, and commercial furor, remained at his writing table, posting letters through a transportation-bound mail service.[84] Likewise, the newspaper editor situated outside of metropolitan areas was increasingly, and not necessarily willingly, a partner in printing and distributing the information generated in the business centers and daily thrust at him by the telegraph.

For Craig, his associates, and New York's AP editors the new technologies of electricity and steam propelled them into a ruling stratum, which was arising around the new central role for news and information in an increasingly complex society. More than a forward step in the collecting and distributing of news on a national scale, Craig's newsbrokerage aided by its partnership with telegraphy was a driving force in Taylor's "new orientation" of business and manufacturing. Singularly and daily imposing itself upon the elites and the smaller newspapers, Craig's news report was an ingredient in businessmen's and speculators' decisions, a guide to opportunities and misfortune.

Among the three institutions along the newsbroking interface, telegraphy made the greatest institutional strides in the years immediately preceding the Civil War. A second generation of developers, urged on by telegraphy's central role in the nation's institutional life, had finally realized that profits, indeed survival, depended on alliance and territorial sovereignty. The six "nations" and the subsequent association of regionally autonomous telegraphic giants, even if intended by some of its architects as a momentary truce in cutthroat competition, abruptly consolidated telegraphy's growth and erected a seemingly impenetrable common technological fortification that excluded the nation's editors and newsbrokers. That some telegraph leaders sought to assimilate newsbroking into the new consolidation made telegraphy even more dangerous to journalists, who after a decade were accustomed to controlling their own news dispatches.

Had cooler heads not prevailed in 1860 and, one suspects, had there not been a residue of fear in telegraph circles for the editorial mischief that metropolitan newspapers could accomplish by pitting public opinion against the telegraphic cartel, Craig's news monopoly might have been swept away on the eve of the Civil War. The New York Associated Press could have survived membership changes within its ranks, but the partnership, with its attendant monopoly over the nation's news flow, would have been useless to its members if national newsbroking had fallen into the hands of telegraph proprietors. To newspaper editors outside of New York City, a change in newsbrokers might have delivered a better news report than Craig's AP reports, which beyond the city were widely perceived as benefiting primarily Craig's seven patron editors. It, thus, became crucial to the AP editors in New York City to retain control over newsbroking, if only to avoid a newsbroking vacuum into which other newspaper editors might be drawn. And, with transcontinental and transatlantic projects on the drawing boards, telegraphers could not have afforded a spate of adverse publicity about their cartel. This, however, would not be the last time telegraphy coveted newsbroking's power. Twice more after major consolidations in telegraphy—in 1866 following Western Union's emergence as a national monopoly and in 1882 after Jay Gould gained control of Western Union in exchange for Western Union's absorption of Gould's telegraph interests—journalistically controlled newsbroking was, as we shall see in Volume 2, threatened by a telegraphic takeover.

Chapter 7
NEWSBROKING IN THE CIVIL WAR

In 1860 the telegraphic reports scarcely exceeded fifteen hundred words a day for such cities as Pittsburgh, Cleveland, Cincinnati, Detroit, Chicago, and St. Louis. . . . All of this changed with the breaking out of the war. The "Associated Press" supplemented its reports of routine business with accounts of the movements of troops. . . and with patriotic appeals. . . . People acquired the habit of reading daily papers, and new and improved machinery was constructed to meet the increasing circulation.

William Henry Smith, "The Press as a News Gatherer," *Century*
(August 1891)

In the weeks following the shelling of Fort Sumter, and certainly after the first battle of Bull Run late in July 1861, journalism's prospects improved substantially. News of hostilities on home soil would send exhilarating and fearsome shock waves through the nation. Many, perhaps even some reporters, would die. War would bring a feast of spectacular news events, tempered by the inevitable famine wrought by censorship and a shortage of communication facilities. While the war's later stages were literally a life-or-death struggle for some Southern newspapers and the Confederacy's newsbrokerage, Northern newspaper journalism, largely unthreatened physically, hugely advanced its fortunes during the conflict.

The New York Associated Press, on the other hand, did not fare as well as its patron and client newspapers. Its national news monopoly shrank with the cutting of the two main arteries into the South. Its correspondents, in addition to suffering federal censorship, submitted to the role of semi-official mouthpiece for the Lincoln administration. It encountered growing hostility among Midwestern clients and the brief challenge of another newsbrokerage. Its news report, qualitatively as well as quantitatively, fell behind the telegraphic exploits of the Union's leading newspapers in covering the war. And a Confederate newsbrokerage had a brief life apart from AP. This chapter will discuss these wartime developments. Because literature abounds with journalism's Civil War performance,[1] this account focuses narrowly on newsbroking during the war.

General agent Daniel H. Craig learned early that this war would bring out the journalistic instincts of many editors taking his AP news report. In mid-April 1861, the *Chicago Tribune* expressed its "dissatisfaction with the meagerness of the information brought us by the arrangement of the associated Press, and with the unreliability of that dished up by the sensation papers of the metropolis," and announced that

> we have determined to incur the great expense of a special
> correspondent at the seat of government, and daily special
> dispatches copious enough to give our readers a correct idea
> of all passing events which have a bearing upon the great
> issues now presented to the people of the West.[2]

Throughout journalism editors dispatched themselves or their trusted subordinates to Washington or the battlefields to get the regional slant or to augment or supersede Craig's report.

In part, this journalistic activity was prompted by the ease of access to the scenes of fighting. Despite the changing, at times arbitrary, censorship of news dispatches, correspondents "were accorded the most liberal privileges" during the Civil War, according to James G. Randall.

> Government passes were put into their hands; they had
> the use of government horses and wagons; they were given
> transportation with baggage privileges on government
> steamers and military trains. They enjoyed the confidence of
> admirals and army commanders, and were seldom at a loss to
> obtain the information they desired.[3]

J. Cutler Andrews lists 436 Northern and Southern correspondents in Washington, Richmond, and the war zones, only twenty-six of whom (6 percent) had newsbrokerages as their primary affiliations.[4] The newsbroker found himself in a crowded field, one that could challenge his credibility, equal his speed, and exceed the length and detail of his dispatches. Whereas Craig, according to Andrews, had thirteen Associated Press correspondents in the field,[5] his seven patron New York City papers had 198 correspondents (57.9 percent of the total Northern press corps) in their employ at some point during the war. The Southern Associated Press had four correspondents,[6] and when that agency was replaced by the Confederate Press Association, the latter had ten correspondents.[7] No newsbroker controlled the flow of this war's news. In fairness, preserving his news monopoly may not have been foremost in Craig's mind when hostilities broke out. Staying afloat in a turbulent sea of nationalized telegraph lines, coping with government management of the news, establishing relations with a new administration in Washington, and trying to get accurate accounts from far-flung battlefields would challenge even a man of Craig's abilities in so unprecedented a news situation.

The first blow to newsbroking occurred on April 19, 1861, five days after the fall of Fort Sumter, when militia took control of the Washington office of the American Telegraph Company. Communication in and out of the capital was chaotic and unpredictable for the next month.[8] By mid-May both governments were moving to secure their own telegraphic systems for military purposes. The Confederate Congress authorized President Davis to seize the telegraph and "supervise communications passing through, so that none be conveyed of military operations, or calculated to injure the Confederate States, or give aid and comfort to their enemies."[9] Already in late April the federal government had begun assembling personnel to operate a military system in the North.[10]

On May 20, 1861, federal marshals seized all telegrams left in Northern telegraph offices for transmission to the South, an effort to expose Southern sympathizers and traitors operating in the North.[11] The next day officials of the American Telegraph Company conferred on the Long Bridge over the Potomac at Washington on what to do about the company's telegraphic lines between North and South.[12] The decision was to cut the line—and AP's link to the Southeast. This was done on June 1,[13] the northern section to be controlled, as before, by Edwards S. Sanford, and the southern section, reorganized as the Southern Telegraph Company, to be controlled by Dr. William S. Morris, a Southern stockholder in the old American company.[14] At the same time federal troops took possession of the telegraph offices in Louisville, cutting off AP's other line to the South.[15] Like the American, the Southwestern Telegraph Company was split into two corporations, one for Kentucky with offices in Louisville, the other for the Confederate side.[16]

The telegraph was "for the first time employed to direct widely separated armies and move them in unison," says the wartime manager of the War Department's telegraph office.[17] And the Civil War was the first to be telegraphed in large measure to a waiting reading audience.[18] Telegraphy would for the first time not only provide

241

same-day or overnight war coverage, but would also invite close governmental scrutiny of correspondents' copy. After February 2, 1862, the telegraph throughout the North was supervised by the military,[19] and news dispatches telegraphed from the field either came under scrutiny by field generals or were fed through Washington censors before proceeding to newsrooms. Vexatious changes in censorship regulations and uneven censorship from time to time and place to place constantly complicated the newsbrokers' work.

The continuing problem of censorship was foreshadowed on July 21, 1861, by news organizations' confusion with the first Battle of Bull Run, the Union's first major military outing. Early AP dispatches told of Union successes, and after AP's John Hasson arrived from the battlefield, he dictated to Lawrence Gobright, AP's Washington bureau chief, a story of a stunning Union victory. Hasson, however, had left the battlefield too soon. The tide had turned, and federal forces were in full retreat. Hasson and Gobright, after depositing their erroneous dispatch at the telegraph office about 11 P.M., discovered the true outcome at Bull Run from those arriving later from the scene and hurriedly filed a new, updated dispatch. Unknown to them, however, military censorship had stopped transmission of all press dispatches reporting the Union defeat, not releasing them until the next morning. The AP dispatches the next morning in New York papers gave a totally false impression of this first Civil War battle.[20]

LINCOLN AND THE ASSOCIATED PRESS

For the most part, AP received favored treatment from the Lincoln administration during the war, despite the suspicions of Secretary of War Edwin M. Stanton that AP was dominated by Democrats. Biographers report that Stanton "hindered [AP's] agents as much as he could."[21] He may have developed this view because only a minority of the New York City AP partnership newspapers were generally pro-administration during the war and because Gobright had Democratic leanings.[22] Another basis for Stanton's distrust may have been the fact that the AP's president from its inception until August 1861 was Gerard Hallock. As noted in chapter 6, he was forced to relinquish control of the *New York Journal of Commerce* at the start of the war because of his pro-slavery, pro–Southern rights editorial posture.

President Lincoln, on the other hand, was the first president to dispense with the practice of using a newspaper as an official organ.

He turned his news over to the Associated Press. Culver H. Smith indicates that rather than this being a bold Lincoln stroke, the end of official organs in Washington, D.C., may have been in the offing for three administrations prior to 1861. Party organs "had produced more headaches than votes" during the 1850s, says Smith, and the growth of a Washington corps of correspondents had put the president in more direct contact with newspaper readers. "The presidents and party leaders," says Smith, "were now showing more concern about the favor of certain metropolitan newspapers with wide circulation."[23] Those papers could most effectively be reached through AP's network.

For Lincoln, additionally, elimination of the administration organ was urged by two factors. Congress created the Government Printing Office on June 23, 1860, Smith reports,

> to end interminable, time-consuming arguments about
> printers, prices, and patronage.... [T]he quantity of printing
> had become too large to handle efficiently under the old
> system [of awarding printing contracts to faithful party
> newspapers], and too expensive.[24]

The new printing office completed the printing required by the last session of the outgoing Congress and officially opened for business on Lincoln's inauguration day, leaving the new president with no subsidies or contracts to bestow on Washington papers.

Throughout most of 1861 the press and various administrative departments warred over the release of information. Censorship was heavy-handed or uneven, reporters pestered harried administration officials for scraps of information, some newspapers circumvented official censorship by mail or express delivery of dispatches. In June 1861 the AP carried a suggestion "from an official source" that editors meet in Washington to devise an effective system of releasing official information. Nothing came of the suggestion.[25] In August AP's Gobright and other correspondents were negotiating with officials over military censorship, but again nothing resulted.[26]

The dilemma of regularizing censorship and the release of information persisted throughout the war, but the first sign that AP was the official conduit of the Lincoln administration came in late November 1861 when Secretary of War Simon Cameron, with the concurrence of other departments, agreed that

> all *official* documents of whatever kind, emanating from the
> Departments, shall be delivered to the general agent of the

Associated Press at Washington—and to him alone—for
prompt and simultaneous transmission to such papers as may
desire to receive them by telegraph.[27]

Informally, friendly relations between Lincoln and the AP had
begun with exclusive release to AP agents of the president's first in-
augural address shortly before he delivered it. Gobright says that although Lincoln had written his address in Springfield and had had
copies of it printed at the office of Springfield's *Illinois State Journal,* the original later underwent extensive revision, and "an exact
copy of [the revision] was furnished to the 'Associated Press' to be
telegraphed."[28] The AP agent who received this final copy was a
twenty-one-year-old *Washington States* reporter named Henry Watterson, who later explained that he had been hired by AP only for
that one event to assist AP's Gobright and Ben Perley Poore with
coverage.[29]

A month later, Gobright says, the administration had taken no
steps that signified a policy. Three days before the siege at Fort Sumter, Gobright, after talking "with numerous prominent gentlemen
in official positions," developed a story draft on "the policy of the
administration," which he directed to "a Cabinet officer" for reaction, approval or rejection. It came back approved, and Gobright
telegraphed it to the Associated Press. This, Gobright claims, "was
the first semi-official announcement" of Lincoln's policies.[30]

Close relations between the departments and AP continued
throughout the war, embracing some extraordinary reciprocity. Gobright was "often being called upon to assist [Lincoln, Stanton, and
Secretary of State William H. Seward] in the preparation of proclamations and other important documents," according to Gobright's
obituary, "which were finally intrusted to his hands for telegraphing."[31] Moreover, early in 1864 Secretary of War Stanton began
writing daily news dispatches capsulizing the day's military messages from the war zones. These Stanton telegraphed to Major General John A. Dix of the New York military district, who delivered
them directly to the NYAP. After protests by Washington, D.C., editors about this practice, Lincoln convinced Stanton to release his
"war diary" entries in Washington rather than New York.[32]

At the time Vicksburg hung in the balance, Gobright reports, he
asked Lincoln for the latest news from the West. The president, saying he had nothing new and could not sleep without further word,
invited Gobright to accompany him to the War Department to see if
any late reports had arrived. As they approached the telegraph

room, a messenger rushed up to the president with a telegram reporting a Union defeat at Vicksburg. Shaken by the news, Lincoln told Gobright "in an admonitory tone: *'Don't say anything about this—don't mention it.'* "[33] In another instance of cozy relations, a message from Thomas A. Scott of the War Department to Craig on October 31, 1861, asked the newsbroker to "please use the following message for out-bound vessel, and see that it is properly used on other side of the water," referring to the departure of a transatlantic steamer from New York. The message, which was strenuously pro-Union, read as follows:

> The power of the loyal States girds the rebels closer and closer. Five hundred thousand troops on an arc stretching from Kansas to Cape Hatteras are slowly but surely pushing the rebellion into the interior of the slave States, where it will inevitably perish. There is no abatement of the military spirit in the free States. Now that the harvest is fully ended volunteers for the war fill up regiments with astonishing alacrity. It is unquestionable that the determination to restore the Union and to accept of no compromise whatever with the slavery propagandists increases daily. The annual fall elections in the North and West have resulted almost without opposition in sustaining the policy of the Federal Government.... An immense naval expedition sailed for an unknown destination on the coast of the Atlantic cotton States on the 29th. It took out 30,000 men of both services, and was composed of thirty-one large transport vessels, sixteen steam gun-boats, and eight men-of-war....[34]

It is not known whether Craig actually included this dispatch on the next steamer bound for Great Britain, thus serving as a Union propagandist.

In another instance a message from Chief of Staff Daniel Butterfield to Gobright requested the latter to "please have the following dispatch telegraphed confidentially to the editors throughout the country." The dispatch, signed by General Joseph Hooker, gave the ground rules by which reporters could cover Hooker's army, then commented:

> After any fight the reporters can open their fire as loudly as they please.... These rules being observed, every facility possible will be given to reporters and newspapers in this army, including the license to abuse or criticize me to their hearts' content.[35]

In the field, AP agents, like any war correspondents, could strike up friendships with military personnel that might be rewarding. George W. Tyler, who supervised AP's Louisville office, was one of only two war correspondents (Henry Villard being the other) General William T. Sherman had friendly relations with.[36] Historian Andrews says that Tyler, an elderly man and a Harvard graduate, made AP's news reports available to Sherman. "Every evening about nine o'clock Sherman came to the Associated Press office to find out what news had come over the wire," Andrews says. "Often he remained there until the closing hour, three o'clock in the morning, discussing the issues of the day with whoever happened to be there."[37]

After Vicksburg had finally fallen to the Union forces, Sherman pushed off from Chattanooga in May 1864 toward the Atlantic coast. Even during his trek to the sea, Sherman maintained contact with Tyler. Writing Tyler on September 7, 1864, from "In the Field, Atlanta, Ga.," Sherman tersely described his tactical approach to Atlanta and its capture. "I am now writing in Atlanta, so you need not be uneasy," wrote Sherman. "If this is not success, I don't know what is." He signed it "Your friend, W. T. Sherman."[38] On September 27 Sherman, still in Atlanta, wrote Tyler to correct an AP dispatch that reported refugees from Atlanta were being robbed of everything they had before Union troops sent them back to rebel lines, because "I know that the people of the North, liable to be misled by a falsehood connived for a special purpose by a desperate enemy, will be relieved by the assurance that . . . real kindness has been extended."[39] A third recorded correspondence from Sherman to Tyler, dated November 4, 1864, from Kingston, Ga., asks Tyler to "dispatch me to-morrow night and the next night a summary of all news, especially of [presidential] elections, that I may report it to Governor Brown at Milledgeville. . . ."[40]

The semi-official status AP occupied as disseminator of government dispatches, however, was a double-edged sword. The price of a successful news monopoly in the North was making room in the news report for government pronouncements, sometimes more propagandistic than newsworthy. And it was a status that apparently followed AP into the postwar years, as indicated by William Aplin, an AP staffer in New York City, who described AP's operations in 1870.

> The regular Associated Press telegrams are what would be called, in Europe, "semi-official." . . . The local agents, on

account of their presumed fairness, and because they have it in their power to bring despatches before so many readers, have the run of official records everywhere, often where the "special" would not be tolerated. The Government appreciates the power of the Associated Press. The Washington agent frequently has his news brought to him by the heads of the Departments. But the Washington news is not always startling, . . . [at times involving] matters that the Government is more interested in getting printed everywhere than the public is to read.[41]

Government dispatches failed to brighten Craig's noticeably dull news report of the prewar days, but they did lend credibility and indispensability to the AP—both for newspaper editors and readers and for the government.

All was not official dispatches and cozy relations, however, between AP and the Lincoln administration. On five occasions AP or one of its correspondents had scrapes with federal authorities during the war. The first incident involved William Barr, [42] an AP agent at Louisville, who was arrested at his home on September 19, 1861, charged with sympathizing with the rebel cause and using his AP position to advance the insurrectionary cause.[43] Barr's job had been to work alongside Tyler in Louisville, filing AP reports to newspapers in New Orleans and intermediate points.[44] Presumably this function had ended when troops occupied the telegraph offices in border states and shut down telegraphic traffic heading into the South.

Tyler wrote Craig on October 5, assuring the AP general agent that Barr's troubles did not stem from his AP duties. He was arrested, Tyler wrote, "for giving counsel and advice in letter and otherwise to Governor Harris and other Confederates." Barr's chances of release are "entirely hopeless," Tyler continued, the evidence of treasonable activity being "overwhelming."[45] Meanwhile, after being held for a short time at Broward's Hotel, Jeffersonville, Ind., Barr was transferred to Fort Lafayette Prison in New York City harbor, and on November 1 he was moved to Fort Warren Prison in Boston harbor.[46]

Sometime before October 15 Craig wrote Barr, assuring him that the Southern editors would support his family and added, "If not, you can draw on me," to which Barr replied, "God bless Mr. Craig."[47] But Craig later changed his opinion of Barr. On December 30 Barr was offered his release if he would take the oath of allegiance to the Union. He declined, and, writing Craig, said, "I hold this plain ground: I am a citizen of Kentucky; I have been illegally taken from my State. The power that holds me and proposes terms has no just right to hold me or release me." Apparently referring to an attempt by Craig to get him to take the oath, Barr continued, "I have more confidence in the vitality of justice in this country than you seem to have," adding that his wife will expect no further assistance from Craig. Craig's endorsement on the copy of this Barr letter in the War Department files is blunt: "From what I know of Barr I should say that his past conduct entitles him to expect nothing better than he has received. I would rather see him hanged than released with conditions."[48]

Barr was again offered his freedom in exchange for the oath on January 31, 1862; again he refused. During January, however, Barr proposed to Secretary of State Seward that he be exchanged for someone in the South, "particularly among telegraphic experts who would gladly come North if they had an opportunity...."[49] Support for this possibility came from a petition of New Orleans editors to Confederate Secretary of War J. P. Benjamin, on January 24, 1862, observing that Barr

> was arrested solely in consequence of his zeal in the cause of
> the independence of the Southern Confederacy.... His
> usefulness to the press of the Confederate States as a
> telegraphic operator cannot be exaggerated. We beg that you
> will exert your influence to have Mr. Barr liberated and
> restored to his family and to his country.[50]

Barr was released to the custody of the War Department on February 15, 1862, and six days later he was ordered released by the Secretary of War.[51] He became the telegraphic correspondent for the *Memphis Appeal* at Senatobia, Miss., which Andrews notes was an important news center in the western theater of operations. In May 1863 Barr was arrested by Yankee raiders in Senatobia but was released "after a brief period of captivity in the North."[52] Barr reappeared after the Civil War as the Southern Associated Press's chief agent, filing a report in Washington, D.C., for the Southern press.

No other AP agent endured as extended an imprisonment as Barr's, but they were not immune from suspicion and even detention for brief periods. Seward wrote Major General N. P. Banks on October 23, 1861, that Theodore Barnard, the AP agent assigned to Banks's forces in the Shenandoah Valley, was to be watched. Seward said,

> Information which leaves no room for mistake satisfies me
> that until last May [Barnard] was an agent of the disunionist
> press in [Washington, D.C.]. You will I think do well to have
> his correspondence strictly observed and to guard against any
> treachery on his part.[53]

Barnard was apparently never arrested. Historian Louis M. Starr identifies him as the AP correspondent at the Battle of Gettysburg in July 1863,[54] and Andrews notes that earlier that same year he was assisting the AP correspondent Sid Deming with coverage of the Army of the Potomac.[55]

Deming while with the Army of the Potomac was arrested on January 21, 1863, on orders from Stanton. There is no record of the arrest in the *Official Records of the Rebellion*, but the incident is recorded in a letter from *New York Herald* war correspondent S. M. Carpenter to the paper's managing editor, Frederic Hudson. Carpenter says Deming was charged with being a "dangerous man," whose " *'future reports'* of the operations of the army, it is feared, will be detrimental to the cause of the country." Carpenter then confided that the "secret of his arrest" was that Deming was "too warm an admirer" of Gen. McClellan.

> The arrest is regarded here as an outrage. . . . The order
> fell among us like a thunderbolt in its startling effect. . . .
> [Stanton] is framing his own gillotine [*sic*], and a spirit is
> breeding in this army that will make mischief with those in
> authority, unless a change of programme is introduced
> soon.[56]

Six months later Deming turned up covering the Gettysburg battle,[57] apparently as quietly released as he had been unofficially detained.

Two actual or supposed Associated Press dispatches ran afoul of official censorship, and since both have attracted some attention in the literature, they will receive only brief discussion here. Charles C. Fulton had been Baltimore agent for AP since Alexander Jones's days as general agent. In mid-1853 Fulton purchased a half-interest in the *Baltimore American* and became not only its editor, but during the Civil War a special correspondent for the paper.[58] In Baltimore, a hotbed of secessionism where Union forces committed twelve acts of press suppression during the war, eight of them permanently closing newspaper offices, Fulton was the Lincoln administration's only real newspaper friend.[59]

On a special four-day War Department pass to observe military operations in Virginia in June 1862,[60] Fulton witnessed much of the decisive Seven Days' Battles of the Peninsula Campaign, in which the Confederates suffered heavy losses from McClellan's army and eventually retreated toward Richmond. Fulton returned to Baltimore late on Saturday, June 28, with an exclusive account of the Union victories. On Sunday morning, as a courtesy, he telegraphed a summary of his notes on the battle to the War Department, was summoned to Washington that day to report in person to Lincoln and Stanton the good news of a Union victory, and late on Sunday returned to Baltimore by special train.

Nothing had appeared in print about the battles Sunday night when Fulton finally put his observations in story form for the *American*. Also that night he wired Craig in New York, offering AP his account.

> I am writing for the American a detailed account of events
> at White House, before Richmond and on the Peninsula,
> during the last four days, including facts obtained from
> Washington, having been sent for by special train to
> communicate with the President. If you desire it, and will
> give due credit, I will send it to you. It will make four or five
> thousand words. We have the grandest military triumph over
> the enemy, and Richmond must fall.
>
> C. C. Fulton

Two hours later Fulton wired Craig again saying he had been refused permission to send any of his story, explaining that Stanton "decides that nothing can be telegraphed relative to affairs on the Peninsula." Craig, thus denied the lengthy account of a Union victory, inserted instead in his Sunday night news report Fulton's two personal telegrams to the AP, focusing on the lines "grandest military triumph," "Richmond must fall," and "facts obtained from Washington." The last statement, as military authorities informed Fulton, was a "flagrant and outrageous violation of the confidence with which you were treated." By carrying his information out of the battle zone, Fulton evaded McClellan's telegraph censors, and since McClellan's army was at that moment busily establishing new headquarters, the War Department considered Fulton and his eyewitness accounts from Virginia a potentially serious leak of military intelligence.

Thus, on Monday morning Fulton found himself arrested and en route to Fort McHenry Prison, where he resided for forty-eight hours before being released amid a chorus of negative press reaction to his confinement. Fulton had been the hapless victim of Craig's blundering release of his confidential telegrams, but it is interesting to note that neither Craig nor his staff were subsequently arrested in the imbroglio. Meanwhile, Fulton's *American* reprinted the exchange of messages between him and the military authorities. These, in turn, were picked up and printed by the Southern press as further evidence of the Lincoln administration's ineptness. And in the North, less than loyal Union journals made much of the exchange, the *New York World* calling the blunder "the most egregious, not to say the most despotic. . .of which Secretary Stanton has been guilty since he first undertook a censorship of the telegraph and the press."

Two years later the *New York World* and disunionist colleagues at the *New York Journal of Commerce* were the object of federal suppression in the famous bogus draft proclamation incident. Apart from the political and legal implications of this episode, both well recorded in the literature, the bogus proclamation illustrates the workings and shortcomings of Craig's system of delivering news dispatches to New York City papers. Loss, theft, substitution, or addition of dispatches was always possible so long as a lad trotted through the late-night city streets delivering AP's flimsies, and it is a wonder that more deceptions and blunders had not been perpetrated on the system over the years.

In the proclamation incident[61] the regular AP report was not tampered with, but two persons who knew AP's delivery system distributed a late dispatch purporting to be a Lincoln proclamation calling 400,000 men to military service by the end of the month. The purpose of the hoax was for its perpetrators to profit in the gold market.[62] One result of the hoax was the only known instance in which Lincoln personally signed an order to suppress newspapers.[63] Joseph Howard, Jr., city editor of the *Brooklyn Daily Eagle*, and Francis A. Mallison, an *Eagle* reporter and former AP manifolder, met in a private home in Brooklyn the night of May 17, 1864, and prepared the bogus proclamation. They parted company at about eleven o'clock, Mallison taking the manifold copies over to Manhattan to direct their delivery to New York's six morning AP papers.[64] An attempt was made at each newspaper office to deliver the proclamation between three and three-thirty in the morning, an hour or so after the last regular AP delivery. A messenger boy found the *Tribune*'s editorial rooms locked and could not locate the composing room entrance, but copies were delivered at the *Sun, Herald, Times, World,* and *Journal of Commerce*. The *Sun*, which traditionally went to press early, was too far along with its press run to include the dispatch in its morning edition for May 18.

The *Times*'s night editor did not recognize the handwriting on the dispatch and sent it, with a query, to the AP office. AP replied, "The proclamation is false as hell and was not promulgated through this office. The handwriting is not familiar." The *Herald* printed 20,000 or 25,000 papers containing the bogus dispatch before it was discovered as a hoax, and all *Herald*s containing the fake dispatch were destroyed. *Herald* staffers suspected the dispatch when early copies of the *Times* and *Tribune* arrived without the proclamation in their telegraphic news columns. Since none of the responsible editors were at the *World* or *Journal of Commerce* when the dispatch arrived, unsuspecting compositors set the late dispatch in type, as was the custom with late AP flimsies, and inserted it in the telegraphic news columns "on the fly."[65]

Part of the authorities' concern over the fraudulent proclamation arose from the fact that May 18 was also steamer day in New York City, and such news, if circulated in Europe, might have harmed Washington's already shaky relations with Great Britain. Bundles of the offending papers were retrieved from the steamer moments before it was to depart. Meanwhile, the dayside AP staff picked up the proclamation from the two papers and, believing it to be the result of the papers' reporting enterprise, included it in AP's day report for the local and out-of-town papers. Craig queried Gobright in Washington about how AP could have missed it the previous night. Frantically, the military authorities, assuming it had reached New York overnight by telegraph, searched telegraph offices and arrested operators and managers in both New York City and Washington. Finding no log of such a proclamation in the telegraph system, the authorities then concentrated on the Associated Press and the two New York papers. Gobright finally wired Craig that the proclamation was a fraud and that AP was suspected of having been involved. Craig fired a kill order onto his news circuits in an effort to restrain his subscribers from publishing the dispatch and then went in search of a culprit.

After satisfying himself that none of his overnight AP staff was responsible for the dispatch, Craig suggested to authorities that the proprietors of a new newsbrokerage in Washington, an independent news room, operated for several Midwestern newspapers by Henry Villard, Adams S. Hill, and Horace White, might be responsible. Villard was held and questioned for two days,[66] Hill was kept under surveillance, and White was summoned to Stanton's office and questioned for several hours. It should be noted that Craig was apparently never arrested, nor was he even under serious suspicion. The government's investigation was stymied at this point—no serious suspects, not even a clear understanding of where the bogus proclamation came from. A Lincoln cabinet meeting that morning was almost totally preoccupied with discussion of the dispatch. Seward suggested suspending the papers, Stanton indicated a willingness to take official steps to that end, and finally, shortly before 2 P.M., May 18, Lincoln signed an order directing the New York commander, Major General John A. Dix,

> to arrest and imprison. . .the editors, proprietors, and
> publishers of the [two] newspapers. . . . You will also take
> possession by military force, of the printing establishments
> . . .and prevent any further publication therefrom.

Gerard Hallock, who had been forced to sell the *Journal of Commerce* to preserve its mailing privileges at the start of the war, was discovered in the paper's offices and was arrested "with great courtesy." *Journal of Commerce* publisher David M. Stone and *World* editor Manton Marble could not be immediately located. Upon learning of Hallock's arrest, *Journal of Commerce* editor William Cowper Prime rushed to Dix's office, arriving just as an order rescinding the arrest order arrived. Historian Harper supposes that Lincoln reconsidered the arrest order on the basis of investigation by Dix, who, it is clear from the correspondence, was not eager to arrest leading New York editors. Hallock was released after a few hours of detention, but the two papers remained under military suspension until their regular morning editions on May 23, five days later.

Meanwhile Marble offered $500 and Craig $1,000 for information leading to the solution of the mystery of the bogus dispatch. Four New York AP editors wrote Lincoln on May 19, explaining Craig's delivery system, guessing that "an ingenious rogue, [who knew] the manner in which the editor were supplied with much of their telegraphic news, could, by selecting his time and opportunity," deliver false news to the papers. The editors asked that the suppression of the two papers be lifted, commenting that "The fraud. . .was one which, from the circumstances attending it and the practices of the Associated Press, was extremely natural and very liable to have succeeded in any daily newspaper establishment in this city. . . ." On May 21 the New York press reported that Howard had been jailed. Mallison's arrest soon followed. When the *World* finally reappeared, two days later, Marble published an open letter to Lincoln, condemning the suppression and accusing Stanton of being the moving force behind the repressive measure. Howard was confined to Fort Lafayette for fourteen weeks and then became the official recorder at the Union military headquarters in the East. After the war he resumed his journalism career, first with the *New York Times* and then, after stops at three other papers, as editor of the *New York Star*, a paper that supported the American Press Association in opposition to the AP.

OTHER CIVIL WAR NEWSBROKERAGES

Although Associated Press was the dominant wartime newsbrokerage, three other such agencies attained some degree of effectiveness during the war. On the one hand, Midwestern editors began asserting both their independence from Eastern press influence and their dissatisfaction with the news report served up by Easterners' AP. This led, in turn, to creation of the so-called independent news room in Washington, a news service to supplement AP's reports for Eastern and Midwestern papers, and to the formative stages of the Western Associated Press, a Midwestern AP eventually seeking equal footing with the New York AP. (Western AP's development is discussed in Volume 2.) On the other hand, Southern editors, cut off from Craig's AP reports and facing wartime publication without adequate news-gathering facilities, formed the Press Association of the Confederate States of America, the prototype of the postwar cooperative news-gathering organization.

Historian Tom Reilly provides an excellent look at the independent news room.[67] Its founders were Henry Villard, Horace White, and Adams S. Hill. Villard had continued as correspondent for the *New York Herald* after he followed Lincoln from Springfield, Ill., to Washington, D.C., filing occasional dispatches also for the *Cincinnati Commercial* and *Chicago Tribune*. In October 1862, Villard, reporting from the Western Front, became associated with the *New York Tribune*.[68] After graduating from Beloit College in 1853, White joined the *Chicago Journal,* and after two years with that paper he was briefly the Chicago agent for the New York Associated Press. After a short involvement with the free state movement that included John Brown, he became a reporter for the *Chicago Tribune,* which made him its Washington correspondent at the outbreak of the Civil War.[69] Hill was a Harvard Law School graduate who became head of the *New York Tribune*'s Washington bureau during the war.[70]

Both Villard and Hill had by the start of 1864 severed their association with the *Tribune*, principally because editor Horace Greeley did not maintain a consistent editorial policy and at times imperiously criticized Villard's reporting. As they cut their *Tribune* ties, Villard and Hill had independently devised, they later learned through conversation, similar plans to establish a Washington-based news agency to supplement Associated Press reports and to serve a number of Midwestern papers that had regularly criticized the AP news reports on which they had to rely.[71] The two reporters' plan, now including Midwesterner White as a third partner, matured around the first of February 1864, their client list including the *Chicago Tribune*, St. Louis *Missouri Democrat, Cincinnati Commercial, Rochester* (N.Y.) *Democrat, Springfield* (Mass.) *Republican,* and *Boston Advertiser.* Reilly finds some common threads among these papers.

> They were all Republican...; they had prospered during
> the war and were expanding; they were not particularly
> satisfied with the coverage supplied to them by the New York
> Associated Press, and the editors of four of the six were
> among the best outside the New York metropolitan
> area....[72]

Villard is unclear as to whether the independent news room was intended as a competitor of the AP. Late in life he characterized the undertaking as "the first news agency in competition with the Associated Press," and as an "undertaking, which was bitterly attacked by the Associated Press for disturbing its monopoly."[73] But at the time the agency was taking shape, Villard wrote *New York Tribune* managing editor Sydney Howard Gay that in Washington

> some of the newspapermen...got up a story that [Hill and I]
> had had a row with the *Tribune* and were going to run a sort
> of opposition. Of course, it is absurd.... I wish to say I have
> nothing to do with any other N.Y. paper, have had and have
> now the kindest feelings toward the *Tribune* and everybody
> connected with it except [for Greeley].[74]

In fact, as Villard was making plans to return to the battlefield a month later, he wrote Gay offering his services as correspondent, presumably as a spinoff of his work for the independent news room.

The news room was soon making its presence felt. Villard's ingenuity had secured release of an exchange of correspondence between Lincoln and Secretary of the Treasury Salmon P. Chase regarding the Pomeroy Circular, a statement concerning Chase's presidential stature in the forthcoming election written by Senator Samuel C. Pomeroy of Kansas. The story broke in the agency's six client newspapers on March 3, 1864. Two months later Villard was with General Ulysses S. Grant's army engaged in the Wilderness Campaign. As the engagement blossomed, Grant shut down telegraphic contact with the outside world, leaving Washington and the North's journalists anxious and guessing about the outcome. Villard rode out of the battle area to Washington with the first news of the bloody, indecisive battle, another scoop for the three-man news agency. The independent news room provided a full report of Washington happenings and whatever Villard might be covering in the battlefield, Hill and White confining their coverage to Washington. Reilly notes that on the day the agency covered the Lincoln-Chase exchange over the Pomeroy Circular, its report also included: a statement by Stanton on continuation of draft bounties, news items from Southern newspapers, the status of Grant's promotion to lieutenant general, results of several congressional elections in Missouri, and the status of a whisky tax bill in the Senate.[75]

Craig, burdened with official dispatches, facing a chorus of complaints from Midwestern papers, and yielding much of the better war coverage opportunities to independent or special correspondents, saw in the Hill-White-Villard operation a menace that could scoop him and encourage Midwestern editors to oppose his AP service. When the *New York Journal of Commerce* and *World* published the bogus presidential proclamation in May 1864, Craig, as we have seen, blamed the independent news room for the treachery. On May 20 Craig moved an AP dispatch charging Villard, Hill, and White with fabricating the false proclamation.

> It may be of interest to the public and the press, who were so terribly imposed on in the publication of the great bogus proclamation, to know that in the city of Washington there has of late existed a body of news gatherers, styling themselves the representatives of the Western Press, composed of Messrs. White, Hill, and Villard, who have for some time been sending daily dispatches to . . . points at the West.
>
> These persons are in no way connected with the Associated Press. . . . It appears, as we learn from the well

informed correspondent of the *Commercial Advertiser,* that on Tuesday night [May 17] a dispatch was sent by members of this Western Press Association, or purported to have been sent by them announcing that there would be a proclamation, calling for a new draft, about the 1st of July....

Whether the bogus Proclamation was concerted by one of the Association, or whether another person based it upon their news, is not yet officially known. It is fair to infer, however, that either some member of the above Association was the author of the bogus Proclamation, or that some person connected with them, knowing the fact that a call was about to be made, wrote the Proclamation upon the predictions furnished by their dispatches.... The Provost Marshal of Washington is giving the matter a thorough investigation, and all the above persons will be critically examined in reference to this great outrage upon the public and the press.[76]

Reilly reveals the ferocity of the Western papers' response to Craig's underhanded accusations. The *Cincinnati Commercial* and *Chicago Tribune* as recipients of AP news reports printed Craig's attack on May 21, following it with strong rebuttals. After supporting and approving the efforts of the independent news room trio and denigrating "a considerable portion" of Craig's work for AP as being "the repetition to the Western press of the news gathered by the New York [newspapers'] specials at Washington," the *Commercial* called Craig's story "a most mean outrage."

Mr. CRAIG knew when writing his card that he was insinuating a charge that was false and scandalous. We understand his game perfectly. He desires to withdraw attention from himself. He is the responsible man of the New York Associated Press, and through that organization the bogus proclamation was telegraphed to all the Western cities, without an express statement of its character, some hours after it was known in New York to be a forgery....

The *Commercial* reported that although Craig's office in New York was telling the *New York Times* at 3:30A.M. that the proclamation was "false as hell," that same office moved the proclamation to the Western papers and did not send a kill order on the story for "eight hours and a half after it was pronounced a forgery in the Associated Press office in New York!" The paper concluded:

> Before Mr. CRAIG's insinuations against others are taken
> as of any account, he must explain his own conduct. . . . [T]he
> original outrage of the forger, whoever he may be, was vastly
> transcended by the publicity given the forgery through the
> Associated Press. . . .[77]

The same day the conspirators were being identified and arrested, as we have seen, the Western papers published their re-
sponses to Craig's charges. Villard was immediately released, and
"although no apologies were made to him or his colleagues," says
David Homer Bates, "some choice scraps of news later found their
way to the office of the syndicate, which supplied material for new
'scoops,' and had a soothing influence generally."[78] White's biographer notes that the proclamation fracas left no lasting scars on either side. While the news agency benefited from subsequent War
Department news leaks, White defended the government two
months later against press criticism that Jubal Early's forces which
overran the Shenandoah Valley had been overestimated by the government.[79]

Villard made one more journey to the battlefront, at Petersburg
in June and July 1864, and came away weary of war and disheart-
ened by the carnage. On September 14, 1864, he sailed for Europe,
where his older sister was dying. He did not return to the United
States until April 15, 1865, after the war was over and the same day
Lincoln was shot.[80] Hill and White, meanwhile, had continued the
news room, confining their coverage to the Washington scene, until
the end of hostilities, when White returned to Chicago to become
editor of the *Tribune.* Hill stayed on in journalism until 1868, when
he entered academic life, teaching and writing about rhetoric and
oratory until his retirement in 1904.[81]

While newsbroking in the North was alive with competition and
criticism, the Southern editor during the war faced the quite different problem of finding a newsbrokerage that could survive long
enough to become effective. The prewar beginnings of the Southern
Associated Press,[82] as previously noted, amounted largely to receiving a news report from the New York AP at Washington. When the
north-south telegraph trunks were severed at the start of the war,
Southern papers were forced to fend for themselves. The literature
presents the Southern press as being more provincial, more old-
fashioned, and less numerous than its Northern counterpart. Daniel
J. Kenny counted eighty-four dailies in the eleven Confederate
states as of 1861, only 18.7 percent of Kenny's total of 450 dailies in

the nation.[83] In reality, the 1860 census data showing that 20.3 percent of the nation's free population lived in the eleven Confederate states[84] suggest that the South's press may not have been disproportionately small.

T. C. De Leon offers some telling comments about the Southern press of 1861.

> Northern newspapers came to the South; and except for matters of local information, or local policy, a large class of her readers drew their inspiration chiefly from journals of New York. . . .
>
> These papers were far ahead of those of the South—except in very rare instances—in their machinery for collecting news and gossip; for making up a taking whole; and in the no less important knowledge of manipulating their circulation and advertising patronage. The newspaper system of the North had been reduced to a science. Its great object was *to pay*. . . .
>
> In the South the case was entirely different. Even in the large cities, newspapers were content with a local circulation; they had a little-varying clientele which looked upon them as infallible; and their object was to consider and digest ideas, rather than to propagate, or manufacture them.[85]

There were, in other words, still many strong political newspapers in the South, operating as the region's dominant journalistic force and going largely unchallenged by a middle-class press and aggressive news-gathering. Cut off from Craig's reports, the Southern press experimented with several newsbroking systems during the war years as beleaguered editors fought to survive and cooperate while the waves of war lapped at their towns and submerged their modest telegraphic network. Although newsbroking in the Confederacy was something of a ragtag affair, it did produce one significant milestone: the organization of a cooperative newsbrokerage more closely resembling postwar agencies than those operating before and during the war in the North.

As the Confederacy took shape, according to historian E. Merton Coulter, news-gathering agencies emerged in New Orleans, Nashville, and Montgomery. Nothing can be found regarding the New Orleans and Nashville agencies. The Montgomery agency, centered at the temporary seat of the new government, was operated by William H. Pritchard, editor of the *Augusta Constitutionalist* and Southern AP's new agent in South Carolina, Georgia, and Alabama before telegraphic contact with the North was cut off. When the Confederate government was moved to Richmond early in June, Pritchard opened a newsbroking office in that city, apparently retaining his residence in Augusta and perhaps an affiliation with the *Constitutionalist*. His news agency is commonly referred to in the literature as the Southern Associated Press. When Pritchard died in Richmond on March 24, 1862, his son, William H. Pritchard, Jr., took over the enterprise. Meanwhile Southern editors became restless about relying on the Pritchard agency.[86] Denied a voice in its operation, yet forced to accept its dispatches or shoulder the expense of sending special correspondents to the capital, Southern editors began taking steps in early 1862 to free themselves from Pritchard's AP. John S. Thrasher, who was to become superintendent of the Press Association of the Confederacy, later called Pritchard's operation "a limited system of news reports" that by the latter part of 1862 "was found to be unsatisfactory to the publishers and the public."[87]

Meanwhile the "combined Press of Richmond" established "a more widely extended and perfect organization," Thrasher continues.[88] This new agency, retaining the name "Associated Press," was centered in Richmond and was controlled exclusively by the Richmond newspapers. It went into operation on November 3, 1862, with John Graeme, Jr., as its general manager in the capital. A notice in the *Richmond Dispatch* explains that to "the full extent of the resources of the Association, agents will be appointed at every important point in the Confederacy, and special arrangements will be made to obtain news from the army and from the North." The notice asked editors to report their previous telegraphic tolls for receipt of Pritchard's AP dispatches as a guide to "charges under the new system." Finally the notice asserted that a "large majority of the daily journals in the Confederate States have united to form an Associated Press."[89]

It was true that the Southern journals found themselves exchanging a newsbrokerage controlled by the Pritchards for one controlled by the Richmond press, but Southern journalism was by no means "united" behind the new Richmond-based AP. Back in January 1862, six newspapers from lower and western Confederate states called for a meeting of Southern editors to discuss several problems. One of the six, the *Memphis Appeal*, described the problems in the following uncompromising terms:

> Universal complaint is found with the present unorganized
> and imbecile arrangement by which the Southern press are
> supplied with telegraphic reports. These reports are vague
> and unsatisfactory, unmeaning, unreliable, and, in many
> instances, flagitiously false. They come to us in a roundabout
> way, after two or three repetitions by as many agents, thus
> securing exaggeration as well as additional expense. They are
> doled out by self constituted and incompetent monopolists,
> who are growing fat and insolent through their extortionate
> earnings from the press. Reform is needed.[90]

Another paper calling for a meeting, the *Charleston Mercury,* observed that "It is high time for the journals of the South to be making arrangements for a permanent, extended, better organized,
and, at the same time, more economic news agency."[91]

The meeting was scheduled for Atlanta on March 26, 1862, and
fourteen days before it was to convene, the *Atlanta Southern Confederacy* carried the following list of topics to be discussed:

1. The Telegraph. Plea for a united news gathering agency.
2. Paper. More adequate and less uncertain supply needed.
3. Mills, Postage, etc. Convention could influence Congress.[92]

Only a handful of the nineteen invited newspapers[93] attended
the Atlanta meeting, reported the *Savannah News,* because of

> the disturbing state of affairs, and the fact that most of the
> Western papers, which were very deeply interested in the
> movement, have lately passed into the hands of the enemy.
> The press of Virginia was kept away because of affairs.[94]

It should be noted, however, that only the *Examiner* and *Whig* in
Virginia were invited to this meeting. Representatives did come
from Charleston, Savannah, Columbus (Ga.), Augusta, Macon, Atlanta, Memphis, and Knoxville, and, after passing a few resolutions,
the group agreed to meet later in Richmond.[95]

Nearly ten months passed before Southern editors tried again to
convene an editorial convention. This one, on January 3, 1863,
arose from a call by the *Montgomery Advertiser.* Originally slated
for Richmond, the meeting was moved to Macon at the urging of the
Augusta papers. Historian Rabun Lee Brantley, paraphrasing the
Macon Telegraph, gave as the meeting's purpose "to have present at
its sessions, printers, pressmen, agents, and reporters, so that a bet-

ter understanding of what news really was could be brought about."[96] Only one representative from Richmond and a few from Georgia papers attended, and after informal discussion of arrangements with the Associated Press recently set up by the Richmond press, and of the continuing paper shortage, the meeting adjourned. Joseph Clisby, editor of the *Macon Telegraph* and chairman of the meeting, was instructed to send circulars urging attendance of all daily papers in the Confederacy at another meeting, this one on February 4, 1863, in Augusta.

Publishers of twelve newspapers[97] showed up at Augusta, most of them from the southern tier of Confederate states and none from Richmond. During February 4 and 5 the Press Association of the Confederate States of America was created—a constitution was enacted, directors were elected, and the new association's relations with the Richmond and Charleston press were discussed.[98] The *Macon Telegraph* afterwards described the meeting in constructive terms.

> It was a gathering of a strictly business character, connected more particularly with the collection and distribution of news by telegram. It was made the first of an annual series of meetings, at which gathering from all parts of our widely extended Confederacy, the profession will annually renew and extend their acquaintance with one another, and re-establish and cultivate those feelings, principles and professional courtesies, the loss of which have done so much to degrade the character and diminish the influence and usefulness of the newspaper press.[99]

It is difficult to know whether the Press Association was simply a reaction to a New York AP–style Richmond press agency or whether more constructive and creative motives dominated its formation. Clearly, however, the Richmond papers were not participants initially, but merely sent to the Augusta meeting, through Graeme and L. T. Blome of the Richmond AP, a communication "setting forth the objects, services, and difficulties attending that association in furnishing news by telegraph."[100]

The Press Association constitution outlined an association of Confederate publishers to secure "early, full and reliable intelligence by telegraph" to be governed by a board of directors. Headquarters were to be in Augusta, and the PA's constitution reserved to the sitting board the right "in case the Richmond papers or any of them, join the Association" to "add to their number by electing a

Director for that city and section."[101] The same olive branch was held out to the press of Charleston in discussion following ratification of the constitution.[102] The majority of daily journals in the Confederacy were on the road to establishing a cooperative newsbroking association.

The Press Association's organization was novel among newsbrokerages, as Arthur T. Robb observed in 1949,[103] foreshadowing the system of newsgathering and self-governance that would subsequently be adopted by most of the new post–Civil War regional APs and eventually by the national AP. While the PA constitution provided for members' input, PA's superintendent, J. S. Thrasher, contributed substantially to PA's newsbroking innovativeness. According to the constitution, the PA's primary object was "to arrange, put in operation, and keep up an efficient system of reporting news by telegraph, which shall be under the exclusive control, and employed for the exclusive benefit of the members thereof."[104] Each member newspaper had one vote in the election of a president, secretary-treasurer, and a board of five directors, each director overseeing the district in which he resided. The board established overall policy, employed a superintendent and assistants, and assessed members "fairly and equitably" for the cost of operating the association.

The constitution required members "in localities where there are no Press Agents, to transmit all news of interest occurring in their vicinity to the nearest Agency," this obligation to be shared in communities where two or more members were located. Although the terms of the association did not "restrict individual enterprise in obtaining special dispatches," the constitution said, "combinations between members to obtain dispatches outside of the Association, excluding others from a joint participation on equal terms, will be deemed inconsistent with the spirit of the Association." Membership was open to daily papers publishing in the Confederacy on February 5, 1863, as long as they paid an "initiation fee" of $50 and made written application "expressing concurrence with the Articles of the Association and pledging adherence to its regulations." The association, therefore, bound Confederate publishers to a mutually advantageous, cooperative news-gathering and distributing system that was governed by a representative board of directors. All were to contribute to the good of the whole, both in news dispatches and in telegraphic tolls, and the resulting news report was "for the exclusive benefit of the members." Thus, control of Confederate newsbroking would be in the hands of at least a majority of the representatives of the Southern press rather than a few journals located in Richmond.

Dr. Robert Wilson Gibbes, publisher of the *Columbia South Carolinian,* was the first president, and N. S. Morse of the *Augusta Chronicle and Sentinel* was elected secretary-treasurer. The new board was heavily loaded with Georgia publishers: G. W. Adair, *Atlanta Southern Confederacy;* W. G. Clark, *Mobile Advertiser and Register;* J. R. Sneed, *Savannah Republican;* James Gardner, *Augusta Constitutionalist;* and Joseph Clisby, *Macon Telegraph.*[105] The board first met only hours after ratification of the constitution and agreed to hire a superintendent at $3,000 per year (within three months the salary was increased to $5,000 "in view of the enormous cost of living at the present time")[106] and began to set up working rules.[107]

John S. Thrasher took charge of the Press Association superintendency on March 9, 1863. Outside of a checkered journalistic past, only a fervent pro-slavery attitude fitted Thrasher for his PA chores. Born and educated a Yankee, Thrasher accompanied his parents to Cuba when he was fifteen or sixteen years old. After clerking in a mercantile house for more than a decade in Cuba, Thrasher fell in with revolutionaries in 1848, editing an anti-Spanish propaganda newspaper for thirteen months. This editorial activity led to his court martial and brief imprisonment on the northern coast of Africa, from which he was rescued by the intercession of the American minister in Madrid. He next turned up in New Orleans, editorially aiding the cause of annexation of Cuba to the United States. In 1855 he secured a position with the *New York Herald* as a correspondent, traveling in Mexico and South America for the next four years. It is not clear, however, when he gravitated to the Confederacy prior to taking the PA position.[108]

The same day that Thrasher officially joined PA, a news report was first filed to PA members, who, totaling thirty-one dailies, were the bulk of the old Associated Press client list previously served by the Richmond AP newsbrokerage.[109] By the time of Thrasher's first quarterly report to the board, dated May 13, 1863, PA membership stood at forty-four papers, including the original thirty-one, plus four dailies in Richmond, two in Charleston, six other dailies, and one tri-weekly.[110] Thrasher said the list "comprises every daily journal in the Confederacy."[111] The adversities of war had whittled PA's membership down to forty-two by October 13, 1863, and to forty-one by January 14, 1864.[112] The new agency inherited the old Associated Press contract with the Southern Telegraph Company (the Confederate portion of the prewar American Telegraph Company network), which limited the weekly total of news transmitted to 3,500 words and the daily total to 1,000 words.[113] The same limits were in a contract Thrasher negotiated with the Southwestern Telegraph Company on April 9, 1863. Any portion of the report exceeding these limits was transmitted at ten cents per word. For this service, each PA paper paid $12 per week, excluding added assessments for reports exceeding daily and weekly limits.[114]

Thrasher concentrated on three areas of PA operations. First, he struggled to implement the board's and the constitution's mandate that members serve as PA's principal agents, thus eliminating the expense of employing many correspondents. In a circular dated March 13, 1863, to PA members, Thrasher announced that

> In order to devote the funds of the Association more effectually to the procuring of intelligence from the scene of active army operations, I . . . at as early a day as possible shall discontinue all paid agents at points where journals, members of the Association exist, except Richmond.

This step, he said, would eliminate paid agents in ten locations where PA members existed and allow for additional agents "at points of great public interest" where member papers were not located.[115]

Results were uneven, but Thrasher was optimistic, as this comment in mid-1863 indicates:

> I . . . do not doubt that with some practice on the part of the Press, . . . the habit of sending a telegraphic synopsis of news to their compeers, will become as fixed a habit in every well conducted Editorial room, as is that of sending copy to the foreman.[116]

By October, although Thrasher had "the satisfaction to report that improvement has been noticed in the working of the mutual system," he was still prodding members, suggesting the board find some way of enforcing compliance with the mutual system.

> In the present absence of such means, there is only a moral obligation upon the members to comply with the duties of fellowship, which does not receive that equal attention that the equal receipt of benefits renders incumbent upon all.[117]

In January 1864 he repeated his request for sanctions against unco-operative members,[118] but this was obviously a losing battle.

The second area of Thrasher's emphasis was taking the fat out of the news report. Hemmed in by daily and weekly word limits, Thrasher warred against telegraphic dispatches that "consist mainly of a diarrhoea of words with an extreme paucity of facts."[119] His answer to this problem was to excise articles, pronouns, conjunctions, prepositions, adjectives, and auxiliary verbs, which were, he said, "seldom necessary to convey meaning, particularly if the language employed in treating every subject were divided into short sentences." He computed that two-fifths of news report language could be dropped.[120]

After some members criticized the new policy, Thrasher fired off a circular on May 1, 1863, to the PA membership defending his clipped news report.

> I believed that it was not...the object of the Press Association to reduce all its members to one procrustean level in the editing of news reports, and that it was not its duty, nor that of its Superintendent, to supply the want of a knowledge of geography, of the history of current events, of the antecedents of men who came into public notice, and of industry, intelligence and tact in preparing for readers the matter sent.[121]

He offered several examples of dispatches in telegraph and published form. The one below is a published version, the italicized words missing in the telegraphic form.

> OKALONA, April 25.—Our cavalry engaged *the* enemy yesterday at Birmingham. *The* fight lasted 2½ hours. *The* enemy *were* completely routed, *with* 15 killed *and a* large number wounded. Col. Hatch *of the* 2d Iowa cavalry was seen *to* fall from his horse, which ran into *our* lines and was captured. Our loss *was* one killed *and* twenty wounded. *The* destruction of *the* bridge prevented pursuit.[122]

The above example, in which fifty-four telegraphic words expanded to sixty-nine words in print, was the least extreme example Thrasher offered, eliminating only 21.7 percent of the word count on the telegraph. Other examples ranged from a 27.3 percent to a 36.4 percent reduction in wordage.

Thrasher did remarkably well staying within his 3,500-word weekly limit. In the first three weeks (March 9–29, 1863) his report averaged 1,884 words per week. In the next three months (March 30–June 27) he averaged 2,315.7 words per week; in the following three months (June 28–September 26) he averaged 3,039.7 words per week; and in the final three months of 1863 (September 27–December 26) he averaged 3,356.8 words per week. In only eight of these forty-two weeks did he exceed his limit: 4,036 words, June 28–July 4; 3,528 words, August 23–29; 3,628 words, September 20–26; 4,712 words, October 4–10; 4,410 words, October 11–17; 3,772 words, November 29–December 5; 3,606 words, December 6–12; and 4,769 words, December 13–19.[123] One may detect in these figures the impact of news reports of Gettysburg (June 27–July 4), Chickamauga (September 19–20), and Chattanooga (November 23–25).

Copyright was Thrasher's third area of emphasis. His first tour of the Confederacy on behalf of the PA convinced him that PA's news reports could be stolen by unauthorized parties without compensation to the PA. Numerous private "clubs" had been formed to receive and distribute among their members the latest telegraphic news dispatches; some weekly journals were actually privately published news letters for club members. Beyond this club movement, which threatened the profitability of PA dailies and the confidentiality of PA's news report, Thrasher detected among telegraph officials some inclination to use PA's reports to establish their own newspapers. In his report of October 13, 1863, Thrasher announced that the Press Association news report was protected by the Confederacy's copyright law, requiring each day's report in each member newspaper to be headed:

REPORTS OF THE PRESS ASSOCIATION
Entered according to act of Congress in the year 1863, by
J. S. Thrasher, in the Clerk's office of the District
Court of the Confederate States for the Northern District
of Georgia.[124]

Thrasher reports, however, that some members "from inattention, or other motives" were "very careless in their observance of the requirements" of the law and PA's copyright rules, by not including the above heading.

The Richmond press refused to publish the heading. PA's Richmond agent, John Graeme, Jr., put the matter simply.

> The Press here will not insert the copyright title.... The
> copyright is unpopular, so to speak, with the Richmond

> publishers. . . . [T]hey listened with but little patience to
> anything I have to say on that and kindred subjects, though
> otherwise very courteous to me. I also called their attention
> this week to the pledge [of PA membership, required to be
> signed by all PA members]. They repudiate it, and reiterate
> that they will do nothing more than pay all reasonable
> charges for news. They want neither copyright, circulars,
> pledges or aught else but the news.[125]

But Thrasher had his way, for on November 3, the heading first appeared in the *Richmond Dispatch,* and there it remained until August 24, 1864, when the heading "Reported Specially for the 'Daily Dispatch' " replaced it.

By early 1864 Thrasher was at pains to maintain contact with trans-Mississippi newspapers and agents as Union successes in the West denied ever larger portions of the Southwestern telegraph system to him. His newspaper membership was increasingly in disarray, papers being silenced by Union troops or dashing ahead of advancing Northern lines. Although his administrative reports were remarkably free of comment and anxiety during the war, Thrasher observed at the start of his report on October 13, 1863, that

> During the quarter now transpiring, the labors in
> organizing an efficient system of reporting news by telegraph
> have been greatly increased by the unfortunate events
> attending the pending war, while the results attained by our
> efforts have been, by the same cause, largely diminished.[126]

Thrasher had made his headquarters in Atlanta, accessible to both the Southwestern and Southern telegraph companies' lines, but by mid-1864 Atlanta sat squarely in the path of General Sherman's march from Chattanooga to cut the Confederacy in half. On September 1 General John Bell Hood evacuated the city; Sherman entered Atlanta the next day. The PA headquarters had been moved to Macon and was serving thirty-eight dailies in August 1864 when four of those troublesome Richmond papers, *Dispatch, Enquirer, Examiner,* and *Sentinel,* notified Thrasher that they were withdrawing from the PA to form the Mutual Press Association. The *Richmond Whig* remained PA's only voice in the capital.[127]

In mid-October 1864, notices appeared in the four Richmond papers announcing their new wire and offering to "members" who were "accessible by telegraph, all important news from [Richmond], together with [a] synopsis of interesting Congressional proceedings." Out-of-town recipients of this report were to arrange for their own agents to receive the report, to pay the transmission tolls themselves, rather than being assessed through the Mutual Press Association, and "to forward to the General Agent all important news" from their communities. To become members of the Mutual agency, papers outside the capital were asked to contribute $5 per month in advance to the treasurer in Richmond. Agents and officers of the new agency were all Richmond people.[128]

A "Reports of the Richmond Daily Press" credit line appeared in the *Dispatch* from October 14 to 20. On October 21 the credit line "Reports of the Mutual Press Association" first appeared; it continued sporadically until mid-November, after which the paper gave little evidence of receiving telegraphic dispatches, relying instead on newspaper exchanges. The loss of the Richmond papers appears not to have affected PA, whose new president, W. G. Clark of the *Mobile Advertiser and Register,* stated in October 1864 that PA served eight more papers than it had two months earlier.[129] Thrasher meanwhile had left PA operations to John Graeme, Jr., on September 5, 1864, traveling to the trans-Mississippi region to organize coverage in one of the few remaining Confederate strongholds. He did not return to Macon until near the end of January 1865.[130]

Historian Andrews observes that "the Confederate press was unable to conceal the low ebb to which public morale in the South had fallen in the first weeks of January 1865." Finding "fewer journals, fainter voices," Andrews calls the Southern press both "heartsick and confused."[131] The end of hostilities in April found the Press Association still supplying dispatches to its few remaining members. Andrews notes PA dispatches in the Augusta papers "as late as May 2, although by that time all organized resistance to Federal authority east of the Mississippi River had ceased."[132] The Press Association, despite a lean news report, a thin staff, a diminishing membership, and eventually the hopelessness of its nation's cause, had in its two years exhibited a system of organizing newsbroking both previously untried and subsequently widely adopted. Thrasher, in his last published superintendent's report, dated January 12, 1864, alludes to the "novelty of the attempt" by Confederate publishers to form a mutual cooperative. He viewed the PA as

an association, which should combine the Press in one
common effort in behalf of the common good, and present
the first known instance of an union of the whole Press of a
Country for the purpose of collecting and diffusing
intelligence of general interest to the people. . . .

> Under the operations of this system, the publisher of
> limited means and small circulation for his journal is enabled
> to present to his readers daily news reports from all parts of
> the country on a footing of perfect equality with the richest
> publisher in the land.[133]

Thrasher's pet projects—mutual exchange of news, brevity in the
news report, and copyright protection of the report—would, as we
shall see in Volume 2, interest journalists and newsbrokers for the
next half-century.

THE WARTIME NEWS REPORTS

The nation quaked and recoiled at Shiloh, Antietam, Vicksburg,
Gettysburg, Chickamauga, and Atlanta, and all the others. No
longer simply post office names or specks on a map, this peculiarly
American collection of names would forever tell the story of a divided people's hopes and fears carried into deadly battle by legions
of coarse men and frightened boys. Politically, economically, and
emotionally the Civil War overshadowed all in the nineteenth century that had preceded it and profoundly affected most of what
came after it to the turn of the century. Between 33 and 40 percent
of the combined Union and Confederate military forces were killed
or wounded during the four-year war, making it the costliest war in
U.S. history. The winner's losses exceeded the loser's by over
100,000.

Confined primarily to wooded and rural areas, small towns, and
Confederate soil, the war actually spurred many sectors of Northern business and finance. Union newspapers added Sunday editions,
extras on weekdays, more pages, and many more readers during the
war, capitalizing on the daily parade of graphic and moving eyewitness accounts from the battlefields, and on rumors, death lists, and
official dispatches. Despite pesky off-and-on censorship, occasionally disrupted telegraphic communications, and infrequent threats
of battlefield injuries, this American Civil War was a marvelous ex-
cursion for hundreds of correspondents on both sides. They
stretched their literary and nationalistic legs, walked out to a distant ridge to scout the fortunes of "our forces" and "the enemy,"
describing their sightings in excited personalized hour-by-hour im-
agery, and dispatched their accounts over such signatures as "Ag-
ate," "Personne," "Galway," "Gamma," or simply "B." As in every
other age, the Civil War was nominating journalism's, as well as the
nation's, next generation of leaders and legends.

The newsbrokerages, however, saw little of this splendid sport. Pipelines for governmental dispatches or pronouncements of officials who were safely tucked away in the two half-nations' capitals, Associated Press, the independent news room, and the Press Association shunned the spicier and more varied cuisine of the newspaper field correspondent. The number and prominence of the New York AP partners' own field correspondents relegated Daniel H. Craig and his AP staff to routine official matter in the main. In an 1863 annual report, Craig had little to say about his small corps of correspondents.

> During most of [1862] we have had a correspondent at
> Gen. McClellan's Headquarters and another with Gen. Banks
> and others on the Upper Potomac. At present we have but
> one correspondent with the army of the Potomac, Mr. T.
> Barnard, who was formerly one of Mr. Gobright's assistants at
> Washington.[134]

An example of AP's coverage of a major battle is found in AP's dispatches from Gettysburg as they appeared in New York's *Tribune* and *Times* on Monday, July 6, 1863. In addition to official dispatches issuing from Washington, D.C., AP relied on one field reporter, Theodore Barnard,[135] whose dispatches received "semi-official" status by being passed by field censorship. His dispatches reveal a Union bias common among most Northern correspondents, full of phrases like "enemy's guns," "our left wing," and "the Rebels." Barnard's work, however, lacked the literary quality, emotionalism, or personal involvement so often found in colleagues' war zone accounts.[136]

Gettysburg coverage filled all of page one and half of page eight in the *Times* and all of pages one and twelve and part of page seven in the *Tribune*. The AP dispatches accounted for 23 percent of the *Tribune*'s coverage, which otherwise included specials from Melville D. Landon ("M.D.L.") and "B.F.C." in Baltimore; "Beta" at Hanover, Pa.; and R. D. Francis, Josiah Rhinehart Sypher, and T. C. Grey ("T.C.G.") at the battlefield. In the *Times* the AP dispatches occupied 38.3 percent of the total space devoted to Gettysburg, the paper otherwise using "Whit" at Harrisburg, and Lorenzo Livingston Crounse and Samuel Wilkeson at the battlefield.

The specials in both papers are far more lively and engaging than the AP reports. Crounse leads his dispatch with: "Another great battle was fought yesterday afternoon, resulting in a magnificent success to the National arms." Wilkeson begins with: "The experience of all the tried and veteran officers of the Army of the Potomac tells of no such desperate conflict as has been in progress during this day." In the *Tribune*, one correspondent concluded with:

> The result amounted to a rout. Cavalry has been sent out to harvest the stragglers. Gen Hayes is said to have covered himself with glory. General Doubleday fell fighting gallantly, saying, as a ball pierced his head, "I'm killed! I'm killed!" Gen. Hancock thinks he is not killed, but seriously wounded. And thus night has drawn her mantle over another bloody day, but a day so bright with deeds of heroism and grand results, with patriotic devotion and sublime death, that the page of History shall glitter with that light.

Deep in Grey's dispatch to the *Tribune* one finds:

> Our men were nerved to the highest pitch of enthusiasm during the fight, and cheer after cheer was heard above the din of battle as our brave fellows rolled back at each assault the ragged legions of the enemy. Men with severe wounds, when being carried from the field to the hospitals, were heard cheering as the intelligence that we were driving the enemy was communicated to them.

In contrast, AP's second dispatch from the battlefield ended with:

> Too much credit cannot be given to our batteries, who for hours stood to their guns under a broiling sun and surrounded by the missiles of death, retiring only to give their positions to others, when their caissons and limbers were exhausted of ammunition. The infantry engaged also nobly did their duty, and the enemy to-day at their hands have received the greatest disaster ever administered by the Union forces. All officers award the highest honors to Gen. Meade, for the able generalship he has displayed since he assumed command, and particularly for his coolness, decision, and energy on this memorable 3d of July.

Throughout the war, AP's copy occupied calmer, more factual, and less emotional ground than that of its members' correspondents. Without glint or glitter, AP concentrated on apolitical (except for a pro-Union cast), abbreviated, and official reporting. Newsbroking dispatches were no longer unique and desirable because of their technological advantage; they had, instead, quickly become the workhorses of journalism's war coverage, outclassed and outdistanced by flashy, fast thoroughbreds.

Craig's feelings about his wartime position as official mouthpiece are not recorded, but constraints imposed on him by his New York principals have to have been worrisome. He feared his service beyond New York City was too thin, too susceptible to criticism to guarantee AP's continued national superiority. At the start of 1863, with Midwestern editors already grumbling their disapproval of AP's meager offerings, Craig addressed his New York City editors in stern terms.

> It is due to the outside Editors to say that they pay you in *cash* nearly one half of your whole expenses. . . and yet you do not make any arrangements whatever for news except such as you deem important to your own interests—neither adding to or [*sic*] subtracting from your news arrangements anything on account of the outside press.[137]

Craig counseled not cutting adrift any newspapers then receiving the AP service, either in the city or outside, and not raising the rates for the AP service.[138] He then raised the specter of competition.

> An opposition News Association, properly organized, with even a few hundred dollars per week, from this city, as a foundation, would speedily and surely extend all over the country, to the very serious detriment of your Association. Of this I have not a particle of doubt. It is a great mistake to suppose that the Associated Press hold a monopoly of any news. *First come, first served* is the only rule known by honest telegraphers. . . .[139]

Midwestern editors' criticism could not be ignored by Craig, and his local editors, awash with stunning and sensational war copy, needed convincing that their shortsightedness about a meatier news report threatened the AP's existence. As Volume 2 shows, Craig's worst fears would be realized in the post–Civil War years, but Craig would not be around to deal with the problem. The other wartime newsbrokerages fared no better than AP in gathering a comprehensive news report. Tom Reilly discovered, as noted above, that the independent news room of Villard, White, and Hill moved a largely news feature report—heavy with Washington observations, sprinkled only occasionally with Villard dispatches from the field of battle. Western editors, although they complained about Craig's reports, did not drop the workhorse AP but augmented it with the independent news room's reports.

In the South newsbroking conditions were worse. With a 3,500-word weekly limit, Thrasher's Press Association dispatches were far leaner and sketchier than Craig's. A PA report in the March 10, 1864, *Richmond Dispatch* consists of eight dispatches from only five locations. Thrasher apparently was not the official government pipeline. Rather, the general impression in the South was that in sequence two Richmond dailies served as official organs for the Jefferson Davis administration. The *Richmond Enquirer*, according to popular belief, occasionally carried unsigned articles by Davis and Secretary of War (and later of State) Judah P. Benjamin during the early part of the war. In August 1862 the paper was named by Adjutant General Samuel Cooper to publish official government orders.[140] The other apparent Davis mouthpiece was the *Sentinel*, which at the start of the war published in Alexandria, Va., and later moved to Richmond, where it issued its first number on March 11, 1863.[141]

Some vestiges of the old party organ system that Lincoln had abandoned in favor of the Associated Press persisted in the Confederacy, denying the PA Davis's official communiques. But unlike the North, where party labels retained some of their old meaning among editors, if not prestige and patronage during the war, Southern editors responded to the single cause of the Confederacy and its prosecution of the war. The more monolithic political and economic structure of the South before and during the war allowed its editors to avoid sharp party divisions among themselves, and, as Thomas C. De Leon suggests, to respond largely from personal viewpoints.[142] The PA reports examined by the author reflect a paucity of sources, correspondents, and resources. There is also in the PA report and in the Confederate press generally a preoccupation with news reports in Northern newspapers. Orange Court House, a community sixty-five miles northwest of Richmond, was a major exchange point through which Northern papers entered the Confederacy; that dateline on dispatches reporting comment and coverage of various Northern journals appeared regularly in the PA reports during 1864.

The PA reports, as one might expect, are much shorter and sketchier than AP's coverage of Gettysburg described above. The Gettysburg coverage by the Southern papers and the PA presents a quite different substantive and journalistic picture. Early coverage of the battle, for example, in the *Richmond Dispatch* on Tuesday, July 7, 1863, contained exchange dates of July 2–4, relying primarily on the *New York World* and *Herald* and telegraphic dates of July 5–6, datelined Martinsburg, Va., thirty-six miles southwest of Gettysburg. The exchange copy was inconclusive about the outcome of the battle, but the Martinsburg telegraphic dispatches report a clear victory for the Confederacy. The next day's *Dispatch,* while conceding that the battle had been bloody for both sides, still relied on telegraphic reports from Martinsburg claiming victory for the South. So far no official dispatches had been issued on Gettysburg. In the vacuum left by official silence and by a newsbrokerage unable to get its own reporter to the scene and facing limited telegraphic channels, editors and their readers swam in treacherous waters.

Finally on July 9—three days after the outcome was reported in New York's dailies—the *Dispatch* carried its first official Gettysburg dispatch, dated July 8, to J. A. Seddon, secretary of war, claiming "a decided and telling advantage over the enemy. . . . So far the victory is ours." The carefully phrased telegram implies that the battle has not ended. On that inconclusive note the paper's coverage of the battle ended.

No doubt there was deception and a considerable insufficiency of information on both sides of the battle lines during the war. The AP's reports consisted of more, longer, and more recent dispatches than its Southern counterpart. And for better or worse, AP was favored with government's steady stream of official dispatches. Throughout the war Craig had the support of leading papers, the reports of field correspondents, and the services of a full and functional telegraph system. Meanwhile in the South, Thrasher, who faced an indifferent and at times hostile officialdom, severe financial and telegraphic limitations, and too few members and independent sources of news accounts, generated a news report of marginal value at best. In both North and South, however, unashamed overarching nationalism was the reporting norm.

DISCUSSION

The forces encircling youthful newsbroking and telegraphy in the Civil War were lusty, persistent, and inevitably overpowering. As two American governments gradually established a wartime footing with each other anticipating the conflict ahead, they impinged increasingly upon the activity of individuals and the private sector. Newspaper journalism, enjoying the fruits of twenty years of unimpeded technological growth, a steady tradition of aggressive newsgathering, and an expanding reading audience, tolerated the sting

of censorship for the chance to intermingle with the nation's ultimate news event as a point of personal pride and professional obligation.

The press, both North and South, determined to exercise its full
constitutional right in the face of censorship, mob action, and even
death itself, flooded the battlefields and capitals with correspondents, poking into officers' tents and government's offices, clamor-
ing for a better view and an earlier word of victory or defeat for the
readers back home. Officials and officers struggled to withhold sensitive military information from the hordes of prying correspondents while seeking ways to inform, manipulate, and capture public
opinion for their cause. Harold L. Nelson summarizes the dilemma:

> The press . . . was enamored of freedom and insensitive to
> the damage that battle plans and armies might suffer from
> news reports that got into print within hours or days after
> dispatch. The government, its armies dependent as in no
> previous war upon the efforts and support of the whole
> people, was insensitive to the people's needs for maximum
> information about the war. . . . By war's end, there was
> perhaps the dawn of understanding within both institutions:
> in the press, that total war meant some compromise of
> democratic forms, including even freedom of the press; in the
> government, that a people tutored in access to news needed
> information when war came if its maximum support was to
> be elicited.[143]

Government's heavy hand, while felt periodically by the press,
grasped telegraphy firmly by early 1862. North-south telegraph circuits were cut, messages were seized, and finally telegraphy was nationalized, turning both nations' primary communications systems
to military service. The press, meanwhile, ran in high gear throughout the hostilities. As readers demanded more and later news from
the government and the battlefield, newspapers, at least in the
North, introduced a regular schedule of additional daytime editions.
In New York City where James Gordon Bennett's *Herald* had endured the wrath of God-fearing people and the indignity of a sporadic "holy war" waged by journalistic colleagues for publishing a
Sunday edition for nearly twenty years, Sunday quickly and quietly
filled with news competitors during April and May of 1861. As war
loomed on the horizon, the *New York Tribune* announced perfec-
tion of a stereotyping process that permitted double and triple the
hourly production of newspapers through the use of multiple print-

ing plates cast from the original hand-set type.[144] As long as the armies kept their sharpshooters and caissons in the countryside, safely away from the news rooms and the eager, growing reading public, the Civil War was a splendid opportunity to extend and perfect wartime correspondence, to editorialize about military strategy, and to capitalize on the public's growing habit of consuming news.

While war was a tour de force for editors and their correspondents, newsbrokers had to be content with all of war's discomforts and few of its glories. Daniel H. Craig's patron editors skimmed the cream of Civil War coverage with their own staffs and consigned Craig's AP to official military dispatches and bland routine snippets of battlefield coverage. The strength of Craig's prewar news monopoly had proved to be its wartime weakness, because the AP network was precisely the national news system the Lincoln administration needed to reach Northern newspaper readers with Union pronouncements. Craig, the old "indefatigable" battler, must have viewed his wartime lot remorsefully, his inability to duplicate patron New York editors' stunning battlefield coverage leaving him vulnerable to criticism from Western editors, who relied primarily on AP for their war coverage.

John S. Thrasher's Press Association of the Confederacy was even more limited than the AP. Hemmed in by a less cooperative national administration that was caught up in a losing military effort and by skimpy access to the more modest Southern telegraph system, Thrasher fought to make a newfangled cooperative agency work in the face of reluctant or desperate Southern editors and of belligerent, outdated political journalism in Richmond. Craig, whose postwar fortunes looked better with each passing month after the tide was turned at Gettysburg, fretted over a growing chorus of editorial discontent with AP in the West and threats of competition in the Midwest and from an independent news room in Washington. Thrasher, riding the gradually diminishing hopes of the Confederacy eventually to a standstill, preoccupied himself with news report brevity, membership cooperation, and copyright.

Except for their government-appreciated ability to reach many readers quickly and their owner-appreciated ability to dragnet many localities for tidbits of news each day, newsbrokerages had failed by the end of the Civil War to develop a journalistic presence that would ensure their permanence and have a marked impact on newspapers and the public. The key to this failure was newsbroking's assigned role as nonpartisan, impersonal, summary capsulizer and fragmentizer of the nation's variegated news scene. The Civil War was the high-water mark of what Joseph M. Webb has called American journalism's "romantic" reporting. The dramatic, eyewitness, chronological news accounts so common during this war reflect an assumption, as Webb explains,

> that man is primarily a feeling, emotional, instinctual being, ...that the Reality to be reported is primarily internal, inside human beings.... [I]nstead of an atomistic view of reality, [romantic reporting] assumes a wholistic view, assuming that life cannot be understood when it is cut up in little pieces.[145]

This complex, multidimensional, and personal reporting style had been the norm in American newspapers from their colonial origins, first examining the issues of revolution, then shaping the dialogue among emerging political parties, and more recently exploiting a wide range of serious and frivolous news topics for the benefit of emerging middle-class readers. War gave romantic reporting its ultimate subject to explore.

Few in 1865 would have agreed with the notion that "rational" reporting (the historical alternative to romantic reporting, according to Webb) assigned to newsbroking since its inception would within three decades supplant romantic journalism. Newsbrokers were safety nets or backstops, protecting editors from missing routine sensations or official deliberations beyond their communities; the newsbroker's reports had to shun flavor, fervor, and fullness. Webb explains that rational reporting, which the author feels characterizes newsbroking reports from the start, makes the assumption

> that Reality is essentially an external phenomenon understood via the senses; ...the assumption that human beings are fundamentally alike and it is their similarities that count; ...and...that to understand Reality it must first be cut up into pieces with each piece digested separately.[146]

Romantic reporting, by stressing a writer's personality and emotions and his or her intimacy with reality, retained strong ties to an oral, interpersonal communication tradition that was alien to the printed page but still evident in mid-nineteenth-century American society. It is interesting to ponder that newspaper content at that time reflected a society that the newspaper format neither catered to nor attracted in large numbers. And it is strikingly consistent with that notion to observe that, according to U.S. census data, daily newspaper circulations in 1860 equaled only 29.1 percent of total urban population and only 5.4 percent of total U.S. free population.[147] Moreover, only 50.6 out of every one hundred children between the ages of five and nineteen were enrolled in school in 1860. Ten years later only 2 percent of persons seventeen years old were high school graduates and 20 percent of the total population was illiterate—including 11.5 percent of the white population and 79.9 percent of the Negro and other nonwhite population.[148]

Newspapers had captured the elite reader and were reaching for the middle-class reader, at least in metropolitan areas, but large pockets of society remained untouched personally by print journalism. And newspapers, among their circle of readers, still reflected the oral, romantic tradition that characterized business and social intercourse among people. Walter J. Ong asserts that "the media in their succession do not cancel out one another but build on one another."[149] Newspaper writing, at least through the end of the Civil War, reflected, in diversity and complexity, the orality of American life.

As the turn of the century approached and as numbers and circulations of newspapers continued to grow, rational reporting and the impact of newsbroking gradually superseded romanticism in journalism. No longer having to meet their readers on terrain reflecting both print and oral traditions, the turn-of-the-century newspaper wrapped itself in rational news accounts, which at least were more consistent with print's inherent static and linear emphases. By then, newsbroking's reports would play a far more prominent role in both the newsroom and the living room. Back at the end of the Civil War, however, newsbroking's product and operation were still immature and subservient to a newspaper journalism which while influencing elite and institutional circles still had not realized its potential impact on society as a whole.

In Volume 2 of this work, *The Nation's Newsbrokers: The Rush to Institution, from 1865 to 1920*, the post–Civil War growth of newsbroking is traced through episodes of telegraphy's renewed efforts to control news flow, of struggles among AP's regional organizations, of serious competition for AP resulting in collusion, discovery, and warfare, and of new competition for AP made vigorous by a world war.

NOTES

Preface

1. "Newsbroking" is used in this work to avoid the various implications of current terminology intended to signify Associated Press, United Press International, and their predecessors. The literature offers a variety of terms as labels for the subject of this book, but each term may carry possibly misleading political, economic, or technological connotations. "Press association" either emphasizes AP's cooperative structure or refers to various state or national organizations of publishers. "News-gathering agency" and "news service" also refer to a variety of journalistic activities well beyond the scope of this study. The same is true of "news agency," which may also have the connotation of governmental news or propaganda activities. When this study began more than two decades ago, "wire service" seemed sufficiently unambiguous and, in light of trade press usage, widely accepted as an appropriate name for the subject of this book. Although the author used "wire service" in previous published work on this subject, growing satellite delivery of the "'wires'" news reports begun in the early 1980s may render this term technologically obsolete in the near future. While the author does not strive to introduce new or obscure terms to our lexicon, the failure of available terms to avoid ambiguity leads to the adoption of "newsbroker," "newsbrokerage," and "newsbroking" as precise and unslanted labels for the subject of this book.

2. Victor Rosewater, *History of Cooperative News-Gathering in the United States* (New York: D. Appleton, 1930).

3. Oliver Gramling, *AP: The Story of News* (New York: Farrar & Rinehart, 1940).

4. Joe Alex Morris, *Deadline Every Minute: The Story of the United Press* (Garden City, N.Y.: Doubleday, 1957).

5. Biographical material on Rosewater and his family is from: *Dictionary of American Biography*, s.v. "Rosewater, Victor"; "The Rosewaters and the 'Bee' of Omaha," *Review of Reviews* 13 (June 1896): 709–10; and the Rosewater Family Papers, American Jewish Archives, Cincinnati, Ohio.

6. The author's doctoral dissertation, completed in 1965 at the University of Illinois, Urbana, focuses on the epistemological problem of identifying and measuring institutional growth, using newsbroking as a convenient communication institution on which to test a systemic

model proposed in that dissertation. See the author's *The American Wire Services: A Study of Their Development as a Social Institution* (New York: Arno, 1979).

7. Walter J. Ong, *Interfaces of the Word: Studies in the Evolution of Consciousness and Culture* (Ithaca, N.Y.: Cornell University Press, 1977), p. 329.

8. Stuart Bruchey, *The Roots of American Economic Growth, 1607–1861: An Essay in Social Causation* (New York: Harper & Row, 1965), pp. 214–15.

Chapter 1

1. Clarence S. Brigham, *Journals and Journeymen: A Contribution to the History of Early American Newspapers* (Philadelphia: University of Pennsylvania Press, 1950), pp. 58–59.

2. Frank Luther Mott, *American Journalism: A History, 1690–1960,* 3rd ed. (New York: Macmillan, 1962), pp. 154–55. See also Mott's "The Newspaper Coverage of Lexington and Concord," *New England Quarterly* 17 (Dec. 1944): 489–505; and Allan R. Pred, *Urban Growth and the Circulation of Information: The United States System of Cities, 1790–1840* (Cambridge, Mass.: Harvard University Press, 1973), esp. pp. 35–77.

3. Pred, *Circulation of Information,* p. 12, relying on Colin Cherry, *On Human Communication,* 2nd ed. (Cambridge: M.I.T. Press, 1966), p. 22.

4. Mott, *American Journalism,* p. 48.

5. Pred, *Circulation of Information,* p. 13.

6. George Rogers Taylor, *The Transportation Revolution, 1815–1860,* vol. 4 of The Economic History of the United States (New York: Rinehart, 1951), pp. 15, 31. This volume offers a valuable overview of transportation's development in the first half of the nineteenth century. For a summary of examples and descriptions of antebellum road conditions see Balthasar Henry Meyer, ed., *History of Transportation in the United States before 1860* (Washington, D.C.: Carnegie Institution, 1917).

7. Wheaton J. Lane, "The Early Highway in America, to the Coming of the Railroad," in *Highways in Our National Life: A Symposium,* ed. Jean Labatut and Wheaton J. Lane (Princeton, N.J.: Princeton University Press, 1950), p. 75.

8. See n. 1 in the Preface for a discussion of the labels used and avoided in this book.

9. Quoted in Alfred McClung Lee, *The Daily Newspaper in America: The Evolution of a Social Instrument* (New York: Macmillan, 1937), p. 483.

10. Ibid.

11. Mott, *American Journalism,* p. 161, relying on J. P. Bretz, "Some As-

pects of Postal Extension into the West," *Annual Report* of the American Historical Association (1909), 146–47.

12. Pred, *Circulation of Information,* p. 78.

13. Pred, ibid., p. 80, provided the following data on the expansion of postal service:

	1790	1800	1810	1820	1830	1840
Population per Post Office (Thousands)	52.4	5.9	3.1	2.1	1.5	1.3
Population per Mile of Post Routes	2,095.47	254.46	198.43	130.87	120.01	109.93

These rates of expansion are very similar, with post offices growing only slightly faster.

14. Carl H. Scheele, *A Short History of the Mail Service* (Washington, D.C.: Smithsonian Institution, 1970), pp. 68–69.

15. Lee, *Daily Newspaper,* p. 485.

16. Ibid., p. 488.

17. John C. Miller, *Sam Adams, Pioneer in Propaganda* (Boston: Little, Brown, 1936), p. 266.

18. Quoted in Arthur M. Schlesinger, *Prelude to Independence: The Newspaper War on Britain, 1764–1776* (New York: Knopf, 1957), p. 17.

19. "Journal," Papers of the Committees of Correspondence, Boston Public Library, Boston, Mass.

20. Ibid.

21. Ibid., minutes for August 19, 1773, meeting.

22. Mott, "Newspaper Coverage," p. 505.

23. Ibid., pp. 492–93.

24. Edwin Emery, *The Press and America: An Interpretative History of the Mass Media,* 3rd ed. (Englewood Cliffs, N.J.: Prentice-Hall, 1972), pp. 79–80.

25. Anthony R. Michaelis, *From Semaphore to Satellite* (Geneva: Henri Studer, 1965), pp. 11, 13; and Laurence Trumbull, *The Electro-Magnetic Telegraph with an Historical Account of Its Rise, Progress, and Present Condition* (Philadelphia: A. Hart, 1853), p. 18.

26. Henry O'Rielly, "Christopher Colles, and the First Proposal of a Telegraph System in the United States...," *Historical Magazine* 15 (April 1869): 263, with corrections made by O'Rielly in the magazine's May

1869 issue, p. 329; and Alvin F. Harlow, *Old Wires and New Waves: The History of the Telegraph, Telephone, and Wireless* (New York: D. Appleton-Century, 1936), p. 26.

27. Christopher Colles, *A Survey of the Roads of the United States of America, 1789*, ed. Walter W. Ristow (Cambridge, Mass.: Belknap Press of Harvard University, 1961).

28. O'Rielly, "Christopher Colles," p. 263; and Robert Greenhalgh Albion, *The Rise of the New York Port (1815–1860)* (New York: Scribners, 1939), p. 218.

29. Quoted in O'Rielly, "Christopher Colles," pp. 262–63.

30. Ibid., p. 263.

31. A careful account of the early development of Agence Havas is in Robert W. Desmond, *The Information Process: World News Reporting to the Twentieth Century* (Iowa City: University of Iowa Press, 1978), pp. 134–40. In contrast to the U.S. newsbrokerages, which arose primarily as a service to newspapers and as a result of efforts of editors, the Havas agency arose amid a general absence of individual newspaper news-gathering initiative in France, served private subscribers as well as newspapers, and received a governmental subsidy from an early date.

32. Lee, *Daily Newspaper,* p. 481.

33. Norval Neil Luxon, *Niles' Weekly Register, News Magazine of the Nineteenth Century* (Baton Rouge: Louisiana State University Press, 1947), pp. 305–6.

34. Pred, *Circulation of Information,* p. 31.

35. Quoted in Robert Greenhalgh Albion, *Square-Riggers on Schedule: The New York Sailing Packets to England, France, and the Cotton Ports* (Princeton, N.J.: Princeton University Press, 1938), pp. 174–75.

36. Joseph T. Buckingham, *Specimens of Newspaper Literature with Personal Memoirs, Anecdotes, and Reminiscences,* 2 vols. (Boston: Charles C. Little & James Brown, 1850), 1:89.

37. Isaiah Thomas, *The History of Printing in America with a Biography of Printers and an Account of Newspapers,* ed. a committee of the American Antiquarian Society, 2nd ed., 2 vols. (Albany, N.Y.: J. Munsell, 1874), 2:40.

38. Frederic Hudson, *Journalism in the United States from 1690 to 1872* (New York: Harper, 1873), p. 172. Hudson says a "Colonel Pickering is the authority" for this account.

39. Buckingham, *Specimens,* 2:104.

40. Hudson, *Journalism,* pp. 179–80. Lee says Lang started a harbor service for his paper in 1795 but gives no source for this year. *Daily Newspaper,* p. 481.

41. "History of 'The Associated Press,'" *Philadelphia Press* as reprinted in *Chicago Times,* November 27, 1858. Mott reports that the *Daily Advertiser* was founded on March 1, 1785. *American Journalism,* p. 116.

42. Buckingham, *Specimens,* 2:169–70. It is difficult to pinpoint Blake's activities in time. The *Palladium* became prominent after 1801; the *Courier* was founded in 1824.

43. Hudson, *Journalism,* p. 190. The *Journal of Commerce* was founded in 1827; the *Express* appeared in 1836.

44. Buckingham, *Specimens,* 2:170–71. Emphasis in original.

45. Frederick B. Marbut, "Early Washington Correspondents: Some Neglected Pioneers," *Journalism Quarterly* 25 (December 1948): 369–74, 400. Marbut's comprehensive study of Washington, D.C., news, completed twenty-three years after this article, reasserts 1808 as the date of the earliest Washington letter-writing. F. B. Marbut, *News from the Capital: The Story of Washington Reporting* (Carbondale: Southern Illinois University Press, 1971), pp. 24–26.

46. See Gramling, *AP,* pp. 3–7; Melville E. Stone, "News-Gathering as a Business," *Century Magazine* 70 (June 1905): 299–310; and Rosewater, *News-Gathering,* pp. 5–8.

47. Writers' Program, *Boston Looks Seaward: The Story of the Port, 1630–1940* (Boston: Bruce Humphries, 1941), p. 98.

48. Samuel Topliff, *ed. Topliff's Travels: Letters from Abroad in the Years 1828 and 1829 by Samuel Topliff,* ed. Ethel Stanwood Bolton (Boston: Athenaeum, 1906), pp. 3–23.

49. Clarence S. Brigham, *History and Bibliography of American Newspapers, 1690–1820,* 2 vols. (Hamden, Conn.: Archon, 1947, 1962). 2:271–350.

50. "The Reading Room and Marine Diary in the Exchange Coffee House, 1810: Lists of Subscribers from the Society's Collections," The Bostonian Society *Publications* 8 (1911): 121–31.

51. William L. King, *The Newspaper Press of Charleston, S.C.: A Chronological and Biographical History Embracing a Period of One Hundred and Forty Years* (1872; reprint ed., Charleston, S.C.: Lucas & Richardson, 1882), p. 105. For several months in 1832 James Gordon Bennett, whose *New York Herald* would later be an aggressive news-gatherer and a leader in the New York City Associated Press movement, served in the *Courier* office, translating the Havana papers for Willington. Hudson, *Journalism,* p. 262.

52. King, *Newspaper Press,* pp. 106–7.

53. Lee, *Daily Newspaper,* p. 483. Rosewater indicates that the source for this claim is the *Journal's* Semicentennial Edition, January 3, 1870. *News-Gathering,* p. 25.

54. George H. Andrews, *General Webb* (n.p., [1858]), p. 8, Webb Family Papers, Rare Books and Manuscripts Division, The New York Public Library, Astor, Lenox and Tilden Foundations, New York. This fifteen-

page pamphlet is a reprint of an article originally appearing in the *New York Courier and Enquirer* on September 16, 1858, while its subject, *Courier and Enquirer* editor James Watson Webb, was absent from the newspaper office.

55. Lee, *Daily Newspaper,* p. 482.

56. Mott, *American Journalism,* p. 181.

57. Albion, *New York Port,* p. 53.

58. Ibid., pp. 213–19.

59. Ibid., p. 306.

60. Quoted in T. H. Giddings, "Rushing the Transatlantic News in the 1830s and 1840s," New York Historical Society *Quarterly* 42 (January 1958): 53.

61. The pro-Webb faction in the literature includes Willard Grosvenor Bleyer, *Main Currents in the History of American Journalism* (Boston: Houghton Mifflin, 1927), p. 145; Andrews, *Webb;* Rosewater, *News-Gathering,* pp. 14–15; History Reference Council, "Competing for News," *History Reference Bulletin* 10 (March 1937): 97; and James L. Crouthamel, "James Watson Webb," *New York History* 41 (October 1960); 403, and his *James Watson Webb: A Biography* (Middletown, Conn.: Wesleyan University Press, 1969), pp. 28–29. The pro-Hale and Hallock group includes Hudson, *Journalism,* p. 365; T[homas] B. Connery, "Great News Operations—The Collection of News," *Cosmopolitan* 23 (May 1897): 23; [William H. Hallock], *Life of Gerard Hallock, Thirty-Three Years Editor of the New York Journal of Commerce* (New York: Oakley, Mason, 1869), pp. 11–12; and *New York Journal of Commerce,* Centennial Edition, September 29, 1927. David Hale's biographer makes no claim of originality for the *Journal of Commerce* in harbor news-gathering, preferring to comment that the paper's early affiliation with the Association of Morning Papers was "rather a combination of laziness than of enterprise—the object being not so much to obtain news promptly as to insure that no one should obtain news to the disadvantage of the rest." Joseph P. Thompson, *Memoir of David Hale, Late Editor of the Journal of Commerce, with Selections from His Miscellaneous Writings* (New York: Wiley, 1850), p. 54. Sons, biographers, and centennial editions may be discounted on both sides because of possible overzealousness. Andrews, too, might be dismissed as a *Courier and Enquirer* employee, but his account is supported by Bleyer (in *Main Currents*) even though Bleyer also authored the biographical sketches of both Hale and Hallock in the *Dictionary of American Biography.* Hudson and the *Herald,* for which he was managing editor, on the other hand, generally viewed Webb and the *Courier and Enquirer* with greater contempt than Hale and Hallock's *Journal of Commerce.* Connery, Hudson's successor at the *Herald,* may have inherited that viewpoint. In any event, Connery reveals an unsteady grasp of these events by reporting "the first attempted combination by several newspapers . . . was to secure ship news, and was formed by the New York *Gazette,* the *Courier and Inquirer [sic],*

and the *Mercantile Advertiser*. . . ." (As the text indicates, Webb's paper could not have been part of the "first attempt.") Connery, "Collection of News," p. 23.

62. Bleyer, *Main Currents,* p. 145; and Andrews, *Webb,* p. 8.

63. *Dictionary of American Biography,* s.v. "Hallock, Gerard."

64. Quoted in History Reference Council, "Competing for News," p. 97.

65. Hudson, *Journalism,* p. 365. Emphasis in original.

66. Andrews, *Webb,* p. 8.

67. Albion, *New York Port,* p. 306; and Crouthamel, *Webb,* p. 29.

68. Andrews, *Webb,* p. 8.

69. Connery, "Collection of News," p. 23.

70. *Dictionary of American Biography,* s.v. "Hallock, Gerard."

71. Hudson, *Journalism,* p. 346.

72. Rosewater, *News-Gathering,* p. 22.

73. *New York Times,* January 7, 1866, obituary of Gerard Hallock; and Hallock, *Hallock,* p. 278.

74. Crouthamel, *Webb,* p. 68, relying on items in the *New York Courier and Enquirer.*

75. Scheele, *Short History,* pp. 68–69.

76. Hudson, *Journalism,* p. 366.

77. "History of 'The Associated Press.' "

78. Lee, *Daily Newspaper,* p. 486, using quotes from [Isaac C. Pray], *Memoirs of James Gordon Bennett and His Times,* By a Journalist (New York: Stringer & Townsend, 1855), p. 372.

79. Hudson, *Journalism,* pp. 608–9.

80. Lee, *Daily Newspaper,* p. 490.

81. Hudson, *Journalism,* pp. 446, 609.

82. Ibid., pp. 450–51, and [Pray], *Bennett,* p. 249.

83. Lee, *Daily Newspaper,* p. 491.

84. Hudson, *Journalism,* p. 451.

85. *New York Herald,* May 18, 1840, quoted in ibid., p. 452.

86. Martin to Bennett, May 7, 1844, James Gordon Bennett Papers, Rare Books and Manuscripts Division, The New York Public Library, Astor, Lenox and Tilden Foundations, New York.

87. "Great Newspaper Rivalry," *Printers' Circular* 16 (November 1881): 202.

88. Reprinted in Alvin F. Harlow, *Old Waybills: The Romance of the Express Companies* (New York: D. Appleton-Century, 1934), p. 18.

89. A[lexander] L. Stimson, *History of the Express Business, Including*

the Origin of the Railway System in America and the Relation of Both to the Increase of New Settlements and the Prosperity of Cities in the United States (New York: Baker & Godwin, 1881), p. 35.

90. Hudson, Journalism, pp. 520–21.

91. Ibid., pp. 370–71.

92. Ibid., p. 321.

93. Ibid., p. 391.

94. W. F. G. Shanks, "How We Get Our News," Harper's Monthly 34 (March 1867): 513–14.

95. Alexis de Tocqueville, Democracy in America, ed. Phillips Bradley, 2 vols. (1835, 1840; reprint ed., New York: Knopf, 1945), 1:187.

96. Lee reports that between 1790 and 1840 the total number of newspapers increased from 92 to 1,404, a growth of 1,426 percent, and dailies increased from 8 to 138, a growth of 1,625 percent. In the same period U.S. population increased only 334.4 percent. Daily Newspaper, pp. 718, 725.

97. Walter J. Ong, The Presence of the Word: Some Prolegomena for Cultural and Religious History (New Haven, Conn.: Yale University Press, 1967), pp. 53–54, relying on the research of David Diringer and D. J. Wiseman.

98. Bruchey, Roots, p. 213.

99. Pred, Circulation of Information, p. 19.

100. Anthony Smith, The Newspaper: An International History (London: Thames & Hudson, 1979), p. 7.

101. Hudson, Journalism, p. 366.

102. An interesting, latter-day linkage between journalism and transportation was the "newspaper train." A system that made transportation schedules conform to journalism's timetable, the newspaper train was a high-speed, leased locomotive and cars operated by metropolitan dailies to deliver papers to distant communities. The result of accommodating rail officials and favorable rate schedules, the newspaper train existed to some extent for twenty-five years, beginning to disappear in 1900 when the practice "was institutionalized, as the modernizing mail system gradually took over its function." George Everett, "Newspaper Trains: America's First Fling at High-Speed Transmission of the Printed Word" (Paper delivered at the Sixty-third Annual Meeting of the Association for Education in Journalism, Boston, August 11, 1980), p. 10. As in most such journalism-transportation linkages, the system was available to the affluent metropolitan papers. Most dailies at this time and virtually all of them soon after 1900 had to conform to the schedules established by the common carriers and the postal service.

103. The leading exponent of the time-space analytical dichotomy is Harold A. Innis in Empire and Communications (Oxford: Clarendon

Press, 1950) and *The Bias of Communication* (Toronto: University of Toronto Press, 1951). While it is a compellingly simple tool for comparing gross communication systems of centuries or decades in duration, as Innis does, the concept of time-space fails to account for the more finite variations in intercity communication outlined in this chapter. Spatial development clearly warrants attention in historical analyses of communication systems if one wishes to fix the physical networks of transportation and communication available to move information. And the study of the temporal movement of information is crucial to an understanding of time-lag and irregularity. The Innis model to the contrary notwithstanding, time and space are not opposite ends of a continuum, but are compatible, interactive factors, both requiring expression in terms of speed in order to produce an accurate measure of transportation's and communication's ability to move information. Pred, in a series of time-lag maps, appropriately depicts the speed with which information made its way from newspaper to newspaper between 1790 and 1841. Pred, *Circulation of Information,* pp. 37–53, passim.

Chapter 2

1. The ten years beginning in 1838 witnessed extraordinary news events. At home, two close presidential elections (1840 and 1844) highlighted a fluid political scene that included the emergence of the Liberty Party and nativism, while Whigs and Democrats both fought factionalist tendencies within their own ranks. Slavery and national banking continued to bedevil the nation. Boundary disputes—in the northeast, ending in the Webster-Ashburton Treaty; in the northwest, raising the Oregon question; and in the southwest, causing the Mexican War—required both domestic and foreign news-gathering efforts. Abroad, there were unrest in Spain, French adventures in North Africa, and British enterprises in the Orient and the Indian subcontinent. British newspapers were filled with Irish separatism and the famine, anti-Corn Law agitation and eventual free trade. Popular uprisings in Austria, Poland, and Portugal in 1846 and rumblings in Italy in 1847 led in 1848 to a general revolution across the European Continent, spawned in Paris and sparing only Switzerland. Richard B. Morris, ed., *Encyclopedia of American History,* 2nd ed. (New York: Harper & Row, 1970), pp. 180–208; and Edwin Emerson, Jr., *A History of the Nineteenth Century, Year by Year,* 3 vols. (New York: P. F. Collier, 1900), 2:892–1039.

2. "Successful" is used here to remind the reader that, in contrast to some European countries, in the United States semaphore had acquired little practical journalistic use.

3. Martin D. Stevers and Captain Jonas Pendlebury, *Sea Lanes: Man's Conquest of the Ocean* (1935; reprint ed., Garden City, N.Y.: Garden City Publishing Co., 1938), pp. 232–35. Although the *Sirius* and *Great Western* crossings in 1838 have secured a niche in history as inaugurating practical transatlantic steam navigation, steam crossings, some unplanned, dated back to 1819 and the eastbound transatlantic cross-

ing of the *Savannah*. Brief accounts of pre–1838 steam crossings are in "The First Steamship," *Niles' National Register,* September 4, 1847, p. 16; Taylor, *Transportation Revolution,* pp. 113–14; and David Budlong Tyler, *Steam Conquers the Atlantic* (New York: D. Appleton-Century, 1939), pp. 18–28.

4. F. Lawrence Babcock, *Spanning the Atlantic* (New York: Knopf, 1931), p. 30.

5. Frank Luther Mott says, "News from overseas was the great staple of colonial papers. That is what newspaper readers chiefly expected of their papers. . . ." *American Journalism,* p. 48.

6. Ibid.

7. Ibid., p. 154. "Packets" were sailing ships with scheduled departure times. The British government introduced contracts for such scheduled service in early colonial days, to expedite mail deliveries on both sides of the Atlantic and to counteract the general practice of postponing ship departures until all cargo space was filled. Stevers and Pendlebury, *Sea Lanes,* p. 237.

8. Albion notes that British newspapers were less inclined to record ships' departures and arrivals than were American papers, making a similar study of eastbound passages impractical. Because of the prevailing westerly winds, however, "[e]astbound trips . . . were shorter and far more uniform" than westbound trips, comments Albion. *Square-Riggers,* p. 191.

9. To Albion, "common range" means that a packet had as much of a chance of crossing in thirty as in thirty-nine days (and for all intermediate durations). Improved packet design shortened the passages during this period, says Albion, but not appreciably. During the first half of the period, the common range of westbound passages was thirty-one to forty-one days. Ibid., p. 200.

10. Ibid., p. 192.

11. Hudson, *Journalism,* pp. 450–51.

12. Babcock, *Spanning,* pp. 50–51.

13. Scheele, *Short History,* p. 102. Perusal of New York and Boston newspapers for the early 1840s confirms these Cunard crossing times during good weather. Add one to four days depending on the severity of bad weather.

14. Babcock, *Spanning,* pp. 50–51, 74–75. A compilation of record Cunard crossings in 1848 shows that these newest four Cunarders were the line's fastest. With an average westward crossing that year from Liverpool to Halifax of 12 days and 2 1/2 hours, the shortest was the *Europa* in 8 days and 18 hours, and the longest was the *Britannia* in 18 1/2 days. On other legs of the transatlantic crossings the newer Cunarders also attained higher speed in 1848: Liverpool to Boston, the *America,* 10 days and 6 hours; Liverpool to New York, the *Europa,* 10 day and 23 hours; Halifax to Boston, the *Niagara,* 1 day and 5 hours; Halifax to New York, the *Europa,* 1 day and 20 hours;

Halifax to Liverpool, the *Niagara,* 8 days and 12 hours; Boston to Liverpool, the *Niagara,* 10 days and 10 hours; New York to Liverpool, the *America,* 11 days and 11 hours; Boston to Halifax, the *Europa,* 1 day and 6 hours; and New York to Halifax, 2 days and 5 hours. *Niles' National Register,* April 25, 1849 p. 272.

15. U.S. Congress, House Committee on Commerce, *Electro-Magnetic Telegraphs: To Accompany Bill H.R. No. 713,* 25th Cong., 2nd sess., April 6, 1838, Rept. 753, p. 3.

16. Robert Luther Thompson, *Wiring a Continent: The History of the Telegraph Industry in the United States, 1832–1866* (Princeton, N.J.: Princeton University Press, 1947), p. 13. F. O. J. Smith's full name was Francis Ormond Jonathan Smith. He usually used Francis O. J. Smith for his signature, and his detractors often referred to him as Fog Smith. Most telegraph historians, however, refer to him as F. O. J. Smith, and that form will be used here.

17. Ben[jamin] Perley Poore, *Perley's Reminiscences of Sixty Years in the National Metropolis,* 2 vols. (Philadelphia: Hubbard Brothers, 1886), 1:310. Kendall, however, did not become involved with Morse until 1845 when he became Morse's business agent. *Dictionary of American Biography,* s.v. "Kendall, Amos."

18. Samuel F. B. Morse, *Samuel F. B. Morse, His Letters and Journals,* ed. Edward Lind Morse, 2 vols. (Boston: Houghton Mifflin, 1914), 2:82–83.

19. Thompson, *Wiring,* pp. 11–22.

20. Alfred Vail, *Early History of the Electro-Magnetic Telegraph from Letters and Journals of Alfred Vail,* ed. J. Cummings Vail (New York: Hine Brothers, 1914), pp. 16–17.

21. Ibid., p. 17; and John W. Kirk, "Historic Moments: The First News Message by Telegraph," *Scribner's* 11 (May 1892): 654–55.

22. Vail, *History,* pp. 16–17.

23. Kirk, "Historic Moments," p. 655.

24. Ibid.

25. *New York Times,* June 22, 1872, reprinted from the *Journal of the Telegraph.*

26. All or part of this letter is quoted in Alfred Vail, *The American Electro-Magnetic Telegraph, with the Reports of Congress and a Description of All Telegraphs Known, Employing Electricity or Galvanism* (Philadelphia: Lea & Blanchard, 1845), p. 81; and Morse, *Letters,* 2:84–86.

27. William Orton, *A Letter to the Postmaster-General Reviewing the Recommendation of his Annual Report in Favor of a Postal Telegraph* (New York, 1873), p. 4.

28. Quoted in Thompson, *Wiring,* p. 31.

29. Ibid.

30. *Niles' National Register,* July 4, 1846, pp. 273–74.

31. Harlow, *Old Wires,* pp. 338–39.

32. Thompson, *Wiring,* pp. 8–13.

33. Ibid., pp. 39–93, where the reader will find considerably more detail about these arrangements and their participants than space permits here.

34. Morse's original experimental line (Washington, D.C., to Baltimore) and its improved successors under the Morse patent remained the capital's only telegraph line to the north until April 1849, when the North American Telegraph Company opened a line of Bain telegraph equipment between the two cities. Ibid., p. 170. Since a government subsidy had underwritten the original Morse line, the federal government operated it through the postmaster general for nearly a year and a half before turning it over (late in 1846) to Alfred Vail, who ran the Washington office, and to Henry J. Rogers, who ran the Baltimore office. The switch to private ownership followed by several months completion of the Baltimore–New York City line. Even though Congress appropriated additional funds in the spring of 1845 to maintain the Washington-Baltimore line, it was not clear whether the government received any of the line's revenue. Wilhelmus Bogart Bryan, *A History of the National Capital from Its Foundation through the Period of the Adoption of the Organic Act,* 2 vols. (New York: Macmillan, 1914–16), 2:366–68.

35. Thompson, *Wiring,* pp. 43–50: and Alexander Jones, *Historical Sketch of the Electric Telegraph, Including Its Rise and Progress in the United States* (New York: Putnam, 1852), pp. 120–21.

36. Across Manhattan on the East River side, as Philip Hone's diary on October 23, 1845, records: "A leaden pipe was successfully laid on the bed of the East River to cross the Fulton Ferry from New York to Brooklyn, for the conveyance of the wires of the magnetic telegraph. The pipe weighs 6,000 pounds, all in one piece without a joint. This is a pretty specimen of mechanical skill, and I see no doubt of its perfect adaptation to the object, except that which arises from the apprehension of danger to the pipe from the anchors of vessels riding in the stream. . . ." Five days later Hone reports: "My apprehensions in regard to the submarine pipe in the East River have been realized. The ship *Charles* for Liverpool, in weighing her anchor. . . dragged it up, broke the pipe, and of course destroyed the connection. Some other plan must be resorted to." Philip Hone, *The Diary of Philip Hone, 1828-1851,* ed. Allan Nevins, 2 vols. (New York: Dodd, Mead, 1927), 2:748.

37. On January 24, 1846, the company's directors approved a schedule of six crossings each way per day, using railroad conductors, express agents, and messengers. Magnetic Telegraph Company, *Articles of Association and Charter from the State of Maryland of the Magnetic Telegraph Company Together with the Office Regulations and the*

Minutes of the Meetings of Stockholders and Board of Directors (New York: Chatterton & Crist, [1852]), p. 30.

38. Thompson, *Wiring,* pp. 81–116, passim; and Jones, *Sketch,* pp. 77–81, passim.

39. Thompson, *Wiring,* pp. 51–53.

40. [Edwin A. Perry], *The Boston Herald and Its History: How, When and Where It Was Founded* (Boston: Herald, 1878), pp. 6–7.

41. Babcock, *Spanning,* pp. 89–90; and I. N. Phelps Stokes, comp., *The Iconography of Manhattan Island, 1498–1909,* 6 vols. (New York: Robert H. Dodd, 1915–28), 5:1807. Cunard's invasion of New York harbor was significant beyond its impact on news-gathering. Cunard was the first major transatlantic line to build docks on the Jersey City side of the Hudson River, reachable from Manhattan at that time only by river ferry. The new docks were ready for the *Hibernia*'s first arrival. Albion, *New York Port,* p. 221.

42. Portions of this section on transatlantic newspapers appeared in the author's "The Foreign Connection: Transatlantic Newspapers in the 1840s" *Journalism History* 10 (Autumn/Winter 1983): 44–49, 69.

43. Bartlett sold the *Albion* to William Young, son-in-law of A. S. Willington of the *Charleston* (S.C.) *Courier* on May 6, 1848. The paper was still publishing in 1872. Hudson, *Journalism,* p. 313.

44. *New York Albion* 3 n.s. (January 30, 1841): 42. Emphasis in original.

45. Times of London, *Tercentenary Handlist of English & Welsh Newspapers, Magazines & Reviews* (London: Times, 1920), p. 231.

46. *New York Albion* 3 n.s. (February 27, 1841): 75.

47. *New York Albion* 3 n.s. (March 6, 1841): 87.

48. Stevers and Pendlebury, on p. 245 of *Sea Lanes,* report the *President*'s disappearance as the first among the transatlantic steamer class. A good sketch of the year-and-a-half-long life of the ill-fated *President* is in Tyler, *Steam,* pp. 105, 107–10.

49. See the author's "Foreign Connection," p. 46.

50. *New York Albion* 1 n.s. (September 17, 1842): 452.

51. Times, *Tercentenary,* p. 231.

52. Ibid., p. 232.

53. *Willmer & Smith's European Times,* March 4, 1846.

54. The *Chronicle* is not even mentioned in Grant's history of British newspapers. See James Grant, *The Newspaper Press: Its Origin, Progress, and Present Position,* 3 vols. (London: Tinsley Brothers, 1871–72), 3:351–60, where Liverpool's newspaper history is discussed.

55. Frederic Boase, *Modern English Biography,* s.v. "Willmer, Edward."

56. Ibid., s.v. "Willmer, Charles," and *Times of London,* October 18, 1897.

57. Times, *Tercentenary,* p. 234.

58. *Willmer & Smith's European Times,* January 4, 1843.

59. *Willmer & Smith's European Times,* March 5, 1844, and Willmer & Rogers advertisement, Daniel J. Kenny, comp., *The American Newspaper Directory and Record of the Press*...(New York: Watson, 1861), p. xxvi.

60. *Willmer & Smith's European Times,* January 4, 1843.

61. Times, *Tercentenary,* p. 232.

62. The issues the author has personally examined are number 1, January 4, 1843; number 6, April 19, 1843; number 28, March 5, 1844; number 152, March 4, 1846; number 161, May 5, 1846; number 225, August 4, 1847; number 230, September 4, 1847; and number 249, January 29, 1848.

63. Schwarzlose, "Foreign Connection," pp. 48–49.

64. Winifred Gregory, ed., *American Newspapers, 1821–1936: A Union List of Files Available in the United States and Canada* (New York: H. W. Wilson, 1937), p. 469.

65. *Herald for Europe,* July 15, 1846.

66. Gregory, *American Newspapers,* p. 469.

67. Mott, *American Journalism,* p. 580.

68. Crouthamel, *Webb,* p. 94.

69. *New York Tribune for Europe,* September 25, 1850. The 1847–48 founding period for this newspaper is surmised from the fact that this only extant copy of the paper is volume 2, number 70.

70. Augustus Maverick, *Henry J. Raymond and the New York Press for Thirty Years: Progress of American Journalism from 1840 to 1870* (Hartford, Conn.: A. S. Hale, 1870), p. 40.

71. Quoted in Frank M. O'Brien, *The Story of the Sun, New York, 1833–1928,* 2nd ed. (New York: D. Appleton, 1928), p. 96.

72. Daniel H. Craig, *Answer of Daniel H. Craig...to the Interrogatories of the U.S. Senate Committee on Education and Labor at the City of New York, 1883* (New York, 1883), p. 2. The anonymous author of the article "The Boston Herald" repeats this description, adding that Craig released his pigeons about fifty miles outside of Boston. The article also states that W. G. Blanchard, "then connected with the Boston press," received the birds, expanded their dispatches, and printed extra editions "for all the papers subscribing to the enterprise," including extras for the *New York Herald* which were shipped on to New York City by Long Island Sound steamer in advance of the regular mails. *The Bay State Monthly (New England Magazine),* 2 (October 1884): 23–24. Another source explains that "extra editions" in this context meant actually placing the *Herald's* nameplate over the news dispatches which had been set in type in Boston. [Perry], *Boston Her-*

ald, pp. 5–6. Blanchard resurfaces in early 1853, then in the office of the *Boston Mail,* serving as the Boston correspondent for Craig, who by then was the general agent of the New York City Associated Press.

73. Hudson, *Journalism,* p. 596.

74. Craig, *Answer,* p. 2.

75. Two schools of thought exist in the literature on the purposes of and support for the *Romer* adventure. The *Herald* school portrays it as an anti-*Herald* effort of four New York City papers and several in other cities. See, for example, Hudson, *Journalism,* pp. 529–33, which is summarized in Oliver Carlson, *The Man Who Made News, James Gordon Bennett* (New York: Duell, Sloan & Pearce, 1942), pp. 196–98. One biographer of Horace Greeley, however, portrays the *Romer* voyage as "a gigantic conspiracy" against the *Herald* "to overwhelm that naughty and clever paper with defeat." This source links the voyage to the *Tribune, Sun,* and *Journal of Commerce* in New York City and "leading papers in Boston, Philadelphia, Baltimore, and Washington." Francis Nicoll Zabriskie, *Horace Greeley, the Editor,* in the American Orators and Reformers series, ed. Carlos Martyn (New York: Funk & Wagnalls, 1890), pp. 85–86. The *Tribune* school of thought, which fails to mention this as an anti-*Herald* effort, emphasizes the need for foreign news to arrive in New York City as rapidly as in Boston, then the only U.S. terminal for Cunard steamers. An extended discussion of news delivery in New York City in the *New York Weekly Tribune* for April 18, 1846, expresses unhappiness with New York's business and government circles for permitting Boston to be the unchallenged entry point for foreign news for five years. The article refers to maturing arrangements, of which the just-completed *Romer* expedition was only a part, by which New York papers could more rapidly secure foreign news. Without elaborating on these arrangements, the article indicated they were among the *Tribune* and *Sun* in New York and the *North American* and *Public Ledger* in Philadelphia. For the *Tribune* view of the *Romer*'s adventure, see the *New York Weekly Tribune* for April 18 and 25, 1846. Later accounts tend to support the *Tribune* view. See, for example, Charles D. Baker, "Newspaper Enterprise in 1846," *The Journalist,* October 6, 1888, p. 11; and Maverick, *Raymond,* pp. 40–42, 486–90, where Maverick devotes an appendix to reprinting the *Romer* account from the *Weekly Tribune.* A brief account is in *Niles' National Register,* April 25, 1846, p. 128.

76. Baker, "Enterprise," p. 11.

77. Tyler, *Steam,* pp. 150–51, citing the *New York Herald,* February 20, 1846.

78. James G. Riggs and Ralph M. Faust, "New York Becomes the Empire State" in *The Age of Reform,* vol. 6 of the History of the State of New York, ed. Alexander C. Flick (New York: Columbia University Press, 1934), p. 334.

79. Quoted in Thompson, *Wiring,* p. 67.

80. James D. Reid, *The Telegraph in America, Its Founders, Promoters, and Noted Men* (New York: Derby Brothers, 1879), p. 308.

81. Alexander Seward, "The Telegraph and Associated Press," Oneida Historical Society *Transactions* (1881): 156–57. Seward originally read this paper before the society on December 31, 1878.

82. Ibid., p. 158. See the author's "The Nation's First Wire Service: Evidence Supporting a Footnote," *Journalism Quarterly* 57 (Winter 1980): 555–62, for a somewhat more detailed account of these upstate New York events.

83. Manchester & Broyman to The Publisher of the Gazette, New York State Associated Press Papers, Oneida Historical Society, Utica, N.Y., (hereafter cited as NYSAP Papers). The collection consists of a volume of mounted correspondence, contracts, ledgers, and other documents entitled "Associated Press and Free Delivery of Newspapers 1846–47," contributed by Alexander Seward, editor of the *Utica Daily Gazette*. The Oneida Historical Society lists the collection as "New York State Newspapers-Publishers' Correspondence."

84. H. S. Winants to Publisher, *Utica Daily Gazette*, February 6, 1846, NYSAP Papers, "Postscript" was a label used by some 1840s dailies over their latest telegraphic dispatches.

85. Cushman to R. Northway & Co., NYSAP Papers.

86. J. Stringham[?] to Printers of Utica Gazette, NYSAP Papers.

87. Gregory, *American Newspapers,* pp. 438–98.

88. Isaac Butts to Messrs. Northway & Co., NYSAP Papers. Emphasis in original.

89. Since the bulk of the correspondence in the NYSAP Papers consists of letters addressed to the *Gazette,* there are no copies of these early circulars. References to *Gazette* circulars and the terms proposed in letters from the west, however, indicate what Northway and Seward proposed and that they sent circulars on February 12, 14, 16, and 26 and March 10 to various editors west of Utica.

90. James Kinney to Messrs. R. Northway & Co., February 17, 1846, NYSAP Papers.

91. John C. Merrill & Co. to R. Northway & Co., February 18, 1846, NYSAP Papers.

92. George Dawson to Alexander Seward, February 19, 1846, NYSAP Papers.

93. Manchester & Broyman to Messrs. R. Northway & Co., March 4, 1846, NYSAP Papers.

94. Henry Oliphant to R. Northway & Co., March 6, 1846, NYSAP Papers.

95. Manchester & Broyman to Messrs. Northway & Co., March 7, 1846, NYSAP Papers.

96. Jerome[?] & Brothers to R. Northway & Co., March 12, 1846, NYSAP Papers.

97. S. F. Smith to Northway & Co., March 20, 1846, NYSAP Papers.

98. The Preface defines newsbroking, i.e., a wire service, as "the daily collection and distribution of general news dispatches via communication systems among journalists in several communities, a process controlled by an agent or agency." As the previous paragraphs indicate, this developing upstate movement fits this definition.

99. Alfred McClung Lee comes to this same conclusion, saying in reference to the New York State Associated Press, "the 'first' press association for telegraphic newsgathering arose spontaneously as the natural solution of a problem. . . . Rosewater and many others to the contrary notwithstanding, this A.P. antedated the A.P. of New York City by more than a year. . . . [T]his association pioneered in . . . cooperative wire service." Lee, *Daily Newspaper,* pp. 495–96. Apparently not privy to the New York State AP papers at the Oneida Historical Society, Lee based this conclusion on a similar assertion in S. N. D. North, *History and Present Condition of the Newspaper and Periodical Press of the United States, with a Catalogue of the Publications of the Census Year* (Washington, D.C.: Government Printing Office, 1884), p. 106. North, in turn, cites Alexander Seward's 1878 address to the Oneida Historical Society, cited above in n. 81. Beyond Seward's address, North had personal knowledge of the New York State AP. Although born two years after the New York State AP was founded, he became managing editor of the *Utica Morning Herald* after graduating from Hamilton College in 1869. He acquired a financial interest in the *Herald,* an AP paper, remaining as editor of the paper until 1886, when he became editor of the *Albany Express.* In 1885 he was elected president of the New York State AP. *Dictionary of American Biography,* s.v. "North, Simon Newton Dexter." In chapter 3 the first telegraphic dispatches in New York City will be placed at May 2, 1846, identical dispatches appearing on May 7 in more than one newspaper. The New York City Associated Press arose at least eighteen months later. See the author's "Early Telegraph News Dispatches: Forerunner of the AP," *Journalism Quarterly* 51 (Winter 1974): 595–601.

100. W. Lacy to Messrs. Northway & Co., May 27, 1846, and W. Lacy to Alex. Seward, June 13, 1846, NYSAP Papers. Nothing can be found on Lacy other than his affiliation with the *Albany Argus,* which was surmised from the return address on his correspondence with the *Utica Gazette.*

101. Jones, *Sketch,* p. 148.

102. Manchester & Broyman to Messrs. R. Northway & Co., February 28, 1846; Manchester & Broyman to Messrs. R. Northway & Co., March 4, 1846; and A. M. Clapp & Co. to Messrs. R. Northway & Co., March 12, 1846, NYSAP Papers.

103. Use of the "New York State Associated Press" name here anticipates this newsbrokerage's first formal name as part of the Associated Press system after 1867. In 1846 the group apparently had no formal name.

104. Seward, "Associated Press," p. 159.

105. Quoted in ibid.

106. Ibid.

107. Ibid., p. 160.

108. "Proposition to Telegraph Co.," August 5, 1846, NYSAP Papers.

109. Untitled, printed circular, signed T. M. Foote, J. Barber, and A. Seward, Committee, August 18, 1846, NYSAP Papers.

110. Snow to Mr. Seward, April 18, 1848, NYSAP Papers.

111. George Snow to The Editor of the Utica Gazette, undated, NYSAP Papers; and Zabriskie, *Greeley*, p. 80. Snow was apparently a respected New York City journalist. Horace Greeley says, "Mr. George M. Snow, a friend of my own age, who had had considerable mercantile experience, took charge of the Financial or Wall-Street department [of the *New York Tribune* when the paper was founded in 1841] and retained it for more than twenty-two years; becoming ultimately a heavy stockholder in, and a trustee of, the [*Tribune*] concern; resigning his trust only when (in 1863) he departed for Europe in ill health; returning but to die two years later." Horace Greeley, *Recollections of a Busy Life* (New York: J. B. Ford, 1868), p. 139.

112. Untitled, printed circular, August 18, 1846, NYSAP Papers.

113. Gregory, *American Newspapers*, p. 438.

114. Untitled financial and service-loss tabulation for September 9 to October 15, 1846, NYSAP Papers.

115. Henry O'Rielly, "Facts Concerning the 'Cunard Letter,'" *American Telegraph Magazine* 1 (April-May-June 1853): 250, where a letter to O'Rielly from Abbot & Winans is reprinted, listing the subscribers to the Abbot & Winans news report as of August 18, 1852.

116. New York City AP general agent Daniel H. Craig was the architect of AP's operation in the mid–1850s. See chapter 5.

117. Rosewater, *News-Gathering*, p. 134. See Volume 2.

118. Several local, state, and regional AP organizations developed after the Civil War, each representing a corporate or partnership newsbroking cooperative of newspapers, together forming a loose national Associated Press confederation. See Volume 2. The death of the old United Press and formation of a national Associated Press are also described in Volume 2.

119. Thompson, *Wiring*, pp. 139–43, citing Reid, *Telegraph*, p. 144.

120. Hudson, *Journalism*, p. 476.

121. Jones, *Sketch*, p. 122.

122. Hudson, *Journalism*, p. 610. Hudson depicts this predicament—slow telegraphic growth, lack of capacity for transmitting all newspapers' dispatches, and the expense of telegraphing news—as the cause for

the formation of the New York City Associated Press in 1848–49. See chapter 3.

123. Ibid., pp. 476–77. On November 27, 1847, the *New York Herald* reports that "the New York daily press, of which the *Herald* is one of the members, has made arrangements to run a daily line of expresses between New Orleans and New York. . . . These expresses will be continued through the approaching winter, probably up to the period required to complete the telegraphic communications between the two great cities of the Union." Despite the generalized terms in the *Herald's* item, there is no evidence here, or in other sources, that these expresses were the seeds of the New York City Associated Press. This express apparently did not include the *Courier and Enquirer,* and this arrangement seems devised only to gather Mexican War news, and to offset the inefficiency of the postal system and the incompleteness of the Southern telegraph line. Dr. Tom Reilly, a scholar of Mexican War reporting, agrees in correspondence with the author that, in the absence of hard evidence to the contrary, the Mexican War was not the origin of the New York City Associated Press.

124. *New York Herald,* February 28, 1848.

125. Jones, *Sketch,* pp. 132–33.

126. *Utica Gazette,* November 3, 1846.

127. Clipping from *Albany Argus,* November 9, 1846, in "Journalistic Series," vol. 1, Henry O'Rielly Papers, New York Historical Society, New York City.

128. Clipping from *Rochester* (N.Y.) *Daily Democrat* in ibid.

129. Ibid.

130. Quoted in Harlow, *Old Wires,* pp. 178–79.

131. Magnetic Telegraph Company, *Articles,* pp. 25–26.

132. Ibid., p. 48. The company's directors took this action on April 6, 1847.

133. Ibid., pp. 41, 48.

134. Ibid., p. 84.

135. Thompson, *Wiring,* pp. 53–54.

136. Ibid., pp. 54–55, 156–57.

137. Ibid., pp. 220–21.

138. Richard B. Du Boff, "Business Demand and the Development of the Telegraph in the United States, 1844–1860," *Business History Review* 54 (Winter 1980): 465, 479.

139. Hone, *Diary,* 2:849. Emphasis in original.

140. For examples of such reporting, see *Niles' National Register,* December 25, 1847, p. 272; January 22, 1848, p. 323; December 13, 1848, p. 384; and January 10, 1849, pp. 25–26.

141. George S. Merriam, *The Life and Times of Samuel Bowles,* 2 vols. (New York: Century, 1885), 1:26–27.

142. Thomas C. Cochran and William Miller, *The Age of Enterprise: A Social History of Industrial America* (New York: Macmillan, 1942), pp. 27–29.

143. Michael Schudson, *Discovering the News: A Social History of American Newspapers* (New York: Basic Books, 1978), pp. 12–60, passim.

Chapter 3

1. See n. 1 in chapter 2 for a brief summary of these events.

2. In light of the significance accorded the New York State Associated Press in chapter 2 as our first newsbrokerage and to avoid confusion between that upstate organization and newsbroking developments in New York City, the latter will be referred to in this book as the New York City Associated Press until after the mid–1850s, when the city's AP attained a national reputation. This is contrary to virtually all the literature, which calls the city's newsbrokerage the New York Associated Press from its earliest dates.

3. The lithograph is reproduced on p. 239 of John A. Kouwenhoven, *The Columbia Historical Portrait of New York: An Essay in Graphic History in Honor of the Tricentennial of New York City and the Bicentennial of Columbia University* (Garden City, N.Y.: Doubleday, 1953).

4. W[ellington] Williams, *Appleton's New York City and Vicinity Guide* . . . (New York: D. Appleton 1849), p. 7.

5. Stokes, *Iconography,* 5:1735.

6. Williams, *Guide,* p. 12.

7. Alex[ander] Mackay, *The Western World, or Travels in the United States in 1846–47, Exhibiting Them in Their Latest Development, Social, Political and Industrial Including a Chapter on California,* 2nd ed., 3 vols. (London: Richard Bentley, 1849), 1:179–80.

8. Henry Collins Brown, *Glimpses of Old New-York* (New York: Lent & Graff, 1917), p. 79, and a lithograph of a drawing by Aug. Kollner entitled "Wall Street, N.Y., 1847."

9. The building was apportioned as follows: 6 Wall, Harnden's Express Company and Livingston & Company; 10 Wall, Livingston and Fargo Company and the American Express Company (also known as Wells, Butterfield & Co.) and 16 Wall, Adams & Co. *Doggett's New York City Directory* (New York, John Doggett, Jr.) for 1850–51.

10. Stokes, *Iconography,* 5:1796, where the Morse notice to the public of the opening of this office is reprinted.

11. *Doggett's New York City Directory* (1850–51).

12. Ibid.

13. Thompson, *Wiring,* pp. 61, 63–66; and *New York Sun,* September 11, 1846.

14. Thompson, *Wiring,* pp. 69, 81.

15. Reid, *Telegraph,* p. 300.

16. Ibid.

17. Rosewater, *News-Gathering,* p. 70; and Gramling, *AP,* p. 23.

18. Jones, *Sketch,* pp. 121–23, 132, 136.

19. U.S. Department of Navy, Office of the Chief of Naval Operations, Naval History Division, *Dictionary of American Naval Fighting Ships,* 8 vols. (Washington, D.C.: Government Printing Office, 1959), 1:21; and *Niles' National Register,* July 11, 1846, p. 291.

20. *Washington Daily Union,* June 27, 1846. The *Union* was the Polk administration's mouthpiece and could secure such messages to the president as the administration deemed it politic to release.

21. *New York Times,* May 27, 1898.

22. *New York Tribune,* January 30, 1887.

23. Lee, *Daily Newspaper,* pp. 496, 500; and Rosewater, *News-Gathering,* pp. 83–84.

24. Abbot's name appears in journalism history as "Abbott." See Rosewater, *News-Gathering,* pp. 83–84; and Lee, *Daily Newspaper,* p. 500, both of whom may have relied on a single reference to "Abbott and Winans" by Daniel H. Craig in New York Associated Press, *Annual Report of the General Agent* (New York, 186[3]), p. 9. The author's use of "Abbot" is based on the man's own signature (see next note), the more frequent use of "Abbot" in New York City directories, and his obituary cited in n. 21.

25. Abbot to Gents, November 8, 1854[?], Ezra Cornell Papers, Department of Manuscripts and University Archives, Cornell University Library, Ithaca, N.Y.

26. New York City series, vol. 434, p. 17, R. G. Dun & Co. Collection, Baker Library, Harvard University Graduate School of Business Administration, Boston.

27. *Opinion of the Supreme Court of the State of New York in the Case of John J. Kiernan vs. the Manhattan Quotation Telegraph Company and Francis A. Abbot...* (New York: Douglas Taylor, 1876).

28. NYAP, *Annual Report,* pp. 8–9.

29. "The Press vs. the Press, in the Matter of Telegraphic Reports," *American Telegraph Magazine* 1 (October 1852): 10; Jones, *Sketch,* p. 141; and O'Rielly, "Facts," p. 250.

30. All city directories from this period available in the New York Public Library were checked for listings of these newsbrokers. The library's collection contains complete or nearly complete runs of *Doggett's New York City Directory, Rode's New York City Directory, Trow's Directory of New York City,* and *Wilson's Business Directory of New York City.*

31. Schwarzlose, "Early Dispatches," pp. 595–601. In this research the author examined dispatches labeled "Telegraphic News," or the like, in New York City papers to locate the first common telegraphic dispatch appearing in at least two of the three papers studied, the assumption being that the New York editors would use the novel "telegraphic" heading at their first opportunity. Frederick B. Marbut finds identical congressional summaries in the *Herald* and *Tribune* as early as April 29, 1846, but without the "Telegraphic News" heading. See Marbut's "Decline of the Official Press in Washington," *Journalism Quarterly* 33 (Summer 1956): 337–38. He notes that the common dispatches ran in the *Tribune*'s "Southern Mails" column and appeared in the *Herald* without labels or characteristic fanfare. Marbut theorizes that the *Philadelphia Public Ledger* had initiated an express, telegraphing congressional reports to Baltimore, where they were put on a 3 P.M. train for Philadelphia. From there, the telegraph company forwarded the *Public Ledger*'s copy on to New York City. Marbut, *News from the Capital: The Story of Washington Reporting* (Carbondale: Southern Illinois University Press, 1971), pp. 76–77.

32. Nahum Capen, ed., *The Massachusetts State Record and Year Book of General Information, 1847* (Boston: James French, 1847), p. 266.

33. *New York Herald,* July 18, 1846.

34. Schwarzlose, "Foreign Connection," pp. 48–49.

35. "History of 'The Associated Press.' "

36. Shanks, "News," pp. 511–22.

37. William Aplin, "At the Associated Press Office," *Putnam's* 6 (July 1870): 23–30.

38. Hudson, *Journalism,* p. 366.

39. Ibid., pp. 610–11. The author takes "emergency" in this quote to refer to the general inability of the telegraph system to serve the newspapers' individual needs. Hudson in previous paragraphs had concluded his discussion of the Mexican War situation and newsgathering.

40. Reid, *Telegraph,* pp. 29–30.

41. North, *Present Condition,* pp. 106–7.

42. *American Cyclopaedia: A Popular Dictionary of General Knowledge,* ed. George Ripley and Charles A. Dana, 16 vols. (New York: D. Appleton, 1883–84), 12:343.

43. James Melvin Lee, *History of American Journalism,* 2nd ed. (Garden City, N.Y.: Garden City Publishing, 1923), p. 276.

44. L. N. Charles, "Birth Certificate of A.P. on View in Public Library," *Fourth Estate,* February 26, 1927, pp. 11, 27.

45. This document is reproduced in Appendix I of Rosewater, *News-Gathering,* pp. 381–88.

46. George Henry Payne, *History of Journalism in the United States* (New York: D. Appleton, 1920), p. 248.

47. Bleyer, *Main Currents,* p. 402.

48. O'Brien, *Story,* p. 115.

49. Hudson, *Journalism,* p. 611.

50. "Harbor News Association," January 11, 1849, Henry J. Raymond Papers, Rare Books and Manuscripts Division, the New York Public Library, Astor, Lenox and Tilden Foundations, New York. This collection was contributed to the library on August 8, 1951, by Marguerite M. (Mrs. Seymour L.) Holbrook, according to Robert W. Hill, keeper of manuscripts. Letter to the author, November 3, 1967.

51. Richard A. Schwarzlose, "Harbor News Association: The Formal Origin of the AP," *Journalism Quarterly* 45 (Summer 1968): 253–60.

52. William Henry Smith, "The Press as a News Gatherer," *Century* 42 (August 1891): 529.

53. North, *Present Condition,* pp. 106–7.

54. Smith, "News Gatherer," p. 529, perhaps relying on the New York City Associated Press's practice in the early 1870s of reprinting this paragraph in the appendix of its "rules." [New York Associated Press] General News Association of the City of New York, *Rules* (New York: L. H. Bridgham, 1874), p. 11. Rosewater can do no better than to cite Smith and report the same fragment quoted here. Rosewater, *News-Gathering,* p. 62.

55. Rosewater, *News-Gathering,* pp. 64–66.

56. Lee, *Daily Newspaper,* p. 499; Gramling, *AP,* pp. 19, 21; Mott, *American Journalism,* p. 251; and Edwin Emery and Michael Emery, *The Press and America: An Interpretive History of the Mass Media,* 5th ed. (Englewood Cliffs, N.J.: Prentice-Hall, 1984), p. 165.

57. Rosewater, *News-Gathering,* p. 66.

58. Francis O. J. Smith, *An Exposition of the Differences Existing between Different Presses and Different Lines of Telegraph Respecting the Transmission of Foreign News* . . . (Boston: Dutton & Wentworth, 1850), pp. 27–30; and Dan[ie]l H. Craig, *A Review of "An Exposition of the Differences Existing between Different Presses and Different Lines of Telegraph Respecting the Transmission of Foreign News. . ."* (Halifax, N.S., 1850), pp. 17–18.

59. Rosewater, *News-Gathering,* pp. 62–63, relying on Jones, *Sketch,* p. 137, and [Pray], *Bennett,* p. 377.

60. Tom Reilly, "American Reporters and the Mexican War, 1846–1848" (Ph.D. diss., University of Minnesota, 1975), esp. pp. 30–51, and correspondence with the author.

61. Magnetic Telegraph Company, *Articles,* p. 65.

62. Ibid.

63. Ibid., pp. 65, 68.

64. Ibid., pp. 65–67.

65. Rosewater, *News-Gathering,* p. 64.

66. *New York Herald,* March 19, 1848. Emphasis in original.

67. Ibid., March 25, 1848.

68. Ibid., May 2, 1848.

69. Ibid., April 9, 1848.

70. *New York Sun,* May 8, 1848.

71. *New York Herald,* May 9, 1848.

72. *New York Sun,* March 25, 1853, quoted in *American Telegraph Magazine* 1 (February–March 1853): 232.

73. Craig, *Review,* p. 8.

74. The *Hibernia*'s Halifax arrival is reported in the *New York Herald,* May 28, 1848. The *Buena Vista*'s interception of the *Hibernia* is reported in the *Philadelphia Public Ledger,* May 30, 1848. The author is unable to explain why the *Buena Vista,* which, according to press reports, first started for Halifax on May 2, did not intercept a Cunarder for twenty-three days. In that period three Cunarders arrived in America—the *Britannia* in Boston on May 7, the *Cambria* in New York on May 14, and the *Caledonia* in Boston on May 20. Even if, as the author suspects, the *Buena Vista* had orders to intercept only New York—bound Cunarders, the *Cambria*'s news should have been collected by the express steamer.

75. *New York Herald,* May 31, 1848.

76. Smith, *Exposition,* pp. 27–28. (The misspelling of "Enquirer" is probably Smith's mistake, not Raymond's.) The full text of this letter, although altered to include italics and spelling corrections, is in Rosewater, *News-Gathering,* pp. 64–65. An abbreviated version of the letter is in Craig, *Review,* p. 17.

77. Smith, *Exposition,* pp. 28–29. A shortened version of this letter is in Rosewater, *News-Gathering,* p. 65.

78. Smith, *Exposition,* pp. 29–30; and Rosewater, *News-Gathering,* p. 66.

79. Craig, *Answer,* pp. 2–3.

80. Ibid.

81. Ibid.

82. Craig, *Review,* p. 8.

83. The author has found at least four variations on this ship's name: *News Boy, News-Boy, News-boy,* and *Newsboy.*

84. Hudson, *Journalism,* p. 611.

85. James Watson Webb Papers, Yale University Library, New Haven, Conn.

86. *New York Herald,* June 2, 1848.

87. Ibid., June 10, 1848.

88. Ibid., June 26, 1848.

89. Ibid., October 18, 1848.

90. *New York Courier and Enquirer,* October 18, 1848.

91. Craig, *Review,* p. 8.

92. *Boston Evening Transcript,* September 1, 1848.

93. "Harbor News Association," January 11, 1849, Raymond Papers.

94. Rosewater, *News-Gathering,* p. 85.

95. James Wright Brown Collection, New York Historical Society, New York City.

96. William M. Swain, Arunah S. Abell, and Azariah H. Simmons were partners in the founding of the *Philadelphia Public Ledger* in March 1836. Then Abell, with Swain and Simmons underwriting the venture, founded the *Baltimore Sun* on May 17, 1837. Emery and Emery, *Press and America,* p. 146.

97. Hudson, *Journalism,* p. 508.

98. Rosewater says the *Public Ledger's* first *Buena Vista* dispatch was on June 26, 1848. *News-Gathering,* p. 67. This is an error. On June 10 the *Public Ledger* carried the dispatch of the *Acadia's* news, brought by the *Buena Vista,* simultaneously with the New York City AP papers.

99. Joseph Edgar Chamberlin, *The Boston Transcript: A History of Its First Hundred Years* (Boston: Houghton Mifflin, 1930), p. 95.

100. Marbut, "Decline," p. 338.

101. Chamberlin, *Boston Transcript,* pp. 95–96. Craig confirms the formation of this nine-newspaper Boston group in mid–1848, referring to it repeatedly as the Boston Association, and in one place as the Boston Associated Press. *Review,* p. 23.

102. The editors' meeting and the proposal appearing in the *Macon Telegraph* are reported in *Niles' National Register,* September 25, 1847, p. 50.

103. Assuming the editors involved in this newsbroking movement were along the initial Morse telegraph routes through the South, they represented seven states (Virginia, North and South Carolina, Georgia, Florida, Alabama, and Mississippi). These states in 1850 had a combined total of only thirty-three dailies, which is only 13 percent of the nation's total dailies at that time. Lee, *Daily Newspaper,* pp. 715–17.

104. Western Associated Press, *Proceedings* (Detroit, 1876), p. 25.

105. Ibid., pp. 25–26.

106. Ibid., p. 27.

107. Clipping from *Louisville Morning Courier*, November 9, 1847, "Journalistic Series," vol. 2, Henry O'Rielly Papers, New York Historical Society, New York City.

108. Clippings from unidentified newspapers in ibid.

109. The *Pittsburg Weekly Commercial Journal*, January 15, 1848, reports: "Several of our Eastern exchanges complain very much...of the high rates charged for Telegraphic despatches by the lines in their sections of the country." The paper notes that a ten-word news dispatch cost 50 cents on the two hundred–mile New York–Boston line and the same on the five hundred–mile Pittsburgh–Louisville line. Clipping in ibid.

110. *New York Herald*, January 15, 1848.

111. *New York Herald*, January 22, 1848.

112. S. F. B. Morse to Sidney Morse, January 12, 1848, Samuel F. B. Morse Papers, Library of Congress, Washington, D.C. Emphasis in original.

113. *New York Herald*, March 9, 1848; and Thompson, *Wiring*, p. 154.

114. Morse to Smith, March 11, 1848, Francis O. J. Smith Papers, Maine Historical Society, Portland, Maine.

115. Morse to Smith, April 18, 1848, Smith Papers.

116. *New York Herald*, March 10, 1848.

117. Morse to Smith, April 18, 1848, Smith Papers.

118. The failure of this Morse suit was inevitable since the two instruments operated on entirely different principles. Morse's telegraph transmitted dots and dashes by use of a sending key and a receiving device that scribed the code on a strip of paper. House's devices for sending and receiving converted strokes on a keyboard of letters and numbers into combinations of electrical impulses, which, in turn were reconverted into letters and numbers printed on a strip of paper. The printing was done by a revolving type-wheel. House's top transmission capacity of about 2,600 words per hour was about twice as fast as the Morse equipment. Thompson, *Wiring*, pp. 54–55; and Harlow, *Old Wires*, p. 52.

119. *New York Herald*, April 30, 1848.

120. Ibid. Note that this compliment for House's invention comes from the same paper that had stood alone in supporting the Morse system three months earlier.

121. Thompson, *Wiring*, pp. 54–55.

122. *Buffalo Daily Courier*, March 6, [1848], clipping in "Journalistic Series," vol. 3, O'Rielly Papers.

123. *New York Sun*, "Tuesday," March 6 or 7, 1848, clipping in ibid. There is no evidence that the *Sun* ever erected one telegraph pole, let alone a line between Boston and Washington.

124. *New York Tribune,* March 11, 1848.

125. Greeley to Vail, March 23, 1848, Horace Greeley Papers, Rare Books and Manuscripts Division, The New York Public Library, Astor, Lenox and Tilden Foundations, New York.

126. Henry O'Rielly, "Memoranda Respecting the 'Relations between the Associated Press and Henry O'Rielly,'" *American Telegraph Magazine* 1 (April-May-June 1853): 239.

127. Thompson, *Wiring,* pp. 166–67.

128. Various correspondence from Jones to O'Rielly (see text for dates), O'Rielly Papers.

129. Ibid.

130. Thompson, *Wiring,* p. 119.

Chapter 4

1. Gramling, *AP,* p. 20.

2. Ibid.; and Morris, *Deadline.* There are numerous autobiographies that also suffer from excessive corporate loyalty, chief among them being Melville E. Stone, *Fifty Years a Journalist* (Garden City, N.Y.: Doubleday, Page, 1921); Kent Cooper, *Kent Cooper and the Associated Press: An Autobiography* (New York: Random House, 1959); and Hugh Baillie, *High Tension: The Recollections of Hugh Baillie* (New York: Harper, 1959).

3. *New York Herald,* March 3, 1848. *Herald* and *Tribune* circulations are adjusted here to be comparable with other figures in the table.

4. J[oseph] C[amp] G[riffith] Kennedy, *Catalogue of the Newspapers and Periodicals Published in the United States. . .* (New York: John Livingston, 1852), p. 29.

5. Papers of Frederic and Woodward Hudson, private collection of Mrs. Wesley P. Wilmot, Concord, Mass. Hudson's diaries, unfortunately, make only occasional references to Associated Press business.

6. Standard biographical sources, especially the *Dictionary of American Biography* and newspaper obituaries, provide the basis for the following discussion.

7. Morton Borden, "Some Notes on Horace Greeley, Charles Dana and Karl Marx," *Journalism Quarterly* 34 (Fall 1957): 460.

8. Beman Brockway, *Fifty Years in Journalism Embracing Recollections and Personal Experiences, with an Autobiography* (Watertown, N.Y.: Daily Times, 1891), p. 140. The concept of Dana and Hudson being actual editors for the frequently absent Greeley and Bennett is convincingly portrayed by Louis M. Starr in *Bohemian Brigade: Civil War Newsmen in Action* (New York: Knopf, 1954), see esp. pp. 11–25.

9. J[ames] Parton, *The Life of Horace Greeley, Editor of the New York Tribune* (New York: Mason Brothers, 1855), pp. 360–61.

10. J[ames] W. Simonton, *The Associated Press: It Is Not a Monopoly. . .*

(New York: John Polhemus, 1879), p. 2. From testimony before the Railroad Committee of the U.S. Senate, February 17, 1879.

11. Harold Underwood Faulkner, *American Economic History,* 8th ed. (New York: Harper, 1960), pp. 423–25; Henry Campbell Black, *Black's Law Dictionary,* 5th ed. (St. Paul, Minn.: West, 1979), p. 307; and Steven H. Gifis, *Law Dictionary* (Woodbury, N.Y.: Barron's Educational Series, 1975), pp. 46–47.

12. Beach Brothers to Ezra Cornell, September 20, 1849, Cornell Papers.

13. Beach Brothers to Ezra Cornell, October 1, 1849, Cornell Papers.

14. The AP's chief administrator was called "general agent" until 1883, when the title gradually became "general manager."

15. Biographical information on Jones is from *New York Herald,* August 26, 1863; *Dictionary of American Biography; Appletons' Cyclopaedia of American Biography;* and *Who Was Who in America: Historical Volume, 1607–1896,* 2nd ed. (Chicago: A. N. Marquis, 1967).

16. *Doggett's New York City Directory,* various numbers.

17. Victor Rosewater is confused about AP's first location. On page 71 he locates AP's first office at 150 Broadway, but on pages 83–84 he says AP's first office and that of rival Abbot & Winans were across Hanover from each other, with the latter at 3 Hanover. Rosewater, *News-Gathering.* In addition to this internal inconsistency, Rosewater is totally at odds with available city directories on these newsbrokerages' addresses. The directories place AP at 3 Hanover for 1849–57, 58 Beaver for 1857–60, 7 Broad for 1860–61, 145 Broadway for 1861–63, 149 Broadway for 1868–75, 197 Broadway for 1875–79, and 195 Broadway for 1879–1914. The directories fail to record an AP location for 1863–68. They list A & W at 1½ Hanover for 1851–52 and at 4½ Hanover for 1852–55. *Doggett's New York City Directory, Rode's New York City Directory, Trow's Directory of New York City,* and *Wilson's Business Directory of New York City.* One scrap of evidence suggests that for at least part of the 1863–68 period, AP may have been at 148 Broadway. The evidence is a reprint of a letter from Daniel H. Craig, AP general agent, dated June 1, 1863, showing the 148 Broadway address. The reprint is in *The Opening and Closing Arguments of Hon. Thomas M. Hayes and Hon. Francis O. J. Smith . . . on a Motion for a New Trial, in the Case of The State vs. Smith* (Portland, Maine: Brown Thurston, 1866), p. 34. Apparently relying on Rosewater's 150 Broadway reference to AP's first office (and perhaps believing Broadway to be a preferable address to Hanover), the Associated Press has claimed its first office was at 150 Broadway. Gramling, *AP,* p. 23; and "Kent Cooper and the Associated Press," *AP World* 20 (Spring 1965): 32. AP might heed the advice of an 1855 observer who wrote, "As a general rule the finest buildings are on the West Side of [Broadway], called the dollar side, in contradistinction to the eastern [including 150 Broadway], which is called the shilling side." Clarence Cook, "Broadway," in *The United States, Illustrated in Views of City*

and Country with Descriptive and Historical Articles, ed. Charles A. Dana, 2 vols. (New York: Herrmann J. Meyer, 1855), 1:159.

18. Jones, *Sketch,* p. 136.

19. Ibid., p. 148.

20. *[Adams's] Boston Directory.*

21. Robert S. Harper, *Lincoln and the Press* (New York: McGraw-Hill, 1951), p. 156.

22. Ibid.; and J. Thomas Scharf, *The Chronicles of Baltimore, Being a Complete History of "Baltimore Town" and Baltimore City from the Earliest Period to the Present Times* (Baltimore: Turnbull Brothers, 1874), p. 86.

23. *Macmillan Dictionary of Canadian Biography,* 3rd ed. (London: Macmillan, 1963), pp. 414–15, 589.

24. Jones, *Sketch,* p. 148.

25. Ibid., pp. 136–37.

26. Gramling, *AP,* p. 31.

27. Marbut, *News,* pp. 81–82, where Marbut cites an unofficial congressional directory for 1853 that lists New York City AP's reporters as Gobright in the Senate and James W. Sheahan in the House.

28. L[awrence] A. Gobright, *Recollection of Men and Things at Washington during the Third of a Century,* 2nd ed. (Philadelphia: Claxton, Remsen & Haffelfinger, 1869), p. 172, where in an account of conflict in the Kansas territory Gobright reprints a statement by Horace Greeley supporting a Gobright news dispatch, identifying the latter as "the agent of the Associated Press at Washington."

29. Bryan, *History,* 2:414.

30. Jones, *Sketch,* p. 138.

31. Ibid., pp. 138–39. During Craig's administration, according to several sources, newspapers outside of New York City were made to pay assessments on a weekly basis.

32. Ibid., p. 138.

33. Thompson, *Wiring,* p. 223.

34. Alfred Vail, comp. *The Telegraph Register of the Electro-Magnetic Telegraph Companies in the United States and the Canadas Using Professor Morse's Patent, Containing the Rates of Charges for Transmission of Messages* (Washington, D.C.: John T. Towers, 1849), pp. 10–11, 13, 21–22.

35. Jones, *Sketch,* p. 123.

36. Reid, *Telegraph,* p. 196.

37. There were, no doubt, many slips in deciphering the news report codes, but perhaps equally embarrassing was forgetting that one was working with a *code* of real words, rather than the real words themselves. In Jones's code "dead" with a senator's name meant that that senator "after some days' absence from indisposition, reappeared in his seat." One day AP's Senate report noted: "John Davis dead." An eavesdropper in Philadelphia, not conversant with Jones's code, overheard the phrase and passed it on to a non-AP newspaper in Philadelphia, which printed it literally. The news eventually reached Sen. Davis's home state of Massachusetts, where, Jones says, "It drew forth a great number of the most *complimentary eulogiums* on the supposed deceased from the press, which Mr. Davis had the satisfaction of reading." Jones, *Sketch,* p. 133. Emphasis in original.

38. Ibid., pp. 123–31.

39. Ibid., p. 132. Emphasis in original.

40. Estimates of early Morse telegrapher speeds vary widely and most authorities avoid the subject. As one weighs the various reports and legends, it appears that a comfortable conventional operating speed was twenty-five or thirty words per minute.

41. Thompson, *Wiring,* p. 250. Anson Stager, later superintendent of the Union military telegraph system during the Civil War and superintendent of Western Union, claims to have been one of the first to receive by sound. As a Morse operator in Pittsburgh early in 1848, he was forced to complete the incoming news dispatches for the *Pittsburgh Gazette* by sound when his register's recording apparatus broke down. J. H. Kennedy, "General Anson Stager," *Magazine of Western History* 4 (July 1886): 293.

42. Hudson, *Journalism,* p. 607.

43. Newsbroker credit lines are occasionally found on newspaper pages after 1850. Most papers, however, did not credit the source of their telegraphic news, the *New York Times* being an exception in the late 1850s and during the Civil War. Until late in the nineteenth century, newsbrokerages, with the exception of the Confederate Press Association (see chapter 7), were unconcerned about whether members or subscribers gave the appropriate credit for newsbroker reports. Then in the 1890s, as the newsbroker war heated up, newsbrokers urged, largely unsuccessfully, that news copy be credited. Soon after the turn of the century, however, newspaper use of credit lines or logotypes was demanded by newsbrokers as a protection for their news reports' property rights. In the pre–Civil War period, wire copy can be identified only by comparing telegraphic dispatches in two or more known AP or Abbot & Winans newspapers. Generally the dispatches appeared in identical form in all newspapers receiving them, variations arising only in styles of abbreviation and capitalization among the papers.

44. The *New York Herald's* coverage of this story is used here because as

a seven-day-a-week paper the *Herald* offers continuous opportunity to see AP's handling of the story.

45. Jones, *Sketch,* p. 139.

46. Printed circular enclosed in Jones to Henry O'Rielly, October 5, 1848, O'Rielly Papers. Emphasis in original.

47. Jones to Cornell, November 21, 1848, Cornell Papers.

48. "Reminiscences of Craig and the Associated Press," *Flake's Semi-Weekly* (Galveston) *Bulletin,* December 5, 1869, in Manton Marble Papers, Library of Congress, Washington, D.C. The author thanks Carol Smith of the University of Iowa for discovering and copying this clipping for him.

49. Reid, *Telegraph,* pp. 343–44.

50. Ibid., p. 341.

51. Several sources discuss the struggle over news movement on the telegraph circuits between Halifax and New York City. See Thompson, *Wiring,* pp. 226–39; Reid, *Telegraph,* pp. 343–46, 362–69, 608–9; and Rosewater, *News-Gathering,* pp. 75–83.

52. Smith, *Exposition,* pp. 30–31. Smith reproduces the contract, presumably in its original form.

53. Ibid., pp. 32–34.

54. "Reminiscences of Craig" (see n. 48 above). The article describes its source as a "person whose recollection of events for twenty years past is still fresh and whose opportunities were unequalled for observing the progress" of the AP. The author believes this source is James D. Reid.

55. John W. Regan, "The Inception of the Associated Press," Nova Scotia Historical Society *Collections* 19 (1918): 93–114, passim.

56. *New York Tribune,* March 9, 1849.

57. Quoted in Regan, "Inception," p. 101.

58. No source gives a precise time when Craig's plan matured. The New York City newspapers offer no clue, in large part because for each of the next four Cunard arrivals at Halifax some portion of the telegraph line between Halifax and New York was inoperative and the city's press was relying on dispatches mailed from some point north of Portland or was waiting for the Cunarders to proceed on to either Boston or New York.

59. Reid is the only contemporary who described this episode. *Telegraph,* pp. 364–66. Despite numerous opportunities to describe this triumph himself, Craig failed to do so. The Reid account is accepted by Thompson, *Wiring,* pp. 232–33, and by Rosewater, *News-Gathering,* p. 77.

60. Nothing can be found on Dyer except that he is mentioned in this connection in Smith, *Exposition,* p. 10; Craig, *Review,* p. 6; and Rosewater, *News-Gathering,* p. 77.

61. Smith, *Exposition*, pp. 34–35. Smith claims the evening papers sought his help in securing foreign news in time for their deadlines. It is equally possible that Smith contributed to the conditions that led to dividing the Boston press into two camps.

62. Quoted in ibid., p. 24.

63. Quoted in ibid., p. 36.

64. Quoted in ibid., p. 21.

65. Ibid., pp. 24–25.

66. Quoted in ibid., p. 13.

67. O'Rielly, "Memoranda," pp. 241–42.

68. Morse to Smith, January 24, 1850, Smith Papers.

69. Quoted in Smith, *Exposition*, pp. 44–46.

70. Ibid., passim.

71. Craig, *Review*, p. 15–16, 29.

72. Magnetic Telegraph Company, *Articles*, p. 202.

73. Ibid., p. 203.

74. Ibid., p. 208.

75. Receipt dated March 23, 1850, and April 3, 1850, show payments on each date of $25 by the *New York Courier and Enquirer* "for expense of forwarding foreign news from St[eamer] Niagara from Portland to Boston" and "for expense of forwarding foreign news from St[eamer] Canada from Portland to Boston," respectively. Webb Papers.

76. Kendall to Smith, April 1, 1850, Smith Papers.

77. Thompson, *Wiring*, p. 239, relying on the *New York Herald*.

78. Morse, *Letters*, 2:82.

79. Magnetic Telegraph Company, *Articles*, p. 209.

80. Ibid., p. 211.

81. Ibid., p. 212. Emphasis in original.

82. Ibid.

83. Ibid., pp. 205–6, 214–15, 217.

84. Morse, *Letters*, 2:308.

85. Quoted in ibid.

86. Thompson, *Wiring*, p. 190.

87. Ibid., p. 229.

88. Jones, *Sketch*, pp. 139–40.

89. Ibid.

90. Hudson, *Journalism*, p. 612.

91. Connery, "Collection of News," p. 27.

92. *New York Herald,* August 26, 1863.

93. Raw newspaper and circulation totals are from Lee, *Daily Newspaper,* pp. 718, 725; population figures and school enrollment rates are from U.S. Department of Commerce, Bureau of the Census, *Historical Statistics of the United States, Colonial Times to 1970* (Washington, D.C.: Government Printing Office, 1975), pp. 8, 11-12, 369-70. Using this census source and a table of daily circulation totals for the years 1919-62 (Editor & Publisher, *International Yearbook* 43 [1963], p. 215), the author calculates that total daily circulation reached its highest percentage of total population, 36.52 percent, in 1945.

94. Smith, *Newspaper,* pp. 106, 108.

95. See n. 69 for source.

96. Lambert A. Wilmer, *Our Press Gang, or a Complete Exposition of the Corruptions and Crimes of the American Newspapers* (1859; reprint ed., New York: Arno, 1970).

97. Samuel Bowles, "The Newspaper," an editorial in the *Springfield* (Mass.) *Republican,* January 4, 1851, as quoted in Merriam, *Bowles,* 1:98.

98. Hudson, *Journalism,* p. 600.

Chapter 5

1. *Dictionary of American Biography,* s.v. "Craig, Daniel H."; *Dictionary of Literature Biography, American Newspaper Journalists,* ed. Perry J. Ashley, vol. 43, pp. 118-24; Craig, *Answer,* pp. 1-8; the personal research files of Peter R. Knights, History Department, York University; and Jesse A. Barney, *Rumney, Then and Now: History* (Rumney, N.H.: town of Rumney, 1967), p. 210.

2. *Rode's New York City Directory* and *Trow's Directory of New York.* Stuart disappeared from the directories in 1857, and Bridgham did in 1861.

3. Williams, *Guide,* p. lii. The first bridge linking Brooklyn and Manhattan, the Brooklyn Bridge, was not completed until the spring of 1883.

4. Smith, "News Gatherer," p. 529.

5. Ibid.; and NYAP, *Rules,* p. 11.

6. The title is not attached to the fragment quoted by Smith, but it is mentioned in Maverick's *Raymond,* p. 326; and in the first section of AP's 1856 "Regulations of the General News Association of the City of New York," the document replacing this 1851 agreement. The 1856 regulations are reprinted in Rosewater, *News-Gathering,* pp. 381-88.

7. Gramling, *AP,* pp. 28-29. The only serious factionalism the author has found in the New York City AP ranks arose, not among members of readership or political groupings of the papers, but between those seeking to expand individual news enterprise and those willing to rely on the AP's news reports and their partners' special reports. See Volume 2.

8. NYAP, *Annual Report*, pp. 8-9.

9. Jones, *Sketch*, pp. 140-41.

10. Ibid., p. 141.

11. "The Press vs. the Press in the Matter of the Telegraphic Reports," *American Telegraph Magazine* 1 (October 1852): 10.

12. Thompson, *Wiring*, p. 195.

13. O'Rielly, "Facts," pp. 248-49.

14. Reid, *Telegraph*, pp. 345-48.

15. "Mr. O'Rielly's Letter to Mr. Cunard," *American Telegraph Magazine* 1 (October 1852): 15-16.

16. "Telegraphic Movements among the Boston Merchants," *American Telegraph Magazine* 1 (November 15, 1852): 95.

17. Daniel H. Craig, *Letter to F. M. Edson on the House Telegraph Line* (New York, 1853), pp. 16-17.

18. The pamphlet is lost but is described and briefly quoted in "Telegraphic Intercourse between Europe and the United States," *American Telegraph Magazine* 1 (April-May-June 1853): 233-34. Emphasis appears in the magazine version without indication of whether it appeared in the pamphlet.

19. Quoted in "Libels Promptly Repudiated by the Associated Press," *American Telegraph Magazine* 1 (February-March 1853): 232. Emphasis appears in the magazine version without indication of whether it appeared in the newspaper item.

20. *New York Tribune*, March 18, 1853, quoted in "Competition in Telegraphing—Monopoly System in Nova Scotia," *American Telegraph Magazine* 1 (February-March 1853): 213.

21. O'Rielly, "Memoranda," pp. 235-48; and O'Rielly, "Facts," pp. 248-62.

22. O'Rielly, "Facts," p. 258. There is no way of knowing whether emphasis was in the original card or in O'Rielly's quote of it.

23. American Telegraph Company, *Remarks of R. W. Russell, One of the Executive Committee of the American Telegraph Company, in Reply to the Statement of Messrs. Abram S. Hewitt, Cyrus W. Field, Henry J. Raymond, and Others, Made at the Meeting of Stockholders, on June 29th, 1860* (New York: Wm. C. Bryant, 1860), p. 62, quoting a pamphlet published by the Nova Scotia Telegraph Company in 1859.

24. "Indispensable" may seem an exaggeration, but in light of the weak A & W alternative and editors' limited prior experience with newsbroker dispatches, any improvement in length, diversity, or style of reporting would have been seen as progress. Dispatches from the newfangled telegraph were rapidly perceived by editors as essential to a successful newspaper, and Craig's AP dispatches by the mid-1850s dominated telegraphic news movement.

25. The *Boston Evening Transcript* joined Abbot & Winans on June 19, 1851, after A & W beat the New York City AP with the news of a fire in San Francisco. Editorially implying that Craig, "the autocrat of the morning papers," had delayed the AP's dispatch to favor the morning press, the paper on June 20 applauded A & W's 10,000-word fire dispatch, concluding with: "Business is business, Mr. Craig. . . .[T]hanks to the superior enterprise of our correspondents, Messrs. Abbot & Winans, who have guaranteed to give us the latest news. . .,we are bound to have it. . . . When two men ride a horse, one must ride behind. Messrs. Abbot & Winans have the saddle, and Mr. Craig must be content with a seat on the pillion."

26. [Perry], *Boston Herald*, p. 37.

27. "Telegraphic Communication between America and Europe," *American Telegraph Magazine* 1 (January 31, 1853): 157; and "Telegraphic Intercourse," p. 258 (see n. 18 above for source).

28. It will be recalled from chapter 2 that Blanchard was a confederate of Craig's in Boston in the latter's pigeon days of competition with AP.

29. Parton, *Greeley*, p. 296.

30. Bryan, *History*, 2:409.

31. *National Cyclopaedia of American Biography*, s.v. "Gobright, Lawrence A." For selected episodes in Gobright's life, most of them political or personal rather than journalistic, see Gobright's *Recollection*.

32. [Benjamin Perley Poore], "Washington News," *Harper's Monthly* 48 (January 1874): 229.

33. Marbut, *News*, p. 82.

34. George H. Manning, "Bennett Fight Opened Senate to Press," *Editor & Publisher*, July 21, 1934, p. 118.

35. "History of 'The Associated Press.' "

36. Manning, "Bennett Fight," p. 118; and [Poore], "Washington News," p. 229. After reading many columns of early AP Washington news, one is compelled to believe Gobright's claim that "I do not act as a politician belonging to any school. . . ." For the record, however, numerous references in his autobiography, *Recollection of Men and Things at Washington*, indicate his personal political sympathies were Democratic. See especially page 172, where Gobright permits himself to be labeled a Democrat by a Republican editor who was in the process of defending Gobright's work.

37. Letter marked "Private," believed to have been written in 1856, Horace Greeley Papers, Library of Congress, Washington, D.C. Emphasis in original.

38. Printed New York Associated Press circular, signed in type by D. H. Craig, 1854, Cornell Papers.

39. Frederick S. Siebert says the origin of objective reporting was "the growth of cooperative news-gathering associations." Siebert, Theo-

dore Peterson, and Wilbur Schramm, *Four Theories of the Press* (Urbana: University of Illinois Press, 1956), p. 60. John D. Stevens observes that after the Civil War "newspapers began using and emulating the accounts provided by the wire services, written so as not to offend papers of any persuasion. Objectivity became the paramount value in the business, and the journalist found it a comforting one." Stevens and Hazel Dicken Garcia, *Communication History* (Beverly Hills, Calif.: Sage, 1980), p. 103. Donald L. Shaw depicts newsbroker influence growing in the content of local newspapers in "News Bias and the Telegraph: A Study of Historical Change," *Journalism Quarterly* 44 (Spring 1967): 3–12, 31. Others advance contrary notions. Dan Schiller finds objectivity predating newsbroking by being central to the "commercial press." *Objectivity and the News: The Public and the Rise of Commercial Journalism* (Philadelphia: University of Pennsylvania Press, 1981). Michael Schudson, by focusing on "objectivity's" introduction in journalism's lexicon, finds it a uniquely twentieth-century phenomenon. See his *Discovering the News.*

40. *New York Herald,* March 9, 1854.

41. *New York Tribune,* November 13, 1856.

42. Craig disputes such an observation in a pamphlet defending the AP and attacking executives of the American Telegraph Company, saying that the average daily news report between New York and Boston during January was 3,100 words in 1854, 3,700 words in 1856, 4,500 words in 1858, and 3,800 in 1860. D. H. Craig, *"The American Telegraph Company and the Press": A Reply to the Falsehoods of the Executive Committee* (n.p., 1860), p. 4.

43. Craig, *Answer,* p. 5.

44. Donald L. Shaw, "Technology and Conformity: Study of Newsgathering in the American Press, 1820–1860" (Paper delivered at the Fifty-fifth Annual Meeting of the Association for Education in Journalism, Carbondale, Ill., August 22, 1972), p. 16.

45. David H. Weaver, "U.S. Newspaper Content from 1820 to 1860: A Mirror of the Times?" (Paper delivered at the Fifty-ninth Annual Meeting of the Association for Education in Journalism, College Park, Md., August 1976), p. 10.

46. Ibid., pp. 10–11.

47. O'Rielly, "Facts," p. 250.

48. The list includes: *Boston Herald* and *Transcript; Worcester Transcript* and *Spy; Hartford Times; New Haven Register, Journal & Courier,* and *Palladium; New York Evening Post, Commercial Advertiser,* and *Evening Mirror; Albany Journal, Argus, Atlas, Register, Express,* and *Knickerbocker; Troy Post, Budget, Whig,* and *Times; Utica Gazette* and *Herald; Syracuse Journal* and *Star; Oswego Times* and *Journal; Auburn Advertiser; Rochester Democrat, Daily Advertiser,* and *American; Lockport Courier; Buffalo Commercial, Express, Courier, Re-*

public, and *Rough Notes; Binghamton Republican; Newark Daily Advertiser; Philadelphia Inquirer, Bulletin, Sun, Pennsylvanian, News,* and *Argus,* "through whose agent papers in the west and north are supplied with news"; *Baltimore Patriot, Argus, Correspondent,* and *Sun* "in part"; *Washington National Intelligencer* and *American Telegraph; Alexandria Gazette; Richmond Times* "in part"; *Norfolk Herald, Beacon,* and *Argus; Charleston Mercury, Standard,* and *Evening News* ("Quite a number of papers South and in the vicinity of Charleston, S.C., are dependent upon the Mercury for the Telegraphic news"); *New Orleans Picayune; Pittsburgh Journal* "in part . . . and other papers obtaining news from it"; and *St. Louis Republican* "and other papers depending on it for news."

49. O'Rielly, "Facts," p. 250. Emphasis in original.

50. Comparing this list of upstate Abbot & Winans subscribers in August 1852 (see n. 48) with that of the founding papers of the New York State AP six years earlier, one finds the latter still largely intact. Only the *Buffalo Advertiser,* a founding paper and still publishing in 1852, is not on this list. In Albany the *Herald* had ceased publication, the *Express* was founded in 1847, and the *Register* was founded in 1850. The *Troy Times* was founded in 1851, and the *Utica Herald* was founded in 1847. The *Auburn Cayuga Tocsin* disappeared in an 1847 merger. In Buffalo the *Republic* was founded in 1847 and the *Rough Notes* was founded in 1852. Oswego had been added to the telegraph circuit since 1846, and the *Lockport Courier* was founded in 1851. Gregory, *American Newspapers,* pp. 438–98.

51. Frederic Hudson Papers.

52. Ibid.

53. NYAP, *Annual Report,* p. 9; and *Trow's Directory of New York City.*

54. *New York Herald, Times,* and *Tribune* for May 27, 1898.

55. R.G. Dun & Co. Collection, New York City series, vol. 434, p. 17.

56. *New York Tribune,* January 30, 1887; and *The Journalist* 4 (February 5, 1887): 5.

57. Daniel H. Craig, *The Convicted Libeller: Open Published Letter to F. O. J. Smith* (New York, 1863), p. 2.

58. Rosewater, *News-Gathering,* p. 74.

59. Reid, *Telegraph,* p. 362.

60. Craig, *Answer,* pp. 4–5.

61. Western Associated Press, *Proceedings* (1876), p. 27.

62. The New York & Erie Telegraph Company was formed by F. O. J. Smith in February 1848, assisted by Ezra Cornell and John James Speed, Jr., in a move to give Smith's coast-bound Morse franchise access to the potentially lucrative telegraph field to the west. A viola-

tion of the original Morse contracts, which granted franchisees territorial exclusivity, the New York & Erie line paralleled Faxton's, but ran across southern New York state, dipping into Pennsylvania and reaching Lake Erie at Dunkirk and Fredonia. As the company organized on October 2, 1849, Smith, absent and unexpectedly reticent about signing over his patent rights to others for use of Morse equipment on the new line, lost control of the new company to his lieutenant Cornell in a stockholders' vote. On January 15, 1852, the line was sold to Cornell and associates for $7,000 and was reorganized as the New York & Western Union Telegraph Company. Extensive growth west of New York state and the lease or purchase of other lines over the years led to the emergence of the Western Union Telegraph Company as the nation's telegraph monopoly in 1866. See Volume 2. Thompson, *Wiring,* pp. 166–84, 263, 424. For this and later periods a useful record of Western Union's corporate growth is U.S. Interstate Commerce Commission, "Corporate History of Western Union," comp. John T. Marchand, 1914–1922, a typed list and description of companies contributing to Western Union's growth.

63. Cornell to Craige [*sic*], January 4, 1856, Cornell Papers.

64. Craig to Cornell, January 22, 1856, Cornell Papers. Emphasis in original.

65. Craig to Cornell, February 11, 1856, Cornell Papers.

66. Craig to Cornell, February 12, 1856, Cornell Papers. Emphasis in original. It is of historical interest now, but perhaps of news value to Craig that Cornell's line along the Erie Railroad right-of-way was the first in the nation used to dispatch trains, a practice begun on the line by railroad superintendent Charles Minot on September 22, 1851. John F. Stover, *American Railroads* (Chicago: University of Chicago Press, 1961), p. 41.

67. Craig to Cornell, February 22, 1856, Cornell Papers. Emphasis in original. "Phelps" in this quote refers to George M. Phelps, who in 1856–57 improved the Hughes instrument to the point where it could receive a patent on September 23, 1857. By 1870 the Hughes instrument was the standard transmission device on the Western Union circuits. Craig had discovered the device, an invention of Kentucky music professor David E. Hughes, during a trip to the West in 1855. Hughes sold his device to the Commercial Telegraph Company, in which Craig owned a half-interest, on November 1, 1855. Although a printing telegraph instrument similar to Royal E. House's, Hughes's was more efficient, faster, and beyond Morse interests' attempts to claim patent infringement. Thompson, *Wiring,* pp. 303–4; Harlow, *Old Wires,* pp. 52, 245–46; and *Dictionary of American Biography,* s.v. "Hughes, David Edward." For a detailed description of House's printing telegraph, the Hughes instrument, and other early telegraphic devices, see Edward Highton, *The Electric Telegraph, Its History and Progress* (London: John Weale, 1852); Trumbull, *Electro-Magnetic Telegraph;* and Robert Sabine, *The Electric Telegraph* (London: Vir-

tue Brothers, 1867) and *The History and Progress of the Electric Telegraph,* 2nd ed. (New York: D. Van Nostrand, 1869).

68. All information and quotes in the previous three paragraphs are from a copy of a telegram from Craig to Chief Clerk of the [Western] Union Telegraph Office, February 21, 1856, Cornell Papers.

69. Barns to Craig, February 10, 1856, Cornell Papers.

70. Craig to Cornell, February 19, 1856, Cornell Papers. Emphasis and "d——d" in original.

71. Associated Press, *Annual Report* (1896), pp. 156–57.

72. The request, made by Frederic Hudson as AP's agent on September 18, 1850, was aimed at obtaining congressional reports "more expeditiously and correctly than if allowed to have the proceedings sent over with the messages of the public." "There would be less confusion, and consequently fewer errors," said Hudson's request, which was also prompted by an AP desire to expand its daily congressional report to two columns in length. Magnetic Telegraph Company, *Articles,* pp. 236–37.

73. Townsend to Messrs. Cornell and Speed, August 29, 1851, Cornell Papers.

74. Reid, *Telegraph,* p. 369.

75. New York and New England Union Telegraph Company, *The Certificate of Formation and Articles of Association of the New York and New England Union Telegraph Company Together with the Records of the Meetings of the Directors* (Boston: Bazin & Chandler, 1852), pp. 56–61.

76. Craig, *Letter,* esp. pp. 11–13.

77. Thompson, *Wiring,* p. 262.

78. Craig, *Answer,* p. 6.

79. Ibid.; and Reid, *Telegraph,* p. 407.

80. Sources for this account of Field and the Atlantic cable are Thompson, *Wiring,* pp. 299–324; Craig, *Answer,* pp. 6–7; and Reid, *Telegraph,* pp. 369, 404–7.

81. Submarine and transatlantic telegraphy had been the subject of much discussion for several years before Field came on the scene. Tests on a gutta-percha-encased cable to traverse the English Channel were reported as "being entirely successful" in March 1849. *Niles' National Register,* March 14, 1849, p. 176. But salt water quickly corroded the insulation, and a successful channel cable, coated with gutta-percha and encased in lead, was finally opened for business on November 13, 1851. Desmond, *Information Process,* p. 111. Congress had been petitioned for funds to survey a route for a transatlantic cable between England and North America by February

1849. The petition proposed suspending the cable twenty feet below the ocean's surface, held by buoys anchored on the ocean floor. *Niles' National Register,* February 7, 1849, p. 81. By 1856 ideas of a suspended cable gave way to one laid on the ocean floor, and two prime routes were under consideration—one hopscotching from northern Scotland through the Orkney, Shetland, and Faeroe islands to Iceland, then to Greenland and Labrador (proposed by Tal. P. Shaffner) and the other submerged the whole distance from St. John's, Newfoundland, to Valentia Bay, Ireland (Field's proposal and the ultimate route). Marshall Lefferts, "The Electric Telegraph: Its Influence and Geographical Distribution," American Geographical and Statistical Society *Bulletin* 2 (1856): 252–54; and Thompson, *Wiring,* pp. 299–300, n. 2.

82. Reid, *Telegraph,* pp. 404–5.

83. Thompson, *Wiring,* p. 304.

84. Ibid., pp. 304–6.

85. Reid, *Telegraph,* p. 413.

86. Craig to Cornell, August 2, 1857, Cornell Papers. Emphasis in original. William M. Swain, a founder of the *Philadelphia Public Ledger* and *Baltimore Sun,* both allied with the New York City AP from the start, was also an early Morse telegraph investor.

87. The literature about the Atlantic cable is broad and interesting. Brief accounts are in Thompson, *Wiring,* pp. 318–19, 323; and Harlow, *Old Wires,* pp. 219–42. A detailed account by the "historian of the enterprise" is John Mullaly, *The Laying of the Cable or the Ocean Telegraph Being a Complete and Authentic Narrative of the Attempt to Lay the Cable Across the Entrance to the Gulf of St. Lawrence in 1855 and of the Three Atlantic Telegraph Expeditions of 1857 and 1858* (New York: D. Appleton, 1858). A popular treatment written by two *New York Times* staffers in August 1858, before the cable fell silent, is Charles F. Briggs and Augustus Maverick, *The Story of the Telegraph and the History of the Great Atlantic Cable* (New York: Rudd & Carleton, 1858). Among many Field biographies, the first to examine are Samuel Carter III, *Cyrus Field, Man of Two Worlds* (New York: Putnam, 1968) and Isabella Field Judson, ed., *Cyrus W. Field, His Life and Work (1819–1892)* (New York: Harper, 1896). An excellent brief view of the cable project from the perspective of one of its American supporters is Allan Nevins, *Abram S. Hewitt, with Some Account of Peter Cooper* (New York: Harper, 1935), pp. 162–68. For descriptions of the 1857 and 1858 cable attempts in histories of Field's entire effort from 1854 to 1866, see [Anglo-American Telegraph Company], *The Atlantic Telegraph, Its History from the Commencement of the Undertaking in 1854 to the Sailing of the "Great Eastern" in 1866* (London: Bacon, 1866); Henry M. Field, *History of the Atlantic Telegraph* (New York: Scribners, 1866); and Philip B. McDonald, *A Saga of the Seas: The Story of Cyrus W. Field and the Laying of the First Atlantic Cable* (New York: Wilson-Erickson, 1937).

88. *New York Evening Post,* August 5, 1858; Field, *Atlantic Telegraph,* pp. 218–19; and Judson, *Field,* pp. 95–97.

89. *New York Herald,* August 6, 1858.

90. *Boston Evening Transcript,* August 6, 1858.

91. Field telegraphed the following to the AP from Trinity Bay on August 7: "We landed here in the woods, and until the telegraph instruments are all ready, and perfectly adjusted, no communications can pass between the two continents; but the electric currents are received freely. You shall have the earliest intimation when all is ready, but it may be some days before every thing is perfected. The first through messages between Europe and America will be from the Queen of Great Britain to the President of the United States, and the second his reply." Field, *Atlantic Telegraph,* p. 228.

92. *New York Sun,* August 17, 1858.

93. Gobright, *Recollection,* pp. 190–91. Emphasis in original.

94. Desmond, *Information Process,* p. 143. Desmond offers no source for an agreement starting in 1857, while other sources are either silent or vague on the point. A United Nations study dates the first Reuters-AP exchange agreement from 1859. U.N. Educational, Scientific and Cultural Organization, *News Agencies, Their Structure and Operation* (Paris: Georges Lang, 1953), p. 18.

95. Craig, *Answer,* p. 6. Frederic Hudson confirms these facts and gives the following totals of steamers intercepted off Cape Race for the AP during four years: 13 in 1859, 31 in 1860, 34 in 1861, and 46 in 1862. Hudson, *Journalism,* pp. 614–16.

96. "History of 'The Associated Press.' " Beman Brockway says that this was the mode of delivering European news in the United States from "about 1854 till November, 1866, when the Atlantic Cable became operative." Brockway makes the questionable assertion that a "news agent come over on every steamship, and on the voyage he prepared and edited a pretty full summary of news from all the London, Paris and Liverpool papers that had been published after the last previous steamer had left Liverpool. . . ." Brockway, *Fifty Years,* p. 240.

97. "History of 'The Associated Press.' "

98. R. G. Dun & Co. Collection, New York City series, vol. 376, p. 487.

99. This document is reprinted in Rosewater, *News-Gathering,* pp. 381–88, and Charles, "Birth Certificate," pp. 11, 27. Unable to locate an original copy, the author here relies on Rosewater's version.

100. Henry Steele Commager, *The American Mind: An Interpretation of American Thought and Character since the 1880's* (New Haven, Conn.: Yale University Press, 1950), p. 7.

101. Ibid., p. 13.

102. Ibid., p. 18.

103. Leonard D. White, *The Jacksonians: A Study in Administrative History, 1829-1861* (New York: Macmillan, 1954), p. 412.

Chapter 6

1. Lefferts, "The Electric Telegraph," p. 261.

2. *Trow's Directory of New York City* (1856-58).

3. Craig to Cornell, August 2, 1857, Cornell Papers. Most of Craig's AP correspondence prior to 1857 was on unheaded stationery.

4. Thompson, *Wiring*, pp. 310-13.

5. Ibid., p. 313.

6. The territories of the "six nations" were: American—Newfoundland, Nova Scotia, New Brunswick, all of New England, New Jersey, Delaware, Virginia, most of today's West Virginia, North and South Carolina, Georgia, Florida, and southern Alabama; Atlantic & Ohio—Maryland, northern West Virginia, and Pennsylvania east of Pittsburgh; New York, Albany & Buffalo—New York state east of Buffalo; Western Union—western New York and Pennsylvania, Ohio, Indiana, Michigan, Wisconsin, and Missouri south of the Missouri River; New Orleans & Ohio—Kentucky, Tennessee, northern Alabama, Mississippi, Arkansas, and Louisiana; and Illinois & Mississippi—Illinois, northern Missouri, Iowa, and Minnesota. Ibid., p. 315.

7. Ibid., pp. 313-17.

8. See chapter 5, n. 81, for more on Shaffner's cable proposal.

9. Thompson, *Wiring*, pp. 319-23.

10. Ibid., pp. 323-30.

11. Ibid., pp. 325, 331-32.

12. *Debate in the Massachusetts Senate on the Bill to Incorporate the Boston and Halifax Telegraphic Cable Co., March 24 and 26, 1859* (Boston: Henry W. Dutton, 1859). In covering the defeat of the proposal, Craig's AP did not disguise its viewpoint on the proposed Nova Scotia-Massachusetts cable: "The project...was initiated by F. O. J. Smith and F. N. Gisborne, who, by specious misrepresentations, induced a committee of Boston merchants to petition the Legislature for a charter.... The measure is now killed, unless the friends of Smith and Gisborne succeed in carrying a reconsideration, which is doubtful." *New York Herald,* March 29, 1859.

13. Thompson, *Wiring*, p. 320; and Reid, *Telegraph*, pp. 398-402.

14. American Telegraph Company, *Remarks*, p. 62, quoting from a pamphlet published by the Nova Scotia Telegraph Company in 1859.

15. Rosewater, *News-Gathering*, p. 92. One can detect the stingier news dispatch by comparing the *Europa*'s news in New York's AP newspapers for July 28, 1858, with earlier steamer dispatches.

16. *New York Times,* June 4, 1859.

17. American Telegraph Company, Executive Committee, *The American*

Telegraph Company and the New York Associated Press (n.p., 1860), p. 23.

18. Reid, *Telegraph,* p. 423.

19. Thompson, *Wiring,* p. 332.

20. American Telegraph Company, *Remarks,* esp. pp. 56–58.

21. Reid, *Telegraph,* p. 424.

22. Craig, *"American Telegraph Company,"* pp. 21–22.

23. Ibid., p. 22. Emphasis in original.

24. Quoted in American Telegraph Company, *Remarks,* pp. 57–58.

25. In addition to holding positions as secretary, counsel, and executive committee member for the American company, Russell had quietly been buying shares in the old Atlantic Telegraph Company from Peter Cooper, Edward Cooper, Abram S. Hewitt, and Cyrus W. Field. Ibid., pp. 6–12.

26. American Telegraph Company, *American Telegraph Company,* p. 26.

27. American Telegraph Company, *Remarks,* p. 73.

28. Thompson, *Wiring,* pp. 336–37.

29. Ibid., pp. 337–38; and American Telegraph Company, Special Tariff Committee, *The Telegraph and the Press* (n.p., 1860).

30. American Telegraph Company, *American Telegraph Company;* a pamphlet by Craig, dated June 12, 1860, addressed to the American stockholders, referred to in subsequent pamphlets here but which the author cannot locate; American Telegraph Company, *Remarks,* a 74-page pamphlet from which a 23-page *Extract* was also published; Craig, *Reply;* American Telegraph Company, Executive Committee, *Reply of the Executive Committee to the Pamphlet of D. H. Craig, Agent of the New York Associated Press* (n.p., [1860]); and Amos Kendall, *Circular to the Stockholders of the American Telegraph Company* (n.p., 1860).

31. *New York Times,* June 30, 1860.

32. Francis Brown, *Raymond of the Times* (New York: Norton, 1951), p. 162.

33. Quoted in Thompson, *Wiring,* p. 342.

34. Hudson, *Journalism,* p. 615. On p. 521 Hudson notes that Sanford had been an early and successful operator of an express company. Among others, "Sanford performed the more arduous part of running locomotive expresses with the latest news from Europe," Hudson says. Sanford and others "have many a time covered themselves with coal-dust and glory in running a mile a minute on a locomotive for the New York and Philadelphia journals."

35. An 1865 trade press notice reports that the AP-American company contract expired October 31, 1865. "The Association has issued circulars," the notice continues, " to the several telegraph companies to

send in their bids for a new contract. . .to Mr. S. H. Gay, of *The Tribune*." *Telegrapher* 1 (September 25, 1865): 165.

36. Brown, *Glimpses*, p. 87. This site has since been occupied by the New York Stock Exchange.

37. *Wilson's Business Directory of New York City* (1857–60).

38. Reid, *Telegraph*, p. 422.

39. *Wilson's Business Directory of New York City* (1861).

40. Western Union and AP occupied the 145 Broadway address until 1875, when both moved into the new Western Union Building at 195 Broadway, two and a half blocks north of the old address.

41. Mott, *American Journalism*, p. 350. This sketch of the *World* is based on Mott, pp. 350–51; and Hudson, *Journalism*, pp. 182–83, 361, 667–76.

42. Hudson, *Journalism*, p. 668.

43. Hudson in two places suggests the *World* initially received AP news. Ibid., pp. 611, 668. Two other sources, however, say the *World* began receiving AP news only after acquiring the *Courier and Enquirer.* George T. McJimsey, *Genteel Partisan: Manton Marble, 1834–1917* (Ames: Iowa State University Press, 1971), pp. 23–29; and Simonton, *Associated Press*, p. 16.

44. On May 31, 1861, Webb was named minister to Brazil; he remained there for eight years. *Dictionary of American Biography*, s.v. "Webb, James Watson." The *Courier and Enquirer* announced its acquisition by the *World* to its readers in a long story published on June 27, 1861, and reprinted in Hudson, *Journalism*, pp. 669–70.

45. Testimony of Henry George in 1883. U.S. Congress, Senate Committee on Education and Labor, *Report of the Committee of the Senate upon the Relations between Labor and Capital and Testimony Taken by the Committee*, 5 vols. (4 vols. published), 48th Cong., 2nd sess., 1885, 1:481.

46. Harper, *Lincoln*, p. 113.

47. Ibid., p. 114. The other four cited papers were *News, Day Book,* and *Freeman's Journal* in New York City and the *Brooklyn Daily Eagle.*

48. Ibid., p. 115.

49. *Dictionary of American Biography*, s.v. "Hallock, Gerard."

50. *New York Times*, January 7, 1866.

51. *New York Times*, April 3, 1895.

52. Hudson, *Journalism*, p. 373; and *New York Times*, January 7, 1866.

53. *Dictionary of American Biography*, s.v. "Prime, William Cowper" and "Stone, David Marvin."

54. Hudson, *Journalism*, p. 611.

55. Quoted in ibid., p. 370.

56. Hudson reports that the *Express* started in 1836 as "decidedly Whig," then became an organ for Know-Nothingism, and then it "drifted into the ranks of the democracy." In 1872, Hudson says, the paper's circulation was "largely confined to the numerous railway cars and steam-boats running to and from and within the limits of the city, where a numerous class engaged in business in the metropolis do their reading." Ibid., pp. 518–19.

57. Ibid.

58. Lee, *Daily Newspaper,* p. 278; and Mott, *American Journalism,* p. 446.

59. Gregory, *American Newspapers,* p. 466.

60. Associated Press reports were identified by comparing telegraphic dispatches among the *Herald, Times,* and *Tribune* of New York City for November 7, 1860.

61. The states represented in AP's election-night coverage were New York, Massachusetts, Vermont, Connecticut, New Jersey, Pennsylvania, Delaware, Maryland, Virginia, North Carolina, Louisiana, and Rhode Island.

62. The *Herald* had a dispatch from Illinois; the *Tribune* had dispatches from Illinois, Maine, and Indiana; and the *Times* had a dispatch from South Carolina.

63. Most of the variation in length of the copy in type resulted not from selectivity or from editing by the papers (there was almost none of either), but from different typographical formats.

64. Four perspectives are offered in the literature on Villard's coverage of the president-elect: Henry Villard, *Memoirs of Henry Villard, Journalist and Financier, 1835–1900.* edited by his family, 2 vols. (Boston: Houghton Mifflin, 1904), 1:140–52, for the reporter's own impressions; Henry Villard, *Lincoln on the Eve of '61: A Journalist's Story,* edited by Harold G. Villard and Oswald Garrison Villard (New York: Knopf, 1941), consisting of the reporter's dispatches selected and edited by his sons; William E. Baringer, *A House Dividing: Lincoln as President Elect* (Springfield, Ill.: Abraham Lincoln Association, 1945), for the political impact and content of the reporter's dispatches; and Tom Reilly, "Early Coverage of a President-Elect: Lincoln at Springfield, 1860," *Journalism Quarterly* 49 (Autumn 1972): 469–79, for a scholarly overview of the episode.

65. Villard, *Memoirs,* 1:140. See chapter 5 for a discussion of AP's 1856 regulations, still in force in 1860–61.

66. *New York Herald,* February 5, 1861.

67. Baringer, *House Dividing,* pp. 15–16.

68. Villard, *Memoirs,* 1:141.

69. Abraham Lincoln, *Collected Works,* ed. Roy P. Basler, 9 vols. (New Brunswick, N.J.: Rutgers University Press, 1953–55), 4:484.

70. Villard's version of Lincoln's Farewell Address can be found in the morning press of New York City for February 12, 1861. Three other versions are reproduced in Lincoln, *Collected Works,* 4:190. The first of these three versions, in the handwriting of Lincoln and his secretary, John G. Nicolay, was written aboard the train after departing Springfield. Considered the most authoritative version of the extemporaneous speech, it is, with the exception of one sentence, very similar to Villard's telegraphed version. Villard indicates he had secured his copy by asking Lincoln to write it out for him after the train left Springfield. Villard says he later lost that autograph copy of the speech. Villard, *Memoirs,* 1:149. Basler comments that Villard's claim of receiving such a copy "may or may not be true." Lincoln, *Collected Works,* 4:191.

71. *New York Times* and *Philadelphia Public Ledger,* February 12, 1861.

72. *Richmond Dispatch,* February 12, 1861.

73. There is no way of knowing how many Southern papers received AP's report. Sources even disagree on how many dailies existed in the South at the start of the war. The U.S. census for 1860 shows 387 dailies in the nation with only seventy in the eleven states of the Confederacy. Lee, *Daily Newspaper,* pp. 715–17. J. Cutler Andrews believes there were eighty dailies in the Confederacy in 1861. J. Cutler Andrews, *The South Reports the Civil War* (Princeton, N.J: Princeton University Press, 1970), p. 26.

74. Andrews, *South Reports,* p. 55.

75. The Southwestern Telegraph Company resulted from the reorganization in January 1860 of the New Orleans and Ohio Telegraph Lessees. It was a party to the Six-Nation Contract and occupied its predecessor's territory. Thompson, *Wiring,* p. 335.

76. The *Picayune* credits "By the Southwestern Lines" for the bulk of its telegraphic news reports. In the paper's morning edition, however, the April 11 datelines were delivered by the Southwestern line, and the April 10 datelines arrived via the American line. In the afternoon edition of the *Picayune* on April 12, the first news of shots fired at Fort Sumter appeared, arriving via the American line. The news of the firing on Sumter arrived at the *Picayune* in the form of several official Confederate telegrams exchanged between Gen. Pierre G. T. Beauregard and Confederate Secretary of War L. Pope Walker, and an official announcement of hostilities from Walker to D. G. Duncan in Montgomery.

77. The author's tabulation of identical telegraphic dispatches among the several newspapers studied is below. Totals will not match in some cases because one paper may have combined two dispatches into one while another paper ran them separately.

Dispatches appearing in: ...and also appearing in:	Chicago Tribune	Richmond Dispatch	New Orleans Picayune
NYAP Papers	0	5	1

NYAP Papers & *Picayune*	5	1	–
NYAP Papers & *Dispatch*	2	–	1
NYAP Papers & *Tribune*	–	2	7
NYAP & All Regional Papers	2	2	2
Picayune	9	0	–
Dispatch	4	–	–

78. George B. Prescott, *History, Theory, and Practice of the Electric Telegraph* (Boston: Ticknor & Fields, 1860), p. 385.

79. Ibid., p. 386.

80. Taylor, *Transportation Revolution,* p. 398.

81. Pred, *Urban Growth and City-Systems,* see esp. pp. 142–56.

82. Ibid., pp. 147–48.

83. *The Writings of James Russell Lowell,* 12 vols. (Cambridge: Riverside Press, 1890–1892), 5:239, as quoted by James W. Carey and John J. Quirk, "The History of the Future," in *Communications Technology and Social Policy: Understanding the New "Cultural Revolution,"* ed. George Gerbner, Larry P. Gross, and William H. Melody (New York: Wiley, 1973), p. 499.

84. The relative inefficiency of communicating via transportation systems, as compared with electric systems, is discussed in chapter 1. The problem of the individual's communication needs as met or thwarted by a succession of technological innovations is discussed more thoroughly by the author in "Technology and the Individual: The Impact of Innovation on Communication," in *Mass Media between the Wars: Perceptions of Cultural Tensions, 1918–1941,* ed. Catherine L. Covert and John D. Stevens (Syracuse, N.Y.: Syracuse University Press, 1984).

Chapter 7

1. For Civil War journalism, see J. Cutler Andrews, *The North Reports the Civil War* (Pittsburgh: University of Pittsburgh Press, 1955); Andrews, *South Reports;* Emmet Crozier, *Yankee Reporters, 1861–65* (New York: Oxford University Press, 1956); Starr, *Bohemian Brigade;* Marbut, *News,* chaps. 10–11; Harper, *Lincoln;* James E. Pollard, *The Presidents and the Press* (New York: Macmillan, 1947), pp. 312–96; and Culver H. Smith, *The Press, Politics, and Patronage: The American Government's Use of Newspapers, 1789–1875* (Athens: University of Georgia Press, 1977), chap. 17. For aspects of telegraphy during the Civil War see Thompson, *Wiring,* chaps. 26–27; Harlow, *Old Wires,* chap. 13; David Homer Bates, *Lincoln in the Telegraph Office: Recollections of the United States Military Telegraph Corps during the Civil War* (New York: Century, 1907); and William R. Plum, *The Military Telegraph during the Civil War in the United States,* 2 vols. (Chicago: Jansen, McClurg, 1882).

2. *Chicago Tribune,* April 12, 1861.

3. James G. Randall, "The Newspaper Problem in Its Bearing upon Mili-

tary Secrecy during the Civil War," *American Historical Review* 23 (January 1918): 307.

4. Andrews, *North Reports*, pp. 751-59, and *South Reports*, pp. 548-51.

5. Charles T. Babcock; Theodore Barnard; —— Cureau; Sid[ney?] Deming; Lawrence A. Gobright; John Hasson; William D. McGregor, who also wrote for the *New York Herald;* —— Myers; James Oscar Noyes; Samuel J. Rea; R. L. Shelly; George W. Tyler; and E. D. Westfall, who also wrote for the *New York Herald*. Andrews, *North Reports*, pp. 751-59.

6. John Graeme, Jr.; Alexander Gray; Capt. John Kennedy; and —— Loomis. Andrews, *South Reports*, p. 549.

7. Jonathan White Albertson; —— Forbes; John Graeme, Jr.; John E. Hatcher ("Scantling"), who also wrote for the *Mobile Daily Advertiser and Register;* Bartholomew R. Riordan, who also wrote for the *Charleston Mercury* as "Adsum"; —— Sanderson; J. Henley Smith; —— Smoot; A. J. Wagner; and Will O. Woodson. Ibid., pp. 548-51.

8. Thompson, *Wiring*, pp. 374.

9. *Richmond Dispatch,* May 21, 1861.

10. Bates, *Lincoln*, pp. 14-37.

11. *Richmond Dispatch,* May 23, 1861. The *Dispatch* here relies upon the "latest news by express," rather than the telegraph, and quotes the *New York Tribune* on the seizure of telegrams in the North.

12. Thompson, *Wiring*, p. 374.

13. Andrews, *South Reports*, p. 55.

14. Thompson, *Wiring*, p. 374.

15. Andrews, *South Reports*, p. 55.

16. Thompson, *Wiring*, p. 375.

17. Bates, *Lincoln*, p. 11.

18. The young and still-growing telegraph had been used for reporting some events of the Mexican War, but not nearly as extensively as in the Civil War.

19. Joseph J. Mathews, *Reporting the Wars* (Minneapolis: University of Minnesota Press, 1957), p. 88.

20. Andrews, *North Reports*, pp. 92-96; and Gobright, *Recollection*, pp. 316-17.

21. Benjamin P. Thomas and Harold M. Hyman, *Stanton: The Life and Times of Lincoln's Secretary of War* (New York: Knopf, 1962), p. 370.

22. Gobright's autobiography indicates a slight but discernible inclination toward Jacksonian democracy and James Buchanan. See Gobright, *Recollection,* pp. 13-25 and 166-201, esp. pp. 170-72.

23. Smith, *Press, Politics, and Patronage,* p. 231.

24. Ibid., p. 229.

25. Starr, *Bohemian Brigade,* p. 41, quoting a dispatch in the *New York Herald,* June 19, 1861.

26. Harper, *Lincoln,* pp. 130–31.

27. *New York Times,* November 21, 1861. Historian Starr indicates that this agreement was an attempt by AP executive committee members Frederic Hudson and Henry J. Raymond to use the newsbrokerage "to forestall future *Tribune* beats" like a recent one that had hurt the *Herald* and the *Times.* Starr, *Bohemian Brigade,* pp. 72–73. Frederick Marbut, however, emphasizes Secretary of War Simon Cameron's corruption and propensity, quoting Henry Villard, to be "a little too freely at the disposal of the newspaper men, to whom he was by far the most cordial and talkative of all secretaries." Cameron's relations with *Tribune* correspondent Samuel Wilkeson (Cameron gave Wilkeson extraordinary access to official documents and freedom from censorship, and Wilkeson gave Cameron laudatory press coverage) prompted an arrangement to hand official documents directly to the Associated Press, according to Marbut, who does not conjecture on the power of the wire's executive committee to influence the course of events in Washington. Marbut, *News,* pp. 113–14; and Villard, *Memoirs,* 1:172. Elsewhere Marbut contends that Associated Press "took over that part of the administration paper's function which consisted of making public official orders and addresses." Marbut, *News,* p. 121. Also see Marbut's "Decline," pp. 335–41.

28. Gobright, *Recollection,* pp. 288–89.

29. Henry Watterson, "Abraham Lincoln," *Cosmopolitan* 46 (March 1909): 363–64.

30. Gobright, *Recollection,* pp. 312–14, where Gobright reprints his dispatch.

31. *New York Times,* May 15, 1881. A well-known instance of Gobright's intimacy with the administration occurred during his coverage of Lincoln's assassination, during which he apparently enjoyed unimpeded access to the presidential box at Ford's Theatre, the death scene across the street, and the homes of cabinet members. See Gobright, *Recollection,* pp. 348–50. A discussion of his coverage and his assassination dispatches are in Louis L. Snyder and Richard B. Morris, eds., *A Treasury of Great Reporting: "Literature under Pressure" from the Sixteenth Century to Our Own Time,* 2nd ed. (New York: Simon & Schuster, 1962), pp. 150–54.

32. Marbut, *News,* p. 126.

33. Gobright, *Recollection,* pp. 335–37. The military telegraph historian says that "during the Civil War the President spent more of his waking hours in the War Department office than in any other place, except the White House. . . . [H]e visited the War Department telegraph office morning, afternoon, and evening, to receive the latest news from the armies at the front. . . . He seldom failed to come over late in the evening before retiring, and sometimes he would stay all night in the War Department." Bates, *Lincoln,* pp. 2, 7.

34. U. S. Department of War, *The War of the Rebellion: A Compilation of the Official Records of the Union and Confederate Armies,* ed. Robert N. Scott et al., 130 vols. (Washington, D.C.: Government Printing Office, 1880–1901), ser. III, 1:612 (hereafter cited as *Official Records of the Rebellion*).

35. Ibid., ser. I, 27:192.

36. For an indication of General Sherman's general anti-press feelings, see Thomas H. Guback, "General Sherman's War on the Press," *Journalism Quarterly* 36 (Spring 1959): 171–76.

37. Andrews, *North Reports,* pp. 115–16.

38. *Official Records of the Rebellion,* ser. I, 38:pt. 5, pp. 821–22.

39. Ibid., ser. I, 39:pt. 2, p. 481.

40. Ibid., ser. I, 39:pt. 3, p. 700.

41. Aplin, "Associated Press Office," p. 26.

42. His full name was Martin William Barr. War Department records list him as "Martin W. Barr" and "M. W. Barr." *Official Records of the Rebellion,* ser. II, 2:805–29. He was, however, referred to as "William Barr" in the *New Orleans Picayune* for September 23, 1861.

43. *Official Records of the Rebellion,* ser. II, 2:806.

44. Andrews, *South Reports,* p. 55.

45. *Official Records of the Rebellion,* ser. II, 2:809–10.

46. Ibid., ser. II, 2:806; and *New Orleans Picayune,* September 23, 1861.

47. *Official Records of the Rebellion,* ser. II, 2:812. The information is reported in a letter dated October 15, 1861, from Barr to a person named "Hettie."

48. Ibid., ser. II, 2:823, 825.

49. Ibid., ser. II, 2:826.

50. Ibid., ser. II, 2:829. The New Orleans editors who signed the petition were Henry J. Leon, of the *Delta;* J. V. R. Adams, the *Crescent;* William J. Seymour, the *Bulletin;* John Maginnis, the *True Delta;* G. P. Wusse & Co., the *Bee;* and A. M. Holbrook, the *Picayune.*

51. Ibid., ser. II, 2:806, 828.

52. Andrews, *South Reports,* pp. 272, 278.

53. *Official Records of the Rebellion,* ser. II, 2:118.

54. Starr, *Bohemian Brigade,* p. 210.

55. Andrews, *North Reports,* p. 339.

56. Carpenter to Hudson, January 21, 1863, James Gordon Bennett Papers, Library of Congress, Washington, D.C.

57. Andrews, *North Reports,* p. 415.

58. Ibid., p. 26.

59. Harper, *Lincoln,* p. 154.

60. The following account of Fulton's misfortunes was assembled from ibid., pp. 156–59; Andrews, *North Reports,* pp. 212–13; and *Baltimore American and Commercial Advertiser,* July 1–3, 1862.

61. This account relies on Harper, *Lincoln,* pp. 290–303; *Official Records of the Rebellion,* ser. III, 4:386–95; Harold L. Nelson, ed., *Freedom of the Press from Hamilton to the Warren Court* (Indianapolis: Bobbs-Merrill, 1967), pp. 232–47; Starr, *Bohemian Brigade,* pp. 315–19; Mary Cortona Phelan, *Manton Marble of the New York World* (Washington, D.C.: Catholic University of America Press, 1957), pp. 31–37; an excellent detailed account of the incident published by the *New York Journal of Commerce* on March 26, 1870, and reprinted in Hudson, *Journalism,* pp. 374–76; and the *National Cyclopaedia of American Biography,* s.v. "Howard, Joseph, Jr." (The bogus proclamation is reprinted by all the above sources except for Starr and the *National Cyclopaedia.*) Manton Marble's open letter to President Lincoln is in the appendix of the Phelan volume and appears, accompanied by selected press commentary, in a pamphlet, [Manton Marble], *Freedom of the Press Wantonly Violated: Letter of Mr. Marble to President Lincoln,* no. 22 of the Papers from the Society for the Diffusion of Political Knowledge (New York, 1864).

62. The *National Cyclopaedia of American Biography,* s.v. "Howard, Joseph, Jr.," says the dispatch "was intended as a burlesque." Interestingly, the same night these two men were concocting a bogus proclamation calling for 400,000 more draftees, President Lincoln signed an order calling for 300,000 more draftees, but had decided to hold the order for release in July. By July 18, when the draft call was announced, the number of draftees had risen to 500,000. Morris, *Encyclopedia,* p. 239.

63. Harper, *Lincoln,* p. 289.

64. There is no evidence that the *New York Express* received a copy of the proclamation that night. It will be remembered from chapter 6 that the *Express* became an evening paper probably before the war and thus would not have published the late-night AP dispatches until twelve hours later.

65. The *Journal of Commerce* offers an alternative explanation: "Our own remoteness from the offices of other papers forbade any such comparison of notes by our employees" with those of other papers. At Wall and Water streets, the paper was ten blocks away from the Park Row and upper Nassau Street areas where the *Times, Herald,* and *Tribune* were located. And it was six blocks from AP's Broadway offices. Quoted in Harper, *Lincoln,* p. 293.

66. Villard's autobiography gives only a brief account of the independent news room and does not mention the arrest. Villard, *Memoirs,* 2: 267–68.

67. Thomas W. Reilly, "Henry Villard, Civil War Journalist" (M.A. thesis, University of Oregon, 1970), pp. 230–60. This discussion relies heav-

ily on Reilly's penetrating research. Neither Reilly nor this author has been able to identify the source of the name "independent news room." Villard's discussion of this brokerage does not give it a name. Villard, *Memoirs,* 2:267. Murat Halstead, who while a Washington correspondent for the *Cincinnati Commercial* occupied a desk "for a short time" in the news agency's office, calls it simply a "bureau of correspondence." Murat Halstead, "Some Reminiscences of Mr. Villard," *Review of Reviews* 23 (January 1901): 62. Robert S. Harper calls it "a news bureau." Harper, *Lincoln,* p. 294. "Independent news room" first appears in Louis M. Starr's study of war reporting. Starr, *Bohemian Brigade,* p. 291. Since Starr's work, the name has come into general usage and is used here on that basis.

68. Villard, *Memoirs,* 1:217, 319.

69. *Dictionary of American Biography,* s.v. "White, Horace."

70. *Who's Who in America, 1908-09,* 5th ed. (1908), s.v. "Hill, Adams Sherman"; and Reilly, "Villard," p. 232.

71. Friction between the New York Associated Press and some of its larger Midwestern clients had surfaced during 1861-62 over the quantity, quality, and cost of the news report Craig was sending to the West. That conflict is discussed in Volume 2.

72. The four editors Reilly refers to here were the *Cincinnati Commercial*'s Murat Halstead, the *Chicago Tribune*'s Joseph Medill, the *Springfield* (Mass.) *Republican*'s Samuel Bowles, and the St. Louis *Missouri Democrat*'s Benjamin Gratz Brown. Reilly, "Villard," p. 233.

73. Villard, *Memoirs,* 2: 267.

74. Letter dated January 28, 1864, quoted in Reilly, "Villard," p. 235.

75. Ibid., p. 240.

76. Ibid., pp. 248-49, quoting the *Chicago Tribune,* May 21, 1864. (In the last paragraph of his dispatch Craig calls Horace White a "confidential employee of the War Department," but White had resigned that position six months earlier when the independent agency was formed.)

77. Ibid., pp. 250-52, quoting the *Cincinnati Commercial,* May 21, 1864.

78. Bates, *Lincoln,* p. 243.

79. Joseph Logsdon, *Horace White, Nineteenth Century Liberal* (Westport, Conn.: Greenwood Press, 1971), p. 98.

80. Reilly, "Villard," p. 259.

81. *Who's Who in America, 1908-09,* 5th ed. (1908), s.v. "Hill, Adams Sherman."

82. Although it appears certain that the Southern editors had organized themselves to deal with distribution and expenses of a news report south of Washington and Louisville, it is far less clear that their agency had an official title. This Southern brokerage, however, was being referred to as the Southern Associated Press in the Southern

press reports during the first year of the Civil War. See, for example, *Richmond Dispatch,* March 26, 1862.

83. Kenny, *Directory,* p. 120. Kenny's total of 450 dailies in the United States in 1861, compared to U.S. census total of 387 in 1860, indicates different criteria for identifying dailies. Lee, *Daily Newspaper,* p. 717.

84. U.S. Department of Interior, Bureau of the Census, *Population of the United States in 1860* (Washington, D.C.: Government Printing Office, 1864), pp. 592–95.

85. T[homas] C. De Leon, *Four Years in Rebel Capitals: An Inside View of Life in the Southern Confederacy from Birth to Death from Original Notes Collated in the Years 1861 to 1865* (Mobile, Ala.: Gossip, 1892), p. 288. Emphasis in original.

86. E. Merton Coulter, *The Confederate States of America, 1861–1865,* vol. 7 of A History of the South, ed. Wendell Holmes Stephenson and E. Merton Coulter (Baton Rouge: Louisiana State University Press, 1950), pp. 496–97, and Andrews, *South Reports,* pp. 55–58.

87. Press Association of the Confederate States of America, *Minutes of the Board of Directors of the Press Association Embracing the Quarterly Reports of the Superintendent, October and January* (Atlanta: Franklin Steam Publishing House, 1864), p. 57 (hereafter cited as PA, *Minutes*). See also Andrews, *South Reports,* pp. 55–58.

88. PA, *Minutes,* p. 57. In 1860 the "combined Press of Richmond" consisted of four dailies: the *Whig,* opposing succession until 1861, when circumstances forced a reversal in its position; the *Enquirer,* a Democratic organ; the *Examiner,* an extreme successionist journal; and the *Dispatch,* nonpartisan and with a circulation equal to the other three dailies combined. Michael B. Chesson, *Richmond after the War, 1865–1890* (Richmond: Virginia State Library, 1981), p. 11.

89. *Richmond Dispatch,* November 5, 1862.

90. The six aggressive papers were the *Memphis Appeal, Atlanta Southern Confederacy, Savannah Republican, Augusta Constitutionalist, Nashville Republican Banner,* and *Charleston Mercury.* The *Memphis Appeal* was quoted in the *Boston Advertiser,* January 20, 1862.

91. Quoted in Rabun Lee Brantley, *Georgia Journalism in the Civil War Period,* no. 58 in Contribution to Education (Nashville: George Peabody College for Teachers, 1929), p. 91.

92. Quoted in ibid.

93. The invited papers were the *Memphis Appeal, Atlanta Southern Confederacy, Savannah Republican, Savannah News, Augusta Constitutionalist, Nashville Republican Banner, Columbus Times, Montgomery Advertiser, Vicksburg Whig, Nashville Patriot, Augusta Chronicle and Sentinel, Selma Reporter, Richmond Examiner, Charleston Courier, Knoxville Register, Columbus Enquirer, Atlanta Intelligencer, Louisville Courier,* and *Richmond Whig.* Ibid.

94. Ibid., pp. 91–92.

95. Ibid., p. 92.

96. Ibid., p. 93.

97. The publishers in attendance were R. W. Gibbes, *Columbia Southern Carolinian;* G. W. Adair, *Atlanta Southern Confederacy;* J. H. Steele, *Atlanta Intelligencer;* W. T. Thompson, *Savannah Morning News;* W. G. Clark, *Mobile Advertiser and Register;* W. F. Wisely, *Jackson Southern Crisis;* J. R. Sneed, *Savannah Republican;* Charles Stone, *Chattanooga Rebel;* James Gardner, *Augusta Constitutionalist;* S. G. Reid and M. P. Barrett, *Montgomery Advertiser;* Joseph Clisby, *Macon Telegraph;* and N. S. Morse, *Augusta Chronicle and Sentinel.* The proxies of three other newspapers were held by two of the above publishers: *Newbern* (N.C.) *Progress* by Clisby, and *Columbus* (Ga.) *Sun* and *Atlanta Commonwealth* by Morse.

98. Minutes of these organizing meetings, and accounts of the previous attempts to convene an editorial convention, are found in Press Association of the Confederate States of America, *The Press Association of the Confederate States of America* (Griffin, Ga.: Hill & Swayze's, 1863), pp. 5-7 (hereafter cited as PA, *Press Association*). Two early discussions of the Press Association are Quintus C. Wilson, "Confederate Press Association: A Pioneer News Agency," *Journalism Quarterly* 26 (June 1949): 160-66; and Ruby Florence Tucker, "The Press Association of the Confederate States of America in Georgia" (M.A. thesis, University of Georgia, 1950).

99. Quoted in Brantley, *Georgia Journalism,* p. 94.

100. PA, *Press Association,* p. 6.

101. Ibid., p. 8.

102. Ibid., p. 7.

103. Arthur T. Robb authored three articles on the Press Association in *Editor & Publisher* on August 13, 20, and 27, 1949, after PA's documents came to light in the Library of Congress and the Boston Atheneum. He correctly notes that PA's "mutual responsibility" structure was new in 1863 and was not transformed into "a national responsibility" system until the Associated Press of Illinois was formed in 1893. "Account of Southern Editors' Early Try with News Agency," *Editor & Publisher,* August 13, 1949, p. 60.

104. This and other quotes from, and references to, the PA's constitution are from a reprint of the document in PA, *Press Association,* pp. 8-10. When PA editors held their next annual meeting, April 6-7, 1864, in Augusta, they discussed and ratified a new constitution, similar to the original 1863 document in most respects, but incorporating specific penalties for noncompliance by PA members. Arthur T. Robb, "One-Meeting PACS Fought Bootlegging of News File," *Editor & Publisher,* August 20, 1949, pp. 48, 44.

105. PA, *Press Association,* p. 7.

106. Ibid., p. 16.

107. Ibid., p. 11.

108. *Dictionary of American Biography,* s.v. "Thrasher, John Sidney."

109. PA, *Press Association,* pp. 19–20.

110. Ibid., p. 53.

111. Ibid., p. 39.

112. PA, *Minutes,* p. 42.

113. PA, *Press Association,* p. 26.

114. Ibid., pp. 50–52; and PA, *Minutes,* p. 29.

115. PA, *Press Association,* p. 42.

116. Ibid., p. 21.

117. PA, *Minutes,* pp. 11–12.

118. Ibid., p. 52.

119. PA, *Press Association,* p. 45.

120. Ibid., p. 26.

121. Ibid., pp. 45–46.

122. Ibid., p. 48.

123. PA, *Minutes,* pp. 9, 44.

124. *Richmond Dispatch,* November 3, 1863.

125. PA, *Minutes,* p. 14.

126. Ibid., p. 8.

127. Andrews, *South Reports,* pp. 480–81.

128. The officers were James W. Lewellen of the *Dispatch,* president; A. M. Bailey of the *Sentinel,* vice-president; Nathaniel Tyler of the *Enquirer,* recording secretary; R. F. Walker of the *Examiner,* treasurer; and R. M. Smith of the *Sentinel,* John M. Daniel of the *Examiner,* W. B. Allport of the *Enquirer,* and James A. Cowardts of the *Dispatch,* directors. P. H. Gibson was Mutual's general agent in Richmond. *Richmond Dispatch,* October 11 and 12, 1864.

129. Andrews, *South Reports,* p. 481.

130. Ibid., pp. 462, 482.

131. Ibid., p. 482.

132. Ibid., p. 503.

133. PA, *Minutes,* pp. 41–42.

134. NYAP, *Annual Report,* pp. 3–4.

135. Starr, *Bohemian Brigade,* p. 210.

136. See, for example, Whitelaw Reid's account of Gettysburg from the Northern viewpoint, reprinted in Snyder and Morris, *Treasury,* pp. 145–46. The Confederate view of the battle as it appeared in the

Richmond Enquirer is reprinted in ibid., pp. 147-49. Similar reprints of this and other Civil War high points are found in Calder M. Pickett, ed., *Voices of the Past: Key Documents in the History of American Journalism* (Columbus, Ohio: Grid, 1977), pp. 125-39; and Laurence Greene, *America Goes to Press: Headlines of the Past* (Garden City, N.Y.: Garden City Publishing, 1938), pp. 143-65.

137. NYAP, *Annual Report*, p. 8. Emphasis in original.

138. While he lobbied against raising rates, Craig reported his weekly expense at $2,354, or $123,408 for the year, of which $1,067 per week was collected "from all papers outside of the Association," the remaining $1,287 per week being divided among the six morning NYAP partners, each paying $214 weekly. Three evening New York papers, including NYAP partner the *Express,* each paid $119 per week for a smaller daytime report. Ibid. p. 4-5.

139. Ibid., pp. 8-9. Emphasis in original.

140. Andrews, *South Reports,* p. 27; Coulter, *Confederate,* pp. 499-500; and Harrison A. Trexler, "The Davis Administration and the Richmond Press, 1861-1865," *Journal of Southern History* 16 (May 1950) 179, 181.

141. Andrews, *South Reports,* p. 33; and Trexler, "Davis Administration," pp. 192-93.

142. De Leon, *Rebel Capitals,* pp. 288-89.

143. Nelson, *Freedom,* p. xxvii.

144. Starr, *Bohemian Brigade,* p. 31.

145. Joseph M. Webb, "Historical Perspective on the New Journalism," *Journalism History* 1 (Summer 1974): 39.

146. Ibid., p. 38.

147. Lee, *Daily Newspaper,* p. 725, and U.S. Census, *Population. . . 1860,* pp. 592-95.

148. U.S. Census, *Historical Statistics,* pp. 370, 379, 382. For comparison, in 1970 87.9 of 100 children between five and nineteen years of age were enrolled in school, 75.9 percent of persons seventeen years old were high school graduates, and in 1969 1 percent of the population was illiterate, including 0.7 percent of the white population and 3.6 percent of the Negro population.

149. Ong, *Presence,* pp. 88-89.

BIBLIOGRAPHY

COMMENT

Anyone even casually acquainted with journalism history knows that escaping the Associated Press's prominence is impossible if one's research is anywhere in the general regions of news reporting, writing, and technology. Even though the modern AP dates from 1893, the name was affixed to news-gathering from the late 1840s. Most of the pre-1893 literature and primary source material deals with the AP, and well over half of the post-1893 material focuses on AP.

The author took this state of affairs as a challenge to uncover as much material as possible describing Abbot & Winans, the United States Associated Press, the independent news room, the Press Association of the Confederacy, Hasson's News Association, American Press Association, National Associated Press Company, the old United Press, Laffan News Service, Publishers' Press Association, Scripps-McRae Press Association, Scripps News Service, United Press Associations, Hearst's various news agencies, and United Press International. To the limit allowed by his feeble success in this endeavor, the author has attempted to give proper perspective to these agencies in the two volumes of this work. The fact remains, however, that winners, especially if they are self-styled cooperatives of newspapers scattered throughout the nation, are more likely to print and preserve their records, more likely to be written about, and more likely to write about themselves.

From a bibliographic standpoint, the history of newsbroking may be divided into three periods. In the first, extending up to 1865, the student relies on widely scattered and diverse sources for glimpses and mere suggestions about news-gathering activity. Most of the time devoted to this research was spent on following hunches and promising leads in quest of bits of pre-1865 information, not the least of which being some indication of the moment of creation of the New York City Associated Press. Some headway was made here in correcting previously reported misinformation and misimpressions and in bringing additional evidence to the subject. But the modest results of that effort reported in this Volume 1 came after scouring telegraphy's literature, city directories, newspaper files, and the sparse manuscript collections bearing on newsbroking up to 1865. Discovery of the New York State Associated Press papers in Utica, N.Y., was the highlight of this period's research. The impact of this corrective research has been felt principally in Victor Rosewater's *History of Cooperative News-Gathering in the United States.* But many of the manuscript materials were either not available or not catalogued when he prepared his 1930 book, nor were newspaper and periodical files as readily available to him in microform as they are today.

The second bibliographic period, from 1865 to 1900, is characterized by a gold mine of detailed and broad-based evidence arising from many manuscript collections, three of which represent the core of Associated Press operations. The second volume of this research, *The Nation's Newsbrokers: The Rush to Institution, from 1865 to 1920,* seeks to represent that rich resource fully and clearly. While Volume 1 sets the record straight on numerous points and fleshes out the procedural and news report skeleton offered by its predecessors, Volume 2 traverses previously uncharted waters of journalism as a business in the last third of the nineteenth century. The third period, from 1900 to the present, consists increasingly of popular materials of sanitized comment and laundered description. Since the author's purpose in this research is to trace newsbroking's development to institutional status, which occurs roughly by the end of World War I, these volumes have successfully avoided having to deal with most of the thin and syrupy depictions of wire services in the twentieth century.

Listed on the following pages are the roughly 280 sources cited in the text and notes of this Volume 1. The second volume of this work contains its own bibliography of cited sources.

MANUSCRIPT COLLECTIONS

Bennett, James Gordon, Papers, 1861–63. Library of Congress, Washington, D.C.

Bennett, James Gordon, Papers, 1840–51. Rare Books and Manuscripts Division, The New York Public Library, Astor, Lenox and Tilden Foundations, New York.

Brown, James Wright Collection, 1789–1951. New York Historical Society, New York.

Committees of Correspondence, Papers of, 1769–76. Boston Public Library, Boston.

Cornell, Ezra, Papers, 1828–1936. Department of Manuscripts and University Archives, Cornell University Library, Ithaca, N.Y.

Dun, R. G., & Co. Collection, New York City Series. Baker Library, Harvard University Graduate School of Business Administration, Boston.

Greeley, Horace, Papers, 1826–1928. Library of Congress, Washington, D.C.

Greeley, Horace, Papers, 1836–72. Rare Books and Manuscripts Division, The New York Public Library, Astor, Lenox and Tilden Foundations, New York.

Hudson, Frederic and Woodward, Papers, 1817–76. Private collection of Mrs. Wesley P. Wilmot, Concord, Mass.

Marble, Manton, Papers, 1852–1916. Library of Congress, Washington, D.C.

Morse, Samuel F. B., Papers, 1793–1844. Library of Congress, Washington, D.C.

New York State Associated Press Papers, 1846–47. Oneida Historical Society, Utica, N.Y.

O'Rielly, Henry, Papers, 1830–83. New York Historical Society, New York.

Raymond, Henry J., Papers, 1840–97. Rare Books and Manuscripts Division, The New York Public Library, Astor, Lenox and Tilden Foundations, New York.

Rosewater Family Papers, 1841–1940. American Jewish Archives, Cincinnati.

Smith, Francis O. J., Papers, 1818–76. Maine Historical Society, Portland.

Webb Family Papers, 1764–1911. Yale University Library, New Haven, Conn.

Webb Family Papers, 1773–1893. Rare Books and Manuscripts Division, The New York Public Library, Astor, Lenox and Tilden Foundations, New York.

NEWSPAPERS

Baltimore American and Commercial Advertiser
Boston Advertiser
Boston Evening Transcript
Charles Willmer's European Mail (Liverpool)
Chicago Tribune

European (Liverpool)
Herald for Europe (New York)
New Orleans Picayune
New York Albion
New York Courier and Enquirer
New York Evening Post
New York Gazette, or The Weekly Post-Boy
New York Herald
New York Journal of Commerce
New York Sun
New York Times
New York Tribune
New York Tribune for Europe
New York Weekly Tribune
Philadelphia Public Ledger
Richmond Dispatch
Times of London
Utica (N.Y.) *Gazette*
Washington (D.C.) *Daily Union*
Willmer & Smith's European Times (Liverpool)

PERIODICALS

American Telegraph Magazine
Harper's Monthly
Journal of the Telegraph
The Journalist
Niles' National Register
Printers' Circular
Telegrapher

BOOKS AND ARTICLES

[Adams's] Boston Directory. Boston: George Adams, 1848–1852.
Albion, Robert Greenhalgh. *The Rise of the New York Port (1815–1860).* New York: Scribners, 1939.
————. *Square-Riggers on Schedule: The New York Sailing Packets to England, France, and the Cotton Ports.* Princeton, N.J.: Princeton University Press, 1938.
American Cyclopaedia: A Popular Dictionary of General Knowledge. Edited by George Ripley and Charles A. Dana. 16 vols. New York: D. Appleton, 1883–84.

American Telegraph Company. *Extract from Remarks of R. W. Russell, One of the Executive Committee of the American Telegraph Company, in Reply to the Statement of Messrs. Abram S. Hewitt, Cyrus W. Field, Henry J. Raymond, and Others, Made at the Meeting of Stockholders, on June 29th, 1860.* N.p., [1860].

———. *Remarks of R. W. Russell, One of the Executive Committee of the American Telegraph Company, in Reply to the Statement of Messrs. Abram S. Hewitt, Cyrus W. Field, Henry J. Raymond, and Others, Made at the Meeting of Stockholders, on June 29th, 1860.* New York: Wm. C. Bryant, 1860.

American Telegraph Company, Executive Committee. *The American Telegraph Company and the New York Associated Press.* N.p., 1860.

———. *Reply of the Executive Committee to the Pamphlet of D. H. Craig, Agent of the New York Associated Press.* N.p., [1860].

American Telegraph Company, Special Tariff Committee. *The Telegraph and the Press.* N.p., 1860.

Andrews, George H. *General Webb.* N.p., [1858].

Andrews, J. Cutler. *The North Reports the Civil War.* Pittsburgh: University of Pittsburgh Press, 1955.

———. *The South Reports the Civil War.* Princeton, N.J.: Princeton University Press, 1970.

[Anglo-American Telegraph Company]. *The Atlantic Telegraph, Its History from the Commencement of the Undertaking in 1854 to the Sailing of the "Great Eastern" in 1866.* London: Bacon, 1866.

Aplin, William. "At the Associated Press Office." *Putnam's* 6 (July 1870): 23–30.

Appletons' Cyclopaedia of American Biography. Edited by James Grant Wilson and John Fiske. 7 vols. New York: D. Appleton, 1894–1900.

Associated Press. *Annual Report.* Chicago and New York: annual, 1893–.

———. *AP World.* New York: quarterly, 1945–.

Babcock, F[ranklin] Lawrence. *Spanning the Atlantic.* New York: Knopf, 1931.

Baillie, Hugh. *High Tension: The Recollections of Hugh Baillie.* New York: Harper, 1959.

Baker, Charles D. "Newspaper Enterprise in 1846." *The Journalist,* October 6, 1888, p. 11.

Baringer, William E. *A House Dividing: Lincoln as President Elect.* Springfield, Ill.: Abraham Lincoln Association, 1945.

Barney, Jesse A. *Rumney, Then and Now: History.* Rumney, N.H.: town of Rumney, 1967.

Bates, David Homer. *Lincoln in the Telegraph Office: Recollections of the United States Military Telegraph Corps during the Civil War.* New York: Century, 1907.

Black, Henry Campbell. *Black's Law Dictionary.* 5th ed. St. Paul, Minn.: West, 1979.

Bleyer, Willard Grosvenor. *Main Currents in the History of American Journalism.* Boston: Houghton Mifflin, 1927.

Boase, Frederic. *Modern English Biography.* 3 vols. and 3 supps. 1892. New York: Barnes & Noble, 1965.

Borden, Morton. "Some Notes on Horace Greeley, Charles Dana and Karl Marx." *Journalism Quarterly* 34 (Fall 1957): 457–65.

"The Boston Herald." *Bay State Monthly (New England Magazine)* 2 (October 1884): 22–35.

Brantley, Rabun Lee. *Georgia Journalism in the Civil War Period.* Contributions to Education, no. 58. Nashville: George Peabody College for Teachers, 1929.

Briggs, Charles F., and Augustus Maverick. *The Story of the Telegraph and the History of the Great Atlantic Cable.* New York: Rudd & Carleton, 1858.

Brigham, Clarence S. *History and Bibliography of American Newspapers, 1690–1820.* 2 vols. Worcester, Mass.: American Antiquarian Society, 1947. Hamden, Conn.: Anchor, 1962.

———. *Journals and Journeymen: A Contribution to the History of Early American Newspapers.* Philadelphia: University of Pennsylvania Press, 1950.

Brockway, Beman. *Fifty Years in Journalism Embracing Recollections and Personal Experiences, with an Autobiography.* Watertown, N.Y.: Daily Times, 1891.

Brown, [Ernest] Francis. *Raymond of the Times.* New York: Norton, 1951.

Brown, Henry Collins. *Glimpses of Old New-York.* New York: Lent & Graff, 1917.

Bruchey, Stuart. *The Roots of American Economic Growth, 1607–1861: An Essay in Social Causation.* New York: Harper & Row, 1965.

Bryan, Wilhelmus Bogart. *A History of the National Capital from Its Foundation through the Period of the Adoption of the Organic Act.* 2 vols. New York: Macmillan, 1914–16.

Buckingham, Joseph T. *Specimens of Newspaper Literature with*

Personal Memoirs, Anecdotes, and Reminiscences. 2 vols. Boston: Charles C. Little & James Brown, 1850.

Capen, Nahum, ed. *The Massachusetts State Record and Year Book of General Information, 1847.* Boston: James French, 1847.

Carey, James W., and John J. Quirk. "The History of the Future." In *Communications Technology and Social Policy: Understanding the New "Cultural Revolution."* Edited by George Gerbner, Larry P. Gross, and William H. Melody. New York: Wiley, 1973.

Carlson, Oliver. *The Man Who Made News, James Gordon Bennett.* New York: Duell, Sloan & Pearce, 1942.

Carter, Samuel, III. *Cyrus Field, Man of Two Worlds.* New York: Putnam, 1968.

Chamberlin, Joseph Edgar. *The Boston Transcript: A History of Its First Hundred Years.* Boston: Houghton Mifflin, 1930.

Charles, L. N. "Birth Certificate of A.P. on View in Public Library." *Fourth Estate,* February 26, 1927, pp. 11, 27.

Chesson, Michael B. *Richmond after the War, 1865–1890.* Richmond: Virginia State Library, 1981.

Cochran, Thomas C., and William Miller. *The Age of Enterprise: A Social History of Industrial America.* New York: Macmillan, 1942.

Colles, Christopher. *A Survey of the Roads of the United States of America, 1789.* Edited by Walter W. Ristow. Cambridge, Mass.: Belknap Press of Harvard University, 1961.

Commager, Henry Steele. *The American Mind: An Interpretation of American Thought and Character since the 1880's.* New Haven, Conn.: Yale University Press, 1950.

Connery, T[homas] B. "Great Business Operations—The Collection of News." *Cosmopolitan* 23 (May 1897): 21–32.

Cook, Clarence. "Broadway." In *The United States, Illustrated in Views of City and Country with Descriptive and Historical Articles.* Edited by Charles A. Dana. 2 vols. New York: Herrmann J. Meyer, 1855.

Cooper, Kent. *Kent Cooper and the Associated Press: An Autobiography.* New York: Random House, 1959.

Coulter, E. Merton. *The Confederate States of America, 1861–1865.* Vol. 7 of A History of the South, edited by Wendell Holmes Stephenson and E. Merton Coulter. Baton Rouge: Louisiana State University Press, 1950.

Craig, D[aniel] H. *"The American Telegraph Company and the Press": A Reply to the Falsehoods of the Executive Committee.* N.p., 1860.

———. *Answer of Daniel H. Craig, Organizer and Manager of the New York Associated Press, 1850 to 1867,* [sic] *and Originator and Promoter of Machine or Rapid Telegraphing, to the Interrogatories of the U.S. Senate Committee on Education and Labor at the City of New York, 1883.* New York, 1883.

———. *The Convicted Libeller: Open Published Letter to F. O. J. Smith.* New York, 1863.

———. *Letter to F. M. Edson on the House Telegraph Line.* New York, 1853.

———. *A Review of "An Exposition of the Differences Existing between Different Presses and Different Lines of Telegraph Respecting the Transmission of Foreign News, Being a Letter and Accompanying Documents, Addressed to the Government Commissioners of the Nova Scotia Telegraph."* Halifax, N.S., 1850.

Crouthamel, James L. "James Watson Webb." *New York History* 41 (October 1960): 400–22.

———. *James Watson Webb: A Biography.* Middletown, Conn.: Wesleyan University Press, 1969.

Crozier, Emmet. *Yankee Reporters, 1861–65.* New York: Oxford University Press, 1956.

Debate in the Massachusetts Senate on the Bill to Incorporate the Boston and Halifax Telegraphic Cable Co., March 24 and 26, 1859. Boston: Henry W. Dutton, 1859.

De Leon, T[homas] C. *Four Years in Rebel Capitals: An Inside View of Life in the Southern Confederacy from Birth to Death from Original Notes Collated in the Years 1861 to 1865.* Mobile, Ala.: Gossip, 1892.

Desmond, Robert W. *The Information Process: World News Reporting to the Twentieth Century.* Iowa City: University of Iowa Press, 1978.

Dickens, Charles. *American Notes for General Circulation.* 2 vols. London: Chapman & Hall, 1842.

Dictionary of American Biography. 22 vols. New York: Scribners, 1928–44.

Dictionary of Literary Biography, American Newspaper Journalists. Vols. 23, 25, 29, 43, edited by Perry J. Ashley. Detroit: Gale, 1983–85.

Doggett's New York City Directory. New York: John Doggett, Jr., 1842–51.

Du Boff, Richard B. "Business Demand and the Development of the

Telegraph in the United States, 1844–1860." *Business History Review* 54 (Winter 1980): 459–79.

Editor & Publisher. *International Year Book, 1963.*

Emerson, Edwin, Jr. *A History of the Nineteenth Century, Year by Year.* 3 vols. New York: P. F. Collier, 1900.

Emery, Edwin. *The Press and America: An Interpretative History of the Mass Media.* 3rd ed. Englewood Cliffs, N.J.: Prentice-Hall, 1972.

Emery, Edwin, and Michael Emery. *The Press and America: An Interpretive History of the Mass Media.* 5th ed. Englewood Cliffs, N.J.: Prentice-Hall, 1984.

Everett, George. "Newspaper Trains: America's First Fling at High-Speed Transmission of the Printed Word." Paper delivered at the Sixty-third Annual Meeting of the Association for Education in Journalism, Boston, August 11, 1980.

Faulkner, Harold Underwood. *American Economic History.* 8th ed. New York: Harper, 1960.

Field, Henry M. *History of the Atlantic Telegraph.* New York: Scribners, 1866.

Giddings, T. H. "Rushing the Transatlantic News in the 1830s and 1840s." New York Historical Society *Quarterly* 42 (January 1958): 47–59.

Gifis, Steven H. *Law Dictionary.* Woodbury, N.Y.: Barron's Educational Series, 1975.

Gobright, L[awrence] A. *Recollection of Men and Things at Washington during the Third of a Century.* 2nd ed. Philadelphia: Claxton, Remsen & Haffelfinger, 1869.

Gramling, Oliver. *AP: The Story of News.* New York: Farrar & Rinehart, 1940.

Grant, James. *The Newspaper Press: Its Origin, Progress, and Present Position.* 3 vols. London: Tinsley Brothers, 1871–72.

Greeley, Horace. *Recollections of a Busy Life.* New York: J. B. Ford, 1868.

Greene, Laurence. *America Goes to Press: Headlines of the Past.* 1936. Garden City, N.Y.: Garden City Publishing, 1938.

Gregory, Winifred, ed. *American Newspapers, 1821–1936: A Union List of Files Available in the United States and Canada.* New York: H. W. Wilson, 1937.

Guback, Thomas H. "General Sherman's War on the Press." *Journalism Quarterly* 36 (Spring 1959): 171–76.

[Hallock, William H.] *Life of Gerard Hallock, Thirty-Three Years Edi-*

tor of the New York Journal of Commerce. New York: Oakley, Mason, 1869.

Halstead, Murat. "Some Reminiscences of Mr. Villard." *Review of Reviews* 23 (January 1901): 60–63.

Harlow, Alvin F. *Old Waybills: The Romance of the Express Companies.* New York: D. Appleton-Century, 1934.

———. *Old Wires and New Waves: The History of the Telegraph, Telephone, and Wireless.* New York: D. Appleton-Century, 1936.

Harper, Robert S. *Lincoln and the Press.* New York: McGraw-Hill, 1951.

Highton, Edward. *The Electric Telegraph, Its History and Progress.* London: John Weale, 1852.

"History of 'The Associated Press.'" *Philadelphia Press* as reprinted in *Chicago Times,* November 27, 1858.

History Reference Council. "Competing for News" and "Combining to Get News." *History Reference Bulletin* 10 (March 1937): 97–112.

Hone, Philip. *The Diary of Philip Hone, 1828–1851.* Edited by Allan Nevins, 2 vols. New York: Dodd, Mead, 1927.

Hudson, Frederic. *Journalism in the United States from 1690 to 1872.* New York: Harper, 1873.

Innis, Harold A. *The Bias of Communication.* Toronto: University of Toronto Press, 1951.

———. *Empire and Communications.* Oxford: Clarendon Press, 1950.

Jones, Alexander. *Historical Sketch of the Electric Telegraph, Including Its Rise and Progress in the United States.* New York: Putnam, 1852.

Judson, Isabella Field, ed. *Cyrus W. Field, His Life and Work (1819–1892).* New York: Harper, 1896.

Kendall, Amos. *Circular to the Stockholders of the American Telegraph Company.* N.p., 1860.

Kennedy, J[oseph] C[amp] G[riffith]. *Catalogue of the Newspapers and Periodicals Published in the United States Showing the Town and County in which the Same Are Published, How Often Issued, Their Character, and Circulation.* New York: John Livingston, 1852.

Kennedy, J. H. "General Anson Stager." *Magazine of Western History* 4 (July 1886): 287–98.

Kenny, Daniel J., comp. *The American Newspaper Directory and Record of the Press Containing an Accurate List of All the Newspapers, Magazines, Reviews, Periodicals, etc., in the United States*

& *British Provinces of North America, Also a Concise General View of the Origin, Rise, and Progress of Newspapers.* New York: Watson, 1861.

King, William L. *The Newspaper Press of Charleston, S.C.: A Chronological and Biographical History Embracing a Period of One Hundred and Forty Years.* 1872. Charleston, S.C.: Lucas & Richardson, 1882.

Kirk, John W. "Historic Moments: The First News Message by Telegraph." *Scribner's* 11 (May 1892): 652–56.

Kouwenhoven, John A. *The Columbia Historical Portrait of New York: An Essay in Graphic History in Honor of the Tricentennial of New York City and the Bicentennial of Columbia University.* Garden City, N.Y.: Doubleday, 1953.

Labatut, Jean, and Wheaton J. Lane, eds. *Highways in Our National Life: A Symposium.* Princeton, N.J.: Princeton University Press, 1950.

Lee, Alfred McClung. *The Daily Newspaper in America: The Evolution of a Social Instrument.* New York: Macmillan, 1937.

Lee, James Melvin. *History of American Journalism.* 2nd ed. Garden City, N.Y.: Garden City Publishing, 1923.

Lefferts, Marshall. "The Electric Telegraph: Its Influence and Geographical Distribution." American Geographical and Statistical Society *Bulletin* 2 (1856): 242–64.

Lincoln, Abraham. *Collected Works.* Edited by Roy P. Basler. 9 vols. New Brunswick, N.J.: Rutgers University Press, 1953–55.

Logsdon, Joseph. *Horace White, Nineteenth Century Liberal.* Westport, Conn.: Greenwood Press, 1971.

Luxon, Norval Neil. *Niles' Weekly Register, News Magazine of the Nineteenth Century.* Baton Rouge: Louisiana State University Press, 1947.

McDonald, Philip B. *A Saga of the Seas: The Story of Cyrus W. Field and the Laying of the First Atlantic Cable.* New York: Wilson-Erickson, 1937.

McJimsey, George T. *Genteel Partisan: Manton Marble, 1834–1917.* Ames: Iowa State University Press, 1971.

Mackay, Alex[ander]. *The Western World, or Travels in the United States in 1846–47, Exhibiting Them in Their Latest Development, Social, Political and Industrial Including a Chapter on California.* 2nd ed. 3 vols. London: Richard Bentley, 1849.

Macmillan Dictionary of Canadian Biography. 3rd ed. London: Macmillan, 1963.

Magnetic Telegraph Company. *Articles of Association and Charter from the State of Maryland of the Magnetic Telegraph Company Together with the Office Regulations and the Minutes of the Meetings of Stockholders and Board of Directors.* New York: Chatterton & Crist, [1852].

Manning, George H. "Bennett Fight Opened Senate to Press." *Editor & Publisher,* July 21, 1934, pp. 116, 118.

[Marble, Manton]. *Freedom of the Press Wantonly Violated: Letter of Mr. Marble to President Lincoln.* Papers from the Society for the Diffusion of Political Knowledge, no. 22. New York, 1864.

Marbut, Frederick B. "Decline of the Official Press in Washington." *Journalism Quarterly* 33 (Summer 1956): 335–41.

———. "Early Washington Correspondents: Some Neglected Pioneers." *Journalism Quarterly* 25 (December 1948): 369–74, 400.

———. *News from the Capital: The story of Washington Reporting.* Carbondale: Southern Illinois University Press, 1971.

Mathews, Joseph J. *Reporting the Wars.* Minneapolis: University of Minnesota Press, 1957.

Maverick, Augustus. *Henry J. Raymond and the New York Press for Thirty Years: Progress of American Journalism from 1840 to 1870.* Hartford, Conn.: A. S. Hale, 1870.

Merriam, George S. *The Life and Times of Samuel Bowles.* 2 vols. New York: Century, 1885.

Meyer, Balthasar Henry, ed. *History of Transportation in the United States before 1860.* Washington, D.C.: Carnegie Institution, 1917.

Michaelis, Anthony R. *From Semaphore to Satellite.* Geneva, Switzerland: Henri Studer, 1965.

Miller, John C. *Sam Adams, Pioneer in Propaganda.* Boston: Little, Brown, 1936.

Morris, Joe Alex. *Deadline Every Minute: The Story of the United Press.* Garden City, N.Y.: Doubleday, 1957.

Morris, Richard B., ed. *Encyclopedia of American History.* 2nd ed. New York: Harper & Row, 1970.

Morse, Samuel F. B. *Samuel F. B. Morse, His Letters and Journals.* Edited by Edward Lind Morse. 2 vols. Boston: Houghton Mifflin, 1914.

Mott, Frank Luther. *American Journalism: A History, 1690–1960.* 3rd ed. New York: Macmillan, 1962.

———. "The Newspaper Coverage of Lexington and Concord." *New England Quarterly* 17 (Dec. 1944): 489–505.

Mullaly, John. *The Laying of the Cable or the Ocean Telegraph Being a Complete and Authentic Narrative of the Attempt to Lay* the Cable Across the Entrance to the Gulf of St. Lawrence in 1855 and of the Three Atlantic Telegraph Expeditions of 1857 and 1858. New York: D. Appleton, 1858.

National Cyclopaedia of American Biography. New York: James T. White, 1892–.

Nelson, Harold L., ed. Freedom of the Press from Hamilton to the Warren Court. Indianapolis: Bobbs-Merrill, 1967.

Nevins, Allan. Abram S. Hewitt, with Some Account of Peter Cooper. New York: Harper, 1935.

New York and New England Union Telegraph Company. The Certificate of Formation and Articles of Association of the New York and New England Union Telegraph Company Together with the Records of the Meetings of the Directors. Boston: Bazin & Chandler, 1852.

New York Associated Press. Annual Report of the General Agent. New York, 186[3].

[———]. General News Association of the City of New York. Rules. New York: L. H. Bridgham, 1874.

North, S. N. D. History and Present Condition of the Newspaper and Periodical Press of the United States with a Catalogue of the Publications of the Census Year. Washington D.C.: Government Printing Office, 1884.

O'Brien, Frank M. The Story of the Sun, New York, 1833–1928. 2nd ed. New York: D. Appleton, 1928.

Ong, Walter J. Interfaces of the Word: Studies in the Evolution of Consciousness and Culture. Ithaca, N.Y.: Cornell University Press, 1977.

———. The Presence of the Word: Some Prolegomena for Cultural and Religious History. New Haven, Conn.: Yale University Press, 1967.

The Opening and Closing Arguments of Hon. Thomas M. Hayes and Hon. Francis O. J. Smith before the Superior Court of Suffolk County, Mass., Mr. Justice Putnam Presiding, February 26th, 27th, and 28th, 1866, on a Motion for a New Trial, in the Case of The State vs. Smith. Portland, Maine: Brown Thurston, 1866.

Opinion of the Supreme Court of the State of New York in the Case of John J. Kiernan vs. the Manhattan Quotation Telegraph Company and Francis A. Abbot: News Is Property, Its Transmission to Subscribers over Telegraphic Printing Instruments Is Not a General Publication. New York: Douglas Taylor, 1876.

O'Rielly, Henry. ''Christopher Colles, and the First Proposal of a Telegraph System in the United States with Incidental Allusions to the Origin and Progress of Our City Water-Works and of Our State Canals, &c." *Historical Magazine* 15 (April 1869): 262–69.

———. "Facts Concerning the 'Cunard Letter.'" *American Telegraph Magazine* 1 (April-May-June 1853): 248–62.

———. "Memoranda Respecting the 'Relations between the Associated Press and Henry O'Rielly.'" *American Telegraph Magazine* 1 (April-May-June 1853): 235–48.

Orton, William. *A Letter to the Postmaster-General Reviewing the Recommendations of his Annual Report in Favor of a Postal Telegraph.* New York, 1873.

Parton, J[ames]. *The Life of Horace Greeley, Editor of the New York Tribune.* New York: Mason Brothers, 1855.

Payne, George Henry. *History of Journalism in the United States.* New York: D. Appleton, 1920.

[Perry, Edwin A.] *The Boston Herald and Its History: How, When and Where It Was Founded.* Boston: Herald, 1878.

Phelan, Mary Cortona. *Manton Marble of the New York World.* Washington, D.C.: Catholic University of America Press, 1957.

Pickett, Calder M., ed. *Voices of the Past: Key Documents in the History of American Journalism.* Columbus, Ohio: Grid, 1977.

Plum, William R. *The Military Telegraph during the Civil War in the United States.* 2 vols. Chicago: Jansen, McClurg, 1882.

Pollard, James E. *The Presidents and the Press.* New York: Macmillan, 1947.

Poore, Ben[jamin] Perley. *Perley's Reminiscences of Sixty Years in the National Metropolis.* 2 vols. Philadelphia: Hubbard Brothers, 1886.

[———]. "Washington News." *Harper's Monthly* 48 (January 1874): 225–36.

[Pray, Isaac C.] *Memoirs of James Gordon Bennett and His Times.* By a Journalist. New York: Stringer & Townsend, 1855.

Pred, Allan R. *Urban Growth and the Circulation of Information: The United States System of Cities, 1790–1840.* Cambridge, Mass.: Harvard University Press, 1973.

———. *Urban Growth and City-Systems in the United States, 1840–1860.* Cambridge, Mass.: Harvard University Press, 1980.

Prescott, George B. *History, Theory, and Practice of the Electric Telegraph.* Boston: Ticknor & Fields, 1860.

Press Association of the Confederate States of America. *Minutes of the Board of Directors of the Press Association Embracing the*

Quarterly Reports of the Superintendent, October and January. Atlanta: Franklin Steam Publishing House, 1864.

———. *The Press Association of the Confederate States of America.* Griffin, Ga.: Hill & Swayze's, 1863.

Randall, James G. "The Newspaper Problem in Its Bearing upon Military Secrecy during the Civil War." *American Historical Review* 23 (January 1918): 303–23.

"The Reading Room and Marine Diary in the Exchange Coffee House, 1810: Lists of Subscribers from the Society's Collections." The Bostonian Society *Publications* 8 (1911): 121–31.

Regan, John W. "The Inception of the Associated Press." Nova Scotia Historical Society *Collections* 19 (1918): 93–114.

Reid, James D. *The Telegraph in America, Its Founders, Promoters, and Noted Men.* New York: Derby Brothers, 1879.

Reilly, Tom. "American Reporters and the Mexican War, 1846–1848." Ph.D. dissertation, University of Minnesota, 1975.

———. "Early Coverage of a President-Elect: Lincoln at Springfield, 1860." *Journalism Quarterly* 49 (Autumn 1972): 469–79.

———. "Henry Villard, Civil War Journalist." Master's thesis, University of Oregon, 1970.

Riggs, James G., and Ralph M. Faust. "New York Becomes the Empire State." In *The Age of Reform*, vol. 6 of the History of the State of New York, edited by Alexander C. Flick. New York: Columbia University Press, 1934.

Robb, Arthur T. "Account of Southern Editors' Early Try with News Agency." *Editor & Publisher,* August 13, 1949, pp. 60, 56.

———. "One-Meeting PACS Fought Bootlegging of News File." *Editor & Publisher,* August 20, 1949, pp. 48, 44.

———. "PACS Minutes Shed Some Light on Southern Press Coverage of War." *Editor & Publisher,* August 27, 1949, pp. 60, 54.

Rode's New York City Directory. New York: Charles R. Rode, 1850–54.

Rosewater, Victor. *History of Cooperative News-Gathering in the United States.* New York: D. Appleton, 1930.

"The Rosewaters and the 'Bee' of Omaha." *Review of Reviews* 13 (June 1896): 709–10.

Sabine, Robert. *The Electric Telegraph.* London: Virtue Brothers, 1867.

———. *The History and Progress of the Electric Telegraph.* 2nd ed. New York: D. Van Nostrand, 1869.

Scharf, J. Thomas. *The Chronicles of Baltimore, Being a Complete*

History of "Baltimore Town" and Baltimore City from the Earliest Period to the Present Times. Baltimore: Turnbull Brothers, 1874.

Scheele, Carl H. *A Short History of the Mail Service.* Washington, D.C.: Smithsonian Institution, 1970.

Schiller, Dan. *Objectivity and the News: The Public and the Rise of Commercial Journalism.* Philadelphia: University of Pennsylvania Press, 1981.

Schlesinger, Arthur M. *Prelude to Independence: The Newspaper War on Britain, 1764–1776.* New York: Knopf, 1957.

Schudson, Michael. *Discovering the News: A Social History of American Newspapers.* New York: Basic Books, 1978.

Schwarzlose, Richard A. *The American Wire Services: A Study of Their Development as a Social Institution.* 1965. New York: Arno, 1979.

———. "Early Telegraphic News Dispatches: Forerunner of the AP." *Journalism Quarterly* 51 (Winter 1974): 595–601.

———. "The Foreign Connection: Transatlantic Newspapers in the 1840s." *Journalism History* 10 (Autumn/Winter 1983): 44–49, 69.

———. "Harbor News Association: The Formal Origin of the AP." *Journalism Quarterly* 45 (Summer 1968): 253–60.

———. "The Nation's First Wire Service: Evidence Supporting a Footnote." *Journalism Quarterly* 57 (Winter 1980): 555–62.

———. "Technology and the Individual: The Impact of Innovation on Communication." In *Mass Media between the Wars: Perceptions of Cultural Tensions, 1918–1941.* Edited by Catherine L. Covert and John D. Stevens. Syracuse, N.Y.: Syracuse University Press, 1984.

Seward, Alexander. "The Telegraph and Associated Press." Oneida Historical Society *Transactions* (1881): 156–60.

Shanks, W. F. G. "How We Get Our News." *Harper's Monthly* 34 (March 1867): 511–22.

Shaw, Donald L. "News Bias and the Telegraph: A Study of Historical Change." *Journalism Quarterly* 44 (Spring 1967): 3–12, 31.

———. "Technology and Conformity: A Study of Newsgathering in the American Press, 1820–1860." Paper delivered at the Fifty-fifth Annual Meeting of the Association for Education in Journalism, Carbondale, Ill., August 22, 1972.

Siebert, Fred S., Theodore Peterson, and Wilbur Schramm. *Four Theories of the Press.* Urbana: University of Illinois Press, 1956.

Simonton, J[ames] W. *The Associated Press: It Is Not a Monopoly but an Independent Cooperative Union of Newspaper Publishers and Only a Private Business; Congress Has No Rightful Power to Interfere with Its Affairs.* New York: John Polhemus, 1879.

Smith, Anthony. *The Newspaper: An International History.* London: Thames & Hudson, 1979.

Smith, Culver H. *The Press, Politics, and Patronage: The American Government's Use of Newspapers, 1789-1875.* Athens: University of Georgia Press, 1977.

Smith, Francis O. J. *An Exposition of the Differences Existing between Different Presses and Different Lines of Telegraph Respecting the Transmission of Foreign News, Being a Letter and Accompanying Documents, Addressed to the Government Commissioners of the Nova Scotia Telegraph.* Boston: Dutton & Wentworth, 1850.

Smith, William Henry. "The Press as a News Gatherer." *Century* 42 (August 1891): 524-36.

Snyder, Louis L., and Richard B. Morris, eds. *A Treasury of Great Reporting: "Literature under Pressure" from the Sixteenth Century to Our Own Time.* 2nd ed. New York: Simon & Schuster, 1962.

Starr, Louis M. *Bohemian Brigade: Civil War Newsmen in Action.* New York: Knopf, 1954.

Stevens, John D., and Hazel Dicken Garcia. *Communication History.* Beverly Hills, Calif.: Sage, 1980.

Stevers, Martin D., and Captain Jonas Pendlebury. *Sea Lanes: Man's Conquest of the Ocean.* 1935. Garden City, N.Y.: Garden City Publishing, 1938.

Stimson, A[lexander] L. *History of the Express Business, Including the Origin of the Railway System in America and the Relation of Both to the Increase of New Settlements and the Prosperity of Cities in the United States.* New York: Baker & Godwin, 1881.

Stokes, I. N. Phelps, comp. *The Iconography of Manhattan Island, 1498-1909.* 6 vols. New York: Robert H. Dodd, 1915-28.

Stone, Melville E. "The Associated Press." Five-part series in *Century* 69 (April 1905): 888-95, 70 (May 1905): 143-51, (June 1905): 299-310, (July 1905): 379-86, and (August 1905): 504-10.

———. *Fifty Years a Journalist.* Garden City, N.Y.: Doubleday, Page, 1921.

Stover, John F. *American Railroads.* Chicago: University of Chicago Press, 1961.

Taylor, George Rogers. *The Transportation Revolution, 1815-1860.*

The Economic History of the United States, vol. 4. New York: Rinehart, 1951.

Thomas, Benjamin P., and Harold M. Hyman. *Stanton: The Life and Times of Lincoln's Secretary of War.* New York: Knopf, 1962.

Thomas, Isaiah. *The History of Printing in America with a Biography of Printers and an Account of Newspapers.* Edited by a committee of the American Antiquarian Society. 2nd ed. 2 vols. Albany, N.Y.: J. Munsell, 1874.

Thompson, Joseph P. *Memoir of David Hale, Late Editor of the Journal of Commerce, with Selections from His Miscellaneous Writings.* New York: Wiley, 1850.

Thompson, Robert Luther. *Wiring a Continent: The History of the Telegraph Industry in the United States, 1832–1866.* Princeton, N.J.: Princeton University Press, 1947.

Thoreau, Henry David. *Walden, or Life in the Woods.* Boston: Ticknor & Fields, 1854.

Times of London. *Tercentenary Handlist of English & Welsh Newspapers, Magazines & Reviews.* London: Times, 1920.

Tocqueville, Alexis de. *Democracy in America.* Edited by Phillips Bradley. 2 vols. 1835, 1840. New York: Knopf, 1945.

Topliff, Samuel. *Topliff's Travels: Letters from Abroad in the Years 1828 and 1829 by Samuel Topliff.* Edited by Ethel Stanwood Bolton. Boston: Athenaeum, 1906.

Trexler, Harrison A. "The Davis Administration and the Richmond Press, 1861–1865." *Journal of Southern History* 16 (May 1950): 177–95.

Trow's Directory of New York City. Henry Wilson, comp. New York: John F. Trow, 1852–60.

Trumbull, Laurence. *The Electro-Magnetic Telegraph with an Historical Account of Its Rise, Progress, and Present Condition.* Philadelphia: A. Hart, 1853.

Tucker, Ruby Florence. "The Press Association of the Confederate States of America in Georgia." Master's thesis, University of Georgia, 1950.

Tyler, David Budlong. *Steam Conquers the Atlantic.* New York: D. Appleton-Century, 1939.

U.N. Educational, Scientific and Cultural Organization. *News Agencies, Their Structure and Operation.* Paris: Georges Lang, 1953.

U.S. Congress, House Committee on Commerce. *Electro-Magnetic Telegraphs: To Accompany Bill H.R. No. 713.* 25th Cong., 2nd sess., April 6, 1838, Rept. 753.

U.S. Congress, Senate Committee on Education and Labor. *Report of the Committee of the Senate upon the Relations between Labor*

and Capital and Testimony Taken by the Committee. 5 vols. (4 vols. published.) 48th Cong., 2nd sess., 1885.

U.S. Department of Commerce, Bureau of the Census. *Historical Statistics of the United States, Colonial Times to 1970.* 2 pts. Washington, D.C.: Government Printing Office, 1975.

U.S. Department of Interior, Bureau of the Census. *Population of the United States in 1860.* Washington, D.C.: Government Printing Office, 1864.

U.S. Department of Navy, Office of the Chief of Naval Operations, Naval History Division. *Dictionary of American Naval Fighting Ships.* 8 vols. Washington, D.C.: Government Printing Office, 1959.

U.S. Department of War. *The War of the Rebellion: A Compilation of the Official Records of the Union and Confederate Armies.* Edited by Robert N. Scott et al. Washington, D.C.: Government Printing Office, 1880–1901.

U.S. Interstate Commerce Commission. "Corporate History of Western Union." John T. Marchand, comp. Typescript copy, 1914–22.

Vail, Alfred. *The American Electro-Magnetic Telegraph, with the Reports of Congress and a Description of All Telegraphs Known, Employing Electricity or Galvanism.* Philadelphia: Lea & Blanchard, 1845.

———. *Early History of the Electro-Magnetic Telegraph from Letters and Journals of Alfred Vail.* Edited by J. Cummings Vail. New York: Hine Brothers, 1914.

Vail, Alfred, comp. *The Telegraph Register of the Electro-Magnetic Telegraph Companies in the United States and the Canadas Using Professor Morse's Patent, Containing the Rates of Charges for Transmission of Messages.* Washington, D.C.: John T. Towers, 1849.

Villard, Henry. *Lincoln on the Eve of '61: A Journalist's Story.* Edited by Harold G. Villard and Oswald Garrison Villard. New York: Knopf, 1941.

———. *Memoirs of Henry Villard, Journalist and Financier, 1835–1900.* Edited by his family. 2 vols. Boston: Houghton Mifflin, 1904.

Watterson, Henry. "Abraham Lincoln." *Cosmopolitan* 46 (March 1909): 363–75.

Weaver, David H. "U.S. Newspaper Content from 1820 to 1860: A Mirror of the Times?" Paper delivered at the Fifty-ninth Annual

Meeting of the Association for Education in Journalism, College Park, Md., August 1976.

Webb, Joseph M. "Historical Perspective on the New Journalism." *Journalism History* 1 (Summer 1974): 38–42, 60.

Western Associated Press. *Proceedings.* Detroit: annual, 1867–91.

White, Leonard D. *The Jacksonians: A Study in Administrative History, 1829–1861.* New York: Macmillan, 1954.

Who's Who in America. Chicago: A. N. Marquis, 1899/1900–.

Who Was Who in America: Historical Volume, 1607–1896: A Component Volume of Who's Who in American History. 2nd ed. Chicago: A. N. Marquis, 1967.

Williams, W[ellington]. *Appleton's New York City and Vicinity Guide, Giving a Full and Accurate Description of the Great Metropolis and Environs, Public Buildings, Places of Interest, and Location of Churches, Banks, Insurance Offices, Hotels, &c.* New York: D. Appleton, 1849.

Wilmer, Lambert A. *Our Press Gang, or a Complete Exposition of the Corruptions and Crimes of the American Newspapers.* 1859. New York: Arno, 1970.

Wilson, Quintus C. "The Confederate Press Association: A Pioneer News Agency." *Journalism Quarterly* 26 (June 1949): 160–66.

Wilson's Business Directory of New York City. Henry Wilson, comp. New York: John F. Trow, 1849–89.

Writers' Program. *Boston Looks Seaward: The Story of the Port, 1630–1940.* Boston: Bruce Humphries, 1941.

Zabriskie, Francis Nicoll. *Horace Greeley, the Editor.* In the American Orators and Reformers Series, edited by Carlos Martyn. New York: Funk & Wagnalls, 1890.

INDEX

Abbot, Francis A., 117, 121, 133, 185, 219, 301 n.24; biography, 85–86, 185–86; and foreign news rights, 173–76

Abbot & Winans, 64, 162, 205, 207, 209, 211, 337; addresses, 87, 308 n.17; and foreign news rights, 173–76; as Morse ally, 86–87, 118; news report, 138–39, 177–78, 182–84; origins and operations, 85–87, 118–19, 171–78, 185; subscribers, 184–85, 315 n.25

Abell, Arunah S., 22, 305 n.96

Acadia (steamer), 37, 102

Adair, G. W., 264, 334 n.97

Adams, Abijah, 15

Adams, J. V. R., 330 n.50

Adams, Samuel, 7–8

Adams and Co., 24

Agence Havas, 10, 284 n.31

Albany (military sloop), 83–85

Albany (N.Y.) *American Citizen*, 59, 63

Albany (N.Y.) Argus, 59, 61, 67, 133, 316 n.48

Albany (N.Y.) Atlas, 59, 316 n.48

Albany (N.Y.) Express, 297 n.99, 316 n.48, 317 n.50

Albany (N.Y.) Herald, 59, 317 n.50

Albany (N.Y.) Journal, 59, 316 n.48

Albany (N.Y.) Knickerbocker, 59, 316 n.48

Albany (N.Y.) Register, 316 n.48, 317 n.50

Albertson, Jonathan White, 328 n.7

Alden, Hiram O., 216, 218

Alexandria (Va.) *Gazette*, 317 n.48

Allport, W. B., 335 n.128

America (steamer), 37, 102, 112, 150, 152, 290 n.14

American Cyclopaedia: on AP's founding, 93

American Press Association, x, 254, 337

American Telegraph Company, 114, 177, 195–97, 212–23, 230; in Civil War, 241, 264; and Six Nation treaty, 213

Andrews, George H., 16, 127; on New York City AP executive committee, 202

Aplin, William, 246–47; on AP's founding, 91

Army of the Potomac, 249, 271

Asia (steamer), 199

Associated Press, 337. *See also* Associated Press of Illinois; Boston Associated Press; New England Associated Press; New York City Associated Press; New York State Associated Press; Northwestern Associated Press; Southern Associated Press; Western Associated Press

Associated Press of Illinois, x, 64

Association of Morning Papers, 16, 19–21

Atlanta Commonwealth, 334 n.97

Atlanta Intelligencer, 333 n.93, 334 n.97

Atlanta Southern Confederacy, 261, 264, 333 nn.90, 93, 334 n.97

Atlantic & Ohio Telegraph Company: and Six Nation treaty, 213

Atlantic cable. *See* Field, Cyrus W.; Shaffner, Tal[iaferro] P.; Transatlantic

Atlantic, Lake & Mississippi Telegraph Company, 43–45, 107
Atlantic Telegraph Company (England), 197
Auburn (N.Y.) *Advertiser*, 59, 60,
63, 316 n.48
Auburn (N.Y.) *Daily Cayuga Tocsin*,
59, 60, 317 n.50
Augusta Chronicle and Sentinel,
264, 333 n.93, 334 n.97
Augusta Constitutionalist, 259-60,
264, 333 nn.90, 93, 334 n.97

Babcock, Charles T., 328 n.5
Bailey, A. M., 335 n.128
Bain, Alexander: telegraph instru-
ment and system, 45, 70, 111,
113–14, 155, 157–58, 160, 172,
173, 193, 292 n.34. *See also* New
York and New England Telegraph
Company; New York & New
England Union Telegraph Com-
pany
Baltimore American, 133, 249–51
Baltimore and Ohio Railroad, 38
Baltimore Argus, 317 n.48
Baltimore Clipper, 178
Baltimore Correspondent, 317 n.48
Baltimore Patriot, 317 n.48
Baltimore Sun, 105, 133, 178, 185,
305 n.96, 317 n.48; expresses, 22,
65
Bancker, Captain William, 22, 103–
4
Banks, General Nathaniel P., 248,
271
Barnard, Theodore, 248–49, 271,
328 n.5
Barnes, Edmund F., 111
Barns, Jacob, 190–91
Barnum, Zenas, 215, 218, 222
Barr, William, 247–48, 330 n.42
Barrett, M. P., 334 n.97
Bartlett, John S., 48–50
Bassett, William, 22
Batavia *Ohio Sun*, 178
Beach, Alfred E.: as New York
City AP partner, 127–28, 170.
See also New York Sun
Beach, Moses S.: as New York City

AP partner, 127–28, 170; as New
York City AP secretary, 114, 128,
174–75, 202. *See also New York
Sun*
Beach, Moses Y., 51, 82; as New
York City AP partner, 128. *See
also New York Sun*
Benjamin, Judah P., 248, 274
Bennett, George, 132
Bennett, James Gordon, 20, 22,
25, 36, 40, 53, 74, 82, 124, 276,
285 n.51; as New York City AP
partner, 128–29, 170. *See also
New York Herald*
Bennett, James Gordon, Jr., 53
Binghamton (N.Y.) *Republican*,
317 n.48
Blake, Henry Ingraham ("Harry"),
13–14, 285 n.42
Blanchard, W. G., 178, 294 n.72
Bleyer, Willard Grosvenor: on AP's
founding, 93
Blome, L. T., 262
Bogus presidential proclamation,
134–35, 251–54, 256–58, 331
nn.62, 64, 65
Boston Advertiser, 106, 153, 255
Boston and New York Printing
Telegraph Company ("Commer-
cial line"), 152, 193, 194–95,
318 n.67
Boston Associated Press, 153, 185,
305 n.101; origins, 105–6
Boston Atlas, 25–26, 106, 112, 133,
153
Boston Bee, 153
Boston Commercial Gazette: ex-
presses, 21–22
Boston Courier, 13, 105, 106, 153,
232, 285 n.42; expresses, 21–22
Boston Evening Transcript, 104–5,
141, 153, 177, 206, 315 n.25, 316
n.48
Boston Gazette, 15
Boston Herald, 316 n.48; expresses,
21–22
Boston Independent Chronicle, 15
Boston Journal, 106, 141, 153
Boston Mail, 178

Boston *Massachusetts Centinel*, 13, 15
Boston Merchants' Exchange, 146
Boston *New England Palladium*, 13, 15, 285 n.42
Boston *New England Weekly Journal*, 12
Boston Patriot, 15
Boston Post, 106, 153
Boston Repertory, 15
Boston Times, 106, 141, 153
Boston Transcript, 106
Boston Traveller, 106, 133, 141, 153
Boston Whig, 106
Bowles, Samuel, III, 332 n.72
Bridgham, Lewis H., 170, 178
Britannia (steamer), 33, 37, 67, 88, 102, 104, 290 n.14, 304 n.74
British and North American Royal Mail Steam Ship Company. *See* Cunard line
Brockway, Beman, 129, 321 n.96
Brogan, Captain William, 22, 103
Brooklyn Daily Eagle, 251, 324 n.47
Brooks, Erastus, 82, 225; as New York City AP partner, 128, 170. *See also New York Express*
Brooks, James, 82, 127, 225; congressman, 128; as New York City AP partner, 128, 170. *See also New York Express*
Brown, Benjamin Gratz, 332 n.72
Brown, George W., 132
Buchanan, James, 198–99
Buckingham, Joseph T., 13–14, 232
Buena Vista (news boat), 90, 96, 98–100, 102–3, 104, 105, 106, 116, 118, 129, 146, 220, 304 n.74
Buffalo Commercial and *Commercial Advertiser*, 59, 178, 316 n.48, 317 n.50
Buffalo Courier, 59, 316 n.48
Buffalo Courier & Pilot, 59
Buffalo Democrat, 59, 63
Buffalo Express, 59, 316 n.48
Buffalo Morning Gazette, 59–61, 63
Buffalo Pilot, 59–61
Buffalo Republic, 316–17 n.48, 317 n.50

Buffalo Rough Notes, 317 n.48, 317 n.50
Bull Run, First Battle of, 224, 242
Butterfield, John J., 43, 58, 70, 81. *See also* New York, Albany and Buffalo Telegraph Company
Butts, Isaac, 59–60, 76, 121

Caledonia (steamer), 37, 51, 97, 102, 110, 151, 304 n.74
Cambria (steamer), 37, 57, 79, 88, 96–97, 102, 304 n.74
Cameron, Simon, 243–44, 329 n.27
Campaigns. *See* Elections
Canada (steamer), 37
Carpenter, S. M., 249
Carr (Philadelphia newsbroker), 220
Carroll, A., 178
Carter, Thomas, 49
Celeste (news boat), 22
Chappe, Claude, 8
Charles, L. N.: on AP's founding, 93
Charleston (S.C.) *Courier*, 15, 178, 285 n.51, 333 n.93; expresses, 65–66
Charleston (S.C.) *Evening News*, 317 n.48
Charleston (S.C.) *Mercury*, 261, 317 n.48, 328 n.7, 333 n.90
Charleston (S.C.) *Standard*, 317 n.48
Charles Willmer's European Mail (Liverpool), 51
Chase, Salmon P., 256
Chattanooga, Battle of, 267
Chattanooga Rebel, 334 n.97
Chicago Journal, 254
Chicago Tribune, 240, 254–55, 257, 258, 332 n.72; AP report for April 12, 1861, 230, 232–33, 326 n.76
Chickamauga, Battle of, 267
Cincinnati Commercial, 254–55, 257–58, 332 n.72
Cincinnati Gazette, 133
Cisco, Captain, 22
Civil War, 239–79 *passim*; newspapers during, 240, 258–59, 269,

270, 274, 275, 276–77; press–
government relations during,
240, 242–54, 274, 275–76; teleg-
raphy during, 241–42, 276. *See
also names of battles*
Clark, Thomas M., 95–96
Clark, W. G., 264, 269, 334 n.97
Clarke, J. W., 178
Clermont (steamer), 34–35
Clisby, Joseph, 262, 264, 334 n.97
Codes, news. *See* Telegraphy
Colles, Christopher, 9–10, 15
Collins line, 54
Columbia (steamer), 37
Columbia South Carolinian, 263–
64, 334 n.97
Columbian telegraph instrument,
111
Columbus (Ga.) *Enquirer*, 333 n.93
Columbus (Ga.) *Sun*, 334 n.97
Columbus (Ga.) *Times*, 333 n.93
Commodore (steamer), 151
Commercial line. *See* Boston and
New York Printing Telegraph
Company
Committees of Correspondence, 6–
8
Confederate Press Association. *See*
Press Association of the Confed-
erate States of America
Confederate States of America,
228; newspapers in, 258–59, 269,
274
Conqueror (steamer), 150–51
Conrad, R. Y., 109
Cooper, Edward, 323 n.25
Cooper, Peter, 222, 323 n.25
Cooper, Samuel, 274
Copyright of news, 267–68
Cornell, Ezra, 40, 130, 144, 188–
91, 193, 196, 317–18 n.62
Courier and Enquirer (news boat),
18, 20
Cowardts, James A., 335 n.128
Craig, Daniel H., 95, 99, 215, 240,
294 n.72; as AP general agent,
117, 128, 148, 169–201, 206–9,
211–21, 228, 232–33, 236–37,
240–41, 245, 247–48, 252–53,
256–58, 271, 272–73, 275, 277,

315 n.25; attacks Abbot &
Winans, 176–85; attacks Johnson
and Zabriskie, 219–20; biography,
169–70; and foreign news rights,
174–76, 216–18, 332 n.12; and
Halifax expresses, 124, 149–62,
163, 218; and news monopoly,
187–91; personality of, 186–87,
201, 219; and pigeon expresses,
22, 54–55, 102, 116, 146; as telegraph owner, 113, 194–96,
318 n.67; as Western Union ally,
223. *See also* New York City
Associated Press
Crounse, Lorenzo Livingston, 271
Cummings, Alexander, 223–24
Cunard, Samuel, 36–37, 174–75
Cunard line: steamers and service,
22, 36–37, 46–48, 51, 54–55, 88–
89, 99, 102–3, 293 n.41; average
and record transatlantic crossings, 290 n.14. *See also names of
steamers*
Cureau (Civil War correspondent),
328 n.5
Cutler, James, 15

Dana, Charles A., 127, 128–29, 179
Daniel, John M., 335 n.128
Darrow, Lawson R., 148, 154–55
Davidson (Buffalo correspondent),
132
Davis, Jefferson, 232, 241, 274
Delmonico's Restaurant, 222
Deming, Sid, 249, 328 n.5
Dix, General John A., 244, 253
Dyer, E. S., 153–56, 219

Early, Jubal, 258
Eastburn, John H., 25
Eclipse (news boat), 19
Edson, Freeman M., 194
Elections: coverage of 1848 presidential, 142–45; coverage of
1860 presidential, 227–28; gathering returns from, 25–26; instructions to correspondents,
117–18, 142–43
Elliott, James, 14

Erie & Michigan Telegraph Company, 130
Erie Canal, 58
Erie Railroad, 189, 318 n.66
Europa (steamer), 37, 150, 217, 290 n.14
European and General Commercial Intelligencer (Liverpool), 48–50
Evening Edition (news boat), 20
Exchange Coffee House, 14–15
Express companies, 24–25
Expresses. *See* Express companies; Halifax expresses; Harbor newsgathering; Horse expresses; Pigeon expresses; Postal service; Railroad expresses; Steamer expresses and news

Fanny Elssler (news boat), 22, 23
Faxton, Theodore S., 43, 70, 81, 86–87, 172–73, 208, 318 n.62; and New York State AP, 58, 60, 62–63. *See also* New York, Albany and Buffalo Telegraph Company
Field, Cyrus W., 177, 195–200, 212, 214–17, 222, 321 n.91, 323 n.25. *See also* Transatlantic
Forbes (Civil War correspondent), 328 n.7
Fort Sumter, siege of, 231–32, 241, 244
Francis, R. D., 271
Franklin, Benjamin, 5, 7
French, Benjamin B., 69
Fuller, Eugene, 132, 178
Fulton, Charles C., 132–33, 178, 249–51
Fulton, Robert, 34
Fulton, W. W., 178

Gale, Leonard D., 34, 43
Gale, Monroe F., 56–57
Galveston News, 185
Gardner, James, 264, 334 n.97
Gay, Sydney Howard, 255, 324 n.35
Gettysburg, Battle of, 249, 267, 335–36 n.136; coverage of, 271–72, 274–75

Gibbes, Robert Wilson, 263–64, 334 n.97
Gibson, P. H., 335 n.128
Gisborne, F. N., 322 n.12
Gobright, Lawrence A.: as AP Washington chief, 133, 178–80, 181, 242, 252, 271, 309 n.27, 315 n.36, 328 n.5; biography, 178–79; and Buchanan telegram, 198–99; and Lincoln administration, 243–45, 329 n.31
Gould, Jay, 237
Graeme, John, Jr., 260, 262, 267–68, 269, 328 nn.6, 7
Gramling, Oliver, 124, 133, 171
Grand Rapids (Mich.) *Enquirer*, 190–91
Grant, General Ulysses S., 256
Gray, Alexander, 328 n.6
Great Western (steamer), 34–35, 36
Greeley, Horace, 25, 53, 82, 113, 164, 179, 229, 255, 309 n.28; congressman, 128; as New York City AP partner, 128–29, 170. *See also* New York *Tribune*
Grey, T. C., 271, 272
Grout, Jonathan, Jr., 9

Hale, David, 16, 18–19, 82, 124; and founding of AP, 91; as New York City AP partner, 128. *See also* New York *Journal of Commerce*
Haley, John J., 44, 46, 65, 70. *See also* Washington & New Orleans Telegraph Company
Halifax expresses, 146–61
Halifax Sun, 178
Hall, Captain John T., 22, 103, 178
Hall, Samuel, 12–13
Hallock, Gerard, 16, 18–19, 25, 82; and bogus presidential proclamation, 253; as New York City AP partner and president, 103, 127–28, 170, 202, 225; Rebel sympathies of, 224–25, 242. *See also* New York *Journal of Commerce*
Halstead, Murat, 332 nn.67, 72
Hamil, Captain Robert, 22
Harbor News Association, 92, 93,

94, 105, 116, 129, 146, 171, 193, 201
Harbor news-gathering, 13–20, 22–24, 98–105
Harnden, William F., 24–25, 26
Hartford Times, 316 n.48
Hasson, John, 242, 328 n.5
Hasson's News Association, 337
Hatcher, John E., 328 n.7
Haughton, Richard, 25–26
Havas, Charles-Louis, 10. *See also* Agence Havas
Herald for Europe (New York), 53
Hewitt, Abram S., 216, 222, 323 n.25
Hibernia (steamer), 37, 48, 55–56, 99, 104, 293 n.41, 304 n.74
Hill, Adams S.: and independent news room, 252, 254–56, 258
Holbrook, A. M., 330 n.50
Hood, General John Bell, 268
Hooker, General Joseph, 245
Horse expresses, 20–22, 65–66, 149–51, 218
House, Royal E.: telegraph instrument and system, 70, 110, 112, 114, 152, 172, 193, 195, 214, 215, 216, 306 n.118, 318 n.67. *See also* Boston and New York Printing Telegraph Company
Howard, Joseph, Jr., 251, 253–54
Hudson, Frederic, 111, 319 n.72; on AP's founding, 91–92, 94–95; on New York City AP's executive committee, 100, 127–29, 148, 202, 329 n.27
Hughes, David E.: telegraph instrument and system, 177, 189, 192, 195–96, 214, 215, 216, 318 n.67
Hughes, Jeremiah, 41–42
Hunt, Wilson G., 216
Hunter, John, 175, 178
Hunter, William, 5
Hurley, Captain, 22

Illinois & Mississippi Telegraph Company, 213, 232; and Six Nation treaty, 213
Independent news room, 252, 254–58, 270–71, 273, 331–32 n.67, 337

Jackson, Andrew, 20–21
Jackson (Miss.) *Southern Crisis*, 334 n.97
Jarvis, Captain Nathaniel, 98
Johnson, George W. L., 218–20
Jones, Alexander: addresses, 87, 117, 132; as AP general agent, 108, 117–18, 123–24, 128, 132–35, 163, 169, 207; biography, 123, 131–32, 162; as early telegraphic reporter, 83–85, 117–18, 121, 132; and news codes, 135–36; on New York State AP, 172. *See also* New York City Associated Press
Jones, George: as New York City AP partner, 171
Journal of Commerce (news boat), 19

Kendall, Amos: criticism of, 109, 196; as postmaster, 6, 21; and the Six Nations, 213–15; as telegraph developer, 38, 43–46, 69–70, 107, 109–10, 111, 157, 164, 187, 216. *See also* Magnetic Telegraph Company; Morse, Samuel F. B.
Kennedy, Captain John, 328 n.6
Kinney, James, 60
Kneeland, Samuel, 12
Knoxville Register, 333 n.93

Lacy, William, 61, 132–33
Laffan News Service, 337
Lancaster (Mass.) *Gazette*, 170
Landon, Melville D., 271
Lang, John, 13
Lee, James Melvin: on AP's founding, 93
Lefferts, Marshall, 193–94, 212
Leon, Henry J., 330 n.50
Levien, A. D., 178
Lewellen, James W., 335 n.128
Liberation News Services, 8
Lincoln, Abraham, 224–25, 227–30, 329 n.33; and AP, 242–54;

Farewell Address, coverage of, 229–30, 326n.70
Lindsey, Charles, 132–33
Liverpool Chronicle, 50
Liverpool Northern Daily Times, 51
Livingston, Cambridge, 222
Lockport (N.Y.) *Courier*, 316n.48, 317n.50
Loomis (Civil War correspondent), 328n.6
Louisville Morning Courier, 109, 178, 333n.93

McClellan, General George B., 249, 250, 271
McElrath, Thomas, 56; as New York City AP partner, 128, 170. *See also New York Tribune*
McGregor, William D., 328n.5
McGuire, Captain, 56
McKesson, John, 216
McKinney, John, 194–95
Macon (Ga.) *Telegraph*, 106, 261–62, 264, 334n.97
Maginnis, John, 330n.50
Magnetic Telegraph Company, 43–44, 67, 68–69, 77, 81–82, 95–96, 110, 136, 156–57, 159–60, 192, 213, 215–16
Mail. *See* Postal service
Maine Telegraph Company, 147, 196
Mallison, Francis S., 251, 253
Marble, Manton, 224; and bogus presidential proclamation, 253–54
Martin, Robert, 22, 23–24
Medill, Joseph, 191, 332n.72
Memphis Appeal, 248, 260–61, 333nn.90, 93
"Mercator," 113
Merchants' line. *See* New York and New England Telegraph Company
Mexican War: and founding of AP, 91–92, 95, 99, 299n.123; news coverage, 65–67
Milwaukee Sentinel, 71
Minns, Thomas, 15
Minot, Charles, 318n.66

Mobile Advertiser and Register, 264, 269, 328n.7, 334n.97
Montgomery Advertiser, 261, 333n.93, 334n.97
Montreal Herald, 133
Montreal Telegraph Company, 214
Morris, Francis, 215–16, 218
Morris, William S., 241
Morse, N. S., 264, 334n.97
Morse, Samuel F. B., ix, 34, 38, 41, 42, 110–12, 155–56, 164, 187, 215; and New York City AP, 107–14, 126, 156–57, 163–64, 195–96, 216; and the Six Nations, 212–15; system criticized, 65–71, 109–114, 195–96; telegraph instrument and system, 26, 31, 37–39, 40–46, 58–59, 62, 81–82, 95–96, 107, 213–15, 292n.34, 318n.67. *See also* Atlantic, Lake & Mississippi Telegraph Company; Magnetic Telegraph Company; New York, Albany and Buffalo Telegraph Company; New York and Boston Magnetic Telegraph Company; New York and New England Union Telegraph Company; Washington & New Orleans Telegraph Company
Munroe, Isaac, 15
Mutual Press Association, 268–69, 335n.128
Myers (Civil War correspondent), 328n.5

Nashville Patriot, 333n.93
Nashville Republican Banner, 333nn.90, 93
National Associated Press Company, 337
Naushon (steamer). *See News-Boy* (news boat)
Newark Daily Advertiser, 317n.48
Newbern (N.C.) *Progress*, 334n.97
New Brunswick Telegraph Company, 116–17, 147–48, 154, 196
New England Associated Press, 106
New Haven Journal & Courier, 316n.48

New Haven Palladium, 316 n.48
New Haven Register, 316 n.48
New Orleans & Ohio Telegraph
  Company, 213, 326 n.75; and Six
  Nation Treaty, 213
New Orleans Bee, 330 n.50
New Orleans Bulletin, 330 n.50
New Orleans Crescent City,
  330 n.50; expresses, 65
New Orleans Delta, 330 n.50
New Orleans Picayune, 185,
  317 n.48, 330 n.50; AP report on
  April 12, 1861, 230, 232–33,
  326 n.76
New Orleans True Delta, 330 n.50
News-Boy (news boat), 90, 103–5,
  106, 116, 130, 146, 304 n.83
Newsbroking: creditlines, 310 n.43;
  definition of, ix, 281 n.1; early,
  10, 76, 119–21; first newsbro-
  kerage, 58–64; in New York City,
  83–105, 108–19. *See also* Abbot
  & Winans; Associated Press;
  Independent news room; Mutual
  Press Association; News report;
  Press Association of the Confederate States of America; Richmond, combined press of; United
  States Associated Press
Newspapers: in early nineteenth
  century, 27–28; in 1830s–1840s,
  72–74; in 1840s, 82, 119, 162–63;
  in Civil War, 240, 258–59, 269,
  270, 274, 275; in post-Civil War,
  279; in New York City, 82, 124–
  26; statistics, 72, 162–63, 258–
  59, 278, 288 n.96, 313 n.93,
  326 n.73, 333 n.83; transatlantic,
  48–54
Newspaper trains, 288 n.102
News Report: of Abbot & Winans,
  177–78, 182–83; in Civil War,
  270–75, 277–79; copyright of,
  267–68; of New York City AP,
  136, 137–46, 177–78, 180–83,
  227–34, 326–27 n.77; of New
  York State AP, 64; romantic versus rational, 277–78; and telegraphy, 114–16, 164–66, 180–83
New York, Albany and Buffalo

Telegraph Company, 43, 45, 213;
  and New York State AP, 58–63,
  172; and Six Nation Treaty, 213
New York Albion, 48–50
New York American (1819): ex-
  presses, 22
New York and Boston Magnetic
  Telegraph Company, 43–44, 81–
  82, 94–95, 99–101, 105–6, 116,
  159–60, 193; and Halifax ex-
  presses, 146–58. *See also* New
  York & New England Union Tele-
  graph Company
New York & Erie Telegraph Com-
  pany, 130, 317–18 n.62
New York and Mississippi Valley
  Printing Telegraph Company,
  188–89
New York and New England Tele-
  graph Company ("Merchants'
  line"), 155, 158, 193. *See also*
  New York & New England Union
  Telegraph Company
New York & New England Union
  Telegraph Company, 173, 193,
  213, 214, 215, 216
New York & Washington Printing
  Telegraph Company, 215
New York & Western Union Telegraph Company. *See* Western
  Union Telegraph Company
New York Associated Press. *See*
  New York City Associated Press
New York City Associated Press,
  22, 61, 64, 106, 169, 300 n.2, 337;
  addresses, 87, 117, 132, 170, 212,
  223, 308 n.17; and American
  Telegraph Company, 212, 216–23;
  and Atlantic cable, 197–99,
  321 n.91; and bogus presidential
  proclamation, 134, 251–54, 256–
  58; *Buena Vista* episode, 96, 98–
  103, 105, 116; and control of AP
  system, 187–88, 233–34, 236–37;
  correspondents, 132–34, 178–81,
  240–41, 328 n.5; expenses and
  revenues, 134, 182–83, 192, 212,
  336 n.138; and foreign news
  rights, 173–76, 216–18; and Halifax expresses, 146–62; and Lin-

coln administration, 242–54, 275, 277; *News-Boy* episode, 103–5, 116; news report, 136, 137–46, 177–83, 227–34, 246–47, 270–73, 316 n.42, 326 n.76; origins in ship news, 90–105; origins in telegraphy, 108–19; partners in, 125–31, 223–26; structure, officers, and operations, 127–28, 129–31, 134–36, 166–67, 201–6, 224–25. *See also* Craig, Daniel H.; Harbor News Association; Jones, Alexander; Regulations of the General News Association of the City of New York; Telegraphic and General News Association

New York Commercial Advertiser, 125, 186, 212, 232, 256, 316 n.48; expresses, 22

New York Courier and Enquirer, 53, 82, 100, 104; early telegraphic dispatches, 88; expresses, 6, 16, 18–21; as New York City AP partner, 125–29, 170; and *New York World*, 134–35, 185, 224, 225. *See also* Webb, James Watson

New York Courier des Etats-Unis, 212

New York Daily Advertiser: expresses, 13, 16

New York Daily News (1855), 212, 324 n.47

New York Day Book, 324 n.47

New York Democrat, 125

New York Deutsche Schnellpost, 125

New York Enquirer, 16

New York Evening Express. See New York Express

New York Evening Mail, 226

New York Evening Mirror (1844), 125, 316 n.48

New York Evening Post, 14, 40, 125, 177, 212, 232, 316 n.48

New York Evening Star: expresses, 22

New York Express, 13, 40, 69, 82, 225, 325 n.56, 331 n.64; as evening paper, 177, 226; expresses,

22; as New York City AP partner, 125–28, 170. *See also* Brooks, Erastus; Brooks, James

New York Freeman's Journal, 324 n.47

New York Gazette (1788, Lang), 13; expresses, 16, 22

New York Gazette, or The Weekly Post-Boy (1747, Parker-Weyman), 1

New York Globe, 125

New York Herald, 11, 21, 36, 40, 41, 53, 99, 100, 102–4, 110, 134, 162, 177, 249, 251–52, 254, 264, 274, 276, 285 n.51, 294 n.72, 328 n.5; AP report on April 12, 1861, 230–31, 326 n.76; coverage of 1848 revolutions, 96–98; coverage of 1848 election, 143–44; coverage of 1858 Atlantic cable, 197–98; coverage of 1860 election and Lincoln, 227–30; coverage of George Parkman murder, 140–42; early telegraphic dispatches, 87–89; expresses, 1, 6, 22, 23–24, 52, 65–66, 295 n.75; and founding of AP, 91–92; as New York City AP partner, 124–25, 127–29, 170. *See also* Bennett, James Gordon

New York Journal of Commerce, 12, 16, 25, 82, 111, 131, 225–26; and bogus presidential proclamation, 134, 251–54, 256; expresses, 6, 18–22, 65, 295 n.75; and founding of AP, 90, 91–92; as New York City AP partner, 124–28, 170; Rebel sympathies of, 224–25, 242. *See also* Hale, David; Hallock, Gerard

New York Mechanics' Day Book, 125

New York Mercantile Advertiser: expresses, 16, 22

New York Morning Courier, 16

New York Morning Express. See New York Express

New York Morning Star, 125

New York, Newfoundland & Lon-

don Electric Telegraph Company, 195
New York Staats Demokrat, 212
New York Staats Zeitung, 212
New York Star, 254
New York State Associated Press, 106, 126, 132, 209, 338; as first newsbrokerage, 58–64; incorporated, 64; news report, 64; structure and operations, 63–64, 166–67
New York Sun, 11, 51, 69, 82, 110–11, 112–13, 174–75, 251–52; coverage of 1858 Atlantic cable, 198; expresses, 22, 23, 54, 65, 99, 295 n.75; and founding of AP, 90, 92, 93, 94, 124; as New York City AP partner, 124–25, 127–28, 170. See also Beach, Moses S.
New York Times, 128, 177, 221, 232, 251–52, 254, 257, 310 n.43; AP report on April 12, 1861, 230–31, 326 n.76; coverage of 1860 election and Lincoln, 227–30; coverage of the Gettysburg Battle, 271; as New York City AP partner, 170–71, 223. See also Raymond, Henry J.
New York Tribune, 23, 52, 63, 69, 79, 86, 113, 177, 186, 251–52, 254–55, 276, 298 n.111; AP report on April 12, 1861, 230–31, 326 n.76; coverage of Zachary Taylor's death, 145–46; coverage of 1860 election and Lincoln, 227–29; coverage of Gettysburg Battle, 271–72; early telegraphic dispatches, 87–88; expresses, 66, 103–4; as New York City AP partner, 125–26, 127–29, 170; William J. Romer episode, 55–57, 295 n.75. See also Greeley, Horace
New York Tribune for Europe, 53
New York True Sun, 69, 125
New York World, 134–35, 185, 223, 251, 274, 324 n.43; and bogus presidential proclamation, 134, 251–54, 256; and New York Courier and Enquirer, 134–35, 185,
224, 225; as New York City AP partner, 224
Niagara (steamer), 37, 104, 290 n.14
Nicolay, John G., 326 n.70
Niles, Hezekiah, 10
Niles' Weekly Register, 9–10, 15, 41–42
Noah, Mordecai M., 16
Norfolk Argus, 317 n.48
Norfolk Beacon, 317 n.48
Norfolk Herald, 317 n.48
North, S. N. D., 297 n.99; on AP's founding, 92, 93
North American Telegraph Association, 211, 214, 217, 221, 223
North American Telegraph Company, 292 n.34
Northway, Rufus, 59–61, 76, 121
Northwestern Associated Press, x
Nova Scotia Telegraph Company, 148, 156–60, 163–64, 173–76, 216–18
Noyes, James Oscar, 328 n.5
Nugent, R., 178

O'Brien, Frank H.: on AP's founding, 93
Omaha Bee, x
Orange Court House, Va., 274
O'Rielly, Henry, 10, 117; and foreign news rights, 173–76; as Morse competitor, 70, 107, 111–14, 155, 157–58, 159, 160, 173, 192; as Morse franchisee, 43–44, 45; and New York City AP, 113–14, 155–58, 192. See also Atlantic, Lake & Mississippi Telegraph Company; New York and New England Telegraph Company
Oswego Journal, 316 n.48
Oswego Times, 316 n.48

Palmer, Joseph, 132–33
Paris Herald, 53
Park, Andrew W., 15
Park, John, 15
Parkman, George, murder, 140–42
Payne, George Henry: on AP's founding, 93

Penny, Edward Goff, 132–33
People's Telegraph line, 111, 113
Persia (steamer), 228
Petersburg, Battle of, 258
Phelps, George M., 189, 318 n.67
Philadelphia Argus, 317 n.48
Philadelphia Bulletin, 317 n.48
Philadelphia Inquirer, 220, 317 n.48
Philadelphia Journal, 220
Philadelphia News, 317 n.48
Philadelphia North American, 109,
   220, 295 n.75
Philadelphia Pennsylvanian,
   317 n.48
Philadelphia Press, 220; on AP's
   founding, 90
Philadelphia Public Ledger, 41,
   105, 178, 215, 216, 218, 220,
   304 n.74, 305 n.96; expresses, 65,
   295 n.75
Philadelphia Record, 185
Philadelphia Sun, 317 n.48
Philadelphia *United States
   Gazette*, 14
Pigeon expresses, 22, 54–55, 102
Piggott, J. T., 178
Pittsburgh Gazette, 310 n.41
Pittsburgh Journal, 317 n.48
Plymouth (N.H.) *Gazette*, 169–70
Polk, James, 55–56, 84
Pomeroy Circular, 256
Pony expresses. *See* Horse ex-
   presses
Poore, Ben Perley, 244
Portsmouth (N.H.) *Freeman's Jour-
   nal*, 14
Postal service, 235–36; expresses,
   6, 21; and news, 4–6; statistics,
   283 n.13
Postal telegraph, 42
Post Office Act of 1792, 5
Prescott, George B., 233–34
President (steamer), 49
Press Association of the Confeder-
   ate States of America, 240, 254,
   310 n.43, 337; and copyright of
   news, 267–68; and Davis admin-
   istration, 274, 275; membership,
   264, 268; news report, 264–67,
   270–71, 273, 274–75; origins,

260–62; structure, officers, and
   operations, 262–67, 269, 277
Prime, William Cowper: and bogus
   presidential proclamation, 253;
   as New York City AP president,
   225
Pritchard, William H., 259–60
Pritchard, William H., Jr., 260
Providence Journal: expresses, 15–
   16
Publishers' Press Association, 337
Purdy, John H., 216

Railroad expresses, 21–22, 23, 24–
   25, 57, 60–61, 157–58, 159–60
Raymond, Henry J., 221–22, 229;
   on New York City AP executive
   committee, 100–1, 103, 127, 148–
   49, 329 n.27; as New York City
   AP partner, 127–28, 171. *See also
   New York Times*
Rea, Samuel J., 328 n.5
Regulations of the General News
   Association of the City of New
   York, 93, 129, 171, 201–6
Reid, James D.: on AP's founding,
   92
Reid, S. G., 334 n.97
Reid, Whitelaw, 335 n.136
Reilly, Tom, 95, 99, 254–57,
   299 n.123, 331–32 n.67
Reuters Agency: and AP, 199
Rhoades, Ebenezer, 15
Richmond, combined press of, 260,
   262, 333 n.88
Richmond Dispatch, 230, 260, 268,
   269, 273, 333 n.88, 335 n.128; AP
   report on April 12, 1861, 230,
   232–33, 326 n.76; coverage of
   Gettysburg Battle, 274–75
Richmond Enquirer, 268, 274,
   333 n.88, 335 n.128, 335–36 n.136
Richmond Examiner, 261, 268,
   333 n.88, 333 n.93, 335 n.128
Richmond Sentinel, 268, 274,
   335 n.128
Richmond Times, 317 n.48
Richmond Whig, 261, 268,
   333 n n.88, 93
Riordan, Bartholomew R., 328 n.7

Rochester (N.Y.) *Advertiser*, 59–60, 316 n.48
Rochester (N.Y.) *American*, 59–60, 316 n.48
Rochester (N.Y.) *Democrat*, 59–60, 67–68, 255, 316 n.48
Rogers, Henry J., 292 n.34
Romer (news boat). *See William J. Romer*
Rosewater, Edward, x
Rosewater, Victor, x, 338; on AP's founding, 93–96, 100
Russell, Benjamin, 13, 15
Russell, John, 15
Russell, Robert W., 194, 215–16, 218–22, 323 n.25
Ryrie, Captain, 55, 104

St. Louis *Missouri Democrat*, 255, 332 n.72
St. Louis Missouri Republican, 317 n.48
Salem (Mass.) *Gazette*: expresses, 12–13
Sanderson (Civil War correspondent), 328 n.7
Sanford, Edwards S., 222-23, 241, 323 n.34
Savannah (steamer), 289 n.3
Savannah News, 333 n.93, 334 n.97
Savannah Republican, 264, 333 n n.90, 93, 334 n.97
Scott, Thomas A., 245
Scripps-McRae Press Association, 337
Scripps News Service, 337
Seddon, J. A., 275
Selma (Ala.) *Reporter*, 333 n.93
Semaphore: and news, 8–10, 14
Seven Days' Battle, 250
Seward, Alexander, 59–61, 76, 92, 121
Seward, William, 225, 244, 248–29, 253
Seymour, William J., 330 n.50
Shaffner, Tal[iaferro] P., 214, 320 n.81
Shanks, W. F. G.: on AP's founding, 90–91
Shaw, Donald L., 183–84

Sheahan, James W., 179, 309 n.27
Shelly, R. L., 328 n.5
Sherman, General William T., 246, 268
Sibley, Hiram, 211
Silvey, Captain Robert, 22, 103
Simmons, Azariah H., 305 n.96
Simonton, James W., 129–30
Sirius (steamer), 23, 34–35
Six Nations, Treaty of the, 197, 213–14, 236, 322 n.6
Skinner, J. B., 132
Smith, David, 50–52
Smith, F[rancis] O[rmond] J[onathan], 95, 135–36, 173, 174, 187, 192, 193, 207–8, 216, 217, 219, 291 n.16, 317–18 n.62, 322 n.12; congressman, 37; criticism of, 105, 109, 155–57, 160–61, 196, 213; and foreign news expresses, 99–101, 113, 127, 147, 149–61, 163; personality of, 38, 111–12, 159; and Six Nation Treaty, 213–15; as telegraph developer, 37–38, 43–44, 70. *See also* New York and Boston Magnetic Telegraph Company; New York & New England Union Telegraph Company
Smith, J. Henley, 328 n.7
Smith, John Turel, 146, 149–53, 154, 161
Smith, R. M., 335 n.128
Smith, Richard, 132–33, 178
Smith, William Henry, 107; on AP's founding, 93–94
Smoot (Civil War correspondent), 328 n.7
Sneed, J. R., 264, 334 n.97
Snow, George M., 63, 127, 172, 298 n.111
Southern Associated Press, 240, 248, 258, 259–60, 264, 332–33 n.82; news report, 230, 232–33, 326 n.76; origins of, 106–7
Southern Telegraph Company, 241, 264, 268
Southwestern Telegraph Company, 230, 232, 241, 265, 268, 326 n.75

Space and time, 30, 76–77,
288 n.103
Spear, Charles, 194–95
Speed, John James, Jr., 317 n.62
Springfield *Illinois State Journal*,
244
Springfield (Mass.) *Republican*,
255, 332 n.72
Stager, Anson, 310 n.41
Stansbury (of *New York Express*),
127
Stanton, Edwin M., 242, 244, 249,
250, 252–54, 256
Steamer expresses and news, 23–
24, 46–48, 57, 321 n.95; and
Buena Vista episode, 96, 98–103,
116; and foreign news rights,
173–76, 217–18; Halifax ex-
presses, 146–61; *News-Boy* epi-
sode, 103–5
Steamers. *See* Transatlantic; *names
of steamers*
Steele, J. H., 334 n.97
Stimson, Henry M., 133
Stimson, William, 132–33
Stone, Charles, 334 n.97
Stone, David M., 225; and bogus
presidential proclamation, 253;
as New York City AP president,
225
Stuart, Richard, 170, 178
Swain, William M., 41, 105, 196,
215, 305 n.96, 320 n.80
Syracuse Daily Star, 59–60,
316 n.48
Syracuse Journal, 59–60, 316 n.48

Tappan, Arthur, 16
Tappan, Lewis, 16
Tavel, R. A., 15
Taylor, Zachary, 138; coverage of
election, 142–45; coverage of
death, 145–46
Teaser (news boat), 22
Telegraph (news boat), 96
Telegraphic and General News
Association, 94, 108, 118, 129,
170, 201
Telegraphy: in 1840s, 37–46, 119–
20; in 1850s, 212–16, 236; in

Civil War, 241–42, 276; and first
newsbrokerage, 58–64; instruments, 45, 69–70, 79–80, 111–12,
318 n.67; and news, ix, 39–40,
74–77, 115–16, 120, 164–66, 183–
84, 235–36; and news codes, 95–
96, 135–36, 310 n.37; newspaper
criticism of, 64–71, 108–15; in
New York City, 81–83; receiving
by sound, 136–37, 310 n.41; submarine, 44, 292 n.36, 319–
20 n.81. *See also names of
telegraph companies and inven-
tors*
Thomas H. Smith (news boat), 19
Thompson, W. T., 334 n.97
Thrasher, John S., 260; biography,
264; superintendent of Press
Association, 263, 264–68, 269–
70, 273–75, 277
Time and space, 30, 76–77,
288 n.103
Tom Boxer (news boat), 22
Topliff, Samuel, 14–15
Toronto Examiner, 133
Toronto Leader, 133
Townsend, K. S., 127; as New York
City AP secretary, 193
Transatlantic: 1858 cable, 195–200;
1866 cable, 37, 52, 200; news-
papers, 48–53; sailing ships, 23,
34–36; steamers, 36–37, 46–48,
55–57, 96–99, 102–5, 289 n.3
Transportation: and news, ix, 1–
32, 57, 60–62, 65–66, 74–75, 76–
77, 115–16, 235–36, 288 n.102
Traveller (steamer), 57
Treaty of the Six Nations. *See* Six
Nations, Treaty of the
Troy (N.Y.) *Budget*, 59, 316 n.48
Troy (N.Y.) *Post*, 59, 316 n.48
Troy (N.Y.) *Times*, 316 n.48,
317 n.50
Troy (N.Y.) *Whig*, 59, 316 n.48
Tyler, George W., 246, 247, 328 n.5
Tyler, Nathaniel, 335 n.128

United Press (1882–1897), 64, 206,
337
United Press Associations, 337